continued inside back cover

The New
Managerial
Economics

The New Managerial Economics

William Boyes

*The W. P. Carey School of Business at
Arizona State University*

Houghton Mifflin Company   Boston   New York

To my students

Publisher: Charles Hartford
Editor in Chief: Jean L. Woy
Sponsoring Editor: Ann West
Editorial Associate: Tonya Lobato
Project Editor: Amy Johnson
Senior Production/Design Coordinator: Carol Merrigan
Senior Manufacturing Coordinator: Marie Barnes
Executive Marketing Manager: Andy Fisher

Cover Photographer: Harold Burch, Harold Burch Design, NYC

Photo credits: p. 9: Getty Images; p. 29: Getty Images; p. 51: AP/Wide World Photos; p. 68: United Airlines; p. 103: Frans Lemmens/Getty Images; p. 124: © Michael S. Yamashita/CORBIS; p. 151: By permission of The Coca-Cola Company; p. 167: Sergio Piumatti; p. 191: Robert Frerk/Odyssey/Chicago; p. 221: © Frozen Images/The Image Works; p. 240: Getty Images; p. 256: Getty Images; p. 274: AP/Wide World Photos; p. 295: Paul Chesley/Getty Images; p. 322: AP/Wide World Photos; p. 342: Getty Images

Printed in the U.S.A.

Library of Congress Control Number: 2002117599

ISBN: 0-395-82835-X

123456789-QUV-07 06 05 04 03

Brief Contents

Contents

Preface

This text is titled *The New Managerial Economics* to emphasize its novel approach. *The New Managerial Economics* differs from traditional managerial texts, which tend to focus on optimization techniques and quantitative analyses while ignoring the context of problem solving that is so crucial to successful business management. *The New Managerial Economics* focuses on business strategy and the usefulness of economics to the manager. Its objective is to introduce the power of economics to the noneconomist and to illustrate to the economics student how economic tools and techniques can be used to solve business problems.

It is important for both MBA and economics students taking managerial economics courses to understand that economics not only describes why firms do what they do but can also point to strategies for entrepreneurs and managers. While several chapter appendixes provide quantitative discussions to supplement those strategies (covering, for example, topics such as optimization techniques and pricing problems), the main body of the text focuses on logical analysis and the applications of economic conceptual models and intuition. The text does not presume that students have a significant economics background or even have taken an economics course. Yet, for readers with a substantial background in economics, the material in this text should be interesting and rich enough to provide a significant learning experience.

Tour of the Text

In sixteen chapters, this text takes readers through every aspect of business strategy, looking at compensation, culture, structure, governmental influences, and international issues—all the while showing how economics can provide insights into institutions and decision making. Part I, Introduction and Foundation, introduces the language of economics and business, including measures of business performance. Part II, Seeking Competitive Advantage, introduces the strategies firms employ to acquire competitive advantage by looking at the customer (Chapter 4 on Demand), costs (in Chapter 5), and profit maximization (in Chapter 6).

Part III, Sustaining Competitive Advantage, explores the strategies firms use to maintain competitive advantage, strategies economists refer to as creating barriers to entry. This part covers non-price strategies (Chapter 7), pricing strategies (Chapter 8), and the firm's use of research, development, and innovation (Chapter 9). Chapters 10 and 11 examine corporate organization and culture and compensation and personnel issues.

Part IV, Analytic Problem-Solving Tools, gets into the details of problem solving. Chapter 12 looks at capital allocation, or decision making that involves more than one time period. Decisions today affect actions tomorrow; decisions today depend on what is expected to occur tomorrow, and this chapter explores the allocation of capital through different time periods. In Chapter 13 strategic behavior is discussed in the context of game theory. This chapter focuses on how looking at business situations as simple games can lead to insights.

Most business strategy deals with issues the manager can control but there are, of course, factors beyond the control of the manager that can affect a firm. Part V, Looking Outside the Firm, addresses these external factors. Chapter 14 discusses globalization and problems involved with having an exposure to exchange rate changes. Chapter 15 covers the public sector and laws regarding business actions that affect business strategy.

Chapter 16 pulls together much of the information found in this book through a sample strategic audit of Southwest Airlines. The audit focuses on the elements that define Southwest Airline's distinctive capability.

Decision Making at Every Step of the Way

This text is meant to provide a window into the strategic workings of the modern firm—businesses both small and large, domestic and multinational, and businesses that provide a wide array of products and services. Each chapter provides students with a rare glimpse into these firms—beginning with the chapter introductory cases, which profile a specific company undergoing some change or trying to make a critical decision. Near the end of each chapter the case is reviewed, giving students a chance to examine the company's choices in light of underlying chapter concepts. Hundreds of other companies are mentioned throughout the chapters as a way to illustrate specific concepts under discussion. In addition, web links to additional resources—including government and corporate sites—have been added occasionally in the chapter margins to provide students with a means of finding out more about a particular topic or company strategy. A compendium of web resources is provided on the chapter endpapers.

At the end of each chapter, a numbered summary highlights key points covered, key terms defined in the chapter are listed, and a wealth of exercises ask students to evaluate the costs and benefits associated with any business choice. Questions marked with a calculator icon require quantitative analysis. I believe that the best way to grasp major ideas and build confidence in strategic decision making is to practice making decisions, and many of these exercises are aimed at helping students do just that.

An Integrated Text and Supplements Package

The New Managerial Economics is accompanied by a set of carefully constructed supplements that focus on the unique features and approach of this text.

Study Guide

Designed to solidify the key concepts addressed in the text, this carefully prepared supplement by Wm. Stewart Mounts Jr. of Mercer University will be an invaluable resource for students who want to maximize their retention and understanding of course material. Chapter by chapter, the Study Guide walks students through important text concepts in the Overview, Key Concepts for Review, and the Active Review sections and follows up by testing their knowledge through True-False, Multiple-Choice and Short-Answer Questions, as well as more intensive Applications and Problems. Each chapter concludes with an "Extending the Case Study" exploration that challenges students to apply what they have learned to real-world problems and helps them make better managerial decisions. Answers are provided for each of the testing sections so that students can evaluate their own progress and preparation level.

Instructor's Resource Manual

I have written this manual with the unique challenges of teaching Managerial Economics in mind. To guide instructors through every chapter, I have included a Chapter Summary, Teaching Objectives, and Important Terms. For classroom help, Topics and Teaching Suggestions and Answers to Exercises and Quantitative Exercises are offered. Additionally, Internet links are provided in many chapters for instructors interested in further research and exploration of chapter-specific topics.

Test Bank

This comprehensive supplement, written by Wm. Stewart Mounts Jr. of Mercer University, offers nearly 1000 class-tested Mulitple-Choice and True-False questions that will give instructors wide flexibility and creativity in designing tests. For ease of use, answers, level of difficulty, and topic section appear in the margin next to each individual question.

HMClassPrep with HMTesting CD version 6.0

Now instructors will have the flexibility of an electronic resource manual and computerized testing program all in one CD. Available for use on MAC or PC platforms, this powerful tool contains all of the content from the Instructor's Resource Manual in a printable, editable format, and all of the content from the Test Bank in a computerized format that allows for customized and randomized testing and offers classroom administration and online testing options. The HMClassPrep/Testing CD also includes a complete set of PowerPoint slides of full-color figures and graphs from the text.

Website

Both students and instructors will find the text's companion website a useful place for easy-access supplemental material. Chapter summaries, outlines, and Internet links (including any necessary updates to the links provided in the text's margins and end sheets) are provided on the student website (college.hmco.com). Professors who have adopted the text will find downloadable PowerPoint slides and Teaching Suggestions in addition to other useful material. For more information about this or any of the supplements mentioned above, professors may contact their Houghton Mifflin sales representative.

Acknowledgments

This text is a culmination of many years of work. I started teaching the material over ten years ago. Colleagues have used my notes and manuscripts and provided invaluable feedback during the past six years. I want to thank my colleagues and others who have read the manuscript, offered suggestions and criticisms, and provided ideas—especially Paul Burgess and Robert Knox of Arizona State University; Wm. Stewart Mounts Jr., Mercer University; and Ryan Amacher, University of Texas, Arlington. I would also like to thank the following reviewers who provided critical comments on chapters at various stages of completion: David Eaton, Murray State University; Harold W. Elder, University of Alabama; Animesh Ghoshal, DePaul University; William A. Hamlen, Jr., SUNY Buffalo; Raja Kali, University of Arkansas; David Levy, University of Baltimore; Carl B. Linvill, University of Arkansas; Martin Milkman, Murray State University; Kathryn Nantz, Fairfield University; Andrew Narwold, University of San Diego; Michael Nieswiadomy, University of North Texas; and Abdul Qayum, Portland State University.

I am grateful to the hundreds of students—MBAs and undergraduate business and economics majors—who have been subjected to different versions of the materials over the past five or so years. In addition, groups of students at Mercer University and The University of Texas, Arlington, participated in a class test of the preliminary manuscript last year and provided some very valuable feedback. I'd like to thank in particular Richard Spivey, Terrence A. Ussery, Pace Bailey, Jenna Stewart, Jennifer Laster, Bo Warren, Jennifer Spano, Elizabeth Skipper, Lewin Chuachiaco, Robert Gibbon, Rasnida Corker, Kecia Isgett, Tiffany Noell, and Jennifer McGuinness, all students from Mercer University, Macon, Georgia for their useful comments.

In addition to the students in these and my own MBA classes, many business executives have contributed to the presentation of the material. In particular, Gary Tauscher read every chapter and offered many suggestions.

Finally I would like to thank the team of editors at Houghton Mifflin who devoted many hours to this text, including Amy Johnson, Tonya Lobato, Carol Merrigan, Tracy Patruno, and Marie Barnes. This book would not be what it is without the contributions of my editor, Ann West, in her role as critic, colleague, and even occasional collaborator.

W.B.

The New Managerial Economics

PART I

Introduction and Foundation

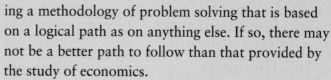

The objective of this text is to introduce the noneconomist to the power of economics and to illustrate to the economist how economics can be of use to managers. Economics not only describes why firms do what they do but can point to strategies for entrepreneurs and managers. Successful management may depend as much on following a methodology of problem solving that is based on a logical path as on anything else. If so, there may not be a better path to follow than that provided by the study of economics.

All fields create their own language. This reduces the problems of communication between specialists in each field. However, it also reduces the ability of nonspecialists to communicate with the specialists. Economics and real-world business each has its own language. Unfortunately, the languages have led to such a separation that many businesspeople think economics is an abstract and useless field. In this book, the two languages are merged. It is shown that popular or faddish business terms are usually based on some economic concept and that economics can yield a great deal of insight about business practices.

This text is titled *The New Managerial Economics* to emphasize that it differs from traditional managerial texts that focus on optimization techniques and quantitative analyses. *The New Managerial Economics* focuses on business strategy and the usefulness of economics to the manager. Its foundation is one of logical analysis and conceptual modeling. It is economics for anyone interested in business, whether that person is an economist or not. One need not have an economics background or have taken an economics course to understand the material in this text. Yet, if one has a substantial background in economics, the material in the text should be interesting enough and new enough to maintain interest and provide a significant learning experience.

In the first three chapters, we introduce some of the language of economics and business. Chapter 1 is an introduction to the topic—a discussion of what leads to success and an illustration of why "there is no free lunch." Chapter 2 provides an overview of economics. In it the intuition of why and how markets work is developed.

Chapter 3 deals with measures of performance. Depending on who is speaking, the objective of the firm is to create value, to maximize profit, to increase shareholder wealth, or to maximize stakeholder wealth. Do these terms mean the same thing? No, they don't. Moreover, focusing on one could mislead the firm, creating disincentives for achieving the objective. To the businessperson, maximizing shareholder value is what business is about. To the economist, maximizing economic profit is the objective of business. In Chapter 3 the concepts are tied together.

CHAPTER 1

Economics and Management

Lincoln Electric

Lincoln Electric was founded by John C. Lincoln in 1895. For decades the company had been one of the leading manufacturers of arc-welding products in the world. At the end of World War II, more than fifty manufacturers of arc-welding products competed in the United States; today only six major manufacturers remain. The vast majority, including such giants as General Electric and Westinghouse, withdrew from the business, primarily because they could not compete with Lincoln Electric. Lincoln Electric's success stemmed from the productivity of its employees. A unique compensation structure that paid piece-rate, rewarding an employee for the number of products that employee produced, created an incentive for employees to work as hard and fast as they could. Each product was identified with the employee responsible for it; if errors in the product occurred, that employee had to repair the product—a task for which no pay was forthcoming. Thus, the company generated a rapid rate of production of high-quality products. The company also makes industrial electric motors, but arc-welding products are its main business. Lincoln Electric has the largest market share in the industry; it has 40 percent of the domestic market for electrodes and welding wires, the consumables that constitute the heart of the business.

In the 1990s, Lincoln Electric acquired manufacturing plants in Europe, Latin America, and Asia. These acquisitions were disastrous, leading to losses of millions of dollars. What was the problem? The company hadn't changed its compensation approach or company policies. What could be done?

The Successful Firm

On average each year, about 7 percent of all firms in the United States are new and 1 percent go out of business. Why do some firms succeed while others fail?

Is It Just Luck?

Luck plays a role in a firm's performance. There are many cases throughout history where luck defined success as much as, if not more than, skill. Consider the Philadelphia pharmacist on his honeymoon in 1875 who tasted tea made from an innkeeper's old family recipe. The pharmacist acquired the recipe and created a solid concentrate of the drink that could be made for home consumption. The pharmacist was Charles Hires, a devout Quaker, who intended to sell "Hires Herb Tea" as a nonalcoholic alternative to beer and whiskey. A friend suggested that miners would not drink anything called "tea" and recommended that he call his drink "root beer." Or how about the luck of a sanitarium handyman named Will Kellogg who was helping his older brother prepare wheat meal to serve to patients in the dining room. The two men would boil wheat dough and then run it through rollers to produce thin sheets of meal. One day they left a batch of the dough out overnight. The next day, when the dough was run through the rollers, it broke into flakes instead of forming a sheet. These wheat flakes were an immediate success.

Irrespective of these and other examples, luck is typically not the primary factor in a firm's performance. If a company relied on luck as its primary strategy, how would the company do? Most business scholars would not expect success from a strategy of waiting for a random draw.

Quality

For an overview of TQM and information about Edward Demming, visit

http://www.ed.gov/databases/ ERIC_Digests/ed396759.html

In the 1970s, many Japanese companies followed the advice of Edward Demming, focusing their efforts on producing quality products; they succeeded—and succeeded wildly—in entering the U.S. marketplace. Is a focus on quality the key to success? A study of 450 firms undertaken in the late 1980s concluded that the single most important factor influencing a business unit's profitability is the quality of its products and services relative to those of rivals.[1] Yet this does not mean that any or all attempts to improve quality will be worthwhile. Consumers may not be willing to pay more just to have a small improvement in quality. SAS Airlines pursued a philosophy of "quality only" in the late 1980s only to find that its costs escalated unchecked. In 1989 then-CEO Jan Carlzon pronounced: "We have to identify and evaluate the business traveler's total service needs . . . our mission is to take care of all their practical details." Two years later, Carlzon's philosophy had changed: "Everything that does not further the competitiveness of our airline activities must be removed, sold or turned into separate entities."[2] From Ford Motor Company we heard that "at Ford quality is job one," but then we also saw the problems associated with the Ford Explorer.

First Mover

Other studies have pointed out that first movers—the first firms to bring out new products—are often the most successful.[3] Standard Oil, Bayer, Kodak, Xerox,

Survival rates for 189 market pioneers versus 320 early followers are presented at http://netec.wustl.edu/BibEc/ data/Papers/fthprukra1115.html

IBM, Coca-Cola, Microsoft, Amazon.com, and Intel are examples of first movers that now have or once had well-known brand names and substantial market advantages due to being the first firm to develop a market or introduce a new product or innovation. Yet VF Corporation, a clothing supplier, has made itself a success by moving second. It allows others to take the risks, and then it jumps in with better distribution and service to take over the market. Most people believe Procter & Gamble invented the disposable diaper business when it launched Pampers in 1961. In fact, the now-defunct Chux had already been going for a quarter-century. Pampers was not a new product; it was just cheaper and aimed at a wider market. The same story can be told about video recorders. An American firm, Ampex, pioneered the product in 1956 but was swept out of the way twenty years later by cheaper models from Japanese manufacturers such as Matsushita and Sony. One study finds that the pioneers in more than fifty markets are leaders in only 10 percent of the markets examined and that, on average, the current leaders in the market entered the market thirteen years after the first mover.[4]

Size/Market Share

For an interesting discussion of market share as a strategy, see http://www.otterbein.edu/home/ fac/brccbly/general/bitsnbytes/ myth.htm

Does size mean success? Are large, dominant firms more successful than smaller firms? On average, as a business's **market share** has risen, its profit rate has also tended to increase.[5] The profit rate does not rise as fast as market share, however. Having a market share of about 10 percent yields a profit rate of about 10 percent, whereas a market share of 60 percent yields a profit rate of about 38 percent.[6] This does not mean that an emphasis on size and market share is necessarily a route to success. Acer is a company that manufactures computers. In its early years it focused so much on market share that it lost sight of profits and very nearly went bankrupt as a result. It has since organized into about twenty separate companies operating under a loose umbrella.

Irrespective of the weak relationship between market share and profitability, most executives want increased market share for their firms. A survey by the consulting company KPMG asking what a company's motive was in launching mergers or takeovers found that over 50 percent said the reason was to raise market share.[7] Yet, achieving mass has virtually no effect on long-term company survival. In 1912 US Steel was the largest industrial company in the world. US Steel is no longer the largest company in the world. In fact, US Steel no longer exists. It was transformed into a different company, USX, after US Steel nearly went bankrupt. USX exemplifies the typical history of large firms.

Great corporations rarely go bust. But their normal fate is to disappear from the scene when, after a period of attrition, they are acquired by more vibrant successors.

There are many cases where rather than celebrating their size, large companies seem to hide it, imitating smaller rivals by shrinking headquarters, slashing layers of management, and subdividing into smaller units. Both AT&T, America's biggest telephone company, and International Telephone and Telegraph (ITT), split themselves into three parts in 1995.

The movement away from size as a panacea has been applauded by two management gurus who have gone so far as to claim that the age of size is finished. Peter Drucker announced that "the Fortune 500 is over." Tom Peters argued that "smaller firms are gaining in almost every market."[8] The average size of companies and workplaces has been falling since the 1970s. This does not mean, however, that size is a guarantee of failure. While Kmart and Sears have experienced serious losses and even bankruptcy while attempting to grow larger, McDonald's, Marks and Spencer, Wal-Mart, Disney, and Toyota have prospered while growing larger.[9] What is important is to know when size is important for success and when it is a detriment.

Mergers and Acquisitions or A Focus on Core Competency   Some firms have found success by merging or combining companies. Typically, one firm acquires another or two firms merge into a single firm. The justifications managers give for a merger or acquisition vary from case to case. General Electric acquired many unrelated firms as an attempt to diversify the risk of focusing on one product—avoiding having all one's eggs in one basket. Rowntree's brands were well known and successful in the United Kingdom but not in the rest of Europe. The acquisition of Rowntree by Nestlé, a Swiss company, enabled the company to have a presence in the U.K. and continental Europe. Philip Morris acquired Miller, a brewery, because it believed that its marketing knowledge could be applied to other products. Sony acquired Columbia Pictures in order to have access to Columbia's film library; Sony had created a certain format for its HDTV and believed that control over the most important films could ensure that other studios would adopt the Sony format. WMX acquired hundreds of firms throughout the world in the 1980s in order to become the largest waste management firm in the world. Quaker Oats, a food company, acquired Snapple, a drink company, in 1994 in order to enhance its product line. Price Club and Costco Wholesale, two discount retailers, merged in order to gain further market share. American Airlines and TWA merged in 2001 in order to become more efficient. Exxon and Mobil merged in 2001 and Chevron and Texaco merged in 2002 to "leverage synergies." Hewlett Packard acquired Compaq in 2002 in order to broaden the product base.

SEC access to mergers and acquisition is provided at http://www.gsionline.com/ma/MandA.html

The explosion of merger and acquisition activity that began in the early 1990s continued into 2001, slowing a little with the recession of 2001–2002 and then picking up steam again in 2002. Despite this activity, evidence points out that mergers and acquisitions typically do not increase the profitability of the resulting firm. For instance, Quaker sold Snapple for a loss, and Price Club and Costco were in disarray less than a year after their merger and these were far from the only failed marriages. A survey of more than three hundred big mergers over the previous ten years by Mercer Management Consulting of New York found that in the three years following the transactions, 57 percent of the merged firms lagged behind their industries in terms of total returns to shareholders. The long-run failure rate is even higher. Over a twenty-five-year period, about half of acquisitions are subsequently divested (split up) and merged companies tend to do worse in terms of stock prices than the market as a whole.[10]

Many analysts have argued that success hinges not on acquiring a diverse set of businesses but on divesting unrelated businesses to focus on a single line of business—a core competency.[11] But here again, counterexamples are easily found. You could look at the success of GE Capital and argue against the view that a business must focus on doing just one thing. Some firms have achieved success by combining the entire production line, or "value chain," in one firm, but others have been better off outsourcing as many activities as possible to other firms.[12] Nike, for instance, does not manufacture its products itself. Instead, it uses independent contractors for the production of its goods and focuses on the marketing of the products.

Globalization

For an interesting perspective on globalization, vist

http://news.bbc.co.uk/1/hi/special_report/1999/02/99/e-cyclopedia/711906.stm

Visit the World Trade Organization's website at http://www.wto.org/

Globalization has been touted as a key strategy for success. Go into the business section of any bookstore, and you will see the word *global* emblazoned on almost every other book. Talk to the executives of almost any company and *globalization* will soon dominate the conversation. The growth of world trade has been tremendous in recent decades. Governments have lowered trade barriers through the GATT (General Agreement on Tariffs and Trade), or what is now known as the World Trade Organization (WTO), and through regional trade agreements such as the European Union (EU), the North American Free Trade Agreement (NAFTA), and Latin America's Mercosur. Over the past decade, foreign direct investment grew four times as fast as world output and three times faster than world trade.

According to the United Nations, there are close to forty thousand transnational companies—companies doing business in more than one nation, three times the figure twenty-five years ago. Together these companies control about a third of all private-sector assets.

Many people look on globalization as the homogenizing of markets, whereby all markets become identical. Some fear this so much that they protest at international trade meetings or even vandalize McDonald's or other firms that seem to be homogenizing the world. But while goods and services may flow more freely among nations than ever before, markets are not homogeneous. When the European Community was formed in 1957, the market for European producers was suddenly many times larger than their domestic markets. The appliance industry was one of the first to market consumer goods extensively across borders. The automatic washing machine was then a new and widely sought product, and demand for it grew rapidly. Indesit and Zanussi, Italian manufacturers, initially dominated the European markets because their size gave them advantages over smaller competitors. But as these companies focused on the same product for every market, others created distinct products for each market. By the early 1980s, Indesit and Zanussi were effectively bankrupt, and the most profitable producers in this industry were those, like Hotpoint in the United Kingdom and Bosch in Germany, that focused on machines designed for specific markets.

There are only a few truly global brands—brands such as Coca-Cola, McDonald's, and Marlboro that are recognized worldwide. Yet, a close look at Coca-Cola's strategy shows that even with such a well-known product, national differences are not ignored. The Coke recipe changes from country to country. The southern Japanese like their Coca-Cola slightly sweeter than do people in Tokyo, and the company obliges. Two thirds of Coca-Cola's Japanese products are made specifically for the local market: "Georgia Coffee," for example, can be seen everywhere in Tokyo but is unknown in Atlanta.

In Japan, McDonald's stumbled until it allowed a local entrepreneur to set up small snack bars in the center of Tokyo, rather than the large suburban eateries used in the United States, and the company began using burgers made with local meat, which is much fattier than that used in America. Moreover, the hamburgers come with optional teriyaki sauce. In Mexico, the burgers come with chili peppers. PepsiCo also adjusts from country to country. It had to rename 7-Up in Shanghai because in the local dialect the phrase means "death through drinking."[13]

Leadership

Some management gurus argue that the secret of success is the person in charge. Jack Welch is credited with the success of General Electric; Bill Gates of Microsoft is looked upon as a visionary. Kenneth Lay was counted among these visionary leaders until the collapse of Enron in 2002. Case studies[14] often emphasize the importance of a single person, like Herb Kelleher of Southwest Airlines, Thomas Watson of IBM, Andy Grove of Intel, and Michael Marks of Marks and Spencer.[15] Most of these case studies spend considerable time on the CEO's personality and background. They often feature an isolated CEO, struggling to resolve the fundamental issues of the company's strategic direction. These cases

When Carly Fiorina took over as the CEO of Hewlett-Packard in July 1999, the Silicon Valley icon had developed an image as a stumbling giant. While HP had seized command of the printer market, in high-margin enterprise computing it had lost ground to rivals like Sun Microsystems. Fiorina instituted a whirlwind of structural and cultural change. Fiorina launched a unified advertising campaign centered around the "rules of the garage," referring to the famous Palo Alto garage (recently bought by HP) where Bill Hewlett and Dave Packard founded the company in 1939. These rules are: Believe you can change the world; Work quickly, keep the tools unlocked, work whenever; Know when to work alone and when to work together; Share tools, ideas. Trust your colleagues; The customer defines a job well done; Radical ideas are not bad ideas; Invent different ways of working; Make a contribution every day. If it doesn't contribute, it doesn't leave the garage; Believe that together we can do anything.

present the reasoning behind attributing a firm's success to a leader. Is success due to a charismatic personality or a visionary leader, or does it occur independently of the person in charge?

There is no doubt that in a few instances the success of a company derives from the personality of the entrepreneur. But no research has been able to identify a set of characteristics of the people in charge that defines success.[16]

Management and Economics

The point of the discussion above is that there is no formula that guarantees success. If there were, then no firm would have an advantage, since all would use the formula. Moreover, it is no more possible to teach someone to be a successful manager than it is to teach someone to be a visionary leader. However, it is possible to provide people with approaches and knowledge that aid them in thinking about business issues and making business decisions—how to identify what is important, to determine which strategies make sense when, and to deal with change. This is the purpose of this text—to learn how to analyze business issues. We will see that economics not only enables us to better understand human behavior, and thus the activities of firms, but provides valuable insights and tools for businesspeople.

The Role of Economics

A businessperson might not find the previous paragraph a very good reason for reading further in this book. Ask businesspeople what they think economics is about. Their answer will be economic forecasting, and most do not think very much of economic forecasting. In fact, in the 1990s, most corporate forecasting departments were disbanded.

Because businesspeople are concerned with costs, firms retain accounting departments or accountants to watch over and measure costs. Most businesses have to determine their prices, which typically is the responsibility of marketing departments. Businesses must deal with internal aspects of the firm, such as employee relations and compensation; this is the responsibility of the personnel or human relations department. Businesses need to interpret the business environment they face—the task of corporate planners and strategic advisers. Many businesses have an ethics department and even a chief ethics officer, another CEO. The economic input into these functions has been minimal. Yet costs, prices, employees, compensation, industries, markets, and behavior are the very subjects with which economics is concerned.

Economists analyze firms, study human behavior and decision making, examine markets and industries, and yet appear to offer the businessperson little help. Every country's chief executive has an economic adviser to turn to for advice on economic policy, but economics has almost no influence on business policy. How many chief executives have an economic adviser? Very few.

Why isn't economics used more by businesspeople when every aspect of business is an important topic in economics? Part of the reason is that businesspeople and economists have not been speaking the same language. Traditionally, economists have studied the role of the firm but have not used their studies to offer advice to business. Businesspeople, looking for practical answers to current problems, have not been inclined to reinterpret economics for their own use and have found the academic studies too abstruse (obtuse and abstract). As a result, management gurus and consultants have filled the void by translating economic concepts into business jargon and coining phrases to catch the attention of businesspeople.

In the 1990s, the management gurus' advice was to flatten the pyramid, become a horizontal organization, eliminate hierarchy from the company, empower the people, open the environment, transform the culture, listen to customers, create a customer-focused organization, and commit to total customer satisfaction. In addition, the leader was to increase value, price for value, write a mission statement, put together a strategic plan, continuously improve, shift the paradigm, think out of the box, reengineer the corporation, and create order out of chaos. The main problem with this advice is that there are costs involved in adopting any of it. But none of the gurus point out the costs. This is where economics is valuable. One of the basic principles of economics is that there are costs involved in any action or decision. In other words, by undertaking one action, benefits from other actions that were not undertaken are forgone. Consider, for instance, the advice "know your customer."

Know Your Customer Knowing your customer means knowing what factors affect their choices. This is not easy. People will often purchase something simply because others are also purchasing that product. Fashions, fads, habits, and other aspects of consumer behavior change.

Knowing your customer is not some esoteric management term. It is basic economics. It simply says: Understand demand. A manager must know whether customers and/or rivals respond to price changes and understand when price and/or nonprice strategies make sense. Whether the firm should advertise, offer guarantees or warranties, improve service or quality, focus on packaging, devote resources to ensuring distribution channels, or introduce new or different products are all decisions that require an understanding of demand.

Economics tempers the enthusiasm of a manager to jump on some management fad or bandwagon by pointing out the costs of undertaking a particular strategy. For instance, consultants often call on the firm to be customer-focused. Yet, while paying attention to the customer makes sense, focusing solely on the customer may result in ignoring other important players in the game of business. Suppliers may be important, as may firms that provide a complementary product. Microsoft benefits when Intel develops a faster chip, and Intel benefits when Microsoft develops new software that strains the limits of existing hardware. Because video required more capacity and speed in microprocessing, Intel wanted someone to develop an inexpensive and widely used video application. To aid that development, Intel spent more than $100 million on ProShare, a videoconferencing system that sits on top of a desktop computer. Because ProShare requires an integrated services digital network, or ISDN, line (lines that have three channels for transmission—two for data and one for voice—each with nearly five times the capability of ordinary twisted copper) and because the phone companies had not been able to sell many ISDN lines, Intel was able to enlist the aid of local phone companies to get people to use ProShare. The phone companies thus subsidized the purchase of ProShare, offering it to their customers for about half of the retail price. All these companies—Intel, ProShare, and the phone companies—recognize the importance of the customer, but it is their relationships with the other firms that have dominated their interest in recent years. Had Intel focused only on its customer—the computer manufacturers—it would not have had nearly the success it has had. Most likely, you would not even recognize the Intel name.

Another illustration of jumping on a bandwagon without consideration of the costs is Johnson & Johnson's move to get rid of hierarchy or to flatten the firm. Johnson & Johnson implemented broadbanding wherein salary grades or differentials are eliminated. But employees saw broadbanding not as a means of fostering employee enrichment but, instead, as the elimination of a promotion path. Instead of increasing performance, broadbanding decreased it.

Total Quality Management Total quality management, or TQM, was the business buzzword of just a few years ago. Managers were told to increase quality or focus on quality and success would follow. In short, it was claimed that quality was free. But economics teaches that there is no free lunch, a lesson business quickly learned when it joined the quality revolution. In November 1989, Florida Power and Light became the first U.S. firm to win the Deming Prize—Japan's award for quality. Two months later, on January 11, 1990, the Florida Public Services Commission denied a rate increase request made by Florida Power and Light. Florida Power and Light wanted the higher rates to pay for the quality improvements it had made and the resources devoted to applying for the award. Florida Power and Light is not alone. Wallace Co. Inc., a Houston-based pipe and valve distributor, won a 1990 Baldrige Award, the top quality award given in the United States. In February 1992, Wallace Co. filed for Chapter 11 bankruptcy. Wallace's quality programs increased on-time deliveries from 75 to 82 percent and the company's market share almost doubled, from 10 to 18 percent, but these improvements came with a cost—about $2 million in additional overhead costs.[17]

When the quality revolution first struck the United States around 1990, several academic institutions were pressured into adopting quality practices as well. In a quarterly newsletter, the dean of the engineering school at a major university proclaimed the school's commitment to quality as follows: No student will be allowed to fail. This sounds terrific, but it could be very costly. Consider the student who does not want to pursue the course of study or who decides that, for the time being, college is for fun, not for attending classes and studying. Is the engineering school going to devote faculty time and other support efforts to ensuring that these students succeed? If so, it will probably fail to provide support to other students—unless the school's resources are unlimited.

In short, quality is costly, and whether it is worth pursuing depends on how much the customers value quality. Quality is not free. Everyone agrees that the Concorde supersonic airplane is a great way to fly, but its much higher operating costs mean that not many people choose it over standard flights. Or consider the case of TWA. In January 1993, TWA was in Chapter 11 bankruptcy proceedings. With nothing to lose, the company decided to take out some of its seats—ten to forty per plane—to increase legroom. TWA called it "Comfort Class." According to the senior vice president of marketing, "We had $10 million. We spent $1 million to take out the seats, the other $9 million to promote it."[18] The skeptics argued that it was too little too late. But customer satisfaction rose; within six months, TWA moved from the bottom to the top of the customer satisfaction rankings. But where is TWA today? It doesn't exist.

How Management Theory and Economic Principles Relate

The demand for quick answers and easy solutions is huge, and many entrepreneurs have responded to the demand. The management "theory industry" is alive and doing very well today. However, good management may involve the opposite of the quick-fix prescriptions.[19] For example, some of the ideas in vogue in the late 1990s included the following:

Activity-based accounting
Benchmarking
Reengineering
Codes of ethics
Core competencies
Corporate culture
Empowerment
Hypercompetition
Lean manufacturing
Market-driven and close-to-customers
Relationship marketing
Strategic alliances and networks
Time-based competition
Total quality management

Business buzzwords are ridiculed in

http://www.buzzwhack.com/

We'll discuss these terms throughout the text. In most cases, we find that the term is simply an exotic way of referring to some basic economic rule or principle. The exotic turn of phrase is as much a marketing ploy to enhance a consultant's reputation as anything. But because the term is advertised as a quick fix to business problems, it may become attractive to managers looking for a solution to their woes. However, as is usually the case, when something seems too good or too easy to be true, it usually is—or, as the economists say, "There's no free lunch." Just a few years ago we heard about such other quick-fix solutions as:

Cash cows, stars, question markets, and dogs
Experience curves
Generic strategies
Intrapreneurship
Management by objectives
Portfolio management
Matrix management
Self-managed teams
Skunk works
Theory Z
Zero-based budgeting
Just-in-time inventory control

What happened to these? We don't hear about them these days.

Many of the prescriptions offered by the management consultants are thought-provoking. The problem is that the adoption of these ideas is typically made without an understanding of what is involved in their implementation or of whether the situation is appropriate for their adoption.

The essence of good management is to determine whether the implementation of a practice increases the value that a firm adds: Does it make money? When does

For more information on corporate governance, see http://www.corpgov.net/index.htm

a customer-only or total quality strategy make sense? When does reengineering make sense, and in what types of firms? Does just-in-time inventory control improve performance? Does downsizing or reengineering improve productivity? Understanding economics enables the manager to answer these questions. Rather than simply grabbing any hand-hold offered, the manager, having knowledge of economics, is more able to choose one that is firmly rooted.

Bob Dylan wrote a song with the lyrics, "The times they are a-changing." This appears to be the case for economics and management as well. Michael Porter, an economist, brought economics to business in his book *Competitive Advantage*. That work spawned the growth of an academic field of study called management strategy. Academic journals devoted to the field, such as *Strategic Management Journal, Business Strategy Review, Journal of Economics and Management Strategy*, and *Managerial and Decision Economics* have emerged. Books by management consultants have begun to introduce economics to businesspeople by translating economic jargon into useful business topics. What this field of strategy and the academic interest in it are saying is that economics potentially has the same role to play in relation to management issues that it currently has for political issues.

The Study of Managerial Economics: How Do We Proceed?

The quick fix or management fad is appealing because business is so complicated. There are so many issues involved in business that it seems impossible to study them. Yet is business any more complicated than biology, astronomy, or chemistry? Biologists, physicists, chemists, and other scientists seeking an understanding of the real world also have an apparently infinite number of details to deal with. The approach they take is to create classification schemes to help them organize thoughts and collect data and to develop simplifying models that help them analyze issues. This is the approach we take in this book as well.

The basis of our analysis is economic reasoning or decision making. What is economic decision making? It is what we have been talking about in this chapter—recognizing that something cannot be acquired without giving up something else. Economists refer to such decision making as comparing costs and benefits and evaluating tradeoffs.

An economic adviser to an executive would require the executive to list his or her goals, to list the options available for achieving those goals, and then to select the option or options needed to reach those goals. The executive would then be required to calculate the costs and benefits of each option. A strategy such as, "we want to be the best at everything," would simply be unacceptable—it is impossible. The executives of Wilkinson-Match, the unsuccessful product of a merger between British Match and razor-blade manufacturer Wilkinson Sword, claimed that their merger would "give both companies substance." What does this tell us? As we noted above, other justifications of mergers support the mergers because they "create critical mass" or they enable the firm "to become a global player." These statements are nothing more than wishes—wish-driven strategies. They make no sense because they ignore the fact that allocating resources to one use means that these resources cannot be used elsewhere. The executive cannot get something for nothing. Executives must evaluate each feasible option by comparing its value and its cost, and that cost is what must be sacrificed in order to attain something. Tradeoffs—-giving up something in order to get something else—lie at the heart of the executive's job. And this is what economics is about.

CASE REVIEW *Lincoln Electric*

The case presents a very brief synopsis of Lincoln Electric. It points out that Lincoln's success was due to the way it paid its employees. The company created a situation in which an employee was rewarded for working fast, working carefully, and being productive. Employees responded by choosing to take short breaks and short lunches and to work as much as they could. They also attempted to produce the highest-quality products possible, since each defect would cost them money. This type of compensation scheme, called piece-rate, enabled Lincoln to become the market leader.

Following the herd, which was stampeding toward globalization, Lincoln Electric acquired manufacturing plants throughout the world. The problem was that none of the Lincoln management team had ever done anything internationally. Moreover, the compensation structure that had led to Lincoln's success did not adapt very easily to other countries and cultures. Consider, for instance, a plant in France, where the typical worker puts in less than thirty hours a week with no less than six weeks of paid vacation. Or consider a plant in China, where a culture of group work permeates the society. The Lincoln Electric compensation structure did not elicit the same response as it did in the United States.

The primary purpose of the chapter was to point out that everything has a cost—there is no free lunch. Each business decision must be undertaken with a view to comparing the costs of the decision with its benefits. Lincoln executives grabbed for the quick fix, expanding into markets where its competitive advantage was not an advantage.

SUMMARY

1. Managerial economics is the study of business decision making and strategy. The economist should be able to provide valuable insights to managers on topics such as costs, prices, markets, mergers, divestitures, globalization, and personnel, since these are the topics of economics.
2. Management is about making choices. Since economics is the study of decision making, it should provide benefits to managers.
3. There is no single formula for success. If there were, it could be taught and learned, and everyone would have it. The formula would then have no value.
4. Choice is selecting one thing or one use of resources over other things or other uses. This means that something must be forgone, or given up, in order to do something else.
5. There is no quick and easy solution to business problems.

KEY TERMS

market share   total quality management

EXERCISES

1. When would being first be a valuable strategy?

2. Look up the latest *Business Week* list of best-selling business books. How many introduce a quick fix?

3. You are to decide whether to implement teams in this course. Describe the costs and benefits of having teams of students work together on papers, exams, and homework. Would you implement teams? Why or why not?

4. Is there a relationship between market share and profit? What could account for this relationship?

5. Why would executives, experienced in business and exposed to business practices over many years, be so quick to grab hold of a management fad?

6. What does the phrase "there is no free lunch" mean?

7. China is the world's most populous nation with 1.25 billion people. Firms look at that population as a huge customer base and are rushing to establish themselves in China. Is this appropriate for all firms? Why or why not?

8. What is meant by the statement that "quality is not free"?

CHAPTER NOTES

1. R. Buzzell and B. Gale, *The PIMS Principles Linking Strategy to Performance* (New York: Free Press, 1987).

2. Thomas S. Robertson, "Corporate Graffiti," *Business Strategy Review,* 6, no. 1 (Spring 1995): 27–44.

3. See, for example, Alfred D. Chandler, "The Enduring Logic of Industrial Success," in C. A. Montgomery and M. E. Porter, eds., *Strategy: Seeking and Securing Competitive Advantage* (Boston: Harvard Business School Publishing Division), 1991.

4. Gerard Tellis and Peter Golder, "First to Market, First to Fail: Real Causes of Enduring Market Leadership," *Sloan Management Review,* 37, no. 2 (Winter 1996), pp. 65–75.

5. See F. M. Scherer and D. Ross, *Industrial Market Structure and Economic Performance* (Boston: Houghton Mifflin, 1990), p. 429; and Richard Miniter, *The Myth of Market Share: Why Market Share Is the Fool's Gold of Business* (New York: Crown Publishers, 2003), pp. 21–34.

6. Miniter, op. cit., note 5.

7. Peter Bartram, "Why Addition Won't Add Up" *AccountancyAge,* February 3, 2000, p. 1; David Henry,"The Urge to Merge," *USA Today,* July 16, 1998, Business Section.

8. As noted in John Micklethwait and Adrian Wooldridge, *The Witch Doctors: Making Sense of Management Gurus* (New York: Random House, Inc., 1996), p. 100.

9. In late 2002 McDonald's had to slow down its rate of growth. Its size was becoming too costly.

10. John Kay, *Why Firms Succeed* (New York: Oxford University Press, 1995), pp. 148–151.

11. See C. K. Prahalad and Gary Hamel, "The Core Competence of the Corporation," in Cynthia Montgomery and Michael Porter, eds., *Strategy* (Boston: Harvard Business School Publishing Division, 1991), pp. 277–300.

12. See James Brian Quinn, Thomas L. Doorley, and Penny C. Paquette, "Beyond Products: Services-Based Strategy," in Montgomery and Porter, *Strategy,* pp. 301–314.

13. Micklethwait and Wooldridge, *The Witch Doctors,* p. 220.

14. Case studies, such as the Harvard Business School cases, typically focus on a specific decision or series of decisions made by a firm at some point in the past. A significant part of the discussion is usually focused on the people in charge.

15. Marks and Spencer is a United Kingdom–based retail department store.

16. Rakesh Khurana, *Searching for a Corporate Savior: The Irrational Quest for Charismatic CEOs* (Englewood Cliffs, N.J.: Princeton).

17. Eileen C. Shapiro, *Fad Surfing in the Boardroom* (Cambridge, Mass.: Perseus Publishing, 1996), p. 175.

18. Quoted in Adam M. Brandenburger and Barry Nalebuff, *Co-Opetition* (New York: Doubleday & Co., 1996), p. 123.

19. Shapiro, *Fad Surfing in the Boardroom*; and John Micklethwait and Adrian Wooldridge, *The Witch Doctors* (New York: Random House, 1996).

CHAPTER 2

Exchange, Efficiency, and Markets

Procter & Gamble: New Product Launch[1]

Over its 160-year history, P&G has accumulated a great deal of industry experience and business knowledge. Part of this experience is not to launch new products without an in-depth understanding of the market. P&G undertakes a great deal of market research and extensive product and market testing before it introduces a product. P&G's success with this approach is exemplified by its well-known and long-lived products: Ivory soap over 100 years old; Crisco shortening over 70; and Tide detergent over 35. Each product is a leader in its market.

Procter & Gamble has developed a new clothes detergent, one that is directed toward the lower-heating washers used in Europe. P&G is considering how to introduce the new product. The issue is whether the new detergent would be the company's first "Eurobrand"—essentially introducing the same product throughout Europe, much as it would in the United States—or whether to create a separate product for each country—something like having a distinct product for Idaho, another for California, and still others for every other state. How should the executives of P&G proceed?

Choices

There is no getting around it: Choices have to be made. One activity is selected and others are forgone. One strategy is chosen and another is forgone. One product is purchased and others are not. You read this page rather than watch TV; you don't do both because your time is *scarce*. Intel devotes $100 million to research and development and in so doing reduces dividends to stockholders by 10 cents. Intel can't both do R&D and increase dividends because its funds are limited. British Telephone (BT) acquires MCI for $21 billion. BT did not have the resources to also acquire Sprint. Any good—product, service, or resource—is scarce. Nonscarce things are either free or are "bads"; for example, disease and garbage are bads. People will give up something to get rid of a bad.

The logic of economics begins with scarcity. Scarcity means that choices must be made; and when a choice is made, one thing is selected and others given up. The things that are given up, or forgone, are the costs of that decision—called *opportunity costs*. There is, then, a cost to everything; this is what the phrase "there is no free lunch" means.

With scarcity and opportunity costs described, the next step is to learn how these things affect behavior. As we'll see in this section, people can increase their gains relative to their costs by specializing in activities they do relatively well and then trading. People are able to get more if they trade than if they did not trade. Trade benefits the trading parties as long as what they give up in the process of making a trade does not cost more than the gains from the trade. There is an incentive, therefore, to find a way to undertake trade using as few resources as possible. This incentive defines the structure of markets and the architecture of firms.

Trade and Exchange

At any moment in time, individuals (as well as firms and nations) are endowed with certain resources and abilities. People can choose to be self-sufficient—using and consuming their resources and output themselves—or they can choose to exchange goods and services with others.

Consider a very simple example involving two nations. China is a nation with 1.25 billion people and vast natural resources. Agriculture represents about one-half of China's economy. The high-technology industries have just begun to develop and are a very small part of the economy. The United States has 300 million people and vast natural resources. Agriculture is about 10 percent of the economy, and high-technology industries are a substantial part of the U.S. economy. Suppose China and the United States each produce the following combinations of agricultural and high-technology products.

If the United States devoted all its resources to agriculture, it would be able to produce 10 units. Conversely, if all U.S. resources were devoted to high-tech products, 10 units of such products and equipment could be produced. China, on the other hand, could produce 4 units of high-tech products and equipment by devoting all its resources to high technology or could produce 8 units of agricultural products by devoting all its resources to agriculture. (See Table 2.1.)

The combinations of the two items that each could produce are illustrated in Table 2.1, a figure known as the **production possibilities curve, (PPC)**. A PPC illustrates the idea of scarcity. The combinations along the line are the maximum

Table 2.1

PRODUCTION POSSIBILITIES

	China	United States
Agriculture	8	10
High Technology	4	10

that can be produced with the given resources; there is no way, with the current resources, to produce any combination outside of the PPC. The United States can produce only those combinations along its production possibilities line (or combinations inside the line). China, similarly, can produce only those combinations along (or inside) its production possibilities line.[2]

The PPC also shows the costs involved in producing any combination of goods. The costs are those combinations that must be forgone or given up. For instance, if the United States produces 10 units of high-tech products, it gives up 10 units of agricultural products. Its opportunity cost of producing 10 units of high-tech products and equipment is, therefore, 10 units of agricultural products. China's opportunity cost of producing 4 units of high-tech products is 8 units of agricultural products. Thus, while China's opportunity cost of producing 1 unit of high technology is 2 units of agriculture, the United States' opportunity cost of 1 unit of high technology is 1 unit of agriculture.

The United States is able to produce more of everything than China but is relatively more efficient at producing high-tech products and equipment. We say that the United States has an *absolute advantage* in high technology and agriculture but a **comparative advantage** in high-tech production. China has no absolute advantage. However, it does have a comparative advantage in agricultural production: It gives up ½ unit of high technology for each unit of agriculture, while the United States gives up 1 unit of high technology for each unit of agriculture.

If each country specializes where each has a comparative advantage—the United States produces 10 units of high technology and China, 8 units of agriculture—they can then trade to get what they want. Suppose China wanted 4 units of high technology. It could devote all its resources to high technology but get no agricultural products. However, the United States might be willing to trade 4 units of high-tech products and equipment, but only if it could get no less than 1 unit of agriculture for each unit of high technology in exchange. Since China is willing to give any amount up to 2 units of agriculture for each unit of high technology, a trade could be arranged.

Suppose China agrees to give up 6 units of agricultural products in return for the 4 units of high-tech products and equipment. Then the United States ends up with 6 units of agricultural products and 6 units of high-tech products and equipment, while China gets 2 units of agricultural products and 4 units of high-tech products and equipment. The United States could have produced only 5 units of agricultural products and 5 units of high-tech products and equipment on its own, so it gains 1 unit of agricultural products and 1 unit of high-tech products with the trade. China by itself could have produced only 4 units of high-tech products and equipment; it gains 2 units of agricultural products with the trade. The **gains from trade** are shown in Figure 2.1 by the consumption point outside the PPC. Each country can get more by specializing and trading than by being self-sufficient.

Figure 2.1

GAINS FROM TRADE

The U.S. PPC indicates the maximum it can produce. Both can gain by specializing and then trading.

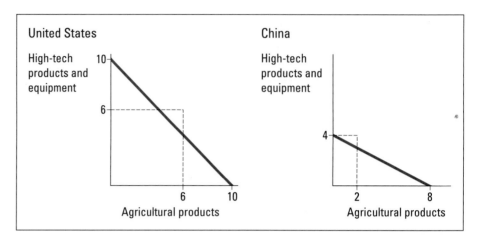

International Trade Voluntary trade occurs because it makes each trader better off. Trade among nations occurs because it makes the citizens of those nations better off than they would be if they could consume only domestically produced products. Trade among individuals occurs because it enables them to consume more than they could produce alone.

Table 2.2 shows patterns of trade between two large groups of countries, the industrial countries and the developing countries. The industrial countries include all of Western Europe, Japan, Australia, New Zealand, Canada, and the United States. The developing countries are, essentially, the rest of the world. The table shows the dollar values and percentages of total trade between these groups of countries. The vertical column at the left lists the origin of *exports* (sales to other countries), and the horizontal row at the top lists the destination of *imports* (purchases from other countries).

As Table 2.2 shows, trade between industrial countries accounts for the bulk of international trade: $2 trillion in value and 48 percent of world trade. Exports from industrial countries to developing countries represent 20 percent of total world trade. Exports from developing countries to industrial countries account for 18 percent of total trade, while exports from developing countries to other developing countries currently represent only 13 percent of international trade.

Because countries differ in their comparative advantages, they tend to export different goods. Comparative advantage is found by comparing the relative costs of production in each country. The cost of producing a particular good is measured in terms of opportunity costs—what other goods must be given up in order to produce more of the good in question.

Productivity differences account for comparative advantage. In other words, if one country can produce some item using fewer resources than another country, then the first country will have a comparative advantage in the production of that item. It takes Japan one-third fewer labor hours to produce automobiles than it takes Germany. Using fewer resources to produce one item means that fewer other items will have to be forgone to produce that first item. Japan has a comparative advantage in producing automobiles.

Technological differences among countries can account for differences in productivity. The countries with the most advanced technology have a comparative advantage with regard to those goods that can be produced most efficiently with modern technology.

Table 2.2

THE DIRECTION OF TRADE (BILLIONS OF DOLLARS AND PERCENTAGES OF WORLD TRADE)

	Destination:	
	Industrial Countries	**Developing Countries**
	Origin:	
Industrial Countries	$1,777 48%	$728 20%
Developing Countries	$664 18%	$461 13%

Source: Direction of Trade Statistics Quarterly (New York: International Monetary Fund, 2000).

Visit the website for the International Trade Association at
http://www.ita.doc.gov/

Trade statistics are available at
http://www.census.gov/ftp/pub/foreign-trade/www/

Another aspect of productivity is that goods differ in terms of the resources required for their production. Countries may have a comparative advantage in those goods requiring more of the resources owned by that country. For instance, countries with a relatively large amount of farmland might have a comparative advantage in agriculture and countries with a relatively large amount of capital might have a comparative advantage in the production of manufactured goods. Countries with a relatively abundant stock of highly skilled labor might have a comparative advantage in producing goods that require relatively large amounts of skilled labor.

Trade is not determined by comparative advantage alone. The products produced by one country must be demanded by another country. A country could have a comparative advantage in producing some good, like sharpeners for disposable razor blades, that no one wants. Trade for the sharpeners will not occur. Citizens in different countries also have different tastes and technological needs, and thus they tend to differ in what they will import. Some goods are more widely traded than others, as Table 2.3 shows. Crude petroleum is the most heavily

Table 2.3

THE TOP TEN EXPORTED PRODUCTS (MILLIONS OF DOLLARS AND PERCENTAGES OF WORLD EXPORTS)

Product Category	Value	Percentage of World Trade
Crude petroleum	$180,565	5.67%
Motor vehicles	155,357	4.90
Petroleum products	80,340	2.54
Motor vehicle parts	77,622	2.45
Data-processing equipment	64,027	2.02
Special transactions	61,508	1.95
Aircraft	57,818	1.82
Transistors, valves, etc.	57,078	1.80
Telecom and high-tech products and equipment	52,973	1.67
Paper and paperboard	46,579	1.47

Source: Data from United Nations Conference on Trade and Development, *Handbook of International Trade and Development Statistics, 1998–1999* (TD/STAT.24), p. 162 (New York: United Nations, 2000).

traded good in the world, accounting for 5.67 percent of the total volume of world trade. Crude petroleum is followed by motor vehicles, petroleum products, motor vehicle parts, and automatic data-processing equipment. The top ten exported products, however, represent only 25 percent of world trade. The remaining 75 percent is distributed among a great variety of products.

Market System

What we found in the previous section is that people (and firms and nations) can consume more if they specialize in the activities in which they have a comparative advantage and then trade with one another to acquire the goods and services they desire than if they are self sufficient—do not trade. But how are the specialized producers to get together or to know who specializes in what, and who determines the terms of trade? The answer depends on how the scarce goods and services are allocated—what the allocation mechanism is.

Allocation Mechanisms

Scarcity of a good means some people will acquire that good and others won't; scarcity of resources means some activities will be selected and others won't. Scarcity would not exist if everyone had everything they wanted. Who or what gets the resources or products depends on the way the resources and products are allocated.

An allocation mechanism is the system by which scarce goods are distributed. Allocation mechanisms in use today include the price or market system, first-come-first-served, various government schemes based on such things as income or age, and luck.

Why are so many allocation mechanisms used? Perhaps we can provide an answer by having you complete a brief questionnaire.

Consider the following situation:

> At a sightseeing point, reachable only after a strenuous hike, a firm has established a stand where bottled water is sold. The water, carried in by the employees of the firm, is sold to thirsty hikers in six-ounce bottles. The price is $1 per bottle. Typically only 100 bottles of the water are sold each day. On a particularly hot day, 200 hikers want to buy at least one bottle of water.

Indicate what you think of each of the following means of distributing the water to the hikers by responding to each allocation approach with one of the following five responses:

  a. Completely fair
  b. Acceptable
  c. Unfair
  d. Very unfair
  e. Totally unfair

1. Increasing the price until the quantity of bottles hikers are willing and able to purchase exactly equals the number of bottles available for sale.
2. Selling the water for $1 per bottle on a first-come-first-served basis.
3. Having the local authority (government) buy the water for $1 per bottle and distribute it according to its own judgment.

4. Selling the water at $1 per bottle following a random selection procedure or lottery.

The following is a similar situation but involves a different product.

A physician has been providing medical services at a fee of $100 per patient and is unable to see more than 30 patients per day. One day the flu bug has been so vicious that the number of patients attempting to visit the physician exceeds 60.

Indicate what you think of each of the following means of distributing the physician's services to the sick patients by responding with one of the following five answers:

a. Completely fair
b. Acceptable
e. Unfair
d. Very unfair
e. Totally unfair

1. Raising the price until the number of patients the doctor sees is exactly equal to the number of patients willing and able to pay the doctor's fee.
2. Selling the services at $100 per patient on a first-come-first-served basis.
3. Having the local authority (government) pay the physician $100 per patient and choose who is to receive the services according to its own judgment.
4. Selling the physician's services for $100 per patient following a random selection procedure or lottery.

Each allocation mechanism is unfair in the sense that someone gets the good or service and someone doesn't. With the price system, it is those without income or wealth who must do without. Under the first-come-first-served system, it is those who arrive later who do without. Under the government scheme, it is those not in favor or those who do not match up with the government's rules who do without. And with a random procedure, it is those who do not have the lucky tickets who are left out.

Since each allocation mechanism is in a sense unfair, how do we decide which to use? One way might be according to the incentives each creates. With the price system, the incentive is to acquire purchasing ability. This means you must provide goods and services that have high value to others and provide resources that have high value to producers—to enhance your worth as an employee by acquiring education or training, to enhance the value of the resources you own—in order to obtain income and wealth. The price system also provides incentives for quantities of scarce goods to increase. In the case of the bottled-water stand described above, if the price of the bottles increases and the owner of the stand is earning significant profits, others may carry water to the sightseeing point and sell it to thirsty hikers—the amount of water available thus increases. In the case of the doctor, other doctors may think that opening an office near the first might be a way to earn more—the amount of physician services available thus increases. The price system creates the incentive for the amount supplied to increase. These incentives ensure that economies grow and expand and that standards of living improve.[3] The price system also ensures that resources are allocated to where they are most highly valued. If the price of an item rises, consumers may switch over to another item or another good or service that can serve about the same purpose. When consumers switch, production of the alternative good rises and thus resources used in its production must increase as well. The resources then are reallocated from lower-valued uses to higher-valued uses.

With the first-come-first-served allocation scheme, the incentive is to be first. You have no reason to acquire an education or improve the quality of your products. Your only incentive is to be first. Yet, first for what? No one will produce anything. Supply will not increase; growth and standards of living will not rise. A society based on first-come-first-served would die a quick death.

A government scheme provides an incentive either to be a member of government and thus help determine the allocation rules or to perform according to government dictates. There are no incentives to improve production and efficiency, or to improve quantities supplied, and thus no reason for the economy to grow. We've seen how this system fared with the collapse of the Soviet Union.

Random allocation provides no incentives at all—simply hope that manna from heaven will fall on you.

It is the incentives created by allocation mechanisms that make the market (price) system "better" than the others. Economists evaluate the outcome of an economic system in terms of **efficiency**. Efficiency is a measure of how well a system satisfies the wants and needs of individual human beings. Because economists assume that people are concerned primarily with regular economic goods and services, an economic system is typically evaluated on how well it satisfies the economic desires of the population.[4] An efficient allocation of resources is one in which no other available allocation that makes someone better off without making another person worse off exists; such an allocation is called **Pareto efficient**. In contrast, an inefficient allocation is wasteful; better use of the available resources would make some people better off without harming anyone else.

For information about online
auctions, visit
http://www.auctionwatch.com/

A system of markets and prices is generally the most efficient means of coordinating and organizing activities. Individuals offer to sell goods and services at various prices, and other individuals offer to buy goods and services at various prices. Without having anyone coordinating the buyers and sellers, the market determines a price for each traded good at which the quantities that people are willing and able to sell are equal to the quantities that people are willing and able to buy. This price is a repository of information. It informs buyers and sellers what they must give up to acquire a unit of the good (that is, their opportunity costs) and thereby lets them know whether their activities have value and in which activities they should specialize.

Day in and day out, without any conscious central direction, the price system induces people to employ their talents and resources in the most effective manner. People do not have to be fooled, cajoled, or forced to do their part in a market system but instead pursue their own objectives as they see fit. Workers, attempting to maximize their own individual happiness and well-being, select the training, careers, and jobs where their talents and energy are most valuable. Producers, pursuing only private profits, develop the goods and services on which consumers put the highest value and produce these goods and services at the lowest possible costs. Owners of resources and capital assets, seeking only to increase their own wealth, deploy these assets in socially desirable ways.

Market Outcomes

The price, or market, system is the predominant allocation mechanism in most industrial societies today. Yet not all exchanges take place through the market system in these societies. Many medical services are provided on a first-come-first-

Figure 2.2
ATTITUDES TOWARD ALLOCATION MECHANISMS

The percent choosing "fair" or "acceptable" is shown along the vertical axis. The allocation mechanisms are shown along the horizontal axis. The red refers to items not related to health.

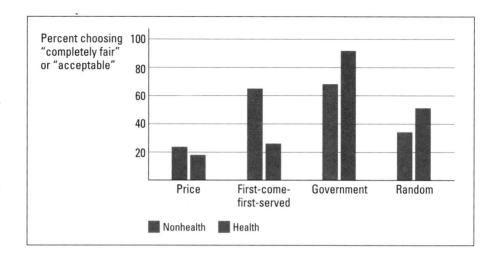

served basis, as are college classes and the use of highways or roadways. Government schemes are also used to allocate many goods—airline routes, radio and television broadcast bands, land use (zoning), rights-of-way at intersections, and many others. Even luck—random allocation—plays a part in the allocation of some items, such as concert tickets, lottery winnings, and other contest prizes.

If the price system is such an efficient mechanism, why is it not universally relied on? One reason is that for some products people do not like the outcome of the price system. For instance, the response of several hundred people to an expanded version of the questionnaire presented earlier indicates that many people prefer something other than the price system, especially for health care. In Figure 2.2, the allocation mechanism is shown along the horizontal axis and the percentage of people choosing either *a* or *b* ("completely fair" or "acceptable") is shown along the vertical axis.

You can see that people feel much less comfortable with the price system for allocating medical goods and services than for other types of goods and services. You can also see that many people simply do not like the outcome of the price system for any good or service—only 20 percent think the price system is fair or acceptable. When people do not like the outcome, they may expend resources to attempt to implement some other allocation mechanism. They lobby the government or attempt to convince voters that some other scheme would be preferable. Thus, in many cases we see allocation mechanisms other than price just because people do not like the outcome of the price system.

Inefficiency

Another reason the price system may not be used is that it is not efficient in certain exchanges. If all costs and benefits are not included in a transaction, then the decisions buyers and sellers make is based on incomplete information and the resulting prices and quantities bought and sold are not efficient. Such costs/benefits are referred to as **externalities;** they are external to the market transaction. Externalities can be positive or negative. If they are negative, they impose costs on others; if they are positive, they grant benefits to others. McDonald's sells its drinks in plastic or Styrofoam cups. Customers discard the cups, often simply throwing them out of the car window. Neither McDonald's nor the customers pay for cleaning up the trash. This is a negative externality. Society as a whole has to pay the costs of cleaning up the trash; those who threw the trash out the window and the McDonald's outlet that put the food and drinks in the plastic containers pay no more than anyone else.

There are 1.5 million cars stolen in the United States each year. An antitheft device called Lojack was first introduced in Boston in 1986 and is now available in most major metropolitan areas. Usually sold to new-car purchasers by car dealers for a one-time fee of about $600, the Lojack system involves a small radio transmitter that is hidden in the car. If the car is reported stolen, the police activate the transmitter by remote control with high-tech equipment provided by the company. About 95 percent of stolen vehicles equipped with Lojack are recovered. By leading police directly to stolen cars, Lojack helps them to shut down "chop shops" that dismantle vehicles for resale of parts. Professional car thieves have no way of knowing whether a car is armed with Lojack. As a result, it is estimated that one auto theft is eliminated annually for every three Lojack systems that are installed. Thus, the benefit to society in terms of less overall auto theft—benefits such as lower insurance costs—exceeds the benefit to the individual owners who install the Lojack system. Society benefits by the sum of the benefits each owner who installs a Lojack system receives and the reduced insurance costs everyone receives. If we subtract the benefits each owner receives from installing the Lojack system from the total society benefits, the remainder is the value of the positive externality.

Externalities refer to situations in which not all costs or benefits are included in a transaction. In other words, people not involved in the transaction receive a benefit or a cost from the transaction. If not all costs and benefits are included in a transaction, then resources may not be allocated to their highest-valued uses. In the case of a negative externality, more resources go into the activity than if the external cost was accounted for. For instance, more Styrofoam cups are produced and sold than if McDonald's and/or customers had to pay the additional cost of cleanup for the discarded cups. In the case of a positive externality, not enough resources go into the activity. For instance, if the benefits of the Lojack system were provided only to the individual buyers, the buyers would receive a lower price and more Lojack systems would be installed. An externality is often referred to as a **market failure** because the market does not take into account all costs and benefits and, therefore, is not efficient.

Another so-called market failure occurs when people can consume a product without having to pay for it. Suppose that whenever you buy a pizza and have it delivered to your house, your neighbors can come over and consume it. You would therefore have no incentive to purchase a pizza. If you do not have the exclusive right (private property right) to the pizza you pay for, you have no incentive to purchase it. As a result, no pizzas would be purchased. This is the type of situation facing national defense. If one person set up a defense network for her property, all others in the neighborhood of that property would also be protected; thus, no one would have an incentive to purchase the defense. This type of market failure is referred to as a **public good**: Anyone can consume the good and it won't affect other people's consumption. As a result, no one pays for the good, and so the good is not produced.

Market failures are often used as the basis for government intervention, that is, for a reliance on a governmental allocation system.[5] Whether these justifications are valid is the focus of a debate among economists. Nevertheless, the government, for example, allocates airwaves (public good), regulates air pollution (negative externality), and provides national defense (public good) based on the argument of market failure.

The Firm's Architecture

Even in the absence of market failure, it is possible that market exchange is not the most efficient allocation mechanism in certain circumstances. For instance, the transactions that occur within a single firm might be too costly (less efficient) to undertake using a market system. The accounting department provides output to the CEO, the production line sends processed microchips to the sales department, and so on, as output is exchanged within a firm. To carry out these transactions via a market system may be inefficient. Can you imagine the accounting department selling the CEO an income statement or balance sheet?[6]

A firm might be thought of as an organization formed to minimize the costs inherent in certain market transactions.[7] Transactions tend to occur in the market when doing so is efficient, and they occur within a firm or some other formal organization when that is efficient. Whether a firm makes or buys—that is, whether it produces a good or service for its own needs or procures it from an outside supplier—depends largely on the cost of managing the transaction within the firm as compared with mediating the transaction through the market. Is it more efficient to have the activities under one roof—within one firm—or to purchase the activities in the market?

Transaction costs include the costs of bargaining and negotiating. They also include the costs associated with one party taking advantage of another because the victim invested in assets that are specifically used in the transaction; this is called a **hold-up.** For instance, a supplier might locate next to a manufacturer with the understanding that their relationship will be a long-term one. Both parties expected gains from trade and had, at least implicitly, agreed to the terms of trade. But once the supplier has invested in a new plant located next to the manufacturer, the manufacturer takes advantage of the supplier by demanding lower prices. The supplier, having invested in the plant, is at a disadvantage in the bargaining process relative to the manufacturer.

Recognizing that a potential trading partner may try a hold-up would necessitate detailed negotiations, written contracts with penalty clauses, or some other protection. All these activities use resources—they are costly. If they are costly enough, one organization may find that it would be less costly to acquire the other or to merge with the other and bring the activity in-house.[8]

Transactions costs of market exchange include the following:

1. The cost of searching for a product or for a supplier willing to sell a given input
2. The cost of negotiating a price (e.g., time, legal fees)
3. The cost of investments and expenditures required to facilitate exchange
4. The cost of avoiding future hold-up problems

If transactions in the market are costly, why isn't the economy just one big firm? The reason is that in-house resource allocations also involve costs. For instance, as firms become larger, it becomes more and more difficult for managers to make efficient decisions. They have to take into account increasing amounts of information; they have to decide what will motivate employees to perform as desired; they have to define and finalize relations with customers and suppliers; they require more assistants to help with the tasks. At some point, it is more costly to have an in-house transaction than to mediate that transaction through the market.

A firm becomes **vertically integrated** when it is more efficient for the firm to carry out transactions between suppliers and producers internally rather than externally. A firm becomes **horizontally integrated** when it is more efficient to include parallel activities within the firm than to use the market.

A firm's organization or structure is referred to as its **architecture**. That architecture includes the boundaries of the firm—how much it does internally and how much it outsources, whether it is "hierarchical" or "flat," and how employees work and are compensated.[9]

Assessing the architecture of the firm is not a matter of ideology or fads. Rather, it involves determining how efficient the architecture is. The most efficient architecture for a firm depends on what the firm does and the market(s) in which it operates. Simply put, the transactions that are carried out within the firm must be more efficient than if they were carried out outside of the firm.

Markets and the Law of One Price

We have discussed the market system but have not defined what a market is or how markets work. Let's turn to that now. A market was once an event that occurred in a particular location at a particular time. Consumers would go there to meet suppliers and compare goods and prices. This is still true of some markets even in the United States. Small "farmers' markets" selling flowers and produce exist in most U.S. cities, and buyers and sellers meet every day in the pit in Chicago's commodity exchange. But these physical markets are now the exception rather than the rule. Nevertheless, as with the historical markets, the boundary of the modern market has a product and a geographic dimension; accordingly, we talk of, say, the New York garment market or the world oil market.

The key aspect in determining the boundaries of a market is the consumers' opportunity to substitute one product for another. People no longer have to walk between market stalls appraising one supplier's price and quality against another's, but if they have information about alternative offers and the opportunity to choose one source rather than another, then that can be considered a single market. The market for travel between Boston and New York consists of air, rail, and highway transportation. The market is not simply the air travel.

Market Boundaries

Firms that define markets too narrowly or too broadly can lose significant amounts of money. Epson, for example, made the error of defining its market too narrowly. In 1989, there were three types of desktop printers on the U.S. market. Dot-matrix printers occupied the low end and laser printers the high end, with ink-jet printers in between. Dot-matrix printers accounted for about 80 percent of total unit sales of desktops and laser printers around 15 percent, with ink-jet printers taking the remaining 5 percent. Typical retail prices were $500 for a dot-matrix printer, $600 for an ink-jet printer, and $2,000 for a laser printer. At that time, Epson was the leading dot-matrix producer and Hewlett-Packard the leader in the laser and ink-jet segments.[10] The laser segment had the highest prices and

Sir Alec Issigonis altered British history with his sketch on a napkin of a small but sporty, fuel-efficient four-passenger family car. That Greek-born engineer who lived in Turkey was the designer of the first Mini, formally the Morris Mini-Minor. Built in response to a gas shortage, the first Minis were released in England in August 1959. Called the Austin Mini Seven or the Morris Mini Minor, the car was fast, fuel-efficient and had room for four. Realizing the little car could hug a road with impressive speed, Formula One designer John Cooper upgraded the engine. The Mini Cooper and the Cooper S, released in 1961, went on to win some of Europe's most prestigious races, including the Monte Carlo Rally. BMW is producing the newest version of the cars and at list price, demand exceeds supply. Would-be customers wait weeks for even a test drive. The sale of one of these cars on an auction site in the USA was $15,000 above list price.

margins and was the fastest growing. So in August 1989, Epson launched a very competitively priced laser printer, the EOL-6000. One week later, HP came out with its LaserJet IIP, priced significantly below the EPL-6000. Epson responded by reducing the price of the EPL-6000 and succeeded in building up to a 5 percent share of the laser printer business by the beginning of 1990.

However, due to the declining prices in the laser segment, HP began to reduce the price of its ink-jet machines. Epson soon discovered that it was losing dot-matrix sales to the ink-jet machines, which were now comparably priced. Epson's core business was squeezed from both ends. Epson had failed to realize that the printers were in the same market—they had simply been positioned differently.

Law of One Price

For an overview of the Big Mac Index, visit

http://www.skfriends.com/
big-mac-index.htm

When the Mazda Miata was introduced in the United States in 1990, the little sports roadster was an especially desired product in southern California. Its suggested retail price was $13,996, the price at which it was selling in Detroit. In Los Angeles, however, the purchase price was nearly $25,000. The identical product, the Miata, was selling for different prices in different markets—the Detroit auto market and the Los Angeles auto market. Several entrepreneurs recognized the profit potential in the $10,000 price differential and sent hundreds of college students to Detroit to pick up Miatas and drive them back to L.A. Within a reasonably short time, the price differential between Detroit and L.A. was reduced. The increased sales in Detroit drove the price there up, while the increased number of Miatas being sold in Los Angeles reduced the price there. The price differential continued to decline until it was less than the cost of shipping the cars from Detroit to Los Angeles.

The process of buying identical products in one market and selling them in another at virtually the same time is referred to as **arbitrage**. Arbitrage results in what is called the **law of one price**: Identical goods selling in different markets have the same price.[11]

Each year *The Economist* magazine carries out a worldwide survey of Big Macs. One such survey yielded the following prices: Tokyo, $4; New York, $3.50; and Phoenix, $1. Does the price differential provide an arbitrage opportunity? Can the Big Macs be purchased in the low-price area and shipped to the high-price area? The answer appears to be no. The reason? Big Macs aren't very portable. By the time the hamburgers were transported, they would not be edible. The law of one price cannot function when products are not portable.

Arbitrage is the market process in operation. It ensures that resources are allocated to their highest-valued uses—that inefficient transactions, inefficient organizations, and inefficiency of any sort wither away.

> **NOTE:** When we speak of arbitrage, it is typically price on which we focus. But arbitrage works on other dimensions as well. If two products are similar but differentiated by quality, the arbitrage will involve buying the higher-quality product and selling the lower-quality one. Then either the quality will be adjusted, so that the two products have about the same quality, or prices will change to reflect quality differences.

Arbitrage is a search for gains. By buying in a low-priced market and selling in a higher-priced market, the trader is able to gain. The search for gains is the market in action—it is competition. Competition drives out inefficiency and ensures that resources are allocated to their highest-valued uses. Think what would occur if resources were not being used efficiently, or in their highest-valued use, by a firm. That firm could not price as low as a firm that was more efficient. The trader would then buy from the low-priced firm; this in turn would force the high-priced firm to lower its price—to become more efficient. If the firm could not achieve that efficiency, then it would have to go out of business. The resources would then be acquired and put into operation in the more efficient firm.

Demand and Supply: Equilibrium

A market can be illustrated as a simple demand and supply diagram, as shown in Figure 2.3. The demand curve represents the buyers; it shows the total quantity that all buyers are willing and able to purchase at each price. The supply curve represents the sellers; it shows the total quantity that all suppliers are willing and able to offer for sale at each price.

Let's digress a moment to define exactly what the demand and supply curves represent. The demand curve illustrates what is called the law of demand. The law of demand consists of five phrases:

Figure 2.3

DEMAND AND SUPPLY

Demand and supply represent a market.

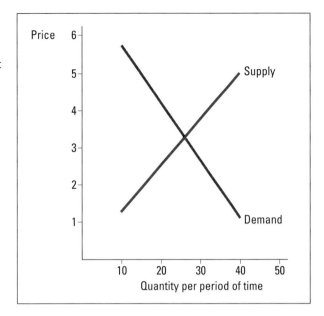

1. The quantity of a well-defined good or service
2. that people are willing and able to purchase
3. during a particular period of time
4. decreases as the price of that good or service increases,
5. everything else held constant.

The first phrase ensures that we are referring to the same item, that we are not mixing different items. A watch is a commodity defined and distinguished from other goods by several characteristics: quality, color, and design of the watch face, to name a few. The law of demand applies to the well-defined good—in this case, a watch. If one of the characteristics should change, the good would no longer be well defined; in fact, it would be a different good. A Rolex watch is different from a Timex watch; Polo golf shirts are different from Izod shirts; Mercedes-Benz automobiles are different from Yugo automobiles. As we discussed in the previous chapter, we may refer to the market just for Rolex watches or to the broader market for watches. The demand being discussed will depend on the market being discussed: There is a demand for watches, and there is a demand for Rolex watches.

The second phrase indicates that people must not only *want* to purchase some good; they must be *able* to purchase that good in order for their wants to be counted as part of demand. For example, Sue would love to own a Mercedes Benz 300C, but the sticker price of $50,000 is too high. Though willing, she is not able to purchase the car. At a price of $30,000, she would be both willing and able; thus her wants would count as an element of demand at a price of $30,000 or less.

The third phrase points out that the demand for any good is defined for a specific period of time. Without reference to a time period, a demand relationship would not make any sense. For instance, the statement that "at a price of $3 per Happy Meal, 13 million Happy Meals are demanded" provides no useful information. Are the 13 million meals sold in one week or one year? Think of demand as a rate of purchase at each possible price over a period of time—two per month, one per day, and so on.

The fourth phrase points out that price and quantity demanded move in opposite directions.

The fifth phrase has to do with things other than the price that affect demand. The phrase "everything else held constant" ensures that anything other than price that might affect demand is assumed to be unchanging.

To move from an individual's demand to the market demand, all the individual demands must be summed. Since not all individuals are identical, the market demand is not simply the number of people involved multiplied by one individual's demand. Instead, each demander must be counted. This means that the market demand will contain the demands of different market segments—senior citizens and children, or high-income and low-income individuals, or college-educated and non-college-educated persons, and so on.

Income, prices of related goods, and tastes or preferences are called *determinants of demand*. When one of the determinants of demand changes, the demand schedule and demand curve will change. For instance, people will buy more of most goods and services if their income rises. So, if incomes rise, the demand curve will shift outward—at each price a higher quantity of goods are demanded.

Also, some goods are related such that when the demand for one changes, the demand for the other also changes. When the price of a microchip increases, the amount of Windows sold declines. These two products are complements. When the price of a Toyota Camry increases, more Ford Tauruses are sold. These two cars are substitutes.

If tastes change, demand will change. For instance, if people learn that some product causes cancer, the demand for that product will decline. People may increase or decrease their desire for a product because of new information or experiences they have acquired.

Economists distinguish between the terms *demand* and *quantity demanded*. When they refer to the quantity demanded, they are talking about the amount of a product that people are willing and able to purchase at a specific price. When they refer to demand, they are talking about the amount that people would be willing and able to purchase at every possible price. Demand is the quantities demanded at each and every price. Thus, the statement that "the demand for U.S. white wine rose after a 300 percent tariff was applied to French white wine" means that at each price for U.S. white wine, more people were willing and able to purchase U.S. white wine. And the statement that "the quantity demanded of white wine fell as the price of white wine rose" means that people were willing and able to purchase less white wine because the price of the wine rose.

On the supply side, there is a law of supply that matches the law of demand. It states that the quantity of some item that people are willing and able to purchase, during a particular period of time, decreases as the price rises and vice versa, ceteris paribus (all else being equal).

Prices of resources used to produce the good or service, technological changes enabling more to be produced with the same amount of resources, expectations of producers, and number of sellers affect supply; if one of these *determinants of supply* changes, the supply schedule and supply curve will change. For instance, sellers will offer more for sale at every single price if their costs are reduced through either lower prices of resources or technological changes. Similarly, producers may offer less or more for sale at each possible price if their expectations

Figure 2.4

EQUILIBRIUM

Demand and supply together determine the market price—the equilibrium price. When demand and/or supply change, the equilibrium changes.

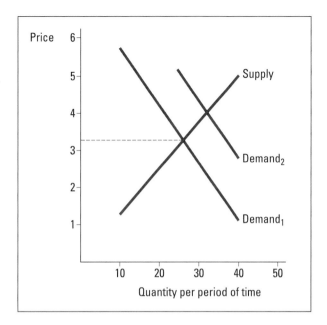

about market conditions change. As more sellers offer a product for sale, the supply increases.

Economists also distinguish between the terms *supply* and *quantity supplied*. When they refer to the quantity supplied, they are talking about the amount of a product that sellers are willing and able to offer for sale at a specific price. When they refer to supply, they are talking about the amount that sellers would be willing and able to purchase at every possible price.

With demand and supply defined, we can now see how the curves can illustrate the operation of a market.

Demand and supply together determine the market price. When price is greater than 3 in Figure 2.4, a surplus would develop—more would be offered for sale than is purchased. To get rid of their excesses, sellers would lower the price. When price is less than 3 in Figure 2.4, a shortage would arise as sellers offer less for sale than demanders want to purchase. Sellers would raise the price. The price at which buyers are willing and able to purchase everything that sellers are willing and able to offer for sale is called the equilibrium, or market-clearing price. At this price neither sellers nor buyers have any reason to alter their behavior.

When something causes demand and/or supply to change, the market-clearing price and quantity are likely to change. In Figure 2.4, demand rises (from Demand$_1$ to Demand$_2$) due to an increase in consumer incomes. This leads to a price increase. Notice that as demand rises, the quantity supplied rises from 30 to 40, but the supply (the entire curve) does not change.

When demand and/or supply change, the market will induce sellers and buyers to alter their behavior and reallocate resources as the market heads toward a new equilibrium—that is, as long as price is able to change. In many markets, buyers or sellers may not like the market outcome and may want a price floor or a price ceiling to be imposed. Rent controls are a specific example of a price ceiling: The rent is not allowed to rise to the equilibrium level. Sugar subsidies are a specific example of a price floor: The price of sugar is not allowed to fall below a certain level.

Figure 2.5
THE LAW OF ONE PRICE

The law of one price states that if an identical good sells for different prices in different markets, market forces will drive price toward equality. In this case, the higher price in the market on the left attracts suppliers while the lower price in the market on the right attracts buyers. The result is a lower price in the higher-priced market (on the left) and a higher price in the lower-priced market (on the right).

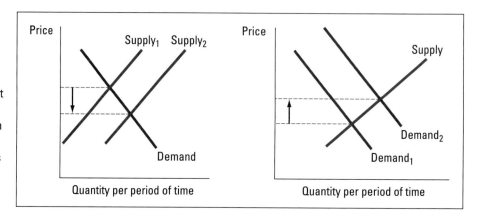

Now consider the law of one price. Suppose Figure 2.5 represents two markets for the same good or service. The market-clearing price is different in the two markets. What will occur? If the good or service is portable and there are no restrictions in entering or leaving either market, the markets will be driven toward the same market-clearing price. Arbitrage will occur; people will buy in the second market and sell in the first. This will drive demand up in the second and supply up in the first. Resources are reallocated to where they are most highly valued, going from market 2 to market 1. The market-clearing price adjusts in each market until there is no room for arbitrage.

CASE REVIEW *Procter & Gamble: New Product Launch*[12]

The case discusses P&G's approach to the European market. It indicates that P&G has to determine whether to consider Europe to be one market rather than designating distinct markets for each country and asks how the executives of P&G should proceed in introducing a new detergent to the European market(s).

Several P&G executives argued that the time was ripe for a common European detergent. Having a single detergent with a single formula and manufacturing structure as well as a single marketing campaign would be a great deal less costly than having separate ones for each nation. Opponents focused on national differences, arguing that the single product would reduce manufacturing costs but would not have the sales of a product designed for each market. They noted that clothes-washing habits vary widely from country to country. Typical washing temperatures are much higher in Europe than the United States. However, lower washing temperatures are more common in some countries where the washing machines do not heat water or where hand washing is still an important segment. European washing machines are front loading with a horizontal rotating drum, whereas in the United States there is an agitator action in a top-loaded machine. The European machines have a smaller water capacity and use a much longer cycle. In Germany, there are fewer grocery retailers than in the other nations. In Italy, the independent corner store is very important. In the United Kingdom, television is in virtually every house, whereas in Spain and Portugal only about 45 percent of households have televisions. The laws affecting business differ considerably as well. In Finland and Holland, phosphate levels in detergent are limited. In Germany, coupons, refunds, and premium offers are not allowed. In other countries, package weight and labeling are regulated.

The issue focused on is the definition of a market. A market is the location where a well-defined good or service is bought and sold. "Well-defined" means that similar but not identical products are substitutes for each other in the consumer's mind. For instance, a detergent for use in Italy might differ in packaging from the one in Germany, but if either could be used in either country, the products are substitutes. In the text, it is mentioned that for short distances, air flights and ground transport are substitutes. The market for travel over short routes then includes both items. If an airline set policies without considering the role of ground transport, it would be leaving out an important aspect of demand—a substitute good.

So, how can P&G determine whether it is speaking of a single market or of different markets? What are the boundaries of the market—all of Europe, each country, or something altogether different? This determination requires that P&G examine the consumers and find out whether they are the same or differ significantly in terms of tastes, preferences, and income. If it determines that Italian consumers have to have some element in their detergent that German consumers refuse to consider, then P&G must consider the markets as distinct—there can be no such thing as a Eurobrand.

P&G's strategy in introducing its new detergent should have been to compare the costs of introducing a Eurobrand to the benefits of this unified approach and to do the same for a distinct introduction to each European country. In each case there are tradeoffs: Choosing the Eurobrand approach means a reduction in marketing and production costs but the potential problem of having defined the market too broadly; choosing the individual market approach means higher marketing and production costs but products more in tune with individual markets. Thus, all costs and benefits should have been compared and the option yielding the greatest benefit over costs chosen. The costs of an action are not simply the out-of-pocket expenses but also what is forgone with each action.

P&G executives had many meetings in which they debated the costs and benefits of the decision. Interestingly, given their extensive experience with market analysis, they failed to appropriately define demand for the Eurobrand. Moreover, they failed to fully define costs. Opportunity costs, such as sales that would not occur because the product was "Euro" rather than "Franco" or "Anglo," were not included. As a result, the Eurobrand launch was not successful. Instead, P&G had to approach its globalization strategy by focusing on each market separately. It set up subsidiaries in each country and designed products and marketing campaigns for each subsidiary.

SUMMARY

1. Specialization according to comparative advantage and then trade enables all parties to gain.
2. Efficiency is the situation in which the most goods and services are produced at the lowest costs and the allocation of goods, services, and resources could not be changed without making someone worse off.
3. Allocation mechanisms are used to distribute scarce goods, services, and resources. Allocation mechanisms in use today include the price system,

government schemes, first-come-first-served, and random allocation (luck). The price system is the predominant mechanism because it is the most efficient. Nonetheless, other mechanisms are used. In some cases, other mechanisms are used because the outcome of the price system is disliked. In other cases, the price system may not be the most efficient; there may be market failures, or transaction costs may be high.

4. A firm is a replacement for a market; trade and exchange occur within the firm. A firm does not use the price system internally because the transaction costs would be too high.

5. The architecture of a firm is its organization. The boundaries of a firm and a firm's architecture are defined by efficiency. Is it more efficient to have an activity carried out in-house or to trade for this activity in the open market?

6. A market is defined by buyers and sellers exchanging goods or services along product and geographic dimensions.

7. The law of one price indicates that identical goods sell for virtually identical prices in different markets. The law holds because of arbitrage—the process of buying where price is low and selling where price is high.

KEY TERMS

production possibilities curve (PPC)
comparative advantage
gains from trade
efficiency
Pareto efficient

externalities
market failure
public good
transaction costs
hold-up
vertical integration

horizontal integration
architecture
arbitrage
law of one price

EXERCISES

1. In most elections, the candidates promise a great deal. For instance, in the 2000 presidential election, it was promised there would be more and better health care; a better environment; better education; and improvements in roads, bridges, sewer systems, water systems, national defense, and Social Security. What economic concept is ignored in such campaigns?

2. If someone invites you to a lunch and offers to pay for it, is it free for you?

3. Evaluate this statement: "You are a natural athlete, an attractive person who learns easily and communicates well. Clearly, you can do everything better than your friends and acquaintances. As a result, the term *specialization* has no meaning for you. Specialization would cost you rather than benefit you."

4. In elementary school and middle school, most students have the same teacher throughout the day for the entire school year. In high school,

different subjects are taught by different teachers. In college, the same subject is often taught at different levels—freshman, sophomore, junior, senior, or graduate—by different faculty. Is education taking advantage of specialization only from high school on?

5. Top officials in the federal government and high-ranking officers of large corporations often have chauffeurs to drive them around the city or from meeting to meeting. Is this simply one of the perquisites of their position, or is the use of chauffeurs justifiable on the basis of comparative advantage?

6. During China's Cultural Revolution in the late 1960s and early 1970s, many people with a high school or college education were forced to move to farms and work in the fields. Some worked as common laborers for eight or more years. What does this policy say about specialization and the production possibilities curve (PPC)? Would you

predict that the policy would lead to an increase in output?

7. In most restaurants, the waiters and waitresses receive a large portion of their compensation through tips from customers. The size of the tip is typically decided by the customers. However, many restaurants put a mandatory tip of 15 percent or so on bills for any group larger than six. Explain why this structure is efficient.

8. In recent years, business consultants and business schools have been stressing teams. It is argued that firms would be better off using teams rather than relying separately on each individual. Evaluate this argument.

9. If the market system is so wonderful, why do firms exist?

10. If transactions are costly, why isn't the economy just one big firm?

11. Xerox underwent a radical reorganization in 1992 in order to stem its decline (its earnings, market share, and earnings per share of stock had all fallen in the 1980s). The reorganization left the information management (IM) division stranded; it was not an integral part of the other divisions. As a result, it could not gather the data necessary to support the various business divisions. Would it make sense to outsource IM? List all the costs and benefits you can for keeping the IM function in-house and for outsourcing the IM function.

12. The following are cost functions from a manufacturing firm whose CEO has called in consultants to help with reengineering. The costs with a hierarchical form—where hierarchical refers to a pyramid type structure with vice presidents reporting to the CEO, managers reporting to vice presidents, associate managers reporting to managers, and so on—are defined as $C = 28,305,600 + 460,300Q$, where C is total cost in dollars and Q is the number of machines sold. The costs with a less hierarchical form (fewer reporting steps) are defined as $C = 22,206,500 + 480,345Q$. What is your recommendation to the CEO regarding the structure of the firm? What must the CEO know in order to make a decision?

13. Suppose the relationship between quantity demanded and price is represented by:

$$Q = -500P + 200I - 400S + 0.01A, \text{ where}$$

P = price

I = income

C = price of complementary product

A = expenditures on advertising

a. Draw the demand curve for Q.

b. Find quantity demanded when $I = \$15,000$, $C = \$300$, $A = \$40$ million. Show that point on the demand curve for Q you drew in part a.

c. Find quantity demanded when $I = \$20,000$, $C = \$300$, $A = \$40$ million. Show that point relative to the point in part b. What has happened to demand?

14. Suppose market demand is represented by

$$Q_d = 3,000,000 - 700P + 200I$$

and market supply is represented by

$$Q_s = 1,000,000 + 400P$$

a. How do you determine the market price?

b. Suppose $I = 15,000$. Can you find market price? Also find quantity supplied and quantity demanded.

CHAPTER NOTES

1. Based on Harvard Business School, Case 9-384-139, by Christopher A. Bartlett; and Harvard Business School, Case 5-388-131, by Christopher A. Bartlett.

2. In this diagram, the PPC is a straight line indicating a constant tradeoff of agricultural products for high-tech products, or vice versa. In reality, the PPC is typically a bowed-out curve illustrating that the additional cost of producing one more unit of a certain type of product rises as more of the resources are devoted to that product.

3. William J. Baumol, *The Free-Market Innovation Machine,* Princeton: Princeton University Press, 2002, examines the incentives of the free market in terms of economic growth.

4. It need not be materialistic. A society believing that glorification of the deity is the goal would be evaluated on that basis, as pointed out in Paul Milgrom and John Roberts, *Economics, Organization & Management* (Englewood Cliffs, NJ: Prentice-Hall, 1992), p. 22. A society believing that military prowess is the goal would be evaluated on that basis.

5. In analyzing whether government intervention makes sense, the question that has to be answered is whether the government allocation system also has failure and inefficiencies. If so, then the costs/benefits of the two alternative systems have to be evaluated.

6. Actually, this is not so far-fetched. Many firms are outsourcing their accounting and budgeting to independent firms.

7. This point was first made in Ronald Coase, "The Nature of the Firm," *Economica* 4 (1937): 386–405. It has since been followed by Armen Alchian and Harold Demsetz, "Production, Information Costs, and Economic Organization," *American Economic Review,* 62 (1972): 777–795; and Oliver Williamson, *Markets and Hierarchies: Analysis and Antitrust Implications* (New York: Free Press, 1975).

8. We'll examine transaction costs and organizational structures in more detail in Chapter 10.

9. Specialization according to comparative advantage and then gaining from trade is a principle older than business. Yet many managers forget the lesson or turn their backs on it to follow along with some management fad. A recent example is reengineering. Reengineering was undertaken in many cases not because it exploited specialization and comparative advantage but because it was popular. A survey of chief financial officers at eighty large American companies in May 1995 pointed out just how faddish it was. According to 29 percent of the officers, the main reason for wanting to do reengineering was cost cutting, but another 26 percent said that is was done simply because "someone important said we should do it" (26 percent).

10. "The Domino Effect: Of Foxes, Printers, and Prices," *Channelmarker Letter,* 2, no. 6 (December 1990): 1–7.

11. Alfred Marshall (1890), a prominent economist of the time stated: "The more nearly perfect a market is, the stronger is the tendency for the same price to be paid for the same thing at the same time in all parts of the market."

12. Based on Harvard Business School, Case 9-384-139, by Christopher A. Bartlett; and Harvard Business School, Case 5-388-131, by Christopher A. Bartlett.

Optimization

Economizing in many respects is optimizing. We want the most for the least. Firms maximize profit while consumers maximize happiness or satisfaction. In this appendix, a few mathematical tools used in optimization problems are discussed. Specifically, it is shown how calculus can be used to analyze unconstrained and constrained optimization problems. We'll begin with a few basic math definitions.

The Concept of Marginal

A **function** is a rule that describes the relation between variables. For each value of variable x, a function assigns a unique value for variable y according to some rule. For example, the function given by $y = 3x$ indicates that the value of variable y is equal to 3 times the value of variable x.

Often in economics we know that some variable y, the *dependent* variable, is a function of some variable x, the *independent* variable, but we do not know the exact algebraic relationship between the variables. In this instance, we write $y = f(x)$, which means that the dependent variable y depends on the independent variable x according to the rule f.

One way to represent a function is with a graph. The graph of a function illustrates the relation between one variable and another with a picture. Figure 2A.1 shows the graph of the function $y = 3x$. In mathematics the horizontal axis usually represents the independent variable and the vertical axis usually represents the dependent variable. In economics, however, we often graph the independent variable on the vertical axis and the dependent variable on the horizontal axis. For example, the demand function, $Q = f(P)$ indicates that the quantity demanded depends on the price P. Price is the independent variable and quantity is

Figure 2A.1

GRAPH OF FUNCTION

$y = 3x$

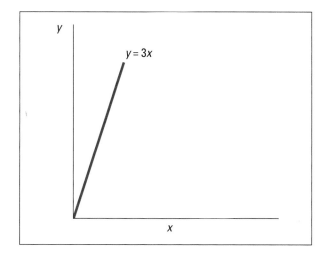

Figure 2A.2

DEMAND CURVE

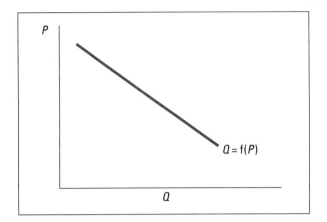

the dependent variable. But we draw the demand curve by measuring price on the vertical axis and quantity on the horizontal axis, as shown in Figure 2A.2.

Economics deals with change. In fact, one of the principal terms in economics, *marginal,* means "incremental," that is, "a change in some variable." For instance, total revenue is *PQ,* price times the number of units of an item that is sold. **Marginal revenue** is the change in total revenue that results from a one-unit change in quantity. Change can be represented with the Greek letter delta, as Δ, so that marginal revenue is shown as:

ΔTotal Revenue/Quantity or $\Delta TR/\Delta Q$.

Similarly, total cost is the cost of producing and/or offering for sale units of an item, *TC.* Marginal cost is shown as:

ΔTotal Cost/Quantity or $\Delta TC/\Delta Q$.

Derivatives

Marginal can also be symbolized as a derivative such as *dTR/dQ* and *dTC/dQ* or the partial derivative $\partial TR/\partial Q$ and $\partial TC/\partial Q$. Whereas Δ represents relatively large differences or discrete changes, the derivative represents very small changes. In fact, the derivative is an infinitesimal change.

$$\frac{dTR}{dQ} = \lim_{\Delta Q \to 0} \left\{ \frac{\Delta TR}{\Delta Q} \right\}$$

A **derivative** measures the change in a dependent variable that comes with a very small change in the independent variables. A **partial derivative** enables us to measure a change in the dependent variable with respect to a very small change in one independent variable, everything else held constant.

Given the function $y = f(x,z)$, the partial derivative of y with respect to x is defined by

$$\frac{\partial y}{\partial x} = \frac{\partial f(x,z)}{\partial x}$$

The primary rules for finding those derivatives or partial derivatives that we use in economic problems are:

If $y = k$, where k is a constant, then $dy/dx = 0$.

If $y = kx^n$ where k and n are constants, then $dy/dx = nkx^{n-1}$.

If $y = f(x)g(x)$ then $dy/dx = g(x)[df(x)/dx] + f(x)[dg(x)/dx]$.

Maximum and Minimum

Often we want to find the maximum or minimum of some function. We identify possible maximum or minimum points by finding the point where the slope of the function is zero. We set the first derivative equal to zero

$df(x)/dx = 0$.

This identifies the point, x^*, where the function is a maximum or a minimum. To know whether it is a maximum or a minimum we would have to know what the function is doing before and after this point, that is, what the slope of the slope is. This is calculated using the second derivative, symbolized as $d^2f(x)/dx^2$. If the second derivative is negative, then the function is concave at the point x^* and the function is at a minimum. If the second derivative is positive, the function is convex at the point x^* and the function is at a maximum.

Constrained Optimization

Often in economics, the optimization involves a constraint; for instance, we want to maximize our happiness but are constrained by how much income we have, or we want to maximize profit but are constrained by how our resources must be used. Suppose that we specify happiness, U, to be a function of the quantity of two goods we have.

$U = f(x,z)$

This is called the **objective function**. But we are constrained by our income, Y.

$Y = g(x,z)$

This is called the **constraint**. This is a constrained optimization problem.

There are two ways to solve a constrained optimization problem. The first way is to solve the constraint for one of the choice variables in terms of the other and then substitute the result into the objective function. The second way is to use Lagrangian multipliers.

To solve by use of Lagrangian multipliers, we start by defining the Lagrangian function

$L = f(x,z) + \lambda([Y - g(x,z)]$

which is the objective function $f(x,z)$ plus the Lagrangian variable λ multiplied by the constraint set equal to zero, $Y - g(x,z) = 0$. We then find the optimal values of x and z by taking derivatives with respect to x, with respect to z, and with respect to λ, and setting each equal to zero.

$$\frac{\partial L}{\partial x} = \frac{\partial f(x,z)}{\partial x} - \frac{\lambda\{\partial g(x,z)\}}{\partial x} = 0$$

$$\frac{\partial L}{\partial z} = \frac{\partial f(x,z)}{\partial z} - \frac{\lambda\{\partial g(x,z)\}}{\partial z} = 0$$

$$\frac{\partial L}{\partial \lambda} = Y - g(x,z) = 0$$

This set of equations is known as the first-order conditions. Notice that the first-order conditions, in this case, involve three equations in three variables, x, z, and λ. So these three equations can be solved for the values of the three variables.

Consider an example of cost minimization. Suppose that company A produces and sells two products, x and z, and that its total cost is given by

$$C = f(x,z) = 4x^2 + 8z^2 - 2xz$$

where x is its output per hour of the first product and z is its output per hour of the second product. The company has contracted with manufacturers to produce a total of 40 units each hour, but any mix of x and z is acceptable. Find the optimal mix if the firm wants to minimize cost.

The Lagrangian function is

$$L = 4x^2 + 8z^2 - 2xz + \lambda(40 - x - z)$$

$$\frac{\partial L}{\partial x} = 8x - 2z - \lambda = 0$$

$$\frac{\partial L}{\partial z} = 16z - 2x - \lambda = 0$$

$$\frac{\partial L}{\partial \lambda} = 40 - x - z = 0$$

Solving the first equation for λ and substituting into the second equation gives

$$16z - 2x - 8x + 2z = 0$$

or $z = 10x/18 = 5x/9$. Substituting this into the third equation and solving for x gives $x = 25.7$. Thus the optimal value for z is $z = 5x/9 = 14.3$. Notice that $x + z = 40$, which is our constraint.

CHAPTER 3

Performance

The Enron Caper

In 2002, Enron Corporation collapsed amid allegations of fraud. The firm was accused of using accounting loopholes to hide its true performance. Yet there are many accounting loopholes and sleights-of-hand that are neither illegal nor Ponzi schemes. Accounting loopholes allow some companies to ignore major costs of

doing business when tallying up their profit. Sears left $2.4 billion in leases it was liable for off its balance sheet. While legal, the maneuver in this case was a major omission, because it wasn't added to the $22.2 billion Sears reported as debt. Even a minor change in the way a company does its accounting can make a huge difference in the bottom line. A company can use various tactics to lower the taxes it pays, change the method it uses to count inventory, or even use profit expected from its employees' pension plans to goose the bottom line. RSA Security, which makes computer security systems, started booking revenue as soon as it sold goods to its distributors rather than waiting until the distributors sold the goods. That change boosted RSA's revenue $1.7 million in the three months ended March 31, 2001. Companies may swap goods in order to help each other look better. The revenue can be booked right away, but the cost of buying the goods can be spread over about three years. Such an arrangement helped Siebel beat analysts' estimates the first quarter of 2001, while most techs were suffering. During the period, Siebel's revenue got a boost from the $38 million in license fees it collected from vendors it bought goods from at about the same time. In the fourth quarter of 2001, Whirlpool topped analysts' expectations; its earnings were up 63 percent from a year earlier. But these numbers did not include $91 million for restructuring that, if included, would have shown a 69 percent decline. Another accounting trick is to have a company divest some portion of its activities but keep a less than 50 percent interest in these activities.

Coca-Cola does this with its bottlers. The advantage is that the debt of the bottlers does not have to appear on Coca-Cola's financial statements. So Enron, the energy-trading company that was at the heart of congressional inquiries in 2002, is not necessarily unique.

What do these accounting practices mean for the ability of investors to measure the performance of firms?

Value

In the previous chapter we noted that the market process results in resources being used where they have the highest value. We also noted that firms are an alternative to market exchange for certain transactions and exist because exchange within them is more efficient than the same transactions would be if carried out in the open market. Efficiency is the cornerstone of success. A firm that is more efficient at providing a product that people want will be more successful than less efficient organizations.

The market process is ongoing or dynamic, which means it is difficult for a firm always to be efficient. A highest-valued use for resources one day might not be the highest-valued use another day. At any point in time, some firms are successful and some firms are not. How do we know which is which? The answer seems obvious, doesn't it? Successful firms are those that are profitable, while unsuccessful ones are those experiencing losses. But the answer is not as straightforward as it seems. Profit can be measured in several different ways, and the ways don't always represent a true picture of success. Not only is the measure of profitability a matter of concern, but many firms or organizations are not for-profit. Their success or failure therefore can't be judged on the basis of profit. In this chapter we discuss measures of performance.

Adding Value

There are many websites that explore adding value or economic value. One of the most interesting is the Stern-Stewart website, found at

http://www.eva.com/

Adding value is one of the current buzzwords of business. It has supplanted *profit maximizing*, perhaps because it is more general. Adding value is an objective not only for for-profit institutions but also for nonprofit ones. The purpose of a charitable organization, university, or tennis or golf club is to create an output that is more valuable than the cost of the inputs used to produce the output. The problem with many nonprofits is that it is difficult to measure the value of output. For instance, St. Mary's Food Bank is a nonprofit organization providing food to homeless people. Its costs are relatively straightforward to measure—the costs of resources used by St. Mary's. It doesn't obtain revenues by selling its output; instead, its revenues come from donations, and the donations arise because donors believe the services provided by St. Mary's are worth purchasing (supporting). Since St. Mary's is by definition nonprofit, its revenues will not exceed its costs. Nevertheless, the charitable institution is adding value if the value of its output—the value of food distributed and other services provided—exceeds the cost of the resources it uses.

Adding value is the purpose of business activity. An organization that adds no value—whose output is worth less than the value of its inputs in alternative uses—has no long-term rationale for its existence. In the long run, organizations that fail to add value will not survive. Inefficient decisions and allocations will eventually be replaced or overturned by more efficient ones.

Economic Profit

Defining added value is easier for for-profit firms than for nonprofit organizations. Nevertheless, for both types of organizations, added value is what remains in the value of output once the costs of the inputs used in the organization have been fully accounted for.

Economists classify inputs into three general groups: land, labor, and capital. Land refers to all natural resources, raw materials, and land and sea; labor includes skilled and unskilled labor; and capital is structures, equipment, and inventories. The costs of these inputs are their opportunity costs—the amount necessary to keep the resource owners from moving the resources to an alternative use. For instance, if a landowner can rent her land to another firm at a higher rate than the current renter pays, then she will. To keep her from renting to another, the first renter must pay her at least equal to what the second would have paid. The landowner has to be paid the opportunity cost of the land if she is to keep that land in its current use. Similarly, an employee must be paid his opportunity cost or he will take an alternative position. Owners of capital also must be paid the opportunity cost of their capital or they will take it elsewhere.

Capital is acquired through loans (debt), sales of ownership rights (shares of stock—equity—for a public company), and earnings retained in the firm (earnings not allocated to owners in the form of dividends). When debt holders lend money to a company, they do so with the expectation that the company will repay the principal, with interest. The interest a company pays depends on the debt holders' expectations of other opportunities, inflation, and risk. The greater the risk, the greater the inflation expected to occur, and the greater the opportunity to earn money elsewhere, the greater the interest rate charged the borrower. Thus, the cost of debt is the interest that is paid on the debt.

Shareholders also consider other opportunities and risk in determining whether to invest in a company. The cost of equity capital is the alternative return that the shareholders could have gotten had they not chosen to invest in this particular activity or company—the investors' opportunity cost. For instance, since shareholders of Microsoft could invest in other businesses, the return from the best of these alternative investments—a return that was forgone when Microsoft stock was purchased—is the cost of investing in Microsoft. And Microsoft must pay its shareholders at least what they expect to get from alternative investments or the shareholders will take their capital elsewhere.

Added value is the excess of revenues over the cost of all resources. Economists refer to this as **economic profit** and distinguish between it and **accounting profit**. The profit figure reported in annual reports, income statements, and other financial reports is accounting profit, often called operating profit or net operating profit. Accounting profit is the value of output less the cost of inputs but not including the opportunity cost of the owner's (shareholders') capital. It may include the cost of debt capital or it may not, depending on the accounting format used.

Economic profit is the difference between the value of output and the opportunity cost of all inputs *including the opportunity cost of the owner's or shareholders' capital*. Consider, as an example, Cisco's reported numbers for 1999 (in millions of dollars):

Sales	12,154
Net income after taxes	2,096
Equity	11,678
Debt	0

Did Cisco add value in 1999? To determine that, the cost of capital has to be subtracted from the net income after taxes. Suppose Cisco's cost of capital was 10 percent; then its equity capital would have cost about $1168 million and its economic profit would have been $928 million.

$$\text{Accounting profit} = \text{Revenue} - \text{cost of land} - \text{cost of labor}$$
$$\text{Economic profit} = \text{Accounting profit} - \text{capital costs}$$

In 2001, Cisco's situation was quite different than it had been in 1999 (again, in millions of dollars).

Sales	22,293
Net income	(1,014)
Total assets	35,238
Equity	27,120
Debt	8,118

Fortune magazine provides several performance measures in its lists of companies at

http://www.fortune.com

For individual firm data visit

http://www.hoovers.com/ (Note that some data may require a subscription.)

A good discussion on accounting and economic profits is available at

http://www.itworld.com/Man/2818/CWST053001/

Cisco's accounting profit was negative, so its economic profit was definitely negative, since the cost of capital had to be subtracted from the negative net income. Its negative economic profit was ($1,014) + ($2,712) = ($3,726) million, where the parentheses indicate negative values.

Negative Economic Profit Economists refer to a firm that subtracts value as having **negative economic profit**. A firm with negative economic profit is using resources that, if used elsewhere, would generate more value. During a booming economy in 1996, such well-known companies as Pepsico, Mobil, DuPont, AT&T, Amoco, Chevron, Boeing, Time Warner, and Turner Broadcasting had negative economic profit. In 1999, while the national economy was still growing, IBM, Exxon, AT&T, Time Warner, Hewlett-Packard, and Mobile, among others, earned negative economic profit. During the recession years of 2001–2002, many companies experienced negative economic profit.

Any firm can earn negative economic profit for a short period of time, but a firm that continually subtracts value will not exist in the long run.[1] According to *Fortune* magazine,[2] automobile companies have been destroying value for several years. What is being said in *Fortune* is that the automobile companies have generated revenues that were not sufficient to pay all opportunity costs. In other words, their economic profit has been negative for several years.

Suppose you are an investor in General Motors. Having experienced 4 percent annual returns over the last ten years, lower returns than you had anticipated, you look at your alternatives. You realize that you could have earned more than double that return by selling your stock in GM and purchasing shares in another firm. If many GM shareholders did this, GM could no longer acquire the use of resources. It would have to go out of business and its resources would be reallocated to more productive uses.

If GM has been destroying value for many years, why hasn't it gone out of business? Because not enough investors have decided they could do better investing in another firm. However, for more than 1 percent of the total firms in the United States each year, investors choose to invest elsewhere and the firms do go out of business.

Zero Economic Profit A firm that neither adds value nor subtracts it is a firm whose revenue is sufficient to pay the cost of all of the inputs it uses—but with nothing left over. This means that the shareholders or owners could have earned an equal, but not better, return in another investment. Economists refer to this as **zero economic profit** or **normal accounting profit**.

If Microsoft had revenues of $8.75 billion and costs of $6.75 billion, it would have an accounting profit of $2 billion. But if the shareholders could have earned 10 percent in an alternative activity and they have invested $20 billion in Microsoft, then Microsoft's economic profit would be zero. Yet the investors would have no incentive to sell Microsoft and purchase something else, since they could expect to earn no more than they do with Microsoft. Zero economic profit is not a bad thing—it says that investors are doing as well as they could have expected to do elsewhere.

Measuring Economic Profit

Economists have long lamented the fact that accountants do not provide a measure of economic profit, arguing that the accounting numbers do not provide appropriate information regarding a firm's performance. More importantly, the accounting numbers provide no information about the allocation of resources. Should the resources be deployed elsewhere? Are there incentives for other firms to enter this industry and begin competing? Only economic profit answers these questions. If economic profit is positive, resources are earning more than their opportunity cost—other resource owners want to do the same and, hence, reallocate their resources to the business. Conversely, if economic profit is negative, resources are not being paid their opportunity cost. The resources will be deployed elsewhere if that situation continues over time.

Cost of Capital

A cost of capital calculator is available at

http://www.financeadvisor.com/finadv/about_sidebar_coc_info.shtml

Cost of capital calculations by industry and by firm are available at

http://www.pwcglobal.com/Extweb/pwcpublications.nsf/docid/748F5814D61CC2618525693A007EC870

Why don't accountants routinely present economic profit in income statements and balance sheets? Partly because they have not been convinced it is necessary, and partly because they have believed that it was too difficult to calculate the cost of equity capital. They argue that since the cost of equity capital is the opportunity cost to investors of leaving their money with a particular firm, that amount is sure to vary from investor to investor; my opportunity cost is not the same as yours.

While a valid point, it does not offset the value of calculating and reporting economic profit. Moreover, the difficulty of calculating the cost of equity capital is not insurmountable. There are several approaches that can be used. The most common approach is a financial model known as the *capital asset pricing model (CAPM)*. The capital asset pricing model calculates how risky a company is and devises a risk premium that must be added to the average cost of equity capital.

What is risk? It is the possibility that some event, usually a bad event, will occur. Suppose you are considering two alternative investments. With the first, you know with certainty that you will get your money back plus an additional payment—the return on the investment. With the second, you may get a return or you may get nothing. If you were going to invest $20,000 of your money in one of these alternatives, you would surely require a higher possible return from the second than the first. Along the same lines, suppose you are looking at a biotech startup company as a possible investment. This investment could return several times the initial investment, but it could also yield nothing. The other option you are considering is an established firm, such as Microsoft, that has been providing a solid return of between 10 and 25 percent per year for the past several years. Clearly, the biotech firm is a much riskier investment than Microsoft and will have to pay a substantial risk premium over Microsoft's cost of capital to entice investors to put their funds into it.

Rather than investing in the risky biotech firm or the less risky Microsoft, investors could decide not to take any risk at all. They could purchase U.S. government financial instruments (government bills and bonds), which are generally considered risk-free because there is virtually no chance that the U.S. government would default.

Studies have shown that, on average and over a long period of time, investors have to be paid somewhere between 4 to 7 percent per year more to invest in company stocks than in U.S. government securities.[3] In other words, the long-term average cost of risk (the risk premium) is between 4 to 7 percent per year. This means that a company of average risk would need to earn a rate of return between 4 to 7 percent more than the U.S. Treasury bond rate in order to reward its shareholders for the risks they had assumed. The average interest rate on long-term U.S. bonds was about 5.5 percent during the late 1990s and early 2000s. This means that a company of average risk would have a cost of capital of about 9 to 12 percent in 2002.

The riskiness of a publicly traded firm is measured by comparing the volatility of its stock price to that of the market, or the average of all firms. Figure 3.1 presents the monthly returns on Intel stock as compared to the market as a whole over a selected two-year period. The dotted line is the Intel return and it, obviously, is more volatile than the market as a whole, illustrated by the solid line. This volatility means that Intel is more risky than the market as a whole. Since investors get about 5.5 percent from a risk-free investment and the average risk premium is about 4.0 to 7 percent, and since Intel is about 1 percent more volatile than the market as a whole, Intel must compensate investors 10 to 14 percent to make them indifferent to keeping their shares of Intel or to purchasing other stock or U.S. government bonds. This is Intel's cost of capital.

The cost of capital for several firms in 1999 and 2001 calculated using the capital asset pricing model is listed in Table 3.1.

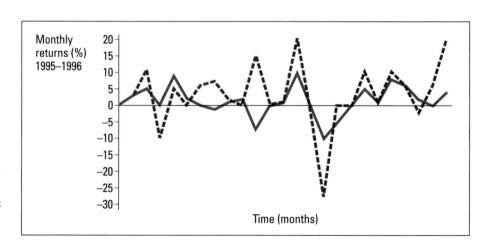

Figure 3.1

INTEL RELATIVE TO THE MARKET

Intel's stock price performance over a selected two-year period is shown as the dotted line. The average firm's performance is shown as the solid line. The greater volatility of Intel's stock is an indication of the riskiness of Intel.

Monthly returns (%) 1995–1996

Time (months)

Table 3.1

COST OF CAPITAL, 1999 and 2001

Company	Cost of Capital, 1999	Cost of Capital, 2001
Intel	12%	12.19%
Coca-Cola	13%	12.31%
General Electric	13.5%	12.47%
Merck	13.5%	10.72%
McDonald's	11.1%	8.83%
Nike	13.5%	10.07%
MIcron Technology	15.6%	13.47%
ebay	15.6%	13.55%
Hershey Foods	12.8%	6.79%

Economic Profit

Economic profit can be calculated once the amount of capital and the cost of capital are defined. To illustrate, consider Wal-Mart Stores. Wal-Mart had $196 billion in revenue in 2001. Its net operating income was $9.5 billion. It had $78 billion in capital, of which $47 billion was debt and $31 billion was equity. Since Wal-Mart has both debt and equity, the cost of capital must include both debt costs and equity costs. Typically, the cost of capital is calculated as the weighted average cost of capital (WACC). The WACC is equal to the cost of debt multiplied by the proportion of total capital made up of debt plus the cost of equity multiplied by the proportion of total capital made up of equity.

$$\text{WACC} = \frac{\{\text{cost of debt(debt)}\}}{\text{total capital}} + \frac{\{\text{cost of equity(equity)}\}}{\text{total capital}}$$

The weighted average cost of capital for Wal-Mart was 11.4 percent in 2001. This is calculated as:

$$.6(15) + .4(6) \qquad \text{(where cost of debt is 6 percent and cost of equity is 15 percent)}$$

Thus, the economic profit for Wal-Mart in 2001 was:

Economic profit = $9.5 billion – $8.89 billion

= $0.7 billion

This is a positive $0.7 billion, indicating that in 2001, a year of recession, Wal-Mart was returning more to its shareholders than they could have expected to get elsewhere at the same risk.

Economic profit is obtained by subtracting the cost of capital from net operating profit after tax (NOPAT). NOPAT is the income derived from the company's operations after income taxes but before all financing costs and noncash bookkeeping entries except depreciation. An illustration using an actual company for the year 2001 is provided in Table 3.2.

Economic profit equals NOPAT less capital charges. Capital charges equal the company's invested capital multiplied by the weighted average cost of capital (WACC). The WACC equals the sum of the cost of each component of capital—short-term debt, long-term debt, and shareholders' equity—weighted for its relative proportion at market value in the company's capital structure. Invested

Line Items	Dollars (millions)	What the Item Means
Total revenues	$16,741	The total revenue of the company for the fiscal year.
Accounting net income from the financial statements	$1,101	The income net to common shareholders as reported in the income statement of the company. Calculations for NOPAT and economic profit start here.
Interest expense Tax adjustment Unusual income	$889 + 87 − 32	Adjustments made to the accounting financial statements to reflect the accounts of the company on a cash and operating basis. Only cash expenses are retained. The only noncash expense remaining is the depreciation for fixed assets. Paper gains or losses are adjusted to a cash basis. For example, the sale of a building for $1 million when its value in the company books is recorded at $400,000 accounts for a $600,000 paper gain, which provides no additional cash to the company.
NOPAT	$2,044	NOPAT is the profit of the company net of all paper losses or gains, on a cash basis, net of income taxes.
Cost of capital	$1,294	The cost of capital is the charge to the company for providing it with all the capital it needs to operate the business. The charge is dependent on the level of risk that investors and lenders take for investing in the company. In this example, the weighted average cost of capital is 7.3% on total capital of $17,726,220.
Economic profit	$750	When the capital charges have been subtracted from NOPAT, the remainder is economic profit.

Table 3.2
ECONOMIC PROFIT

capital is the sum of all the firm's financing, apart from short-term, non-interest-bearing liabilities, such as accounts payable, accrued wages, and accrued taxes. It equals the sum of shareholders' equity, interest-bearing debt (both short- and long-term), and other long-term liabilities.[4]

The Relationship Between Economic Profit and Shareholder Value

Conceptually, economic profit is a better measure of a firm's performance than accounting profit because it recognizes all costs. But sometimes conceptual superiority does not translate into practical advantage. Does it in the case of economic profit? We've already mentioned the reluctance of accountants to measure economic profit. But that is not the practical advantage we are talking about. The practical advantage that is of most importance is whether the measure will help firms be successful. As managers, we want to know whether or not we are using our resources efficiently and appropriately. Only economic profit shows this. As owners, we want to know whether our wealth is being increased or eroded. Only economic profit shows this.

Shareholder Value

Free cash flow discussions and examples are provided at
http://www.spredgar.com/WebHelp/spredgar/theory_of_free_cash_flow.htm

Shareholder value is the primary thing on executives' minds today. What does economic profit have to do with shareholder value?

Is there a relationship between economic profit and stock price performance?[5] A quick glance at stock prices would suggest not. In any one year, some of the top-performing firms will have stock price gains that are above the market average and some will have stock price gains that are below the market average. The reason is that the stock market looks ahead. The value of a stock depends entirely on the economic profits that investors expect a company to produce in the future. Past profits matter only because they play a role in creating expectations about future performance.

As the period over which we look back grows longer, companies we recognize as excellent companies today (that is, ones that generated substantial economic profit) are increasingly likely to have outperformed stock market expectations and today's bad companies to have done worse than yesterday's stock market expectations. Economic profit is a snapshot, a one-year look at a firm's performance, and one year does not make a trend. But economic profit over several years gives

Born of a merger to fend off a takeover, Enron was a profitable pipeline company. But Ken Lay wanted more. Lay brought in Jeff Skilling, first as an in-house consultant, then in 1990 as head of trading. Skilling brought in brilliant dealmakers, put Andy Fastow in charge of the numbers, and told them to do whatever it took to improve the bottom line. The stock price rocketed and Enron was repeatedly named "most innovative company."

a great picture of performance, and this is what the stock market looks at. The present value of all expected future economic profits is what tells us whether a company creates or destroys wealth.

If the connection between economic profit and stock price requires a long time to see, is economic profit a useful piece of information? Are investors patient enough to wait ten or more years before making an evaluation of a firm's performance? Yes, it is, and no, they are not. Investors evaluate how well they think the firm will do tomorrow, next week, six months from now, or next year when deciding whether to purchase the stock of a company. Thus, the phrase "maximizing shareholder value" is often interpreted as a focus on short-term profits even at the expense of long-run losses.[6]

While it might seem that investors demand this short-term outlook by purchasing a company's stock as it earns short-term profits and then selling, this perception is incorrect. Such behavior would create arbitrage opportunities for others. Since the long-term value of the company would be undervalued and the short-term value overvalued, an investor could buy shares of stock long term and sell them short term. This would occur through various financial means, such as futures and options, which would tend to equalize the short- and long-term market values of the company. Thus, focusing on short-term results at the expense of long-term results would drive the shareholder value down, not up, and the short-term stock performance would be low, reflecting the long-term prospects of the firm.

Suppose an investor is considering two firms, A and B. The CEO for firm A is going to carry out an activity that will increase profits next year but lead to losses in the following years. The CEO for firm B, on the other hand, is looking to the long term and wants to increase profits each year. The result of this is that firm B will not increase profits next year as much as firm A does.

Investors, knowing the directions the two CEOs are going in, think to themselves, "I want to own firm A's stock only next year. I don't want to be holding it after that. But I don't want to be the last to sell. In fact, I want to be the first to sell and then the first to own firm B, so that when everyone else tries to buy firm B, I will make a large appreciation. So I should sell firm A's stock before the end of the year—perhaps in month 11. But others will expect me to do that and they will sell in month 10. So I will have to sell before that—month 9, 8 . . . ?"

The process of moving the time of sale forward would continue until the investor realizes that the only way to gain is not to buy stock in firm A at all but instead to buy stock in firm B now. As other investors do the same thing, the stock price of firm A decreases now, not next year, and that of firm B rises now, not next year. The stock price reflects the expected long-term economic profit stream.

This illustration assumed that investors knew with certainty what firms A and B would do. In reality, such certainty does not exist. Investors must gather information and form expectations about future performance. Since the stock price reflects the expected economic profit stream, shareholder value will be a reflection of the current and expected future economic profits of a firm. Thus, maximizing shareholder value should mean the same as maximizing economic profit. It is not a short-term tactic but instead a focus on long-term performance. It is not just an attempt to increase earnings but instead an attempt to maximize the difference between net earnings and the cost of capital.

A stock price is determined by the demand for and supply of shares of that stock. Both demanders and suppliers base their valuation of the price of the stock on expectations of future firm performance. It is the market expectations of future firm performance that determine the price of a share of stock. The price can be represented as the expected value of the future economic profits:

Price = Present value of expected future economic profit

$$P = \sum_{i=1}^{n} \left\{ \frac{E \text{ (economic profit)}}{(1+r)^i} \right\}$$

where $\sum$ is a symbol meaning the sum all items in periods 1 to n and n represents the length of time the market looks ahead. The denominator, $(1+r)^i$, is the discounting factor, where r is the cost of capital. In words, the stock price formula says the price of a stock today is equal to the present value of expected future economic profit.

Based on this formula, what causes the stock price to rise or fall? The answer is revisions of expectations. When expectations are revised upward, the stock price rises because more investors want to buy and fewer want to sell. When expectations are revised downward, the stock price falls because fewer investors want to buy and more want to sell. Thus, when a firm does better than expectations, its stock price will rise, and when a firm does worse than expectations, its stock price will fall.

From the mid-1990s through 2000, Cisco generated very substantial economic profit, a value that was reflected in the high price of its shares. Changes in the market value of Cisco in 2001, therefore, reflected its actual performance relative to its expected performance. Since expectations were high for Cisco, it would have been difficult for the company to have done better than those expectations, and, in the short term, stock price reassessments were as likely to be downward as upward, even though Cisco was earning significant profits. In fact, from March to June 2000, Cisco stock fell 40 percent, from a high of $80 per share to about $50 per share, even though Cisco earnings and profits were rising faster than the market as a whole.

You may have noticed from the formula that the stock price is dependent on n, the length of time for which the market forecasts economic profit. How far ahead do investors look? We can determine this by turning the formula around and asking how many years of firm performance are required to justify the current price of the stock. Instead of plugging numbers into the right side of the formula to find the stock price, we plug today's stock price into the left side, the projected economic profit and cost of capital into the right side, and then increase the number of periods until the right and left sides are equal.[7]

Consider as an example the computer manufacturer Gateway, whose stock price at the beginning of 2001 was $52 per share. In 2001, analysts were making the following estimates:

Sales growth rate	20%
Operating profit margin growth rate	9%
Cost of capital	10%

This enables us to project sales as far as we want at 20 percent per year. If the tax rate is 35 percent then we would subtract 35% of NOPAT from NOPAT. We would also subtract any additional capital expenditures that the firm would make. We calculate this each year until the value divided by number of shares of stock that have been issued equals the current stock price. In this example using Gateway, it took seven years for the expected growth path to reach the 2001 share price of $52.[8] This implies that the market is looking ahead seven years to determine Gateway's stock price.

By carrying out this exercise for different industries, we find that the time period varies from industry to industry but typically ranges from seven years (in high-tech, rapidly changing industries) to at least twenty years (in industries involving patents and other barriers to entry by new firms, such as pharmaceuticals). This is another confirmation of the idea that the stock market's view is long term.

Valuing the Dot.coms

In 1999, Amazon.com's share price was $113 even though the company had not made a positive accounting profit in its entire existence. Amazon was not alone; many of the so-called dot.coms were highly valued without having generated even accounting profits. How could a company without positive profits be valued highly in the stock market? There are two principal ways. One is that investors were speculating or simply gambling that the company would become profitable or that other investors would drive up the price of the stock. A second possibility is that the company had options or strategic choices that were valuable and these options led investors to believe the company would be highly profitable in the future.

An option is a choice: It is something that *enables* a firm to undertake an action but does not *obligate* that firm to undertake the action. A firm may have more or less value depending on the options open to it. For instance, a pharmaceutical firm that has the option of continuing the research on a specific drug may have substantially more value than a pharmaceutical firm without that option even though neither firm has committed to the project. An Internet retailer may have more value than is indicated by its sales or profits because of the options it has to grow its business or to move into related lines of business.[9]

The Internet stock boom of the 1990s reflected elements of both speculation and options. This became evident when the bubble burst and the dot.coms and other stocks came tumbling down in 2000. More than two hundred dot.com shutdowns occurred in 2000 and the price of internet stocks fell 90 percent. At the beginning of 2000, the stock market value of the Internet sector was $881 billion; at the beginning of 2001, it was $208 billion. Why? How could so many have been so wrong about so much? The reasons for the dot.com collapse are relatively easy to list, but to truly understand them it is necessary to cover several of the chapters in this book. We will examine Amazon.com and other option issues in Chapter 12. For now, suffice it to say that the collapse is not X-Files material; it is basic economics.

The Practical Effect of a Focus on Economic Profit

Because stock market valuation is related to economic profit, executives who argue that they are generating shareholder value must keep an eye on economic profit. When this occurs and economic profit is measured and becomes part of the company's financial data and compensation criteria, the business may be altered. A change in focus from accounting profit to economic profit has altered the behavior of many firms.[10] Before Quaker Oats adopted economic profit as its measure of performance, the manager of Quaker's granola bar plant in Danville, Illinois, used long production runs to turn out the various sizes of bars in order to minimize downtime and setup costs. This bolstered operating profits but also resulted in huge inventories of bars that sat in a warehouse until gradually they were shipped to customers. Inventory is not free, however. Capital is tied up in that inventory. Thus, when the company charged the manager for the inventory—that is, the capital tied up in inventory—he switched to short production runs, which reduced net operating profits but increased economic profit.

Prior to focusing on economic profit, Coca-Cola shipped its soft-drink syrup to bottlers in stainless-steel cans, which could be used over and over. The problem was that the steel cans were expensive; they required significant amounts of capital. When the company began focusing on economic profit, it sold off the stainless-steel cans and switched to cardboard containers. The cardboard increased operating costs—but by less than the cost of capital declined.[11] As a result, economic profit rose.

CASE REVIEW *The Enron Caper*

Perhaps the fundamental economic principle brought out by this case is that resources flow to where they are most highly valued. Following the Enron caper, resources have become highly valued in scrutinizing firms' financial reports and other business information to ensure that investors have good information. This and another aspect are pointed out by a book published in 2002—*Financial Shenanigans,* by Howard Schilit. The book is a guide to the ways in which companies fudge their financials. The first edition, published in 1993, was only 191 pages; the 2002 edition is nearly 300 pages. This tells us that more financial shenanigans have occurred from 1993 to 2002. It also tells us that more scrutiny of such practices is occurring.

In the Enron caper, the issue is not necessarily that the information companies have to provide to investors is inadequate, resulting in the need for new laws or regulations. It may simply have been an attempt—as common in the past as today—to look the other way when the market is doing well. Schilit said that Enron's practices are "as bad as it gets," but he also noted that the audited financials of the company raised enough red flags. For instance, in its final quarterly report, the company reported net income of more than $1 billion although cash flow was more than negative $1 billion. Schilit asks, "Shouldn't it have at least caused someone to ask questions?"

We need to put the Enron case and its effects on investors in perspective. It is nothing new—and seems to occur with virtually every stock market boom. Turn back the clock to the 1960s and the rise of the "conglomerates." Diversification was the buzzword on Wall Street. Historically high price/earning (p/e) multiples enabled aggressive companies to raise equity easily and then undertake acquisitions. Gulf & Western, ITT, Litton Industries, LTV Corporation, and Textron were among investors' favorites. The conglomerates employed aggressive accounting techniques to report increases in earnings per share that were largely illusory. ITT acquired more than 100 companies during the decade to become the eleventh-largest U.S. corporation. But after the market collapse of the late 1960s, a congressional study found that ITT's earnings between 1964 and 1968 would have been 40 percent lower than reported if more conservative accounting techniques had been employed. The stock market went into a tailspin following the bankruptcy but then rallied almost 32 percent from its low in the following twelve months. During the late 1970s and into the 1980s, junk bonds were created and with them came the hostile takeover and the leveraged buyout (LBO). Almost half of all major U.S. corporations received a takeover bid during this period. Michael Milken was the undisputed king of the junk bond and his firm, Drexel Burnham Lambert, dominated the market. Drexel had stakes in more than 150 companies by 1986 and Milken earned a bonus of $550 million that year, making him the highest-paid individual to that date in U.S. history. Scandal arose over insider trading involving Milken and Drexel, causing Drexel to close its doors in February 1990 and Milken to be sentenced to ten years in jail. But by the time Milken was sentenced, the benefits of the decade-long changes brought about by the new financing techniques had become evident and a new market upswing was under way.

It seems that each of these accounting nightmares led to a period of investor fear and caution, resulting in a market downturn. Then within a year or two, a rebuilding and market upturn began. This process is as old as capital markets. Down, or bear, markets expose the excesses that accumulate during booms.

So, what do these accounting practices mean for the ability of investors to measure the performance of firms? Is it possible to calculate economic profit? Clearly, such deceptive practices make it more difficult to analyze firm performance. Nonreporting of numbers would make it extremely difficult. But fears that firms will be destroyed and executives imprisoned or impoverished themselves tend to keep firms from outright illegal deception. This means that analysis requires careful scrutiny. This would be the case for any measure of performance. Economic profit is no more prone to being sensitive to accounting practices than any other financial measure, and economic profit provides benefits that straight accounting profit measures do not. It should also be pointed out that even if the capital off the balance sheet is ignored, Enron was not earning a return that exceeded its cost of capital—that is, its economic profit was negative.

SUMMARY

1. The objective of firms is to add value. Added value is measured as the difference between the sales or value of output and the input costs—the opportunity costs. It is called economic profit.
2. While a rather simple concept, the measurement of added value or economic profit is difficult. Somehow, the opportunity cost of capital must be accounted for. One way to do this is to use the cost of capital to a firm of comparable risk, perhaps the cost of capital for the marginal firm in the industry. Another approach is to estimate the cost of capital using the capital asset pricing model (CAPM).
3. Simple accounting measures, such as return on assets, or return on equity market value, or price-to-earnings ratios, simply do not provide a measure of economic profit.

KEY TERMS

added value
economic profit
accounting profit

negative economic profit
zero economic profit

normal accounting profit
shareholder value

EXERCISES

1. Calculate the added value for each of the following firms.

Microsoft:

Value of output	$2,750
Wages and salaries	400
Cost of capital	40
Cost of materials	1,650

Barclays Bank:

Value of output	$5,730
Wages and salaries	3,953
Cost of capital	916
Cost of material	556

General Motors:

Value of output	$50,091
Wages and salaries	29,052
Cost of capital	15,528
Cost of materials	7,507

2. What follows is some standard accounting information for each of the firms shown. Can you tell which firm is the most successful? Explain.

	Boeing	Goodyear	Liz Claiborne	Circuit City
Sales	5601	423	622	1767
Profits	254	26.9	56.2	31.6
Return on sales	4.5%	5.2%	9%	1.8%
Return on equity	10.2	13.9	15	14.5

3. a. With what group of firms would you classify the following for calculating a cost of capital?

Motorola
Hershey Foods
Home Depot
Dillard Department Stores
Coca-Cola

b. A cost of capital figure for each of the firms is listed below. Explain what this figure means.

Motorola	11.6
Hershey Foods	12.8
Home Depot	12.2
Dillard Department Stores	10.5
Coca-Cola	12.0

4. Listed below are financial figures for Abbott Labs. How well is Abbott doing? Explain your answer.

	89	90	91	92	93	94	95	96
Sales ($mil)	5,380	6,159	6,877	7,852	8,408	9,156	10,012	11,014
Net income	860	966	1,089	1,239	1,399	1,517	1,689	1,882
Capital per share (book value/share)	3.08	3.30	3.77	4.00	4.48	5.04	5.58	6.15

5. In measuring economic profit:
   a. How do you deal with a one-time event?
   b. How do you deal with money provided by relatives to get the business started?
   c. How do you handle off-balance-sheet expenses—that is, expenses that are incurred by the firm but are not measured as part of the firm's balance sheet?

6. The following type of report occurs each quarter as firms announce their earnings:

Weaker-than-expected results last week from Exxon Mobil have set a gloomy backcloth for results on Thursday from Royal Dutch/Shell. A consensus of Wall Street analysts polled by Thomson Financial/ First Call had projected ChevronTexaco would report earnings of 70 cents per share. However, the company said that after excluding special items and merger-related expenses in both periods, operating earnings were $931 million (88 cents). Using that math, the company beat the analysts' figure by 18 cents. The company said it lost $154 million in the first quarter, compared with the year-ago quarter, in refining, marketing, and transportation operations. The company said its profit margins in that sector were at their lowest levels since the mid-1990s. Chevron stock closed up 90 cents, to $85.90, yesterday on the New York Stock Exchange.

   a. Why does the stock market react to earnings reports?
   b. What do the earnings reports mean?

7. The manager of Global X is contemplating the purchase of a new machine that will cost $300,000 and has a useful life of five years. The machine is expected to yield cost reductions to Global X of $50,000 in year 1, $60,000 in year 2, $70,000 in year 3, and $80,000 in each year in years 4 and 5. Will the acquisition of the machine add value?

8. You have just been hired as a consultant to help a firm determine which of three options to take to increase shareholder wealth. The following table shows year-end profits for each option. Assume that the risk-free cost of capital is 5 percent and the risk premium is 8 percent.

Option	Profit in Year 1	Profit in Year 2	Profit in Year 3
A	$70,000	$80,000	$90,000
B	$50,000	$90,000	$100,000
C	$30,000	$100,000	$115,000

   a. Calculate the economic profit for each option.
   b. Suppose that the profit figures are based on earnings figures of 10 times profits and that

there are 100,000 shares of stock outstanding. What are the earnings per share for each option?

9. It is often stated that free cash flow is the same as economic profit. Define *free cash flow*. Demonstrate whether it is or is not the same as economic profit.

10. Using the formula given in the text for stock price determination, explain why stock prices move up or down in response to quarterly earnings reports.

11. Using the following balance sheet and income statement information, calculate accounting profit and economic profit:

Balance Sheet	Jan 01
Cash	57
Net receivables	547
Inventories	3,364
Other current assets	332
Total current asssets	4,300
Net fixed assets	9,622
Other noncurrent assets	2,156
Total assets	16,078
Accounts payable	2,163
Short-term debt	82
Other current liabilities	1,150
Total current liabilities	3,395
Long-term debt	5,942
Other noncurrent liabilities	931
Total liabilities	10,384
Total Equity	5,694
Shares Outstanding (mil)	405

Income Statement	
Revenue	36,762
Cost of goods sold	25,335
Gross profit	11,427
Gross profit margin	31.1%
SG&A expense	8,740
Depreciation & amortization	1,001
Operating income	1,686
Nonoperating expenses	385
Income before taxes	1,274
Income taxes	509
Net income after taxes	765

12. Use the following data to calculate economic profit in year 1.

Year	0	1
Sales		1,000
Expenses other than interest		500
Depreciation		200
Earnings before interest and taxes (EBIT)		300
Taxes on EBIT @40%		120
Earnings before interest and after taxes (EBIAT)		180
Current assets less excess cash and securities	300	340
Non-interest-bearing current liabilities	100	120
Adjusted net working capital	200	220
Gross property, plant and equipment	2,000	2,300
Accumulated depreciation	1,000	1,200
Net property, plant and equipment	1,000	1,100
Invested capital	1,200	1,320
Return on invested capital (EBIAT / invested capital)		15%
based on previous year's invested capital		

13. Calculate the WACC—the weighted average cost of capital—using the following data:

Market value of debt = $30 million
Market value of equity = $50 million
Cost of debt = 9 percent
Tax rate = 40 percent
Cost of equity = 15 percent

CHAPTER NOTES

1. Unless the firm is supported by government.
2. December 1996.
3. Bradford Cornell, *The Equity Risk Premium: The Long-Run Future of the Stock Market* (New York: John Wiley & Sons), July 1999.
4. Many analysts argue that the focus of attention ought to be on free cash flow since free cash is what companies have available to make interest payments, pay off the principal on loans, pay dividends, and buy back shares—in other words, to return cash to their capital providers. Free cash flow is calculated as follows:
   NOPAT
   + depreciation and amortization
   − capital expenditures
   − changes in working capital required
   = free cash flow.

You can see from this calculation that free cash flow is really no different from economic profit. It is simply another way to calculate economic profit. Capital expenditures plus changes in working capital required in the free cash flow calculation is the same as the capital costs that are subtracted from NOPAT to yield economic profit.

> Invested capital =
>> Excess cash + working capital required + fixed investment
> Working capital required =
>> Amount of money that must be used to finance inventories and receivables + the amount of operating cash – accounts payable, accrued expenses, and advances from customers

Thus,

> Invested capital =
>> Total assets – short-term non-interesting-bearing liabilities.

which is the same as

> Short-term debt + long-term debt + other long-term liabilities + shareholders' equity

5. Several studies have examined the relationship between economic profit (as measured by EVA, Economic Value Added) and stock price performance. One study followed 241 firms over the period 1987–1993 and found that three accounting measures—return on assets, return on equity, and return on sales—as well as EVA are correlated with stock returns. However, it found that EVA is more highly correlated with stock prices than the other measures. Perhaps even more suggestive of the importance of economic profit is that the turnover of executives is more closely related to EVA than to the accounting measures, suggesting that managers are better served to focus on economic profit than accounting profit. Kenneth Lehn, and Anil K. Makhija, "EVA & MVA as Performance Measures," *Strategy and Leadership* 24, no. 3 (May 1996): 34.

6. Many executives claim that the pressure to perform each quarter forces them to ignore long-term payoffs and focus only on short-term results. The CEO of Bell & Howell noted: "When the typical institutional portfolio in the U.S. has an annual turnover rate of 50% and some smaller ones have turnover rates of more than 200%, it is no surprise that American business is hobbled compared with foreign rivals. The pressure for short-term results puts unnecessary hurdles in the way of sound management." Another CEO agreed: "The only pressure I have on me is short-term pressure. I announce that we're going to spend half a billion dollars at Courtland, Alabama, with a hell of a payout from redoing a mill and my stock goes down two points. So I finally caved in and announced I'm going to buy back some stock, which makes no sense." Stewart III, G.B., *The Quest for Value,* (New York; HarperCollins, 1991), p. 56. A study by Michael Porter concluded that excessive emphasis on short-term results was stifling investment and undermining U.S. competitiveness and that the problem had worsened in the 1970s and 1980s when institutional ownership and takeovers were growing. Porter decried the impatient U.S. investors and praised the patient German and Japanese investors. Michael Porter, *Capital Choices* (Cambridge, Mass.: Harvard Business School Press, 1992); and "Capital Choices: Changing the Way America Invests in Industry," *Journal of Applied Corporate Finance,* vol. 5, no. 2, 1992.

7. Alfred Rappaport and Michael J. Mauboussin use this approach to suggest ways in which investors should pick stocks for their portfolios in *Expectations Investing* (Cambridge, Mass.: Harvard Business School Press, 2002).

8. For details on this and other company calculations, see ibid., p. 74.

9. Options are discussed in detail in Chapter 12.

10. The recognition that it is the economic profit that matters has led to a brisk business in management consulting. Spurred by lucrative fees, consultants are scrambling to help companies install new value-based performance metrics to replace the old standbys of per-share earnings (EPS), return on equity (ROE), and others. The dominant firm in this business is Stern-Stewart, promoting its *economic value added* (EVA). Another major firm in the business is the Boston Consulting Group, whose experts combine cash flow return on investment (CFROI) with a concept they call *total business return.* McKinsey uses the term *economic profit,* while the LEK/Alcar Group push for *shareholder value added* (SVA). These are far from the only consulting firms in the business. The field has become quite crowded, with each firm trying to offer a slightly different measurement tool or metric. *While differing somewhat, all of the metrics attempt to provide a measure of economic profit.*

11. These examples are from Al Ehrbar, *EVA: The Real Key to Creating Wealth* (New York: John Wiley & Sons, 1999), p.141.

Calculating Economic Profit

In the simplest terms possible, economic profit is similar to the concept of net worth to an individual. On the left side of the list below is the definition of net worth for an individual and next to that on the right is the comparable definition of economic profit.

Individual	Business
Salary	Revenue
Less	Less
Nonfinancial expenses	Operating expenses
(food, clothing, utilities,	(cost of goods sold,
insurance, miscellaneous)	SGA, etc.)
Taxes	Taxes
Income before interest	NOPAT
Less	Less
Interest loans	Capital charge
Equals	Equals
Change in net worth	Economic profit

Economic profit can be calculated from a standard balance sheet and income statement.

Sales	11,645	
Less		
Cost of sales	7,037	
Equals		
Operating income	4,608	
Plus		
Interest income	65	
Equals		
Income before taxes	4,673	
Less		
Income taxes	665	
Equals		
Net income after taxes or NOPAT	4,005	
Less		
Capital charges (average IC × cost of capital)		4010.14
Invested capital = total liabilities		
and shareholders' equity		32,870
Weighted average cost of capital		12.2%
Equals		
Economic profit	−5.14	

This calculation of economic profit is straightforward in a couple of ways. First, there are no complicating factors in income or capital costs. Second, it does not include accounting adjustments that some analysts insist are necessary—deferred tax expense, goodwill amortization, bad debt accruals, one-time writeoffs, and restructuring charges. Many analysts claim that these adjustments should be made because they are a necessary part of the company and indicate strategies that will define the company's success in the future. Others argue against the adjustments, claiming that they are manipulations that don't really have anything to say about the performance of the firm in the future.

Remember, what we are trying to measure is the total value added of the company: the total value of output sold less the full opportunity cost of all resources used. What is included and what is not should meet the test of being related to the value of output and the full opportunity cost of all resources used.

Cost of Capital[1]

To calculate the cost of capital to the firm, we must estimate the cost of equity capital and add that to the interest expense of debt capital. The cost of equity capital is typically estimated using the capital asset pricing model (CAPM), which specifies an explicit relationship between the expected return on an asset and the risk of that asset. The expected return is the return required by investors, that is, the opportunity cost of capital. CAPM is a simple model that relates risk and return. Let R^i denote the return on an asset, R^f the return on a risk-free asset, and R^m the return on the entire market of assets. CAPM states that the expected return on the asset is equal to the risk-free rate plus beta (β) multiplied by the market risk:

$$E[R^i] = R^f + \beta^i(E[R^m] - R^f)$$

where E represents expectation.

The beta of the security, denoted by β^i, is the relevant measure of risk for security *i*. Beta is the covariance between the security's return and the market's return, divided by the variance of the market's return. In other words, beta measures the volatility of a company's stock relative to the entire market. If a company has a beta exactly equal to 1, the company has the same risk as the market itself. If a company has a beta that is greater than 1, its stock will probably go up higher than the market if the market is going up; it also will go down farther than the market if the market is falling. The reverse is true for a company with a beta that is less than 1. If the market is going up, the firm's stock will probably go up but by less than the market; if the market is going down, the firm's stock will probably go down but by less than the market. A low-beta firm is less sensitive to swings in the market.

Beta represents the relationship between the monthly returns on the individual stock and the entire market; it is a measure of the volatility of the individual stock versus the market. If beta is 1, then the individual stock has the same volatility as the market. If beta is greater than 1, the stock has a volatility that is greater than that of the market—investors would require a premium to own that more volatile stock as compared to owing an index of the entire market. Intel's beta in 2000 was 1, which means that, during that period, the market and the Intel stock essentially moved up and down together at the same rate.

To use the CAPM to measure a company's cost of equity, an estimate of the company's beta, an estimate of the risk-free rate, and an estimate of the expected market premium $E[R^m - R^f]$ must be obtained.

There are several ways to find an estimate of a company's beta. The easiest is simply to look it up on one of the many published sources. Sources include the Value Line Investment Survey, Yahoo!Finance, and Hoovers. An alternative is to estimate beta yourself. The most commonly used method is with a simple ordinary least squares regression, with the return on the company as the dependent variable and the return on the market as the independent variable. The slope of the regression is an estimate of beta.

To estimate the regression equation, the first thing you have to do is choose a measure of the return on the market. Theory makes three suggestions: (1) The market portfolio should include as many securities as possible; (2) the returns for the securities should include any dividend payments as well as price changes; and (3) the securities in the market portfolio should not be an equally weighted average, but rather a market-value-weighted index. An index like the Dow Jones industrial average falls short on all three points and the Standard & Poor's index is not much better but includes many more stocks. Most academic researchers use the Chicago Center for Research in Security Prices (CRSP) value-weighted index, which includes dividends, and which includes the entire New York Stock Exchange listing.

Most calculations are based on a long-U.S. government bond rate (such as the ten-year Treasury bond) as a risk-free proxy and using a risk premium of about 4 to 6.5 percent. The choice of risk-free proxy and risk premium can have significant effects on cost-of-capital calculations. The choice is not without a little controversy. Some people have recently argued that major changes in economies have led to a reduction in stock market risk and that the U.S. government bond is not entirely risk-free—that the rate needs some adjustment for what is called systematic risk.[2]

Betas are reported by many sources using different time periods and different data. Hoover's presents a sixty-month beta for each firm it reports on and uses the S&P 500 as its measure of the market. Value Line reports a shorter-term beta for each firm it reports on but based on more stocks than the S&P. Every brokerage house provides some measure of beta. Using a reported beta requires making sure that time periods are consistent and measures of the market are appropriate.

With a beta in hand, a firm's cost of equity capital is calculated by multiplying its beta by the risk premium and adding that to the risk-free rate:

Risk-free rate + β(risk premium)

Given an estimate of beta, a risk-free rate, and a risk premium, you can calculate cost of capital using the CAPM equation. Suppose, for the company for which economic profit is calculated above,

beta = 1.2,
risk-free rate = 5
risk premium = 6

This means that the cost of capital is:

5 + 1.2(6) = 12.2%.

Applied to total capital, the capital charges (average invested capital multiplied by the cost of capital) are 32,870 × 0.122 = 4010.14. Economic profit is calculated as NOPAT minus the capital charges:

Since net operating profit after tax (NOPAT) is 4008, economic profit is

4008 – 4010.14 = –2.14

EXERCISES

1. You have the following betas for firms. Calculate the cost of capital for each.

Intel	1.
GE	1.26
IBM	1.2
Merck	1.4
GM	1.1

2. You are analyzing the beta for Hewlett-Packard and have broken the company into four business groups with equity value and betas for each group. Calculate the beta for HP as a company. If the Treasury bond rate is 7.5 percent, calculate the cost of capital.

Business Group	Equity	Beta
Mainframes	$2 billion	1.1
Personal computers	$2 billion	1.5
Software	$1 billion	2.0
Printers	$3 billion	1.0

3. Would it make a difference in the calculation of the cost of capital whether you looked at the short-term U.S. government rate rather than the long-term U.S. government rate as your risk-free rate? Under what conditions would you choose long term? Short term?

APPENDIX NOTES

1. Ibbotson.com provides estimates of the cost of capital for a fee. Betas are available from many sources, some of which are free and some of which involve a small fee, such as Value Line, Standard & Poor's, Barra.com, and Yahoo!Finance. Market-risk premium estimates are available from brokerage houses and advisory firms such as Alcar.com.

2 Discussions about the estimate of the cost of capital are contained in *Cost of Capital: Estimation and Applications* by Shannon P. Pratt (New York: John Wiley & Sons, 1998). The Valuation Technologies website at *http://www.valtechs.com/r3.shtml* provides definitions, discussions, and calculations of cost of capital. Ibbotson and Associates has cost of capital data and information available at *http://www.ibbotson.com/Default.asp* in the "cost of capital" section.

PART II
Seeking Competitive Advantage

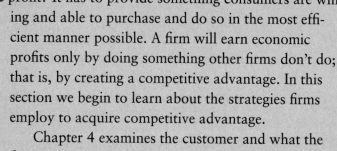

Resource owners want the highest returns possible for the use of their resources. This includes owners of capital as well as shareholders in publicly traded companies, who invest where they expect to get the highest economic profit. How does a firm acquire positive economic profit? It has to provide something consumers are willing and able to purchase and do so in the most efficient manner possible. A firm will earn economic profits only by doing something other firms don't do; that is, by creating a competitive advantage. In this section we begin to learn about the strategies firms employ to acquire competitive advantage.

Chapter 4 examines the customer and what the firm needs to know about the customer. Chapter 5 deals with the costs of doing business. Costs are not simply straightforward expenditures that show up on balance sheets or income statements. Costs include options not undertaken, strategies forgone, and actions that should not have been taken. A firm has to operate as efficiently as it can, producing the products consumers want and are willing to pay for at the lowest possible price. A firm that is not efficient will not last very long in the midst of competition. Thus, a firm must consider all opportunities; it must be sure that the option it does take is better than others it could have taken.

In Chapter 6 we examine profit maximization. We look at the process by which managers decide how much to offer for sale and at what prices. Interestingly, no matter the selling environment in which a firm operates, it follows the same rules for profit maximization. But aside from these basic rules, the strategies involved in maximizing profit vary widely according to whether the firm is one among many or one among a very few.

Demand

The typical supermarket has 30,000 different products on sale at any given time. The manager of that supermarket must determine not only what mix of products to have on hand but where to locate those products and what price to set on each one at any specific time. The typical procedure is to set a price that is a markup

on the cost of the item and leave that price fixed until costs change. A typical hotel must maintain an occupancy rate of over 76 percent to break even. The manager of the hotel must determine the price to charge for each room, whether to require more than one-night stays, whether to favor groups or individuals, and what other services to provide. The usual procedure is to set a series of prices on each room depending on whether the customer is a frequent customer, is staying more than one night, is on business, or is a tourist, but to quote the highest price initially and wait for the customer to request some type of discount. The typical telephone provider receives about seven million calls a year from customers inquiring about services and prices. The company representative usually has access to the customer's billing history and a list of general products or services to try to sell to the customer but is not sure in which of the many products the customer might be interested.

These examples are just a few of the many problems confronting businesses in their relations with customers. Companies do not seem to know much about their customers. For instance, companies often base prices on the anecdotal evidence of a few vocal salespeople or product managers. Even Mercedes-Benz, when it was about to launch one of its A-class models in the German market, initially proposed a price tag of DM29,500, based on little more than the belief that DM30,000 was a psychologically important barrier. Consultants point out that price has a disproportionate effect on the bottom line, far more than greater volumes or cuts in fixed and variable costs. Assuming that volumes stay constant, a

1 percent price increase produces between an 8 percent and 11 percent improvement in operating profits. So does this mean that most businesses should raise their prices? Are these businesses leaving money on the table—that is, not generating the greatest revenue they could by knowing the customer better?

Know Your Customer

There are so many stories in business about the costs of not understanding your customer that it is surprising that most businesses today do not know their customer. What are the consumer's tastes? At what price will consumers purchase the product, and how high a price will they pay? How many consumers will purchase the product? Will consumers purchase any product from any old firm, or are they loyal to a specific firm or product? Does the firm need to devote resources to advertising, to promotion, to packaging or placement or pricing? To answer these questions requires that we understand demand. The first step in that understanding is elasticity.

Elasticity

A useful explanation of price elasticity is provided at http://www.toolkit.cch.com/Text/P03_5230.asp

It is vitally important for the manager to know whether the firm's customers are sensitive to price or whether they are willing to pay a little more to purchase the firm's product. Bayer, Cocoa-Cola, Kodak, Xerox, IBM, and Microsoft are well-known brand names. The products offered by these companies are typically priced above competitive products that are not as well recognized. The reason is that people prefer to deal with the brand-name product rather than purchase a generic one. How far can the brand-name product be priced above rival products? The answer depends on how sensitive consumers are to price.

It is also important for the manager to know whether there are different customer segments that must be appealed to in different ways and from which segment the greatest revenue comes. Also, the manager must determine whether the firm can gain by personalizing the product—determining placement, packaging, and price for each customer or customer segment.

To know these factors is to know the customer. Economists have devised measures of how consumers alter their purchases in response to changes in various attributes of a firm's goods or services. These measures are called elasticities. Elasticities are measured as the percentage change in the purchases of a good or service that results when some attribute is changed by a fixed percent. The reason elasticities are measured in percentage changes is to put all goods and services on a common footing. For instance, to compare a $1 change in the price of a hamburger and a $1 change in the price of an automobile would not make much sense. But to compare a 10 percent change in the price of a hamburger and a 10 percent change in the price of an automobile puts matters in perspective. Let's examine several of the most often used elasticity measures.

Air fares have been dropping for several years. To slow the decline, airlines have formed alliances and attempted to cooperate on pricing. One such arrangement has been Orbitz, the website owned by five airlines—United, Delta, Continental, American, and Northwest. Such attempts rarely work. In 2002, Expedia began to offer many of the special web fares that until now had largely been restricted to Orbitz. As long as customers have many airlines to choose among, the price elasticity of demand for any specific airline will be high.

Price Elasticity of Demand

The **price elasticity of demand** is a measure of the magnitude by which consumers alter the quantity of some product they purchase in response to a change in the price of that product. The more price-elastic demand is, the more responsive consumers are to a price change—that is, the more they will adjust their purchases of a product when the price of that product changes. Conversely, the less price-elastic demand is, the less responsive consumers are to a price change.

The price elasticity of demand is the percentage change in the quantity demanded of a product divided by the percentage change in the price of that product.[1]

Consider the case of Globastar Canada, a provider of satellite-based mobile communications throughout Canada. The company found that its customers were price sensitive when it tried to charge rates as high as $1.50 per minute when customers were able to get rates as low as $.80 per minute elsewhere. The customers flocked to companies offering lower rates, leaving Globastar Canada near bankruptcy. If the quantity of phone calls that are made falls by 3 percent whenever the price of a minute of calls rises by 1 percent, the price elasticity of demand for the telephone calls is 3.[2]

$$e^d = 3\%/1\% = 3$$

Demand can be **elastic, unit-elastic,** or **inelastic.** When the price elasticity of demand is greater than 1, demand is said to be elastic. For instance, the demand for videotape rentals, according to the example of $e^d = 3$, is elastic. When the price elasticity of demand is 1, demand is said to be unit-elastic. For example, if the price of private education rises by 1 percent and the quantity of private education purchased falls by 1 percent, the price elasticity of demand is 1. When the price elasticity of demand is less than 1, demand is said to be inelastic. In this case, a 1 percent rise in price brings forth a smaller than 1 percent decline in quantity demanded. For example, if the price of gasoline rises by 1 percent and the quantity of gasoline purchased falls by 0.2 percent, the price elasticity of demand is 0.2.

The shape of a demand curve depends on the price elasticity of demand. A perfectly elastic demand curve is a horizontal line that shows that consumers can purchase any quantity they want at the single prevailing price, as shown in Figure 4.1(a). An example of a perfectly elastic demand might be the demand for disk drives in PCs. There are many manufacturers of disk drives, and the PC manufacturers do not care which they install in their machines; most consumers have no idea which disk-drive company produced their drives. As a result, if the price of one brand of disk drives is increased, the PC manufacturers are likely to move to another brand. A perfectly elastic demand means that even the smallest price change will cause consumers to change their consumption by a huge amount; in fact, they will totally switch to the producer with the lowest price.

A perfectly inelastic demand curve is a vertical line illustrating the idea that consumers cannot or will not change the quantity of a good they purchase when the price of that good is changed. Perhaps heroin for an addict is a reasonably vivid example of a good whose demand is perfectly inelastic. The addict will pay almost any price to get the quantity that satisfies the addiction. Figure 4.1(b) shows a perfectly inelastic demand curve.

Figure 4.1
DEMAND CURVES

(*a*) Perfectly elastic demand: Demand is so sensitive to price that even an infinitesimal change leads to a total change in quantity demanded. (*b*) Perfectly inelastic demand: The quantity demanded is the same no matter the price. Demand is completely insensitive to price. (*c*) Alternative demand curves: D_1 and D_2 represent straight downward-sloping demand curves. D_2 is said to be more elastic than D_1 because at every single price the elasticity of demand is higher at D_2 than D_1.

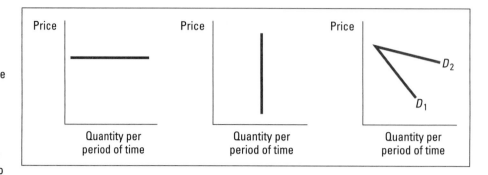

Several firms now focus on price elasticity in the form of revenue management. For examples, see
http://www.khimetrics.com
http://www.revenuemanagement.com/whatisrm.htm

In between the two extreme shapes are the demand curves for most products. Figure 4.1(c) illustrates two demand curves. One is a relatively flat line, D_2, and the other is a relatively steep line, D_1. D_2 is more price elastic than D_1.[3]

Price Elasticity and Revenue

Why is the price elasticity of demand important to a manager? Because there is a close relationship between the price elasticity of demand and total revenue. Total revenue (TR) equals the price of a product multiplied by the quantity sold: $TR = P \times Q$. If P rises by 10 percent and Q falls by more than 10 percent, then total revenue declines as a result of the price rise. If P rises by 10 percent and Q falls by less than 10 percent, then total revenue rises as a result of the price rise. If P increases by 10 percent and Q falls by 10 percent, then total revenue does not change as the price changes.[4] Thus, total revenue increases as price is increased if demand is inelastic, decreases as price is increased if demand is elastic, and does not change as price is increased if demand is unit-elastic. A firm wanting to increase total revenue would lower the price as long as demand is elastic and raise the price if demand is inelastic.

What makes the demand for one product price-elastic and the demand for another price-inelastic? It depends on how many **substitutes** there are, how expensive the item is, and the time period we are talking about. The demand for the services provided by Amazon.com and BN.com are very price-elastic. Consumers who can switch from one product to another without losing quality or some other attribute associated with the original product will be very sensitive to a price change. Their demand will be very elastic. Similarly, Amadeus Petroleum NL is building a commercial biodiesel plant in Perth, Western Australia, to convert low-value tallow, a by-product of the livestock industry, into a high quality diesel fuel, a direct substitute for traditional diesel made from fossil fuels. Once on-line, the price elasticity of demand for diesel will rise considerably. In contrast, when there are few substitutes for a product, the price elasticity of demand for that product is low. Drug addicts have few substitutes that satisfy their addiction; business travelers have few substitutes for the airline routes and times they travel. As a result, the demands for these goods are relatively inelastic.

The elasticity of demand can be very important to business strategy. For instance, would you say that the demand for a specific media—newspapers, periodicals, or television—is price elastic? If customers consider these media as close substitutes then the demand would be price elastic and a price increase by any one of them would lead to decreased revenues as customers switched to others. In Canada, the Competition Bureau was debating this issue in 2002 when considering whether or not it would allow Astral Media Inc (Astral) to acquire a number of radio stations owned by Telemedia Radio Inc. It ruled that the media were not substitutes and thus the acquisitions would not be allowed. The bureau feared that Astral would be able to increase price substantially without losing many sales.

In most cases, a manager would prefer to have the demand for her firm's product be price-inelastic. When the demand for a product is price-inelastic, the firm can increase the price without losing significant business. It is for this reason that firms attempt to create brand names and customer loyalty. Increasing brand-name recognition and customer loyalty toward that brand means that fewer close substitutes exist. It is because of brand-name recognition that Coca-Cola is priced higher than Safeway's cola and Bayer aspirin is priced higher than Walgreen's aspirin.

Because a new car and an exotic vacation are both quite expensive, even a small percentage change in their prices can take a significant portion of a household's income. As a result, a 1 percent increase in price may cause many households to delay the purchase of a car or vacation. Coffee, on the other hand, accounts for such a small portion of a household's total weekly expenditures that a large percentage increase in the price of coffee will probably have little effect on the quantity of coffee purchased. The greater the portion of the consumer's budget a good constitutes, the more price-elastic is the demand for the good. This typically means that the more expensive the item, the more likely that the demand for that item will be price-elastic.

The time period in which we measure the price elasticity is important. If we are speaking about a very short period of time, then the demand for most goods and services will be relatively price-inelastic. With a longer period of time, there are more substitutes available. For instance, the demand for gasoline is very price-inelastic over a period of a month. No good substitutes are available in so brief a period. Over a ten-year period, however, the demand for gasoline is much more elastic. The additional time allows consumers to alter their behavior to make better use of gasoline and to find substitutes for gasoline. The longer the period under consideration, the more elastic is the demand for any product.

Other Demand Elasticities

Since demand also depends on factors other than just price, there are elasticities to measure how much a change in one of these factors affects demand. We can calculate an income elasticity of demand, a cross price elasticity of demand, an advertising elasticity, a promotion elasticity, and others. As we'll see, each of these can be of substantial use to an executive.

Income Elasticity of Demand

For Canadian economic data visit http://www.statcan.ca/english/Pgdb/

For world economic data visit http://rfe.wustl.edu/Data/World/

The total output in the U.S. economy (real gross domestic product, RGDP) is shown in Figure 4.2 for the years 1929–2002. What do you observe in this graph? It presents two important characteristics of the U.S. economy. One is that the U.S. economy has grown over the years. The other is that the growth has not been at a steady pace. At times the economy has grown rapidly, at other times it has grown slowly, and at still other times it has declined. Economists study both of

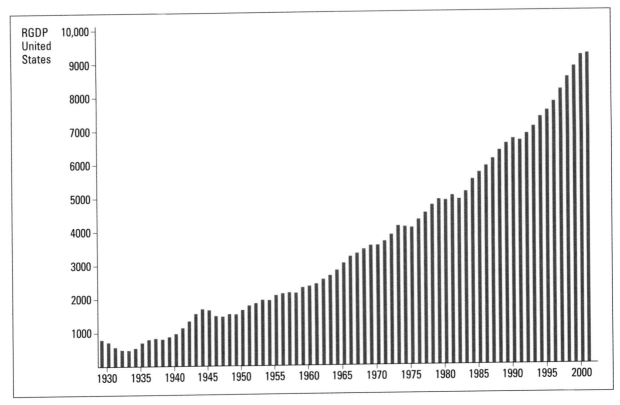

Figure 4.2

ECONOMIC GROWTH AND THE BUSINESS CYCLE

The real output or GDP of the U.S. economy each year is pictured. The picture points out two things: the total output has grown over the years and the growth has not been a steady rise.

Economic data are available at www.economagic.com

these characteristics. They want to know why economies grow and why some grow faster than others. They also study the fluctuations. They want to know what causes the downturns and upturns.

Taking out the growth and leaving just the cycles results in Figure 4.3. Figure 4.3 is, in fact, a picture of business cycles in the United States. Business cycles are important to most businesses. During an upswing in business activity, incomes are growing and sales of many products are rising. During a downswing, incomes are not rising and sales of many products may be declining. But there are firms for which sales rise during downswings and decline during upswings. For other firms, sales are not dependent on the business cycle.

Whenever the economy is strong and incomes are growing, Goldstar Kitchens, a firm specializing in kitchen designs, cabinets, and appliances, does very well. The demand for new kitchen cabinets and appliances increases much faster than does income growth. The problem is that when the economy falls into a recession, Goldstar struggles. Price is a consideration for Goldstar, but it is not price so much as income that affects Goldstar's business. The manager of Goldstar must know how much demand will change whenever incomes change. In contrast, sales of the Australian company Billabong, makers of surfer and other leisure wear, seem not to be sensitive to income growth. The company has experienced sales growth in Japan, whose economy was in recession, and in North America during years of growth and recession. A manager would like to know whether or not the level of income or rate of growth of national income would affect the sales of his firm. A measure known as the **income elasticity of demand** would inform the manager about how sensitive sales are to income changes. The income elasticity of demand is a measure of the responsiveness of consumer pur-

Figure 4.3

BUSINESS CYCLE

Taking out the growth part of Figure 4.2 leaves just the cycles.

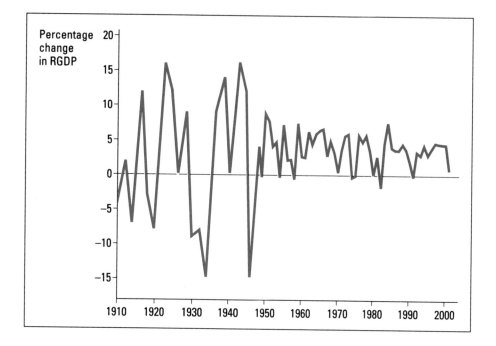

chases to income changes; it is defined as the percentage change in demand divided by the percentage change in income, everything else held constant.[5]

We do not say that demand is elastic or inelastic when referring to income elasticity. Instead, we may refer to some item as a luxury good or an inferior good, or we may call a good a cyclical good or a countercyclical good. A *luxury good* is one for which the income elasticity is very high—some value significantly greater than 1.0. A high income elasticity value tells us that a 1 percent increase in income will lead to a greater than 1 percent rise in demand. A high income elasticity means that as long as the economy is growing and incomes are rising, sales are rising. But if the economy slows and/or incomes decline, sales decline. A *normal good* is one for which the income elasticity is positive but probably less than 1.0 or near 1.0. Hotel rooms are a normal good—occupancy rates rise when incomes rise and fall when incomes fall. These goods are also called **cyclical goods** since their sales vary with the business cycle (levels of income). An *inferior good* is one for which the income elasticity is negative, meaning that as income rises, demand falls. Bankruptcy services are an inferior good—sales of bankruptcy services rise when income falls and decline when income rises. These are also called a **countercyclical goods** since as the business cycle rises (as incomes rise), demand falls, and vice versa. Billabong clothing appears to be noncyclical, rising even when incomes are not, at least in 2001 and 2002. This could be due to it being in the midst of a fad where young people the world over want to join in the Billabong revolution or could be due to Billabong entering new markets and thus experiencing growth even though incomes in Australia or in North America were not rising in 2001.

Cross-Price Elasticity

The latest version of the Windows operating system is more valuable on a computer having the most powerful version of a microchip than on a less powerful machine. The operating system and the microchip are complements. A **complement** to one product or service is any other product or service that makes the first one more attractive. Hot dogs and mustard, cars and auto loans, televisions and videocassette recorders, television shows and *TV Guide* are examples of complementary products and services. The Canadian companies Liqui-Box, a manufacturer of packaging systems for pumpable food products for institutional applications and DuPont Canada, a diversified science company that produces food products, generate complementary products. When the demand for the food products rises, the demand for the packaging systems rises.

Firms that produce complementary products are called *complementors*. DuPont Canada and Liqui-Box are complementors. Microsoft and Intel are complementors. Microsoft benefits when Intel develops a faster chip, and Intel benefits when Microsoft pushes forward in software development. Unless customers feel the need to upgrade, they won't continue buying the new Intel chip. For this reason, Intel has sought out other complementors such as ProShare and local phone companies to increase the demand for video applications that extend the limits of the microprocessor chips.

In 1913 General Motors, Hudson, Packard, and Willys-Overland, together with Goodyear tires and Prest-O-Lite headlights, set up the Lincoln Highway Association to develop America's first coast-to-coast highway.[6] The association built several miles along the proposed transcontinental route. The roads so complemented the cars that more cars were sold; this in turn increased the demand for roads. In 1916 the federal government committed its first dollars to building roads; by 1922 the first five transcontinental highways had been completed.

Complements and substitutes are an important aspect of business. While businesses may seek complementors, they want to distance themselves from substitutes. A business does not want a large number of substitutes for its product. The more substitutes, the more price-elastic is demand.

The **cross-price elasticity of demand** measures whether goods and services are complements or substitutes. Goods that are close substitutes for each other will have high positive cross-price elasticities. As the price of one good—say, Trek bikes—rises, the quantity demanded of other bicycles—Specialized, for instance—rises. If the two brands of bikes are considered virtually the same by most consumers, then a small price change in one will significantly affect the demand for the other. Goods that are complements have negative cross-price elasticities. As the price of movie tickets rises, the quantity of popcorn consumed declines. Movies and popcorn are used together—they are complements. If the cross-price elasticity is near zero, the goods are not very related—they are not really either substitutes or complements.

The cross-price elasticity is defined as the percentage change in the demand of one good divided by the percentage change in the price of a related good.[7]

A firm whose products have high positive cross-price elasticities with other products must be very conscious of what the related product's firm is doing. A strategy of altering demand will dramatically affect the related firm. A move to "value pricing" or "everyday low prices" by Federated Department Stores affected other department stores and specialty apparel stores. The rivals had to respond quickly or they would be impacted by the altered demand for Federated Department stores. However, should the price of Coca-Cola rise, the demands for coal, gas, or other sources of energy are unlikely to change. These products are not substitutes for each other. Genesis Microchip Inc. of Ontario Canada just entered the microchip market a few years ago. As a relatively small firm, it had to maintain a vigilant eye to the major manufacturers like Intel. A decrease in the price of Intel products could dramatically affect the demand for Genesis's products.

An elasticity measure could be calculated for anything that affects demand. For instance, it is not unusual for firms to want information on how advertising expenditures affect demand or on how sales forces affect demand. The calculation of these elasticities is similar to the calculation of price, income, and cross-price elasticities.

Elasticity Estimates

The PIMS (profit impact of market strategies) survey of major American firms obtained annual expenditures and performance data for about 1,500 business units. Using these data, the price elasticity of demand, as well as the elasticities of demand with respect to advertising, promotion, and sales force, are calculated.[8] The elasticity of demand with respect to advertising is the percentage increase in quantity sold resulting from a 1 percent increase in spending on media advertising. The elasticity of demand with respect to promotion is the percentage increase in quantity sold resulting from a 1 percent increase in expenditures on promotions. And the elasticity of demand with respect to sales force is the percentage increase in quantity sold resulting from a 1 percent increase in sales force expenditures. The average estimated values are:

Price elasticity	0.985
Advertising elasticity	0.003
Promotion elasticity	0.008
Sales force elasticity	0.304

What do these elasticities mean? The price elasticity of demand of 0.985 indicates that, over the price range examined in the study, a 1 percent change in price would lead to just less than a 1 percent decline in sales.

Advertising elasticity relates expenditures on advertising to sales. A 1 percent increase in expenditures on advertising would generate just a 3/100 percent increase in sales. Does this mean that firms spend too much on advertising? No. This low elasticity simply measures the impact on sales from increasing advertising expenditures by 1 percent. It doesn't say anything about the costs of the advertising. Similarly, a 1 percent increase in promotion expenditures generates a 8/100 percent increase in sales. Does this mean that resources should be allocated away from advertising toward promotion? No, all the numbers tell us is the impact on sales of a 1 percent increase in advertising expenditures or a 1 percent increase in promotion. We do not know the amount of expenditures on advertising or on promotion. Perhaps many more dollars have been spent on promotion than on advertising. For instance, suppose that $100 million has been spent on promotion and $1 million on advertising. Then a 1 percent increase in promotion would be $1 million, while a 1 percent increase in advertising would be $10,000. In this case, it might be more profitable to allocate the money to advertising rather than promotion.

Computer technology has enabled firms to get much better information about their customers and the elasticities of demand. Consider the petroleum industry, for example. Some petroleum companies have typically priced higher on the strength of their brand names, while others have aimed to offer the lowest prices.

Most retailers look at their sites, factor in overhead, and try to price slightly lower than their competition, with price increases or decreases being fairly uniform across all grades of fuel. "Pricing has been looked at as an art in the petroleum industry, something you determine by gut feel, reacting to what everybody else is doing. If you raise or lower prices, it's usually a couple of cents across the board for all grades of gasoline," said Don Spears, managing director of pricing systems and consulting for Tulsa-based MPSI Systems Inc.[9]

Computer technology allows retailers to determine price elasticity relationships quite readily. Elasticity models operate through a daily evaluation of pricing factors, site by site, that are stored on a running database. The process starts by entering historical price, volume, and competitive data for use by the model, with continual fine-tuning accomplished through daily data updates. Typical elasticity estimates for a single retailer, according to the pricing company MPSI Systems Inc., are 6 for regular, 4.5 for mid-grade, and 3 for premium: A 1 percent change in price will result in a 6 percent loss in volume for regular, a 4.5 percent loss in volume for mid-grade, and a 3 percent loss in volume for premium.

Computer technology is enabling many "low-margin" industries to improve their margins by knowing their customers better. The supermarket business is a prime example. Companies such as KhiMetrics and Customer Analyst provide the technical means to gather detailed information at the checkout counter. This information is then fed into a central computer and analyzed. The results are then used to determine prices on the products for the next day, week, or month.

Software companies create pricing models for businesses—even for retail businesses such as supermarkets that have more than thirty thousand products for sale at any one time. These software firms offer a service they call revenue management. Their results are a significant improvement in revenue. KhiMetrics is finding that its clients are adding about 1.9 percent to sales and from 3 percent to nearly 5 percent on profit margins.

Petroleum retailers, supermarkets, and many other firms are increasing profits because they better understand the customer. Computer technology enables firms to keep records of each customer—what they like and don't like, how sensitive they are to prices, and so on. A firm whose managers do not understand elasticities may be at a competitive disadvantage.

CASE REVIEW *Knowing the Customer*

Are businesses leaving money on the table? The short answer is yes, they are. As we have seen in this chapter, how customers respond to price depends on several characteristics, and these must be known to understand consumer behavior. A price increase will result in a revenue increase only if the price elasticity of demand is less than 1 or inelastic. It is quite amazing that the majority of companies use ad hoc pricing procedures. A survey conducted in October 2001 among the members of the U.S.-based Professional Pricing Society found that about 38 percent tried to determine a price based on value, cost, and competition; 25 percent narrowed it down to value versus competition; and 18 percent relied on cost-plus or some formula based on margin or return on investment; while the remaining firms chose other methods.

With the technologies available today, these ad hoc procedures are costly. Knowing the customer requires more than guessing or relying on some feeling about psychological aspects. It requires information, and that information can be obtained and utilized. The science of knowing the customer is referred to as revenue management. For example, *revenue management system* (RMS) vendors are incorporating new techniques such as group rates, guest history, and application service provider (ASP) technology to provide hotels an affordable and automated way to increase revenues. Data are collected, analyzed, and then stored in an easily retrievable format.

Most revenue management systems are "real-time," meaning that each transaction is immediately fed into a large database that can be called up immediately. For instance, Bell Canada's database can be used to pull not only the customer's history but also psycho-demographic information and other sales flags, such as whether the customer is at high risk of switching carriers. Part of knowing the customer is knowing when customers are satisfied or are about to leave for a competitor—and what to do about it.

Revenue management systems are offered by a growing number of companies. Satmetrix provides firms with a measure of the degree of customer loyalty and determines what needs to be done to maintain or improve that loyalty. In essence, the company measures the price elasticity of demand: Is it low enough; that is, is there a firm or product loyalty? KhiMetrics provides large retail operations scientific real-time pricing. Scanner data are collected and analyzed, and then price elasticities, cross-price elasticities, and other measures are calculated and used to set prices. KhiMetrics has found that its customers have significantly increased profits simply by adopting the technological approach to knowing the customer.

SUMMARY

1. Know your customer. This phrase means understand the demand curve and know the values of the elasticity measures.
2. The price elasticity of demand is a measure of the sensitivity of customers to price changes.
3. There is a relationship between price elasticity of demand and revenue. When the price elasticity of demand is less than 1 (inelastic), an increase in price increases revenue. When the price elasticity of demand is greater than 1 (elastic), an increase in price decreases revenue.
4. The more substitutes, the more time involved, and the larger the proportion of the consumer's budget devoted to the item, the greater is the price elasticity of demand.
5. Income elasticity is a measure of the sensitivity of demand to changes in income, with the price and other factors held constant. A cyclical good is one for which the income elasticity of demand is positive. A noncyclical good is one for which the income elasticity of demand is near zero. A countercyclical good is one for which the income elasticity of demand is negative.
6. The cross-price elasticity of demand measures the relationship between two goods. A negative cross-price elasticity means that as the price of one good (or service) rises, the demand for the other good (or service) falls. These goods are complements. A positive cross-price elasticity of demand means the goods are substitutes—as the price of one rises the demand for the other rises.

KEY TERMS

price elasticity of demand
elastic
unit-elastic
inelastic

substitutes
income elasticity of demand
cyclical goods

countercyclical goods
complements
cross-price elasticity of demand

EXERCISES

1. The HD Company has introduced a television with substantial technological advantages over existing televisions in picture, sound, and programming characteristics. The HD Company has decided to introduce only a few products initially at a very high price. They will then introduce more products at a reduced price. What is the basis for the pricing strategy? What conditions are necessary for this strategy to be more successful than merely introducing a huge number of products at a lower price?

2. For each of the following pairs of goods or services, identify the one for which the price elasticity of demand is greater and explain why.

   Coffee/Starbucks coffee
   Tuition at a public university/tuition at a private university
   Emergency room medical service/annual physical exam
   Movies in the afternoon/movies at night
   Prescription medicine/over-the-counter medicine

3. Although water is essential to life no matter where one lives, the demand for water differs across regions. In one study it was found that the price elasticity of demand for water in all regions of the United States ranged from 0.39 to 0.69.

   a. Why is the demand for water price-inelastic?

   b. In those regions where outdoor use of water makes up a relatively large portion of total use, the price elasticity is high. Why?

   c. The demand for water in the summer months is greater than in the winter months. Explain why.

4. Many proponents of public transit argue that the service should be provided free to the public in metropolitan areas in order to reduce pollution and traffic congestion. Estimates by economists found the price elasticity of demand for public transit to be 0.17. The economists also found the cross-price elasticity of demand with the automobile to be 0.10.

   a. What will free public transit mean to the use of the public transportation service?

   b. What will free public transit mean to the use of the automobile?

5. The income elasticity of demand for automobiles in the United States was estimated by a government agency to be between 2.5 and 3.9.

   a. What does this mean?

   b. If incomes rise by 10 percent, what happens to the purchase of automobiles?

6. Suppose you are the manager of a firm that has discovered an innovation that enhances the power of a microchip by 1,000 times. What would you do with that unique resource—your innovation? Would you sell the chip to Intel and Motorola and allow them to market the chip under their own brand name (a private label)? Would you sell the chip directly to manufacturers such as IBM and Macintosh under your own label?

7. Many retailers will use short-term price cuts to attract customers. These often include "loss-leaders," products sold at a loss for a short time. Why would a firm ever sell at a loss?

8. The demand curve slopes downward, illustrating the law of demand. What about the so-called prestige good, the situation in which the higher the price of a product, up to some point, the greater is the quantity demanded?

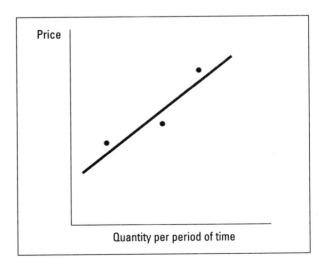

Does the prestige good run counter to the law of demand? The answer is no. Explain why.

9. In 1998 an agreement known as the Tobacco Resolution was reached between a group of U.S. states and the tobacco industry. The agreement required the tobacco companies to pay the states $246 billion over twenty-five years. The tobacco companies are going to have to raise prices to be able to pay the states. Economists have found that cigarette smoking declines about 4 percent for every 10 percent increase in cigarette price. Will the tobacco companies be able to pay the $246 billion without affecting their profits? Explain.

10. Develop a marketing strategy for a store with very limited floor space that sells the following goods having the cross-price elasticities shown.

First Item	Second Item	Cross-Price Elasticity
Coffee bean grinder	Coffee maker	−0.04
Gold mesh coffee filter	Coffee maker	−2.70

11. The Rolls Royce Corporation, a maker of aircraft engines, determines that the demand for its product is

$$P = 2{,}000 - 50Q,$$

where P is the price in dollars of an engine and Q is the number of engines sold per month.

a. To sell twenty engines per month, what price would Rolls Royce have to charge?

b. If it sets a price of $500, how many engines will Rolls Royce sell per month?

c. What is the price elasticity of demand if price equals $500?

d. At what price is the price elasticity of demand equal to unit elasticity?

e. What price will maximize revenue?

12. The XYZ Company's marketing officials report to the company's CEO that the demand curve for the company's products is:

$$P = 3{,}000 - 40Q$$

where P is the price of a unit of the product and Q is the number sold per month.

a. Plot the demand curve.

b. Indicate the elastic range, inelastic range, and unit-elastic point.

c. What price will maximize revenue?

13. The marketing department of a firm finds that the demand function for the product the firm sells is

$$Q = 500 - 3P + 2P_r + 0.1I$$

where Q is the quantity demanded of its product, P is the price of its product, P_r is the price of its rival's product, and I is per-capita disposable income. At present, $P = \$10$, $P_r = \$20$, and $I = \$6{,}000$.

a. What is the price elasticity of demand for the firm's product?

b. What is the income elasticity of demand for the firm's product?

c. What is the cross-price elasticity of demand between its product and the rival's product?

CHAPTER NOTES

1. $e_d = \partial \ln Q_d / \partial \ln P = [\partial Q_d / Q_d] / [\partial P/P]$, where e_d represents the price elasticity of demand, $\partial \ln Q_d$ is the percentage change in the quantity demanded (the derivative of the logarithm of quantity demanded, which is the change in Q_d divided by the base quantity demanded or the initial quantity demanded), and $\partial \ln P$ is the percentage change in price (the derivative of the logarithm of price, which is the change in price divided by the base price or initial price).

2. Notice that we say 3 rather than −3. According to the law of demand, whenever the price of a good rises, the quantity demanded of that good falls. Thus, the price elasticity of demand is always negative, which can be confusing when referring to a "very high elasticity" (a large negative number) or to a "low elasticity" (a small negative number). To avoid this confusion, economists use the absolute value of the price elasticity of demand and thus ignore the negative sign.

3. Demand curves need not be straight lines. The straight line is used to illustrate demand concepts because it incorporates most of the important aspects of demand.

4. These are based on very small incremental movements. When using larger discrete amounts, the results are only approximate. For instance, if price is $1 and quantity is 100, then revenue is $100. A 10 percent rise in price to $1.10 and a 10 percent fall in quantity to 90 means that revenue is $99.

5. The income elasticity of demand is
$$Y_e = \partial \ln Q_d / \partial \ln Y = [\partial Q_d / Q_d]/[\partial Y/Y]$$
which is the percentage change in quantity demanded divided by the percentage change in income.

6. Drake Hokanson, *The Lincoln Highway: Main Street Across America* (Iowa City: University of Iowa Press, 1988).

7. It is represented mathematically as

$$cp_e = \partial\ln Q_d^a/\partial\ln P^b = [\partial Q^a /Q^a]/[\partial P^b/P^b]$$

where Q_d^a is the demand for good a and P^b is the price of good b.

8. M. Hagerty, J. Carman, and G. Russell, "Estimating Elasticities with PIMS Data: Methodological Issues and Substantive Implications," *Journal of Marketing Research* 25, no. 1 (February 1988): 1–9.

9. Quoted in Keith Reid, "The Science of Pricing," *Business and Management Practices* 5, no. 2 (March 2000): 33–35.

CHAPTER 4 APPENDIX A
Consumer Behavior

Consumer behavior is the basis for price and other elasticities of demand. In this appendix we look more closely at consumer behavior. We also examine elasticities using the mathematical material discussed in the appendix to Chapter 2.

Consumer Choice

Most of us believe that all we need—all any reasonable person needs—is a little more than what we have. But whether you are a Peruvian peasant farmer living on $500 a year or an American physician living on $500,000 a year, the consumption decisions you make are those appropriate to your income, and you will still not get enough of everything you might want. This causes people to choose among the different things they value. People choose to consume more of one thing but at a cost of having less of something else. It is this need for making choices that leads to the law of demand and the various elasticities of demand.

Indifference Analysis

The law of demand says that people are willing and able to purchase a smaller quantity of an item when the price of that item rises, everything else remaining unchanged. To illustrate the link between the choices people make and the law of demand, we'll look at consumer behavior under the assumption that people are rational—that they can compare costs and benefits and that they prefer more to less of any good or service. Under this assumption and confronted with a limited income, we can show that consumers will increase the quantity demanded of some item as the price of that item falls, everything else remaining unchanged. The approach we'll use to demonstrate the law of demand is called **indifference analysis**. With indifference analysis, we enable consumers to reveal their preferences by making choices. All possible combinations of goods are presented. Consumers will choose those combinations they prefer over other combinations and indicate those among which they are indifferent. But just having a set of preferred combinations does not mean consumers have the income to purchase those combinations. They must decide how to allocate their budget or income among the combinations of goods. The exact combination chosen by consumers is the one that maximizes their happiness (what is called utility) given the prices of the goods and the consumers' income.

Let's begin by defining an indifference curve. An **indifference curve** is a graph showing different combinations of goods among which the consumer is indifferent. Suppose we consider Alberta's preferences for two food products, milk and meat. We have measured quarts of milk along the vertical axis and pounds of meat along the horizontal axis of Figure 4A.1. There are infinite combinations of the two goods—everywhere including and between the two axes. Indifference curves are drawn by finding those combinations of goods to which Alberta is indifferent. For instance, in Figure 4A.1, bundle A is 10 pounds of meat and 15 quarts of milk while bundle B is fifteen pounds of meat and ten pounds of milk. Alberta indicates that she is indifferent between them; she doesn't care which she

Figure 4A.1

COMMODITY BUNDLES AND INDIFFERENCE

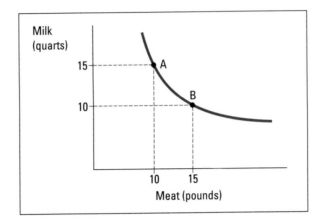

has. Connecting these two and all other combinations of the two goods among which Alberta is indifferent yields an indifference curve. The indifference curves slope downward to the right because if one bundle has less meat than another yet is equally attractive to Alberta, it must have more milk. Alberta makes tradeoffs by giving up meat for milk. She would not be indifferent between a bundle having 10 quarts of milk and 20 pounds of meat and one having 10 quarts of milk and 10 pounds of meat. The consumer always wants more.

Although the consumer always prefers more to less, the more the consumer has of a good, the less is the value to the consumer of having a little more of that good. As you move downward and to the right along the indifference curve to bundles with less milk and more meat, additional milk becomes more valuable and additional meat, less valuable. Notice that starting at combination A, Alberta is willing to give up 12 quarts of milk to get 5 pounds of meat, but then only 7 quarts of milk to get an additional 5 pounds of meat, and finally only 5 quarts of milk to get 8 pounds of meat. Economists say that the marginal utility of a good gets smaller the more of that good a consumer has. That is why indifference curves all have the same general shape—the curve gets flatter as you move downward and to the right. Every possible bundle of goods is on some indifference curve; the curve showing all bundles equivalent to that one. If all of those curves were drawn, the graph would be solid black. Curves I_1, I_2, and I_3 in Figure 4A.2

Figure 4A.2

INDIFFERENCE CURVES

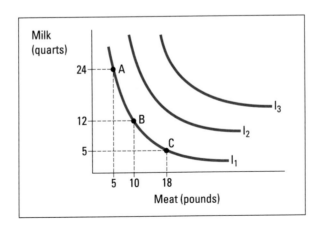

are just three that could have been drawn. Notice a few things about the indifference curves.

1. Every indifference curve must slope downward and to the right so long as the consumer prefers more of each good to less.
2. Indifference curves cannot intersect. If they did, this would contradict the assumption that more of a commodity is preferred to less. For example, consider Figure 4A.3, in which two indifference curves, I_1 and I_2, intersect. At point C, the intersection point, the bundle is the same on both curves. But point E is preferred to point D, thus contradicting the idea that the consumer is indifferent between combinations C, D, and E.
3. The farther out from the origin an indifference curve is, the more that all bundles on it are preferred to all bundles lying on curves below it. In Figure 4A.2 all combinations along I_3 are preferred to all combinations along I_2, which are preferred to all combinations along I_1. In other words, more is preferred to less.

Although we all want more, we are not able to have everything that we want. For instance, let's suppose that Alberta had just $25 on her when she entered Safeway (and let's assume no immediate access to other funds). The amount the consumer has to spend is called the budget or income constraint. The budget line is drawn once prices of the commodity bundles (milk and meat) are specified. We'll assume that milk costs $1.00 a quart and meat $2.50 a pound. This enables us to draw the budget line: purchasing only milk with $25 would allow Alberta to purchase 25 quarts of milk. Purchasing just meat would allow Alberta to buy 10 pounds of meat. The budget line is shown in Figure 4A.4. Alberta can purchase any combination along the budget line and below it.

If Alberta had $40, she could purchase 16 pounds of meat at $2.50 per pound or 40 quarts of milk at $1.00 per quart. This would be shown as the budget line, running from 40 on the vertical axis to 16 on the horizontal axis in Figure 4A.4. As income (the budget) rises and everything else remains the same, the budget line shifts out, representing the idea that the consumer can now purchase more of everything.

If the price of milk rises from $1.00 per quart to $1.50 per quart and the total budget is $25, the budget line rotates in along the milk axis, illustrating the idea that the consumer can now purchase less milk, everything else remaining the

Figure 4A.3

INTERSECTING INDIFFERENCE CURVES

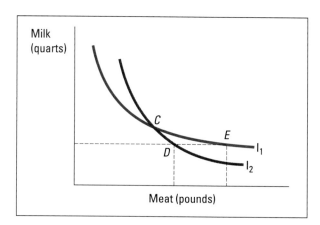

Figure 4A.4
THE BUDGET LINE

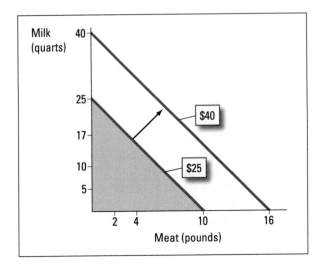

same, as shown in Figure 4A.5. With $25, Alberta could purchase 10 pounds of meat at $2.50 per pound or 16.6 quarts of milk at $1.50 per quart.

By placing the budget line and the indifference curves on the same graph, we can illustrate the consumer's maximizing point—where the consumer gets the most happiness (utility) for the least expenditure.

In Figure 4A.6, notice that Alberta could purchase any combination equal to or less than her budget line. But she gets the greatest satisfaction by purchasing at the highest indifference curve she can. That point is point A along indifference curve I_2. She would prefer to be along a higher indifference curve, such as I_3, but cannot afford to spend that much. She much prefers being along I_2 than along any indifference curve below I_2.

Having obtained the maximizing point, we can now discover what occurs as the price of one good changes while everything else remains the same. As the price

Figure 4A.5
A PRICE RISE AND THE BUDGET LINE

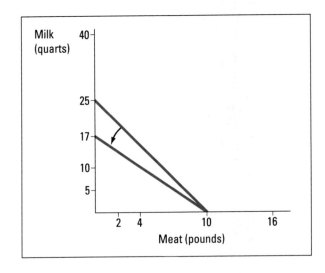

Figure 4A.6

THE OPTIMIZING POINT

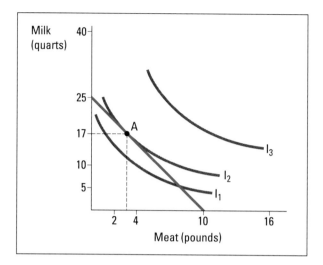

of milk rises, Alberta purchases less milk and more of the now relatively less expensive good, meat. This is illustrated in Figure 4A.7. As the price of milk rises, Alberta trades off, or substitutes, meat for milk. As the price of an item increases, everything else remaining the same, the consumer will make substitutions, purchasing less of the now more expensive item. If we plot the price of milk against the quantity of milk demanded by Alberta, we end up with her demand curve. This is shown in Figure 4A.8.

We have examined Alberta's choices and her personal tradeoffs between milk and meat. The steepness of her demand curve depends on how much Alberta is willing to change her purchases when the price changes. Another consumer would have different preferences and different tradeoffs. We could derive a demand curve for each consumer. Then adding all the individual demand curves (horizontally) would give us the market demand. The steepness of the market demand curve would depend on how all consumers together respond to a price change. If they

Figure 4A.7

A PRICE RISE

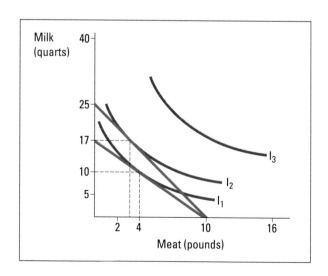

Figure 4A.8

ALBERTA'S DEMAND CURVE

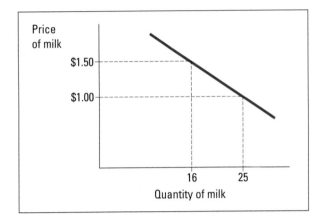

are willing to give up a lot of milk when the price of milk rises, then the demand curve for milk would be flatter than if they are willing to give up just a little milk when its price rises.

Calculus Approach

Consumer choice can be represented in terms of calculus. The consumer is posited to have a preference function or what is called a utility function—$U = U(x_1, x_2)$—where the two goods (milk and meat) are represented by x_1 and x_2. The budget constraint is specified as $B = p_1 x_1 + p_2 x_2$, where p_1 and p_2 are the prices of the goods x_1 and x_2. The optimization is set up as follows (called a Lagrangian optimization or constrained optimization problem, as discussed in the appendix to Chapter 2):

$$L = U(x_1, x_2) + \lambda[B - p_1 x_1 + p_2 x_2]$$

To find the bundle of goods at which the consumer obtains the greatest satisfaction or utility that the consumer's budget allows, we differentiate with respect to x_1, x_2, and λ, and set each equal to zero. The results—the first-order conditions—are:

$$\frac{\partial U(x_1, x_2)}{\delta x_1} - \lambda p_1 = 0 \tag{1}$$

$$\frac{\partial U(x_1, x_2)}{\delta x_2} - \lambda p_2 = 0 \tag{2}$$

$$B - p_1 x_1 + p_2 x_2 = 0 \tag{3}$$

We can solve the three equations for the three unknowns, x_1, x_2, and λ. When we do this, we derive demand functions for the two goods. There are some other interesting results presented in the first-order conditions. Notice that if we divide equation (1) by equation (2), we obtain the rate at which consumers substitute the two goods:

$$\frac{\partial U(x_1, x_2)/\partial x_1}{\partial U(x_1, x_2)/\partial x_2} = MRS = \frac{p_1}{p_2} \tag{4}$$

The ratio on the left side of equation (4), the marginal utility of x_1 to the marginal utility of x_2, is the rate at which a consumer is willing to substitute x_2 for x_1

and remain indifferent. This is called the **marginal rate of substitution (MRS).** The MRS is the slope of the indifference curve. The price ratio is the slope of the budget line. When the two slopes are equal, the consumer is optimizing. The consumer gains the most happiness (the greatest utility) at the point where the marginal rate of substitution between two goods is equal to the price ratio of those goods.

Equation (4) tells us that when the price of one item rises, everything else the same, the consumer will substitute out of that more expensive good. Suppose, for instance, that the price of x_1 rises. This causes the ratio p_1/p_2 to rise. This means that the ratio of marginal utilities is smaller than the ratio of prices. The consumer will reallocate expenditures. By purchasing less of x_1, the marginal utility of x_1 decreases—the more you have of something, the less valuable another unit of that something is to you. Thus, the ratio of marginal utilities rises as the consumer reduces expenditures on x_1. The consumer continues to reallocate expenditures until the ratio of prices is once again equal to the ratio of marginal utilities.

Psychology of Consumer Behavior

You might think that the consumer behavior we have described using indifference curves and the marginal rate of substitution is very unrealistic. "No one calculates the ratio of marginal utilities and ratio of prices and ensures they are equal. People aren't that rational—no one is a computer, and a computer would be required to make calculations like this." Yet, although the theory might be considered unrealistic, it still pretty much describes how consumers behave. People do tend to behave as if they were totally rational (could and do calculate ratios of marginal utilities and prices) and had perfect information. But tendencies don't mean they always do this.

Are Consumers Ever Rational?

Is it rational to drive twenty minutes to a discount grocery store to save $10 but to spend hundreds of dollars a year on the gas-guzzling car used for the trip? Is it rational to chance running out of gas to pass one station because you know a station offering gas at 2 cents a gallon less that is just about a mile away? Is it rational to pay more for clothing simply because it is "in style"? Is it rational to invest in the stock of companies for no better reason than that other investors are doing the same?

Is it rational to take a lesser deal while turning down a better deal? Consider, for instance, a bank offering free checking. The free checking requires a balance of $1,500 in the account; without such a balance, the fee for the account is $5 a month. People routinely choose the free checking. Is this rational? The free checking means you are giving up the interest you could earn on that $1,500, something to the tune of 5 percent. The cost of $5 per month is $5/$1500 = .00033, or about 3.5 percent per year. So, isn't it irrational to choose the 5 percent rather than the 3.5 percent cost?

These types of decisions, made all the time, are not irrational. They are not perfectly rational as economic theory has defined the term, but they are not irrational. A story about a honeymooning couple in Las Vegas provides an illustration of why such behavior is not irrational. Knowing they were headed for Vegas and knowing they did not have a lot of money, the couple decided they would spend only a certain amount. Once that was gone, they had to return home. So after a couple of days, the amount had been spent. The couple was spending their last night in their hotel prior to returning home. The wife was asleep and the husband, wide awake, noticed a $5 chip that they had saved as a souvenir. Strangely, the number 12 was flashing in the groom's mind. Taking this as an omen, he rushed to the roulette tables, where he placed the $5 chip on the 12; sure enough, the winner was 12, paying 35 to 1. He let the winnings ride and kept on winning until he had won $262 million. He then let it ride once more and lost. Broke and dejected, he walked back to his room. "Where were you?" asked his bride. "Playing roulette" he responded. "How did you do?" she asked. "Not bad. I lost five dollars."

This story captures what is referred to as playing with the house's money. The idea is that people do not feel something belongs to them unless it comes out of their own pocket. In terms of people's feelings and behavior, opportunity costs are not always the same as out-of-pocket costs. This is why some retailers ask the customer to "take it home and see how it looks." Others charge "no interest for 12 months" or provide it "free for 90 days." And, of course, we've all heard that "you are already a winner." A purely rational being would never differentiate out-of-pocket from opportunity costs.

Another example of how people behave that is not strictly rational is provided by the following quiz:

Who is happier?
   A, who wins the office football pool for $100 and also wins a bowling contest for another $50.
   B, who wins the office football pool for $150.

Who is less unhappy in the following situation?
   A, who ruins the carpet in his apartment and must pay the landlord $100.
   B, who loses $25 but also ruins the carpet in his apartment and must pay the landlord $75.

The choice of most people in these two cases is A, although in both cases A and B end up with exactly the same amount. In the first case, A is happier because she wins two events. In the second case, A is less unhappy because he has just one loss. Although the gains or losses are the same for choices A and B, people want to *separate gains* and *combine losses*. The idea is captured in the statement that "you shouldn't wrap all the Christmas presents in one box." People like to have their gains occur several times rather than all at once. Conversely, people feel better if they must pay something or incur a loss to have it occur all at once. A purely rational being would rate a $1 loss (gain) and two 50-cent losses (gains) the same and a $1 gain or two 50-cent gains as equivalent.

Framing

Another aspect of behavior that might be considered irrational is that people tend to place prices and other aspects of products and services in a frame; that is, they compare price or other aspects of a good or service to some reference. (We discuss framing in terms of price strategies in Chapter 8.) A frame is simply a point of reference. People make decisions in the context in which the problem is presented. It is the idea that transactions, prices, and so on have a frame of reference, something to which consumers can compare different choices.

A frame most people have implicitly available is some sense of "fairness." There is a simple exercise called the ultimatum game that illustrates how this frame works. You have a fixed sum of money, say, $10. You then give the entire amount to half of the people assembled, the group we'll call givers. You tell them that they can keep whatever portion they choose, 1 to 10, as long as someone in the other half, the group we'll call receivers, accepts what they choose to give away. The givers have to decide how much of the $10 to keep for themselves and how much to offer to the receivers. Each giver writes the allocation on a piece of paper. The papers are collected and randomly allocated to the receivers. If the receiver accepts what the giver offers, the two keep the split of the $10. If the receiver rejects, then both giver and receiver get nothing.

Since $1 or even 1 cent is better than zero, you would expect the givers to choose to keep virtually everything for themselves and offer the receiver the smallest amount possible. Interestingly, however, givers tend to choose to give either $4 or $5 to the receivers; very seldom do they choose to give $1, $2, or $3. They never give more than $5. An offer of $1, $2, or $3 is nearly always rejected by the receivers. Once in a while $4 is rejected. What does this mean? It means that people are not thinking of the $1 as marginally better than zero—their reference is not zero but instead something more "fair." In fact, fairness is the crucial aspect. A fair split is $5 and $5, and that is the reference people implicitly have in mind.

People will reject something they perceive as not being fair. During a snowstorm, does the local hardware store raise the price of snow shovels? During a hurricane, do the grocery stores raise the price of food and water? The answer is not if they want to retain business. The old saying is: "If you gouge them at Christmas, they won't be back in March."

When people must make decisions without having perfect information, they often use things they are familiar with or are used to more than would seem to be the case described by economic theory. Familiarity leads to decisions that might appear irrational because people are more comfortable with a familiar situation than an unfamiliar one. Consider the following quiz.

(1) In four pages of a novel (about 2,000 words), how many words would you expect to find that have the form "_ _ _ _ ing" (seven letters that end in *ing*)?

   0 1–2 3–4 5–7 8–10 11–15 16+

Now that you have answered the first part, answer the following:

(2) In four pages of a novel (about 2,000 words), how many words would you expect to find that have the form "_ _ _ _ _n_" (seven letters with an *n* in the sixth position)?

   0 1–2 3–4 5–7 8–10 11–15 16+

You may have noticed that the second option includes the first—in other words, the answer to the second has to be larger than the answer to the first. Yet, because people are familiar with -*ing* they tend to think there are more options for it. This choice of familiarity also shows up in answers to:

Which is more common in New York City, murder or suicide?

Although suicide is much more prevalent than murder, many people think the answer is murder. The point is that the more familiar people are with something (here, news reports of murders in New York), the more likely they are to choose it.

Anchoring

Another way in which people make decisions is called anchoring. Here is another quiz:

You have five seconds to estimate the value of $1 \times 2 \times 3 \times 4 \times 5 \times 6 \times 7 \times 8$.

Now, if at another time you are given five seconds to do the same for $8 \times 7 \times 6 \times 5 \times 4 \times 3 \times 2 \times 1$, you will most likely end up with different results. The first case is always smaller than the second. The reason is that the guesstimate had been "anchored" to the higher numbers early in the sequence (but still nowhere near the correct number of 40,320).

These decision rules and others similar to them were derived by two psychologists, Daniel Kahneman of Princeton University and the late Amos Tversky of Stanford University. In the 1970s they carried out a series of pioneering studies revealing how humans behave in the face of uncertainty. In standard economic theory, people are perfectly rational. But Kahneman and Tversky studied actual human behavior by means of laboratory experiments. Their experiments showed that people can make choices that don't provide them with what would appear to be the best outcome. The upshot of these studies is that people tend to resort to rules of thumb—heuristics—that can mislead them when they try to make decisions based on limited or uncertain information. But being misled does not mean these people are not maximizing their utility or happiness. The maximization is just occurring with the use of heuristic decision making.

Kahneman and Tversky's research has added to the economist's understanding of individual behavior. Economists now talk about "bounded rationality" rather than strict rationality. Bounded rationality recognizes that people do use frames, familiarity, anchoring, and other heuristic rules to make decisions when they don't have perfect information. But bounded rationality does not change the basis of decision making—that people want to have the greatest happiness they can obtain given limited resources and income. In 2002, Kahneman received the Nobel Prize in Economics for this research.

Marginal Revenue and Demand Elasticities: Calculus

Irrespective of how people make decisions, they do purchase less of an item when the price of that item increases, everything else remaining the same. How much less is measured by the price elasticity of demand. The price elasticity of demand is defined to be the percentage change in quantity demanded divided by the percentage change in price. Percentage change is the change divided by a base: $\Delta Q/Q$ is the percentage change in Q and $\Delta P/P$ is the percentage change in price. The price elasticity of demand, e^d, then is

$$e^d = \frac{\Delta Q/Q}{\Delta P/P}$$

which can be rewritten as

$$e^d = (\Delta Q/\Delta P)(P/Q)$$

In terms of derivatives, the price elasticity of demand is

$$e^d = (\partial Q/\partial P)(P/Q)$$

The relationship between marginal revenue and price elasticity of demand can be shown using the definition of marginal revenue:

$$MR = \partial TR/\partial Q = P + Q(\partial P/\partial Q)$$

Marginal revenue is equal to P, the price of the last unit sold, plus the amount by which revenue declines because all units sold are now sold at the lower price of the last unit sold, $Q(\partial P/\partial Q)$. Rearranging terms by taking out P,

$$MR = P[1 + (Q/P)(\partial P/\partial Q)]$$

And since the price elasticity is $(P/Q)(\partial Q/\partial P)$, we can write marginal revenue as

$$MR = P(1 - 1/e^d)$$

So you can see that when $e^d = 1$, $MR = 0$; when $e^d = \infty$, $MR = P$; and when $e^d > 1$, $MR < P$.

Consider an example. Suppose the demand function is

$$Q = -400P + 200Y - 400S + .01C$$

where P is the price of Q, Y is income, S is the price of substitutes, and C the price of complements. Given the value of $Y = \$20,000$, $S = \$400$, and $C = \$3,000$,

$$Q = 400P + 200(\$20,000) - 400(\$400) + .01(\$3,000) = 3,840,030 + 400P$$

Suppose we want to calculate the price elasticity when $P = \$5,000$. The derivative of Q with respect to P is $\partial Q/\partial P = 400$. Multiplying $\partial Q/\partial P$ by P/Q gives us the price elasticity, $P/Q = 5,000/3,840,030$. Multiplying 400 by P/Q yields

$$400(.001302) = 0.52$$

The price elasticity of demand at that point is 0.52.

Income elasticity and cross-price elasticity are calculated in the same manner as the price elasticity. The income elasticity is $(\partial Q/\partial Y)(Y/Q)$ and the cross-price elasticity of demand is

$$(\partial Q_a/\partial P_b)(P_b/Q_a)$$

where a and b are two goods.

CHAPTER 4 APPENDIX B
Market Research

In April 1985 the Coca-Cola Company announced that it was replacing original Coke with a reformulated cola, what has become known as New Coke. Never before had a company voluntarily ceased production of a best-selling product and replaced it with an entirely new one. What motivated this bold and shocking move? Research. Over a period of about two years, 180,000 blind taste tests had been done. The blind tests showed that Pepsi-Cola was preferred to Coke because Pepsi was sweeter. In order to counter the "Pepsi challenge," Coke had to be perceived as being sweeter. This was the basis for New Coke—its formula produced a much sweeter cola. As is well known, consumers reacted violently against New Coke and the plan to take the original Coke off the market. How could Coca-Cola, with its two-year research program and a $4 million budget, have misread consumer reaction so terribly?

The short answer is that market research is difficult. The objective of market research is to learn about the customer, but how one approaches the problem is a science in itself. Some of the approaches and issues involved with market research are discussed in this appendix. This is only an introduction to the subject—entire texts and treatises exist on the subject.

Data

We know that demand depends on the price of the product, the prices of related products, tastes, preferences, size of the market, incomes, and other factors. We know that elasticity measures the responsiveness of consumers to changes in any of these factors holding all others fixed. But it is necessary to put actual numbers to this theory if we are to formulate strategies for a firm. How do we get those numbers?

There are two sources of data, primary and secondary. Primary data are data collected for a specific purpose and used for that purpose. Secondary data are data collected for one purpose and used for another.

Primary Data

A great deal of market research involves obtaining information about the market. The most direct way to obtain information about anything is to ask for it. To find out what factors influence demand, one approach is to simply interview potential consumers: "How much would you be willing to buy if the price of this product were X? If it were Y?" Consumers might be asked what their current consumption behavior is and how they would respond if a certain product were available at a 10 percent discount. Or interviewees might be asked how they would expect others to behave. A great deal of market research involves simply asking consumers what their attitudes are and how they will behave. When data are gathered in this manner, they are called primary data.

Primary data can be gathered by observing the relevant actors and settings. Researchers for an airline might meander around airports, airline offices, and travel agencies to hear how travelers talk about the different carriers. They could fly on various planes to observe the quality of in-flight service. Data can be collected from credit card purchases of tickets or from Internet purchases of e-tickets. This research might yield some useful hypotheses about how travelers choose their air carriers. The next step would be to refine those hypotheses. This is often done using focus groups.

Focus Group The focus group interview consists of a small number of people (typically six to twelve) who are gathered together and asked to express their thoughts and feelings on an issue, product, or some other subject. Focus groups are used in such areas as new product development, product testing, package design, brand-name selection, advertising copy, and promotion research.

The Buick division of General Motors used focus groups to help develop the Regal two-door, six-passenger coupe introduced in 1987. The effort began more than three years prior to introducing the car, when Buick held about twenty focus groups across the country and asked what features customers wanted in a new car. Who were the customers? Those wealthy enough to afford a $14,000 price tag. At this time the price was about $1,000 to $2,000 more than the average price of a new car, which meant an annual income of $40,000 or more. All the participants, gathered in every major geographic region of the country, had purchased new cars within the past four years. What these groups indicated was that the customers wanted a legitimate back seat, at least twenty miles per gallon gas consumption, and zero to sixty miles per hour acceleration in eleven seconds or less. They also wanted a stylish car, but they didn't want it to look like it had just landed from outer space.

After Buick engineers created clay models of the car and mock-ups of the interior, the company went back to yet another focus group. This group reacted positively to the suspension but disliked the oversized bumper and the severe slope of the hood. The result was the Regal.

Focus groups also helped to refine the advertising campaign for the Regal. Participants were first asked which competing cars most resembled the Buick in terms of image and features. The answer was Oldsmobile, a sister General Motors division. In response, Buick was repositioned above Oldsmobile by focusing on comfort and luxury features such as full six passenger seating, wood-grain instrument panels, velour-type fabrics, and special stereo systems.

Consumer goods companies have been using focus groups for many years, and an increasing number of service firms—newspapers, law firms, hospitals, and public service organizations—are now using them. Focus group interviews may be the first step in the research process for many types of problems. Because they are used in the early stages of the research process, their primary usefulness is not in providing precise quantitative information but rather in providing qualitative descriptive information.

Focus groups are a useful research tool, but they have severe limitations. First, focus groups are conducted in extremely contrived conditions. In the real world, people are bombarded by many more choices than they are in a closed room with a rigid set of questions. Second, the results depend greatly on the ability of the group's moderator. Third, people often say one thing in public but act in a totally different way when they're actually shopping in a store. For example, ask a group of moms if they'd prefer Cereal X, a healthy blend of grain, nuts, and berries, or Cereal Y, a Coca-Puffs copy with twice the sugar. Guess which they'll pick. Guess which will sell better.

Focus groups informed the Cadillac division of General Motors that they would prefer the Allante to the BMW and Mercedes-Benz sport coupes it was compared with. The Allante looked sleek enough to merit positive reviews by the focus groups, but when it was driven and found to be less powerful, have less room, be less leak-proof and noisier than the European cars, sales went nowhere. Moreover, the Allante debuted in 1987 at a sticker price of $57,000, a much higher price than the comparable BMW and Mercedes-Benz automobiles.

Surveys   A survey can be undertaken in several ways—mail or email, telephone, or direct or personal interviewing. Personal interviewing is the most versatile of the three methods. The interviewer can ask more questions and can record additional observations about the respondent, such as dress and body language. Personal interviewing is the most expensive method and requires more administrative planning and supervision than the other two. It is also subject to interviewer bias or distortion.

Personal interviewing takes two forms, arranged interviews and intercept interviews. In arranged interviews, selected respondents are contacted and appointments made for the interview to take place. Intercept interviews involve stopping people at a shopping mall or busy street corner and requesting an interview.

Not all interviewers today are human. Some companies are using toll-free telephone numbers to solicit marketing information via telephone. For example, in 1993 Pepsi-Cola sent a direct-mail piece to a million households that drank Diet Coke, offering them a chance to call an interactive 800 number, talk to Ray Charles, and possibly win a prize. But first they had to use their touch-tone phone to answer a series of market research questions designed to help Pepsi understand Diet Coke households. More than half a million people called and were greeted by Ray and the Uh-Huh Girls.

The arranged interview attempts to uncover underlying motivations, prejudice, and attitudes toward sensitive issues. It has been used in brand-name research to understand consumers' perceptions and responses to names and in copy and concept evaluations wherein respondents are asked what they recall or what they feel after listening to an advertisement.

In the typical application, buyers are asked to express their intentions to purchase a product class and/or brand, among other queries. Usually they are able to express their intentions to purchase as a matter of degree and with respect to a particular time horizon. The responses of buyers are then added up and used to generate potential market estimates and brand shares. A typical intention question is:

What is the probability that you will purchase a television within the next year? Circle the appropriate probability

0 0.1 0.2 0.3 0.4 0.5 0.6 0.7 0.8 0.9 1.0

Mechanical devices are sometimes used in marketing research. Galvanometers measure the subject's interest or emotions aroused by exposure to a specific ad or picture. The tachistoscope flashes an ad to a subject with an exposure interval that may range from less than one hundredth of a second to several seconds. After each exposure, the respondent describes everything he or she recalls. Eye cameras study respondents' eye movements to see where their eyes land first, how long they linger on a given item, and so on. The audiometer is attached to television sets in participating homes to record when the set is on and to which channel it is tuned.

Buyer Intentions One of the basic problems with marketing research using primary data is that what people say they will do is often different from what they actually do. Intentions are not always related strongly to behavior. One reason is that people's needs, judgments, and evaluations change between the time of measurement of their intentions and the opportunity to act. Also, events change, economic conditions fluctuate, competitors come and go, prices jump up or down, and so on. In addition, people often don't want to admit how they actually feel or what they will be likely to do, instead saying what they think the interviewer wants to hear.

The Oobie illustrates the problem. The Oobie was a plastic clam-shaped toy with two eyes and an address label on it. Developed by Parker Brothers in the early 1970s, the Oobie was supposed to be a toy dedicated to friendship. The idea was for a child to write a note to a friend, put it in an Oobie, and simply leave it somewhere in public. Then whoever happened to come upon the Oobie would pick it up and help it along on its journey. Surveys by Parker Brothers indicated that the toy would do well. Parents said they liked the "It's a small world" lesson of the toy and would definitely buy it for their children. However, once on the market, parents took a rather different view. They started to think that reliance on the potential kindness of strangers was a real problem. A pervert could easily pick up the Oobie and pay a visit to the child listed on the address label.

It's common practice to use purchase intentions to predict sales of a new flavor of cereal or potato chip or a new category of product, such as nonfat cookies. But there is very little predictive content in those surveys. In fact, people generally aren't reliable predictors of their own long-term purchasing behavior for any type of good, new or old, durable or not. Asking consumers if they intend to buy a computer in the next year or two, for instance, will not generate responses that match up very accurately with actual sales. A survey of approximately a hundred previously published academic and industry-sponsored studies encompassing two hundred products and sixty-five thousand consumers found that although consumers gave what the consumers thought were honest responses when asked whether they would try a product initially, their actual behavior had little relationship to their intentions.[1]

Another example is the research carried out on the possible introduction of a new sport utility vehicle.[2] Surveys and focus groups pointed out that consumers would purchase the SUV if it was safe. Yet the actual purchases depended not at all on safety.

In the New Coke debacle, the research focused on taste preferences, but it did not measure the abiding emotional attachment to Coke. Most of the taste tests were blind comparisons that did not take into account the total product gestalt— the name, history, packaging, image, and so on. Moreover, the people who were surveyed were not told that the old Coke would be taken away and the new one substituted. In addition, the intention surveys and taste tests were not directed toward the proper market segment. Although most colas are consumed by a younger segment of the population, Coke's following was an older segment. And even though the younger segment liked the sweeter taste, Coke's core market preferred the less sweet formulation.

Experiment Experimental research calls for selecting matched groups of subjects, subjecting them to different treatments, controlling extraneous variables, and checking whether observed response differences are statistically significant. To the extent that extraneous factors are eliminated or controlled, the observed effects can be related to the variations in the treatments. The purpose of experimental research is to capture cause-and-effect relationships by eliminating competing explanations of the observed findings.

True experiments are usually conducted in a laboratory, where maximum control of experimental stimuli is possible and external biases can be eliminated. A field experiment is similar to a lab experiment, but it is conducted in the real world. Less control is possible in the field experiment, with the consequence that extraneous unknown forces might be at play, but the field experiment offers the advantage of being performed in a realistic setting, thereby overcoming the artificiality of the lab setting.

Firms use field experiments primarily to test new products, prices, or advertisements. For example, American Airlines might introduce in-flight phone service on one of its regular flights from New York to Los Angeles at a price of $25 a phone call. On the same flight the following day, it might announce the availability of this service at $15 a phone call. If the plane carried the same number and type of passengers on each flight and the day of the week made no difference, then any significant difference in the number of calls made could be related to the price charged. The experimental design could be elaborated further by trying other prices, replicating the same prices on a number of flights, and including other air routes in the experiment. To the extent that the design and execution of the experiment eliminate alternative hypotheses that might explain the results, the research and marketing managers can have confidence in the conclusions.

Dick's Supermarkets selected seventy-five to a hundred scanner numbers, or SKUs, in categories such as peanut butter, orange juice, canned vegetables, and baby foods. Three stores were designated as test sites, alternating control stores (no changes) with price-change stores. The price was lowered on a certain brand of orange juice, and the price was raised on a brand of canned vegetables for a period of four weeks. Comparing the control stores with the price-change stores, Dick's found an increase in sales of 29 percent for the orange juice and 20 percent for the vegetables. Dick's also calculated cross-price elasticities. It found that yogurt and granola bars have a cross-price elasticity of negative 10 percent—that is, customers are likely to purchase one item in conjunction with the other. In another test, canned milk at full retail price was placed near a display for discounted pie fillings, and the test stores noted a 24.5 percent revenue increase for those items.[3]

Secondary Data

Secondary data are data gathered for one purpose and used for another. One source of secondary data for a firm wanting to estimate its demand would be the historical data available from the firm's actual sales, prices, and other relevant information. Another source would be comparable firms' historical records or the historical records of comparable products. Government statistics provide much of the secondary data used in economic research. Typically, the data are readily available at various government agency websites. Private firms also provide data, typically for a fee. These, too, are typically available on websites.

While secondary data avoid the problem of primary data wherein people say one thing and do another, there are limitations of the use of secondary data as well. If an existing firm wants information about how consumers will react to a price change, then secondary data are well suited to providing an answer. The estimate of the demand function based on actual prices and sales will provide a very good and reliable estimate of the reactions to a price change. If, however, a totally new product is to be introduced in the market and the manufacturer wants information about how consumers will react, secondary data will be less reliable. The market researcher might find a closely related product and use its historical record to provide information about the new product. But the new product will surely have different characteristics, or there may not even be a comparable product. So, how can the demand be estimated? Often in such cases, firms will have to rely on primary data; they will try to generate data by introducing the product in select but limited locations and then varying price and other important attributes of the product. These "test markets" function much like an experiment, generating data that could be used to estimate demand.

APPENDIX NOTES

1. Andrea Ovans, "The Customer Doesn't Always Know Best," *Harvard Business Review,* Vol. 76 (May/June 1998): 12–13.
2. See Harvard Business School, Case 596-0036, Land Rover North America, Inc.
3. Kenneth L. Robb, "Data Warehouse Success Story: A DataSage Solution for Dick's Supermarkets," *Business and Management Practices* 9, no. 8 (September 1999): 86–87.

CHAPTER 5

Costs

CASE *Mrs. Fields' Cookies*[1]

At nineteen, Debbi Sivyer married economist and financial adviser Randy Fields, then twenty-nine. Debbi often provided cookies to Randy Fields' office, and his clients loved the cookies. Bored with cooking only as a hobby, Debbi convinced Randy that she should start her own cookie business. They borrowed $50,000

and in August 1977 opened the first Mrs. Fields' store in Palo Alto, California. By 1982, stores had been opened in San Francisco and other areas in northern California and a macademia nut operation had been set up in Hawaii.

Debbi's objective was to run each store as she had run the original Palo Alto store. The first common feature was the structure of the stores. Each store was typically divided into two areas, the ovens and the retail area. Customers were drawn into the store by the openness of the design and by the aroma of hot cookies fresh from the ovens plainly in view. The operation of each store was standardized by a computer system tied into the headquarters. Each store's personal computer accessed a sophisticated store management system designed by Randy and the MIS organization. Menu-driven applications included day planning, time clocks, store accounting and inventory, and others. One application dialed the headquarters' computer, deposited the day's transactions, and retrieved any mail for store employees. A store manager's day began in the back room at the personal computer. After entering workday characteristics, such as day of the week, school day or holiday, weather conditions, and so on, the manager answered a series of questions that caused the system to access a specific mathematical model for computing the day's schedule. The manager was subsequently advised how many cookies to bake per hour and what the projected sales per hour was. The manager would enter the types of cookies to be made that day, and the system would respond with the number of batches to mix and when to mix them. The cookie mixes were created in Park city, Utah, company headquarters, and shipped to each of the stores daily.

By 1982, the company was doing so well that international expansion was put on the agenda. It was decided that Japan, Hong Kong, and Australia would be the first international arenas for Mrs. Fields. By 1990, Mrs. Fields was huge, with almost a thousand stores in eight countries. But in 1990, the company posted a net loss of $8.8 million even with revenue of $130 million. By 1991 the company had been sold at a value well below its mid-1980's peak. What happened? Why did the company grow at an amazing rate only to find that its costs rose even more?

Costs and Output

Telecom firms have been virtually wiped out during the late 1990s and early 2000s. In the 1990s, WorldCom was pointed to as a model telecom and its CEO, Bernie Ebbers, was admired as a model leader. Ebbers began buying long-distance telephone time as a commodity and reselling it through a company called Long Distance Discount Service (LDDS). After renaming LDDS WorldCom in 1995, Ebbers began focusing on growth. Within just three years, he had acquired more than seventy-five companies to become a telecom giant. WorldCom purchased MCI in 1998 and attempted to acquire Sprint in 1999 but was denied by antitrust regulators. Then the bottom fell out. On April 30, 2002, WorldCom's market value was just 4 percent of its value at its peak. Why? WorldCom's debt was overwhelming; it owed billions just from its purchase of MCI. It declared bankruptcy in July 2002 and attempted to reorganize with fewer costs.

General Electric has been the world's most admired company for years and its former CEO, Jack Welch, lauded as the best leader in business. GE is essentially two companies—its industrials and its financial segment, or GE Capital. GE Capital purchases more than a hundred companies each year, retaining or restructuring those that are profitable and discarding those that are not. It has had one of the fastest-growing and most stable earnings streams over the past couple of decades. In August 2000 GE's shares were selling for $60. On April 24, 2002, GE's shares had fallen below $33, valuing the company more than $260 billion less than its worth at the peak. The reason? Many argued it was GE's rapid growth. Others claimed that it was fallout from the Enron collapse and that possible earnings manipulations on the part of GE were weighing heavily in investors' attitudes toward the company. GE began to focus on costs.

Knowing the customer means understanding demand. But demand is just revenue. It is not profit. Profit is revenue minus costs, so knowing the customer is only one of the issues the firm must consider. As stories like the above two regarding WorldCom and GE illustrate, companies cannot ignore their costs. Stories like these appear almost daily in the business press. Companies find that they are not adding value and thus begin tackling their costs. Instead of expanding, they begin to contract, selling off parts of their business and reducing the number of employees—downsizing operations or reengineering the business. Some firms undergo major changes, while others make relatively minor alterations. Some firms are able to recover and increase their profitability. Other don't make it. They never seem to solve the problem of why their costs are too high. In this chapter we begin to examine costs. Once one understands costs, it becomes clear why executives often lose sight of their target—to add value—when they are focusing on costs. It also becomes clear why executives might lose sight of costs when focusing on some other activity of the firm.

The Law of Diminishing Marginal Returns

The costs of doing business are the costs of resources used in the business. A firm may have a manager and other employees; may use buildings and equipment; and may consume electricity, water, and raw materials. Each resource has a cost; the firm's total cost is the sum of the costs of the resources.

What happens to costs as a firm produces more? It depends on the combinations of resources used to create the firm's output and the cost of these resources. Amazon.com has increased sales each year of its existence, but, at the same time, it has not earned a positive profit. While sales and thus revenues have risen, so have costs.

The relationship between costs and output depends on the underlying relationship between output and inputs. WMX has 16,000 garbage trucks and 180,000 employees; FedEx has 25,000 planes, 50,000 trucks, and 280,000 employees; Rayovac has 2,400 employees and J. Crew, 6,000. Would FedEx be better off with fewer planes and more trucks? Would WMX be better off with more trucks and fewer employees? Would Rayovac or J. Crew be better off with more employees? The answers depend on the relationship between output and inputs.

Suppose that the various technological possibilities for a small airline are captured in Table 5.1. With one mechanic servicing the planes, the company can generate 30,000 passenger-miles if the airline has five airplanes, 100,000 passenger-miles if it has ten airplanes, 250,000 passenger-miles if it has fifteen airplanes, and so on. With a second mechanic working on the planes, output is increased with each quantity of airplanes; five airplanes now generate 60,000 passenger-miles, and so on. The airline could produce about the same amount, say 340,000 to 360,000 passenger-miles with several different combinations of mechanics and airplanes—three mechanics with ten airplanes, two mechanics with fifteen airplanes, or one mechanic with twenty airplanes. And several other output levels can be produced with a number of different combinations of mechanics and airplanes.

What combination or combinations does the airline use? It depends on where the airline is now. Suppose that the airline had previously leased or purchased ten airplanes and cannot change the number of planes for at least a year. The airline can alter the number of mechanics it uses but not the number of airplanes during that one year period. Thus, the options open to the airline are only those under the column label "10" airplanes in Table 5.1. This is referred to as the short run because at least one input is fixed. The **short run** refers not to a chronological amount of time but rather to the length of time just short enough that at least one input is fixed. The **long run** is a period of time just long enough that all resources are variable. Again, this is not a chronological period of time but a period of time long enough that everything is variable—a time period that varies from firm to firm.

The relationship between quantities of a variable resource and quantities of output is called the **law of diminishing marginal returns (DMR)**. The law of diminishing marginal returns states that as additional units of the variable resource are used in combination with a fixed amount of other resources, total output at first rises, initially quite rapidly and then more slowly, and eventually declines.

Table 5.1
PRODUCTION COMBINATIONS

Number of Mechanics	Number of Airplanes							
	5	10	15	20	25	30	35	40
0	0	0	0	0	0	0	0	0
1	30	100	250	340	410	400	400	390
2	60	250	360	450	520	530	520	500
3	100	360	480	570	610	620	620	610
4	130	440	580	640	690	700	700	690
5	130	500	650	710	760	770	780	770
6	110	540	700	760	800	820	830	840
7	100	550	720	790	820	850	870	890
8	80	540	680	800	830	860	880	900

Diminishing marginal returns is a physical law—it applies everywhere. It describes the situation where a flower bulb is placed in a small container and covered with good soil. As the plant is watered, it begins to grow. So more water must mean more growth right? Obviously not; everyone knows that the plant will eventually die if one continues adding more and more water. In a *New York Times* review of Madonna's performance at Madison Square Garden, writer Jon Pareles noted, " 'The Girlie Show' recognizes the diminishing returns of explicitness,"[2] meaning that additional amounts of explicitness generated reduced additional amounts of audience appreciation.

Diminishing marginal returns limit the effort to improve passenger safety during collisions by installing air bags in cars. The air bags open on impact to keep the passengers from contact with the car. The first air bag added to a car increases protection considerably. The second adds an element of safety, particularly for an adult front-seat passenger. Additional bags also add some safety—for instance, the side-impact bags protect the passengers from injuries due to collisions on the doors. Each additional air bag adds less additional safety. Eventually another air bag would actually lessen protection because the bags would interfere with each other. As successive units of the variable resource, air bags, are placed on the fixed resource, the car, the additional amount of protection provided by the air bags declines. This is diminishing marginal returns.

Diminishing marginal returns show up in Table 5.1 whenever one of the resources is fixed and the other is variable. For instance, when the number of airplanes is fixed at ten, then the first mechanic increases total output from 0 to 100,000 passenger-miles. Increasing the number of mechanics from one to two increases total output to 250,000 passenger-miles, an increase of 150,000 passenger-miles. The third mechanic raises total output to 360, an increase of 110. The fourth mechanic increases output to 440,000 passenger-miles, an increase of 80,000 passenger-miles. The additional output produced by an additional unit of the variable resource diminishes.

From Production to Costs

To illustrate how the law of diminishing returns defines the relationship between costs and output, let's consider a very simple example. Suppose the cost per mechanic is $1,000 and that this is the only cost the airline has. Then, the total costs

Table 5.2

TOTAL, AVERAGE, AND MARGINAL COSTS

Total Cost	Output	Average Total Cost	Marginal Cost[a]
$0	0	—	—
$1,000	100	$10	$10
$2,000	250	$ 8	$ 6.67
$3,000	360	$ 8.33	$ 9.09
$4,000	440	$ 9.09	$12.50
$5,000	500	$10	$16.67
$6,000	540	$11.11	$25
$7,000	550	$12.73	$100
$8,000	540	$14.81	—

[a]This is the average of the individual unit marginal cost. The marginal cost of $10 for the first 99 units indicates that the average marginal cost of units 1 through 100 is $101, and so on for units 101–250, units 251–360, etc.

are calculated by multiplying $1,000 by the number of mechanics necessary to produce the output. Notice that as output rises, total costs rise, but the two do not rise proportionately. Initially total output rises more rapidly than costs, and then costs rise more rapidly than output. This is shown in Table 5.2.

Total cost is the number of mechanics from Table 5.1 multiplied by $1,000. Output is taken from column 3 in Table 5.1—the output generated by various combinations of mechanics and ten airplanes. The **average total cost (ATC)** is the cost per unit of output and is derived by dividing total cost by the quantity of output. Average total cost is shown in column 3 of Table 5.2: Notice that average total costs fall initially and then rise as output rises. **Marginal cost (MC)** is the change in cost caused by a change in output and is derived by dividing the change in total cost by the change in the quantity of output. It is, essentially, the additional cost that comes from producing an additional unit of output. Marginal cost is shown in the last column of Table 5.2; it, too, falls initially and then rises as output rises. The reason that average total cost initially falls and then rises is the law of diminishing marginal returns. As one more mechanic is added, output initially rises a great deal (the additional cost is $1,000 and a great deal of output results). Eventually, as one more mechanic is added and costs rise by another $1,000, output rises only a small amount—the cost of generating a given amount of output rises.

Fixed and Variable Costs Costs can be presented in financial statements in many different ways. The most common procedure is to distinguish between overhead and direct costs. *Overhead costs* are those costs that are not directly attributable to the production process. They include such items as taxes, insurance, premiums, managerial or administrative salaries, paperwork, and the cost of electricity not used in the production process. *Direct costs* are those costs directly attributable to production—materials, supplies, equipment, and so on.

Economists don't find the distinction between overhead and direct costs to be as useful to their analyses as that between fixed and variable costs. *Fixed costs* are costs that do not change as the volume of production changes. *Variable costs*, on the other hand, are costs that depend on the volume of production. Insurance premiums, taxes, and managerial salaries are fixed costs. They must be paid regard-

In the petrochemical industry, larger producers have reduced fixed costs by consolidating and shutting down higher-cost facilities and lowered variable costs by investing in new supply sources. In the short run, revenues must cover variable costs for a facility to continue in operation. A restructuring of the relative sizes of fixed and variable costs can alter the short-run strategies of firms. Higher variable relative to fixed costs mean that a firm has fewer options regarding temporary closures; lower total costs mean more likelihood of positive profits.

less of how much is produced. Electricity used to operate the production process is a variable cost, increasing as the quantity of output produced is increased. Many resource costs include elements of both fixed and variable costs. If employees work overtime or new employees are brought on board when the firm is producing more output and then released during reductions in output, then the costs of labor are variable. But long-term labor contracts fix labor costs during the period of the contract, so that during any period shorter than the period of the contract, labor costs are fixed.

To this point we have made the simplifying assumption that the only costs facing the airline are labor costs. Clearly, there are other costs of running an airline. For most airlines, land, materials, and fuel make up about 50 percent of costs, wages and salaries about 33 percent, and capital costs about 17 percent. So we need to consider these other costs.

Suppose there are labor, capital, and land costs that have been allocated to either variable or fixed costs, as shown in the first three columns of Table 5.3. Column 1 lists the total quantity (Q) of output produced. Column 2 lists the **total fixed costs** (**TFC**)—costs that must be paid whether the firm produces or not. Fixed costs are \$10—this is what must be paid irrespective of whether any output is produced. Column 3 lists the **total variable costs** (**TVC**), costs that rise or fall as production rises or falls. *Total costs (TC),* the sum of total variable and total fixed costs, are listed in column 4.

With costs divided into fixed and variable, there are three measures of average or per unit costs—average total, average fixed, and average variable. Each is derived by dividing the corresponding total costs by the quantity of output. **Average**

A tutorial on managing your business and fixed and variable costs can be found at
http://www.toolkit.cch.com/ text/P06_7510.asp

Table 5.3

COST SCHEDULES

Output (Q)	Total Fixed Costs (TFC)	Total Variable Costs (TVC)	Total Costs (TC)	Average Fixed Costs (AFC)	Average Variable Costs (AVC)	Average Total Costs (ATC)	Marginal Costs (MC)
0	$10	0	10				
1	10	10	20	10	10	20	10
2	10	18	28	5	9	14	8
3	10	25	35	3.33	8.33	11.6	7
4	10	30	40	2.5	7.5	10	5
5	10	35	45	2	7	9	5
6	10	42	52	1.66	7	8.66	7
7	10	50.6	60.6	1.44	7.2	8.6	8.6
8	10	60	70	1.25	7.5	8.75	9.4
9	10	80	90	1.1	8.8	10	20

fixed costs (AFC) decline as output rises because the total fixed cost, $10, is divided by a larger and larger number as output rises. **Average variable costs (AVC)** and average total costs (ATC) first decline and then rise, because of the law of diminishing marginal returns. Marginal costs (MC) are listed in column 8. Marginal costs initially fall and then rise as output rises.

The average and marginal cost schedules are plotted in Figure 5.1. The AVC curve reaches a minimum at the output level of 5 to 6. The ATC curve lies above the AVC curve by the amount of the average fixed costs, since ATC = AFC + AVC. The ATC curve declines until output level 7 and then rises. The MC curve begins below the AVC and ATC curves and declines until output level 5, where it begins to climb. The MC curve passes through the AVC curve at the minimum value of the AVC curve and then continues rising until it passes through the ATC curve at the minimum point of the ATC curve.

Applying variable costs in airline pricing is discussed in

http://www.conservativemonitor.com/opinion/2001009.shtml

Figure 5.1

THE COST CURVES

The average and marginal cost curves are plotted using data in Table 5.3. The AVC and ATC are U-shaped, reflecting the law of diminishing marginal returns. The AFC continually declines since it is just a constant amount divided by larger and larger amounts. The MC lies below the average cost curves initially and then rises to intersect the ATC and then AVC at their minimum points.

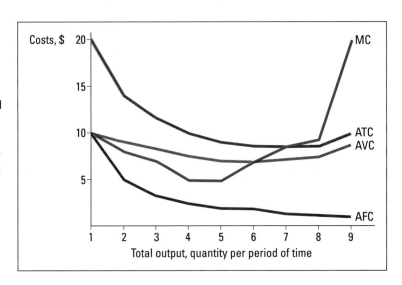

NOTE: Statements like "We need to spread the overhead" sound somewhat like the concept of declining average fixed costs—fixed cost per unit of output declines as output rises. But overhead may also include variable costs. Thus, the need to spread the overhead refers to reducing the total costs that are not directly attributable to the production process. The more a firm can keep its overhead costs the same and increase its volume of production, the more those overhead costs look and act like fixed costs. But the two are not the same thing.

The law of diminishing marginal returns defines the relationship between costs and output in the short run for every firm, no matter whether that firm is a billion dollar a year corporation or a small proprietorship. Obviously, the size or scale of the companies will differ, but the general nature of the relationship between short-run costs and output will not.

The Planning Horizon: The Long Run

Akio Morita, the founder of Sony Corporation, came to America in 1955 to sell a small transistor radio his company had developed.[3] He received an offer that seemed irresistible: A chain store would buy nearly 100,000 radios. Amazingly, Morita turned it down. Why? Morita knew Sony did not have the capacity to produce that many radios. Sony's capacity was less than a thousand radios a month. An order of 100,000 would mean hiring and training new employees and expanding facilities even more. The executive of the chain store was totally stunned. Morita explained his position to the chain store buyer. He drew a curve that looked something like the lopsided letter U, shown in Figure 5.2. He explained that the cost per unit for 5,000 units would be quite high, the beginning of the curve. For 10,000 units, the per-unit costs would fall. For 50,000 units, the per-unit cost would begin to climb. At 100,000 units, the cost per unit would be exorbitant.

If Sony had to increase its production to complete an order for 100,000 radios and could not get a repeat order the following year, it would be in big trouble. The buyer eventually agreed to purchase just 10,000 radios for his stores. That decision was crucial for Sony. Had Morita succumbed to the lure of the larger order, Sony might not exist today.

Although Morita drew a U-shaped cost curve, it was the long run he was dealing with. He had to decide whether to expand the size or scale of his firm, not simply add more workers or acquire more materials. A firm can choose to relocate or to build a new plant or to purchase additional planes only in the long run or planning stage. A manager can choose any size of plant or building and any combination of other resources when laying out the firm's plans because all resources are variable in the long run. In essence, during the long run the manager compares all short-run situations. In the short run or operating period, a manager can decide whether to produce and how much to produce but is unable to increase the size of the manufacturing plant or to change locations. In the long run the manager can expand, contract, relocate, enter a new business, exit any line of business, or quit doing business altogether.

Figure 5.2

MORITA'S DRAWING

The sketch Morita made regarding the firm's costs reflected a U-shaped curve. But Morita was talking about the long run, not the short run.

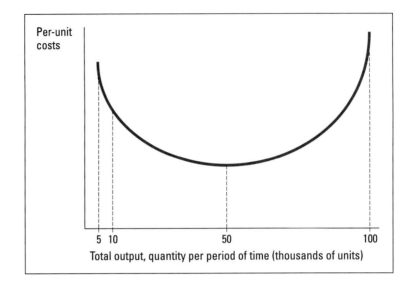

Long-Run Cost Curves

Figure 5.3 shows several short-run cost curves along which a firm could produce. The curve SRATC$_1$ in Figure 5.3 is the cost curve Morita drew (Figure 5.2). The SR in front of ATC indicates that the curve is the **short-run average total cost (SRATC)** curve. Each short-run cost curve is drawn for a particular quantity of the capital resource (a particular plant size, number of production lines, etc.). Once the quantity of the capital resource is selected, the firm brings together different combinations of the other resources with that fixed capital resource to produce output. For instance, if a small quantity of the capital resource is selected, such as the amount necessary to efficiently produce 5,000 units, the firm would operate along SRATC$_1$. If the firm selects a larger quantity of the capital resource, say enough to produce 100,000 units efficiently, then it could operate anywhere along SRATC$_2$.

In 1955 Sony only had the size or capacity illustrated by SRATC$_1$. Sony could produce 5,000 units at per-unit costs of A. If it produced more than 5,000 units, it would move along SRATC$_1$. Once beyond a quantity of 30,000, per-unit costs would rise. It could increase its size in the long run by acquiring more capital. If it chose to be of the size shown by SRATC$_2$ in order to produce the 100,000 units, the per-unit cost would be B. But, having established that size manufacturing facility, Sony would then be vulnerable to a reduction in the quantity produced. For instance, if sales dropped to 30,000, Sony would have to move along SRATC$_2$ by reducing its variable resources until it had time to sell off some of its fixed resources. During that period until it could alter its size, the per-unit costs would be very high, C.[4]

The long run is a planning period—any combination of resources can be selected. Once a specific combination is selected—that is, once a certain size of operation is chosen—the firm must operate along a specific short-run cost curve. In the long run, a firm can choose to operate along any of the SRATC curves. All it needs to do is choose the level of output it wants to produce and then select the least-cost combination of resources with which to produce the chosen output level. Least-cost combinations are represented in Figure 5.3 by a curve that just

Figure 5.3

THE LONG-RUN AVERAGE COST CURVE

The long-run average cost curve is tangent to, or just touches, each short-run average cost curve. For each quantity of the fixed resource, a different short-run average total cost curve is traced out.

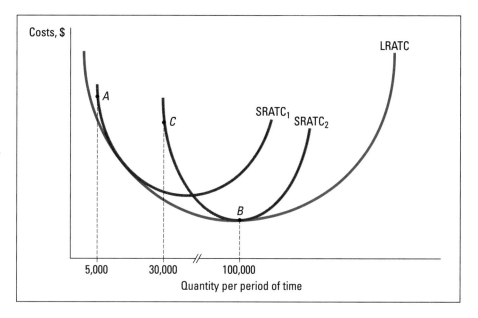

touches or is tangent to each SRATC curve. This curve is the **long-run average total cost (LRATC)** curve—it shows the lowest cost per unit of output for every level of output when all resources are variable.

Economies and Diseconomies of Scale

Both the long-run average total cost and short-run average total cost curves may be U-shaped, but for entirely different reasons. The U shape of the short-run cost curves is the result of diminishing marginal returns, but when the quantities of all resources can be varied, diminishing marginal returns do not occur.

If unit costs decrease as the quantity of production increases and all resources are variable, we say there are **economies of scale**. If unit costs increase when the quantity of production increases and all resources are variable, then we say there are **diseconomies of scale**. If the cost per unit of output is constant as output rises and all resources are variable, then we say there are **constant returns to scale**. Economies of scale account for the downward-sloping portion of the long-run average cost curve, diseconomies of scale account for the upward-sloping portion, and constant returns accounts for the horizontal portion.

Economies of scale may result from the ability to use larger machines that are more efficient than small ones. In 1892, John D. Rockefeller's Standard Oil Company (the precursor of Exxon) dominated the production of kerosene. Kerosene was, at that time, the key product refined from crude oil and was by far America's largest nonfarm export. Standard Oil made 90 percent of all the kerosene produced in the United States. But when Russia's Caspian Sea oil fields were discovered and kerosene began to be shipped from there to the European market, Standard Oil feared that it would lose its domination in Europe. The company had to become more efficient. It did this by closing several small refineries and building three enormous new ones. The huge scale of production in these new refineries led to significant cost reductions. In 1880, plants with a 2,000-barrel-a-day capacity made kerosene for 2.5 cents a gallon. In 1885, with the new plants having a 6,000-barrel-a-day capacity, Standard Oil could make kerosene for less than half a penny per gallon. This allowed the company to price its kerosene in Europe below the Russian kerosene even though the American product had much higher shipping costs.

Sometimes economies of scale result from specialization. Being larger enables companies to use their specially trained labor and management in specific activities rather than over a broad range of activities. This is the reason given for the mergers that took place in the ski business in the 1990s. American Skiing Company acquired most of the New England market, Intrawest owned Quebec's Mont Tremblant and Vermont's Stratton Mountain, and British Columbia's Blackcomb purchased a 33 percent interest in Mammoth Mountain. In Colorado, Vail and Beaver Creek acquired Breckenridge, Arapahoe Basin, and Keystone. The owners claimed that the mergers allowed the companies to standardize operations, consolidate jobs, and gain increased purchasing power.

Creating economies of scale by outsourcing is discussed in http://www.outsourcing-journal.com/issues/may2001/insights.html

Size, however, does not automatically improve efficiency. The specialization that comes with large size often requires the addition of specialized managers. A 10 percent increase in the number of employees may require an increase greater than 10 percent in the number of managers. A manager to supervise other managers may be needed. Paperwork increases. Meetings are held more often. The amounts of time and labor that are not devoted to producing output grow. Managerial inefficiencies need not be the only reason for diseconomies of scale, but they are typically the primary reason.

The U shape of the LRATC curve would occur if there are economies of scale followed by diseconomies of scale. Such a situation often occurs in businesses that both produce and then distribute their output. The generation of electricity has traditionally experienced economies of scale. One huge plant can generate electricity at a lower cost per kilowatt-hour than can several small plants. But the transmission of electricity is a different matter. The farther the electricity has to be transmitted, the greater the loss of electricity and the higher the cost per kilowatt-hour transmitted. At some size, the marginal transmission costs rise more than the marginal generation costs decline. Diseconomies of scale dominate economies of scale.

Many different types of firms face similar problems. Mrs. Fields' Cookies trained the managers of all Mrs. Fields' outlets at its headquarters in Park City, Utah. The training period was referred to as Cookie College. By spreading the cost of Cookie College over more than seven hundred outlets, Mrs. Fields' Cookies was able to achieve economies of scale. However, the company faces some diseconomies because the cookie dough is produced at one location and distributed to the outlets in premixed packages. The dough factory can be large, but the distribution of dough produces diseconomies of scale that worsen as outlets are opened farther and farther away from the factory.

The law of diminishing marginal returns applies to every resource, every firm, and every industry. Whether there are economies of scale, diseconomies of scale, constant returns to scale, or some combination of these depends on the industry under consideration. No physical law dictates that an industry will have economies of scale eventually followed by diseconomies of scale, as is the case for the U shape of the short-run average cost curves. Theoretically, it is possible for an industry to experience only diseconomies of scale, only economies of scale, or only constant returns to scale.

Large Scale Is Not Always Best

Economies of scale result in lower cost per unit of output as the volume of production increases. It might seem, then, that a large firm would always have an advantage over smaller firms, but that isn't necessarily so. Efficiency and specialization are limited by the size of the market, as illustrated in Figure 5.4. A firm of size C ($SRATC_C$) would not have an advantage over a firm of size B ($SRATC_B$). The large firm C could not sell all the output necessary to realize its most efficient output level. If demand is not sufficient to purchase all the output produced by the larger firm, then producing that much output would not make sense.

Examples of production being limited by the size of the market often arises in small developing countries, where the domestic market for manufactured goods is quite limited. The most modern technology for an industry may involve a size whose output exceeds the reasonable market in the country. Sri Lanka, for example, sought assistance from the former Soviet Union to establish a steel mill. The smallest plant the Soviets operated had a capacity of sixty thousand tons of steel a year, but total demand in Sri Lanka was only thirty-five thousand tons a year. As a result, the mill set up by the Soviets could be used only to about 58 percent of its capacity. At that rate of output, the mill operated inefficiently.

Since markets in different countries may not support the most efficient size of a firm or plant, you might wonder why nations don't specialize in industries where they can achieve a scale that is competitive with the most efficient producers and buy from other countries the products for which the domestic market is too small to support competitive production. In fact, there is some evidence that scale economies help determine the pattern of trade across countries. Countries that can achieve an efficient scale of production in an industry such as steel or autos sell products to countries that are unable to produce sufficient scale economies. The problem with this scenario is that many countries do not allow certain goods and services to be purchased from other countries, and, as a result, local firms are the only sources of these goods and services. When protectionism limits the size

Figure 5.4

SPECIALIZATION IS LIMITED BY THE SIZE OF THE MARKET

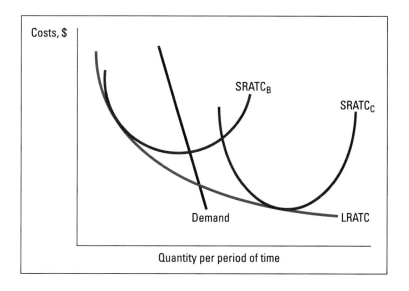

of a market, then the small size of that protected domestic market may mean the use of outdated and inefficient methods of production.

Which is better, to be a large or a small firm? In the 1980s, management consultants believed that it was better to be a small firm. Tom Peters, author of *In Search of Excellence,* argued that the experiences of IBM and General Motors in the early 1980s clearly showed that small firms were better than large ones. It was almost common knowledge that small businesses created eight out of ten new jobs in the United States. Yet, as occurs in most circumstances, blanket statements are subject to exceptions. For instance, while IBM and Daimler-Benz did struggle in the 1980s and early 1990s, IBM has come on strong since the late 1990s. Other large firms—Coca-Cola, McDonald's, and Toyota, for instance—have prospered.

Large firms have found that the flexibility of small firms is something they can copy. Large firms are contracting out (outsourcing) many activities, allowing small firms to provide services that are peripheral to the core business of the large firm. Similarly, small firms are finding that they need the economies of scale larger firms have. More and more firms are creating alliances with other companies or are locating in industrial clusters to simulate the economies of scale of a larger firm. The joint venture, alliance, cluster, or network, enables distinct companies to join forces in order to gain some benefits of larger size without having to merge or combine into one firm. In the power industry, new technologies like microturbines, fuel cells, and sterling engines compete against large central generation stations that have economies of scale. The smaller companies try to create the economy of scale necessary to compete by setting up a large number of small plants at one site. Two recent projects, one near Los Angeles and one near Denver, illustrate this approach. In both cases, the smaller gas-fired units are lined up to produce sufficient power to match those coming from a large generation facility. The same thing is occurring in some farming areas and in some pharmaceutical concerns. Many agricultural entities that raise foodstuffs for cereal are forming joint ventures such as machinery syndicates and contract farming arrangements to achieve economies of scale. Some pharmaceutical firms are outsourcing many activities and then joining in alliances or networks to achieve economies of scale in the activities where such economies exist.

Creating economies of scale for small business is discussed in http://www.credit-to-cash.com/ small_business/economies_of_ scale.shtml

Economies of Scope

Firms producing more than one product may find synergies in their production. For instance, petroleum companies such as Exxon and Mobil produce petroleum and chemical products; pharmaceutical companies produce many different pharmaceuticals; and many other firms produce a full line of different goods. When a firm obtains a production advantage from producing more than one product, we say there are *economies of scope.* These advantages may arise because a production facility used to make one product can also be used to make another, or because by-products of one product are useful in the production of another product, or because the people trained to produce one product can use their training in the production of another product.

In the 1890s, three large chemical companies—Bayer, Hoechst, and BASF—were building huge dye-making factories. Prior to the construction of these large factories, each different dye had been produced in a separate small factory. The new plants were able to produce hundreds of different dyes using the same basic chemical stock. The result was a substantial reduction in costs. This was a case of economies of scope.

Economies of scope occur when the cost of producing two (or more) products jointly is less than the cost of producing each one alone. For example, suppose that the chemical company Boscht produces a thousand tons of a chemical and five hundred tons of a paint per year at a cost of $15 million, whereas producing the chemical alone would cost $12 million and producing just the paint would cost $6 million. Then we would say this chemical company experiences economies of scope.

It is often claimed that an advertising agency can provide many products at a lower per-unit cost than by simply focusing on a single product. In other words, they can carry out many different types of advertising—such as network television, spot television, magazines, special print media, newspapers, radio, outdoor services, and so on—or they can just supply one type of advertising. The cost reduction from joint production for advertising agencies is in the range of 5 to 70 percent.[5]

Firms do not always experience economies of scope—diseconomies can occur as well. Electricity retailing in Australia has been a value-destroying industry for the past decade or so. As a result, two of the major retailers, Pulse and CitiPower, were put up for sale in 2002. It was argued that the purchase of these companies by another would enable the purchaser to restructure so as to gain from economies of scale. But, the acquisition would be successful only if the economies of scale could overcome associated diseconomies of scope. The diseconomies of scope came about because the firms all had several different call centers and billing systems and integrating these would be very difficult; as a result the merging of the system could mean a disproportionately greater cost to manage greater complexity, that is diseconomies of scope, which would lead to higher not lower costs. Thus, for the acquisitions to be successful, the additional per unit costs of diseconomies of scope had to be overcome by the reduced per unit costs arising from economies of scale.[6]

The Experience Curve

Economies of scale result in a downward-sloping long-run average cost curve. This is why the concept of economies of scale is often confused with the *experience*, or *learning, curve*. In the early 1970s, a major consulting company, Boston Consulting Group, published its observations that costs fall as output rises. The company claimed that costs fall by around 15 percent with each doubling of overall output, as shown in Figure 5.5. They called this the experience curve because they believed the declining costs were the result of learning, of gaining experience.[7] In fact, the experience curve mixes or confuses several different factors. For instance, it includes the influence of both learning that is specific to the firm and learning that is general to the industry, and it includes costs that fall with the cumulative amount of output a firm has produced over time and costs that fall with the rate of output (economies of scale) per unit of time.

Figure 5.5 shows experience curves drawn from two industries—aircraft manufacturers and broiler chickens. The apparent similarity of the curves is remarkable, but the causes and the implications are very different.[8] The falling costs of the airline are the result of learning by experience—learning that is mostly specific to Boeing and largely specific to a particular aircraft. There is no experience

Figure 5.5
THE EXPERIENCE CURVE

If the more experience a firm has in producing a particular good results in lower per-unit costs, then the firm has an experience, or learning curve, that slopes downward. In this diagram, experience curves for two industries are shown, one for aircraft and one for chickens.

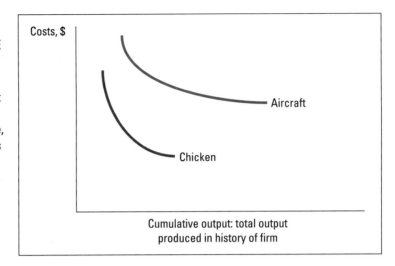

curve for chickens. In the case of chickens, the cost per chicken fell because of the industrywide adoption of a new technology to mass-produce chickens (as opposed to providing free-range chickens) supported by the use of antibiotics. Thus, the experience curve for chickens in Figure 5.5 is misleading. What actually occurred is that the average total cost curve shifted downward.

Experience can be an important advantage to a firm. Aspartame is a low-calorie sweetener much better known by Monsanto's brand name for it, NutraSweet. Aspartame was discovered by accident. In 1965 James Schlatter, a scientist at G.D. Searle & Co., was trying to develop an anti-ulcer drug. While experimenting, he noticed a sweet taste when he combined two chemicals. In 1970 Searle secured a patent on aspartame, and the product was launched in 1983. In 1985 Monsanto acquired Searle. In 1986 the Holland Sweetener Company began building an aspartame plant in Geleen, the Netherlands, to challenge Monsanto's hold on the market. Holland Sweetener was a joint venture between two chemical companies, the Japanese Tosoh Corporation and the Dutch State Mines. With the expiration of NutraSweet's European patent in 1987, Holland Sweetener went after the European market. Monsanto fought back with aggressive pricing. Before Holland's entry, aspartame prices had been $70 per pound. After Holland's entry, they fell to $22 to $30 per pound. At these prices, Holland was losing money.

The problem for Holland was that Monsanto had a huge cost advantage. It had spent the previous decade learning how to cut manufacturing costs; "it marched down the learning curve."[9] Monsanto had developed a name brand, reduced manufacturing costs until they were only 30 percent of Holland's, and developed distribution networks. These factors meant that Holland was not able to compete with Monsanto.

The value of a lower position on the learning curve can induce firms to acquire other firms—firms that have more experience in certain activities. For instance, in August, 2002, Halliburton Energy Services acquired Pruett Industries, Inc., in order to "hit the ground running in regard to field service, for DTS as well as future fiber optic sensors." Halliburton executives said that "Pruett's critical mass of experience and know-how positions us way up the learning curve in the critical installation competencies."[10]

Interpreting Some Business Buzzwords

Reengineering, downsizing, outsourcing, joint ventures—the buzzwords in business are expanding exponentially. In fact, they appear so suddenly and seemingly everywhere that they have been referred to as corporate graffiti.[11] Much like being a successful member of a street gang, to be a successful member of the business gang it is necessary to understand the graffiti. Now that we're familiar with costs, we can examine what a few of the more popular buzzwords mean.

Downsizing

In the early 1990s and again in the early 2000s, **downsizing** was the most important business policy in the United States. Downsizing refers to divesting unrelated businesses to focus on the "core" but, in practice, generally means cutting jobs, particularly jobs at the middle-management level. In the United States, 100,000 jobs were cut in 1989, 300,000 more in 1990, and nearly 600,000 per year from 1991 through 1994. The job-cutting frenzy peaked in 1994, declined in 1995, rose again in 1996, then stabilized through the years of robust economic growth in the United States, Australia, Canada, and elsewhere, 1996–2000, and rose again in the recession of 2001 and into 2002.

Downsizing involves moving down along an existing short-run average cost curve (if one variable remains fixed) or moving to a new short-run average cost curve, one that lies closer in to the origin and encompasses a smaller range of output (if the downsizing is a long-run move wherein all resources are variable). Downsizing could lead to lower or higher per unit costs, depending on how the entrenchment occurs. The typical assumption made for a firm to embark on downsizing is that the firm has allowed itself to become too large and inefficient. For instance, the firm operating at point A on $SRATC_5$ in Figure 5.6, should be operating along $SRATC_4$ to produce Q_5. So, the firm downsizes; it lays off employees with the expectation it will move to the lower cost curve, $SRATC_4$. However, the downsizing could mean an increase in costs if not carried out for the right reasons or in the right way. Suppose a firm downsizes its middle managers and piles the work the dismissed managers used to do on remaining employees. If there was no technological change or other reason for the downsizing, then the remaining employees will become less productive; morale will decline as employees have to perform more tasks for the same pay. Moreover, since each remaining employee has to do more jobs, the benefits from specialization will be reduced.

Accounting costs seem to decline immediately after most firms downsize. Why? Because there are fewer resources being paid. But unless the downsizing results in increased efficiency—that is, unless the firm was previously inefficient—within six months to a year, even accounting costs will rise. In fact, about 75 percent of the firms that underwent reengineering in the 1980s and 1990s have found that their accounting costs rose some six months to a year following the reengineering. And firms in other countries that have pursued downsizing have often found the action to have reduced the firm's viability.[12]

Outsourcing The downsizing and reengineering processes often include outsourcing. **Outsourcing** is the process of purchasing services that used to be performed in-house. More than 75 percent of all businesses outsource some aspect of their

Figure 5.6

DOWNSIZING

The assumption of down-sizing is that the firm is operating inefficiently—along SRATC$_5$, for instance. Downsizing allows the firm to move to an efficient point—say, *B*, along SRATC$_4$.

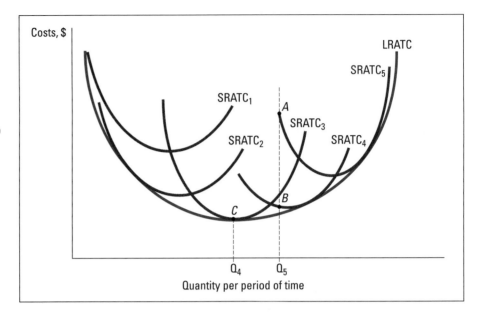

work. The Outsourcing Institute of Jericho, NY, recently found that about 43% of Canadian firms have an outsourcing strategy in place. Of these companies, 91% strategically outsource at least some support and non-core functions. The most common outsourced activities are IT, at 57%, and human resources, bene-fits and facilities management at 41% each.[13] This result is not much different in other developed countries. Outsourcing may be a short-run or a long-run event. It could mean a reduction in certain kinds of tasks within the firm, or it could mean a change in the scale of the firm.

Outsourcing, which is often part of the downsizing process, results from a de-cision to buy rather than to make. It should occur when it has become more effi-cient to purchase the activity rather than make it internally. The two reasons most often given for outsourcing are "improving company focus" and "accessing world-class capabilities." What do "improve company focus" and "accessing world-class capabilities" mean? If these strategies are important, why weren't they being carried out previously? The only reason to engage in downsizing or reengineering is if the firm has become inefficient (or if new technology has been developed that changes the long-run cost curves).

Joint Ventures

In the late 1980s and early 1990s, another phrase in vogue was the **joint venture**. General Motors, for example, created joint ventures and other cooperative arrangements with a wide range of firms in the United States and around the world. But GM was far from alone in engaging in joint ventures. Joint ventures be-tween Japanese and U.S. firms, European and U.S. firms, and U.S. firms and firms in less developed countries such as China and Vietnam have been very popular. For a joint venture to be productive, each firm must have something the other does not. For instance, Toyota had the most efficient automobile production process and GM had access to the U.S. auto market, something not allowed Toyota by the U.S. government. The joint venture gave GM access to the more efficient production process and allowed Toyota access to the U.S. market. In essence, the joint venture enabled the two firms together to produce on a lower average cost curve (to produce and sell more efficiently) than either firm could do alone.

Access to markets is a common reason for a joint venture. U.S. firms found it virtually impossible to operate in China without a relationship with a Chinese company. The Chinese government wouldn't allow U.S. firms to locate facilities in China unless there was an important domestic component to the operations. A joint venture allows a U.S. firm to establish operations in a foreign country—in essence, to establish long- and short-run cost curves that could not have existed without the joint venture. In this case, what the one firm has is access to the market. What the other firm has is product, expertise, and experience. In fact, it is not just U.S. firms that are entering markets via a joint venture. It is a common strategy employed by firms in nearly every country. For instance, in Canada, Bravo Venture Group Inc., established a joint venture providing for the production and sale of ice wine in China and for its possible export to other Asian countries in 2002, and Altachem Pharma's proposed a joint venture in 2002 with Erdos Cashmere Group in China to finance and expedite the development of Altachem's blood technologies.

The Supply Chain

The term **Supply Chain Management** came into use nearly a decade ago and since has become one of the buzzwords of business. Today nearly every business executive—86 percent according to one survey—says that supply chain management is one of the firm's priorities.[14] Yet, nearly as many executives are unsure exactly what a supply chain is and how it can be managed. A supply chain refers to the process of creating and selling a product and encompasses all steps from raw materials through final product. Consider, for instance, the supply chain of gasoline retailing as shown in Figure 5.7.

In Figure 5.7 we see that the first step is extracting crude oil and the last step is putting gasoline into the consumers' gas tanks. The raw material is extracted, transported to the refining locations, distributed to retail outlets, and finally sold to customers. The various steps are said to be down- or upstream from one another. Extraction is *upstream* from the other steps and retail is *downstream*. The entire supply chain or more than one part of the supply chain could be within one firm but need not be and typically is not. Thus, Ecopetrol, Colombia's state-owned oil company, contracts with Brazil's Braspetro oil company and Canadian Petroleum Ltd. to explore and extract the oil. Then, once extracted, the crude goes to Ecopetrol, is shipped by a company like Stelmar from the U.K., to locations such as Houston where companies like ChevronTexaco may refine it and introduce the additives the company desires in its gasoline. Once refined, the gasoline is piped or

Figure 5.7

FACSIMILE OF A SUPPLY CHAIN FOR A PETROLEUM COMPANY

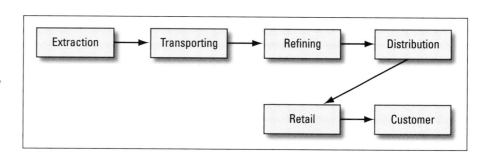

shipped to hubs; trucks then transport the gas to retail locations. Thus, each of these companies does business with an upstream and/or downstream supply chain member. By the way, business carried out between businesses is referred to as business to business or *B-2-B*.

Supply chain management refers to the attempt to ensure that each transaction along the supply chain is efficient. Supply chain management may refer to the case where a downstream firm provides training or technological inputs to an upstream firm in order to reduce the upstream firm's costs or improve the quality of its products; obviously the downstream firm is expecting this activity will reduce the downstream firm's own costs. Supply chain management could refer to a downstream firm forcing upstream firms to deliver products only when the downstream firm needs them—so-called just-in-time (JIT) inventory control. This would reduce costs to the downstream firm by imposing additional costs on the upstream firm. Supply chain management could also refer to an upstream firm increasing the efficiency of a downstream firm so that the downstream firm would purchase more from the upstream firm. This would influence the downstream firm's cost curves and the upstream firm's demand curve.

Three successful applications of supply chain management are provided by Dell, Baxter, and Procter and Gamble. In 1994, Dell was a struggling second-tier PC maker. The company ordered its components in advance and manufactured to inventory. Then Dell began to implement a new business model. It converted its operations to a build-to-order process, eliminated its inventories through a just-in-time system, and sold its products directly to consumers. The results were both lower costs per unit of output and more sales.

In the mid-1980s, Baxter, the hospital-supply company, developed a new partnership with its downstream customers. The company developed a new strategy for managing its customers' inventories within their hospital facilities. A Baxter employee counts the stock in each hospital ward each day and transmits it to Baxter's warehouse, where orders to replenish the stock are made and the order is delivered the next day and restocked by a Baxter employee.

P&G first partnered with Wal-Mart to develop a continuous replenishment system whereby P&G replenishes Wal-Mart's facilities without purchase orders. Based on this experience, P&G systematically shifted its strategic focus toward supply chain-based service innovation—and in the process transformed both the consumer products and retail industries.[15]

In these three examples, the change in supply chain focus resulted in lower costs and increased demand from downstream firms. But, two-thirds of manufacturing companies do not successfully synchronize supply chain operations with their partners, ultimately leading both to added distribution and planning time and to increased costs.[16]

CASE REVIEW *Mrs. Fields' Cookies*

Why did Mrs. Fields' costs grow so aggressively during the company's expansion? By 1990, Mrs. Fields was huge, with almost a thousand stores in eight countries. But the expansion went well beyond economies of scale. The operations could not be maintained in the same way they had when the company had three hundred stores. Managers had to be provided more discretion, but the Fieldses did not want to relinquish what they thought had made them a success. Moreover, the cookie dough was a secret formula and hence was mixed and distributed from one U.S. operation. The stores were too widespread for a single distribution center to function efficiently. The result was that costs rose significantly. In 1990, the company posted a net loss of $8.8 million even with revenue of $130 million. The failure to recognize the limits of size led Debbi Fields to sell nearly 80 percent of the cookie company's stock to four lenders and to resign from the company.

SUMMARY

1. The short-run is a period of time just short enough that the quantity of at least one of the resources cannot be altered. The long run is a period of time just long enough that all resources are variable.
2. According to the law of diminishing marginal returns, when successive equal amounts of a variable resource are combined with a fixed amount of another resource, there will be a point beyond which the extra or marginal product that can be attributed to each additional unit of the variable resource will decline.
3. Total costs are the sum of fixed and variable costs; they are also the sum of direct and overhead costs.
4. Average total costs are the costs per unit of output—total costs divided by the quantity of output produced.
5. Fixed costs are costs that do not vary as the quantity of goods produced varies.
6. Total variable costs rise as the quantity of goods produced rises.
7. Average total and average variable costs fall when marginal costs are less than average and rise when marginal costs are greater than average.
8. The U shape of short-run average cost curves is due to the law of diminishing marginal returns.
9. The law of diminishing marginal returns is a short-run physical property, while economies and diseconomies of scale refer to the long-run.
10. Economies of scale result when increases in output lead to decreases in unit costs when the quantities of all resources are variable.
11. Diseconomies of scale result when increases in output lead to increases in unit costs when the quantities of all resources are variable.
12. Large scale is not always best. The best size depends on the structure of costs and the extent of the market.
13. Downsizing, reengineering, outsourcing, and joint ventures may be short-run or long-run activities. These activities make sense only if something changed such that it has become more efficient to alter the combinations of resources or production techniques.
14. Supply chain management is primarily a focus on reducing costs. The supply chain represents the steps from raw material or resources to finished product and sale to the consumer.

KEY TERMS

short-run	total variable costs (TVC)	economies of scale
long-run	average fixed costs (AFC	diseconomies of scale
law of diminishing marginal	average variable costs (AVC)	constant returns to scale
returns	short-run average total cost	downsizing
average total cost (ATC)	(SRATC)	outsourcing
marginal cost (MC)	long-run average total cost	joint ventures
total fixed costs (TFC)	(LRATC)	supply chain management

EXERCISES

1. Use the following information to list the total fixed costs, total variable costs, average fixed costs, average variable costs, average total costs, and marginal costs.

Output	TC	TFC	TVC	AFC	AVC	ATC	MC
0	$100						
1	150						
2	225						
3	230						
4	300						

2. Use the following table to answer the questions listed below.

Output	Cost	TFC	TVC	AFC	AVC	ATC	MC
0	$20						
10	40						
20	60						
30	90						
40	120						
50	180						
60	280						

   a. List the total fixed costs, total variable costs, average fixed costs, average variable costs, average total costs, and marginal costs.

   b. Plot each of the cost curves.

   c. At what quantity of output does marginal cost equal average total cost and average variable cost?

3. Describe some conditions that might cause larger firms to experience inefficiencies that small firms would not experience.

4. Why would different industries have different degrees of economies or diseconomies of scale?

5. Describe the relation between marginal and average costs. Describe the relation between marginal and average fixed costs and between marginal and average variable costs.

6. Explain why the short-run marginal cost curve must intersect the short-run average total cost and average variable cost curves at their minimum points. Why doesn't the marginal cost curve also intersect the average fixed cost at its minimum point?

7. Consider a firm with a given-sized production facility as described by its existing cost curves.

   a. Explain what would happen to those cost curves if a mandatory health insurance program were imposed on all firms.

   b. Explain what would happen if the plan requires a firm to provide a health insurance program for each employee worth 10 percent of the employee's salary.

   c. How would that plan compare to one that requires each firm to provide a $100,000 group insurance program that would cover all employees in the firm no matter the number of employees?

8. Explain the statement "We had to increase our volume to spread the overhead."

9. Express Mail offers overnight delivery to customers. It is attempting to come to some conclusion about whether or not to expand its facilities. Currently its fixed costs are $2 million per month and its variable costs are $2 per package. It charges $12 per package and has a monthly volume of two million packages. If it expands, its fixed costs will rise by $1 million and its variable costs will fall to $1.50 per package. Should it expand?

10. Explain what reengineering implies for the costs of a firm.

11. Explain outsourcing and what it means for the costs of a firm. Can you see any differences between reengineering, downsizing, and outsourcing? Describe a situation in which downsizing is a short-run event. Describe a situation in which downsizing is a long-run event.

12. Under what conditions would a joint venture make sense? When would a firm not want to enter into a joint venture?

13. "The thing a lot of people don't understand about e-commerce is the degree to which it is a scale business," says Jeff Bezos, CEO of Amazon.com. Where a conventional retailer might have to double its capital spending to double sales, Amazon's costs are largely fixed. "Once our software is written, we can handle a lot of customers with it." Explain what this paragraph means.

14. Suppose the long-run costs of a firm can be represented as the function

$$C = 28,400,300 + 460,200Q$$

where C is total cost in dollars and Q is the number of products.

a. If Q equals 500, what is average total cost?

b. If Q equals 200, what is average total cost?

c. If the entire market is 1,000 products and if all firms have the same cost function, would a firm with a 50 percent market share have any advantage over a firm with a 20 percent market share?

d. What is the marginal cost?

15. Suppose the costs (in cents) per passenger-mile of operating a jumbo jet on flights of 1,200 and 2,500 miles with 250, 300, and 350 passengers aboard is:[17]

Number of Passengers	Number of Miles	
	1,200	2,500
250	4.3	3.4
300	3.8	3.0
350	3.5	2.7

a. What is the marginal cost of one more passenger on a 1,200-mile flight if there are between 250 and 300 passengers.

b. If the number of passengers is 300 and the flight is between 1,200 and 2,500 miles, what is the marginal cost of flying an additional mile?

c. What would the fare on a 2,500-mile flight have to be for a company to cover the operating costs?

16. Given the following long-run total cost function

$$LRTC = 200Q - 24Q^2 + Q^3$$

a. Over what range of output levels does the firm experience economies of scale?

b. Over what range of output levels does the firm experience diseconomies of scale?

17. A hot dog vendor outside the ballpark has a short-run total cost function of

$$C = 2Q^2 + 130$$

a. What is the vendor's marginal cost?

b. How many hot dogs must the vendor cook in order to minimize the per-unit cost of production?

CHAPTER NOTES

1. Based on Harvard Business School, Case 9-189-056; and Tom Richman, "Mrs. Fields' Secret Ingredient," *Inc.* (October 1987): 67–72.
2. Quoted in Cal Thomas, "Have We Hit Bottom on Immorality?" *Arizona Republic,* 20 October 1993, p. B7.
3. Shlomo Maital, *Executive Economics* (New York: Free Press, 1994).
4. Consider another example, but one with an opposite result. In 1998 John Deere joined forces with Home Depot to manufacture tractors for the mass market under Scott's brand name, which is an exclusive brand for Home Depot. John Deere agreed to provide Home Depot with a quality mid-price lawn tractor. Home Depot predicted a demand of 200,000 tractors for the year 2002 and a demand upwards of 349,000 tractors by 2006. John Deere decided to build a factory just to produce the tractor for Home Depot, which amounted to a capital investment of approximately $23.4 million and an expense investment of $12.7 million. The focused factory was built to handle 175,000 tractors in five months. The problem was that Home Depot reduced the forecast by half to 100,000 units, leaving John Deere with excess capacity.
5. A. Silk and E. Berndt, "Scale and Scope Effects on Advertising Agency Costs," National Bureau of Economic Research, Cambridge, MA, Working Paper No. 3463, October 1990.
6. Conor Wynn, "Scope Costs Could Lessen Electricity Scale Savings," *Australian Financial Review,* June 4, 2002; p. 71.
7. Boston Consulting Group, "Perspectives on Experience," Boston Consulting Group, Boston, Mass., 1968.
8. As someone said, the only thing the two industries have in common is wings.
9. *Co-Opetition,* by Adam M. Brandenburger, Barry J. Nalebuff, and Ada Brandenberger (New York: Doubleday, 1997), p. 70.
10. "Halliburton Advances Strategy in Reservoir Performance Monitoring" *PR Newswire,* August 15, 2002.
11. These buzzwords are referred to as graffiti in Thomas S. Robertson, "Corporate Graffiti," *Business Strategy Review,* 6, no. 1 (Spring 1995): 27–44.
12. Emma Connors And Stephen Long, "When Downsizing Becomes Risky Business" *Australian Financial Review,* June 4, 2002, p. 1.
13. "Outsourcing: Buying Best Practices," *Canadian Business,* August 5, 2002.
14. "Bain & Company Survey Shows Supply Chain Still Mismanaged by Most Companies" *Business Wire,* May 28, 2002.
15. William C. Copacino and Jonathan L. S. Byrnes, "How to Become a Supply Chain Master" *Supply Chain Management Review,* March 30, 2002, p. 37.
16. "Industry Survey Reveals a Majority of Manufacturing Companies Fail to Synchronize Supply Chain Operations" *PR Newswire,* August 7, 2002.
17. S. Breyer, *Regulation and Its Reform* (Cambridge, Mass.: Harvard University Press, 1982). It is pointed out that these data were approximately what Boeing said its 747 would cost to operate in 1977 in Edwin Mansfield, *Applied Microeconomics* (New York: Norton, 1997).

Costs and Production

In this appendix, the relationship between marginal product and marginal cost is demonstrated using calculus. It is shown why the law of diminishing marginal returns defines the shape of the marginal cost curve.

The total output a firm can produce or offer for sale depends on how its resources are used. This is represented by the production function

$$Q = f(K,L)$$

representing that output, Q, depends on resources—capital (K) and labor (L). (The production function captures Table 5.1 in the chapter, in which combinations of mechanics and airplanes is shown to generate numbers of passenger-miles flown.)

The marginal product of labor is the additional output created by adding one more worker:

$$\partial f(K,L)/\partial L = MP_L$$

The marginal product of capital is the additional output created by adding one more unit of capital

$$\partial f(K,L)/\partial K = MP_K$$

The law of diminishing marginal returns tells us that as we add more and more labor to a fixed amount of capital, the additional output we obtain may initially rise but will eventually decline. Thus, MP_L initially rises but then declines as L increases for a fixed K. Similarly, the MP_K initially rises but then declines as K increases for a fixed L.

Total cost is the sum of the costs of all resources. Assuming just two resources, land (L) and capital (K), the total cost function is:

$$TC = C(Q) = rK + wL$$

where r is the cost of capital and w the cost of labor.

The firm wants to minimize costs but is constrained by the production relationship; that is, how the resources combine to produce output. Minimizing cost subject to the production relationship is carried out using the Lagrangian function:

$$H = (rK + wL) + \lambda[Q - f(K,L)]$$

Differentiating with respect to K, L, and λ,

$$\frac{\partial H}{\partial K} = r - \lambda\frac{\{\partial f(K,L)\}}{\partial K} = 0 \tag{1}$$

$$\frac{\partial H}{\partial L} = w - \lambda\frac{\{\partial f(K,L)\}}{\partial L} = 0 \tag{2}$$

$$\frac{\partial L}{\partial \lambda} = Q - f(K,L) = 0 \tag{3}$$

Notice that if we divide equation (1) by equation (2), we obtain

$$\frac{r}{w} = \frac{\partial f(K,L)/\partial K}{\partial f(K,L)/\partial L} = \frac{MP_K}{MP_L}$$

or, rewriting,

$$r/MP_K = w/MP_L$$

This tells us that we minimize cost when we use resources to the point where an additional dollar spent on either resource will generate the same additional output.

Marginal cost is the change in cost that results from changing the output a firm offers for sale by one unit. In symbols, $MC = \partial TC/\partial Q$. In the short run, when some costs are fixed, MC is the change in variable costs (since fixed costs do not change): $MC = \partial TC/\partial Q = \partial TVC/\partial Q$.

As we discussed in the chapter, the shape of the marginal cost curve is dictated by the law of diminishing marginal returns. The law of diminishing marginal returns says that as we add additional units of a variable resource to a fixed resource, output rises but eventually at a slower and slower rate. So, if labor is our variable resource, then, since marginal cost is the change in the variable cost, marginal cost is the change in the cost of labor that occurs when we change output.

The cost of labor is the cost per hour of workers multiplied by the number of workers:

$$\text{Cost of labor} = wL$$

So the change in the cost of labor is $w(\partial L/\partial Q)$. This says that the hourly wage multiplied by the number of hours it takes to increase output by one unit is the marginal cost:

$$\text{Marginal cost} = w\,(\partial L/\partial Q)$$

Notice that this expression for the marginal cost involves the marginal product. $\partial L/\partial Q$ is the inverse of the marginal product, $\partial Q/\partial L$, the additional output per unit of labor. So,

$$\text{Marginal cost} = w(\partial L/\partial Q) = w(1/MP_L)$$

The law of diminishing marginal product says that as we increase labor in the short run, we initially get a lot of additional output: MP_L is rising. But eventually, for each additional worker, we get diminishing additional quantities of output: MP_L is declining. This tells us that $1/MP_L$ will initially decline but eventually will rise, which means that marginal cost will initially decline but eventually rise; as a result, we get the U-shape of the marginal cost curve.

Profit Maximization:
Seeking Competitive Advantage

CASE *Kmart*

Does America need Kmart? By its 2001–2002 bankruptcy filing, Kmart created some time to close underperforming stores, walk away from bad leases, and trim debt. Most analysts expect Kmart will survive the bankruptcy—at least for a while. But how is it to thrive in the long run? Some have argued that it must cut

prices. But Kmart should have learned that trying to compete on price was an error because however much it cut prices, Wal-Mart cut more. Kmart hopes to dramatically boost sales and profits in its urban stores by adding a full assortment of groceries—including fresh meat, produce, and bakery products—tailored to each community's ethnic mix. Does this make sense? Kmart has been experimenting with food for a decade but has not made this strategy work. In 2002, it had just 124 supercenters, compared with 1,060 Wal-Mart supercenters. That's one reason Wal-Mart zoomed past Kmart in sales. Shoppers visit supercenters two or three times a week, compared with three visits a month to a typical discount store. Will Kmart survive?

A market need not be a sophisticated, computerized process. It is not a government created entity. It arises when there are gains from voluntary exchange—if one person is willing and able to pay more for something than the person who owns that something finds necessary to sell the item. While online auctions are occurring in the offices in the buildings beyond the park, the simple exchange of food items occurs in this farmer's market. In each case, buyers and sellers are looking for gains from trade—each is seeking a profit.

Seeking Competitive Advantage

A company's resources have to be managed in such a way as to make them worth more than they would be if managed in any other way or by any other firm. In other words, a firm must maximize the value it adds to resources. If it does not, the resources will be reallocated to other, more valuable uses. Maximizing shareholder value, maximizing profit, maximizing value added—these phrases reflect the idea that the objective of business is to create value. The question is, how does a firm create value? How much should it sell and at what price?

Profit Maximization: The *MR* = *MC* Rule

It is simply common sense that if the production of one more unit of output increases costs less than it increases revenue, then producing (and selling) that unit of output will increase profit. The use of the term production here and throughout the text includes services, not just manufacturing output. Offering another unit of service or providing another balance sheet or accounting statement or passenger mile or whatever the unit of a firm's output will make sense if it increases benefits more than it increases costs. And, conversely, if the production of one more unit of output costs more than the revenue obtained from the sale of that unit, then producing that unit of output will decrease profit. This common sense leads us to what economists refer to as their golden rule: Profit is maximized when the additional revenue from producing and selling an additional unit of output equals the additional cost. This is referred to as *MR = MC*, or marginal revenue equals marginal cost.

Marginal cost is the additional cost of producing one more unit of output; *marginal revenue* is the additional revenue obtained from selling one more unit of output. When marginal revenue is greater than marginal cost, producing more will increase profit. Conversely, when marginal revenue is less than marginal cost, producing more will lower profit. Thus, profit is at a maximum when the quantity offered for sale creates a marginal revenue that is equal to the marginal cost: *MR = MC*.

The profit-maximizing rule, *MR = MC*, is illustrated in Figure 6.1, in which the average total and marginal cost curves of producing and selling a product—say, bicycles—are drawn, along with the demand and marginal revenue curves that arise from the firm's customers. According to Table 6.1, the first unit of output costs $1,000 to sell; the marginal cost (additional cost) of the first unit is $1,000. When sold, the first unit of output brings in $1,700 in revenue, so the marginal revenue is $1,700. Since marginal revenue is greater than marginal cost, the firm is better off selling that first bike than not selling it.

The second unit of output costs an additional $800 (Table 6.1, column 8) to sell and brings in an additional $1,500 (Table 6.1, column 5) in revenue when sold. With the second unit of output, marginal revenue exceeds marginal cost. Thus the firm is better off producing two units than none or one.

Figure 6.1

REVENUE, COST, AND PROFIT

Profit is maximized at the point where the marginal revenue and marginal cost are equal.

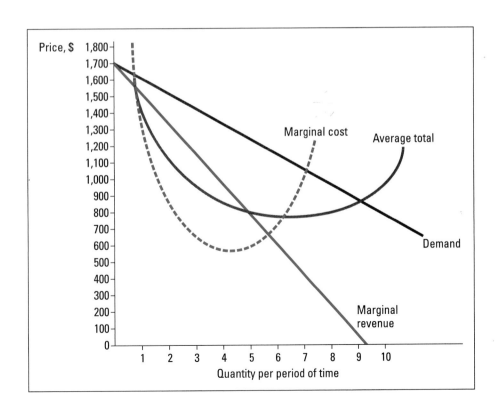

(1) Total Output (Q)	(2) Price (P)	(3) Total Revenue (TR)	(4) Average Revenue (AR)	(5) Marginal Revenue (MR)	(6) Total Cost (TC)	(7) Average Total Cost (ATC)	(8) Marginal Cost (MC)	(9) Total Profit (TR-TC)
0	0	0	0	0	$1,000	—	—	−$1,000
1	$1,700	1,700	1,700	1,700	2,000	2,000	1,000	−300
2	1,600	3,200	1,600	1,500	2,800	1,400	800	400
3	1,500	4,500	1,500	1,300	3,500	1,167	700	1,000
4	1,400	5,600	1,400	1,100	4,000	1,000	500	1,600
5	1,300	6,500	1,300	900	4,500	900	500	2,000
6	1,200	7,200	1,200	700	5,200	867	700	2,000 Profit Maximum
7	1,100	7,700	1,100	500	6,000	857	800	1,700
8	1,000	8,000	1,000	300	7,000	875	1,000	1,000
9	900	8,100	900	100	9,000	1,000	2,000	−900

Table 6.1

NUMBERS ASSOCIATED WITH FIGURE 6.1

Profit continues to rise until the sixth unit of output is sold. The marginal cost of selling the seventh unit is $800 while the marginal revenue is $500. Since marginal cost is greater than marginal revenue, profit declines if the seventh unit is sold. The firm can maximize profit by selling six units, the quantity at which marginal revenue and marginal cost are equal.

Figure 6.1 provides a great deal of information about business behavior. The demand curve may be different (steeper or flatter) depending on the price elasticity of demand, or the position of the cost curves might be different depending on cost conditions, but irrespective of these, profit is maximized when $MR = MC$. Every decision a manager or owner makes comes down to comparing marginal revenue and marginal cost. Should the firm increase advertising expenditures? If the MR from doing so is greater than the MC, then yes. Should the firm hire another employee? If the MR from doing so exceeds the MC, then yes. This decision-making approach shouldn't be any surprise to you. It is how you make decisions as well. You compare your marginal revenue (your additional benefits) of doing something to your marginal costs. If your marginal revenue exceeds your marginal cost, you do it. Nike used to say "Just Do It." What they ought to have said is "If MR exceeds MC, then do it."

Is the *MR = MC* Rule Useful in the Real World?

If we know marginal revenue and marginal cost, determining the quantity to offer for sale and the price to charge is straightforward. The problem is that marginal revenue and marginal cost are typically not known. Accountants do not report them. Accountants allocate costs among activities or across departments;

they do not calculate the incremental cost of producing one more unit. Moreover, as we saw in previous chapters, all opportunity costs are not reported in accounting statements. So calculating marginal cost is not straightforward. In addition, for a firm producing millions of units of a product, one more unit would seem to be a trivial thing to worry about. Just to emphasize how the economists' golden rule, $MR = MC$, is not recognized in business, a search of newspapers and magazines over the two-year period 1998–2001 using "marginal revenue" or "marginal cost" as keywords on the Lexis-Nexus system turned up a total of twenty-two articles. In none of them did the $MR = MC$ topic come up. Why do economists pay so much attention to marginal revenue and marginal cost if they are not used in the real world?

Although accountants do not provide marginal cost information and although executives say they pay no attention to marginal cost or marginal revenue, these concepts come into play in their decision making. Consider, for instance, how an airline decides to price its services. The price of seats varies considerably depending on when one flies, whether one stays over on a Saturday night, and when one purchases a ticket. Often an airline flying with some empty seats will sell the seats at the last moment very inexpensively. In fact, the price of the seat is often below the average per-passenger cost of flying the plane. The average per-passenger cost of Southwest Airlines to fly is one of the lowest in the industry, about $0.07 per mile. Yet Southwest will often sell some of its seats on distances of a thousand miles for $25. Why? Because $25 is significantly more than $0. In addition, the incremental cost of adding one more passenger is nearly zero. Thus, the marginal revenue of the seat, $25, is greater than the marginal cost, near zero. The executives of Southwest Airlines know that they are better off selling the seat. They know this not because they know that marginal revenue is greater than marginal cost or because they have calculated marginal cost, but because they know they make more profit by doing so.

Another illustration is provided by an executive of CarQuest, an auto-parts distributor. The executive, John Albano, having a degree in business, knows the theory of $MC = MR$. Yet he says that the pricing of parts is often more art than science. He says that the manager responds to customers; if customers complain about a price being too high, then the price is lowered. Conversely, if sales are brisk for a part, the price of that part is raised a little. In essence, Albano is describing the practice of finding the quantity where $MR = MC$ and pricing according to demand.

The profit-maximizing rule, $MR = MC$, may not be on executives' lips or in their manuals or part of their current graffiti, but it does describe their behavior. It provides a framework for understanding business behavior.

Selling Environments: Market Structures

A firm's behavior is dictated by the type of selling environment in which the firm operates. Selling environments are what economists call **market structures.** There are four market structures economists consider to represent nearly every type of business behavior: perfect competition, monopoly, monopolistic competition, and oligopoly.

Table 6.2 summarizes the characteristics of the four market-structure models used to illustrate business behavior. The name of the market structure is listed in

Table 6.2
CHARACTERISTICS OF SELLING ENVIRONMENTS

Market Structure	Entry Condition	Number of Firms	Product Type
Perfect competition	Easy	Large	Identical
Monopoly	None	One	One
Monopolistic competition	Easy	Large	Differentiated
Oligopoly	Impeded	Few	Identical or differentiated

column 1. The next three columns are the characteristics of the market structure—the entry conditions, the number of firms, and the product type of the firms. **Differentiated products** are perceived by consumers as having characteristics that products offered by other sellers do not have. **Standardized products** are perceived by consumers as being identical; these are often referred to as commodities.

Perfect Competition

Perfect competition is a market structure characterized by a very large number of firms, so large that whatever any one firm does has no effect on the market. In the perfectly competitive market structure, all firms sell an identical product and anyone can begin a business or close a business and exit the industry without difficulty. Because of the large number of firms, consumers have many choices of where to purchase the good or service, and there is no cost to the consumer of going to a different place to make the purchase. Since the products are identical, consumers do not prefer one store to another or one brand to another. In fact, there are no brands—only identical generic products. For instance, wheat from one farm is identical to wheat from another farm; scrap metal from one firm is identical to scrap metal from another firm; personal computer disk drives from one firm are identical to disk drives from another firm. Entry is easy and potential entrants are ready to enter immediately upon observing that existing firms are earning positive economic profit. Buyers and sellers have complete and perfect information: Buyers know the price and quantity offered by each firm; each firm knows what the other firms are charging and how they are behaving.

Distinguishing Between the Individual Firm and the Market One thing that is often confusing to students when learning about perfect competition is the difference between the individual firm and the market. The market is the sum of all firms and all consumers. It is represented by the downward-sloping demand curve and the upward-sloping supply curve that we are so familiar with; it is what people are thinking about when they speak of markets. Again, a market is the sum of all firms and consumers. When we look at one firm selling in a perfectly competitive market, we are just taking one of these many, many participants in the market and isolating it.

The individual firm in a perfectly competitive market is a **price taker** since the firm must sell its goods and services at the price determined in the market. The individual firm cannot charge more because no one would purchase from that firm

Figure 6.2

THE PERFECTLY COMPETITIVE MARKET AND FIRM

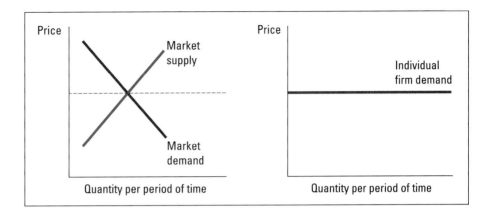

and it won't charge less because it could sell all it wants at the market price. Figure 6.2 shows the market and next to that the individual firm's demand.

Whereas the market quantity may be in the billions of units, the individual firm's may be in the hundreds; the individual firm is just a very small part of the market. The horizontal demand curve means that the marginal revenue is the price—each additional unit sold brings in additional revenue equal to the price at which it is sold and all products are sold at the same, market price. The demand curve and the marginal revenue curve are the same horizontal line.

Profit Maximization for the Perfectly Competitive Market The perfectly competitive market is often referred to as a **commodity market.** What is meant is that consumers see no differences among the products and an individual firm has no control over the price. Another aspect of a perfectly competitive market people allude to when they say a market has become a commodity market is the result that no firm can sustain positive economic profit. To see this, let's consider what occurs when a single firm does earn a positive economic profit.

Figure 6.3 illustrates the individual firm in a perfectly competitive market maximizing its profit. The firm will offer Q_p for sale at a price of P_p. The firm earns

Figure 6.3

PROFIT MAXIMIZATION FOR THE PERFECTLY COMPETITIVE FIRM

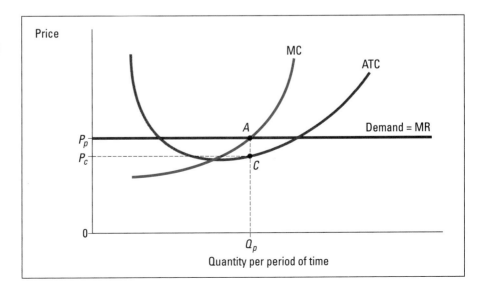

Figure 6.4

**ENTRY INTO
THE PERFECTLY
COMPETITIVE MARKET**

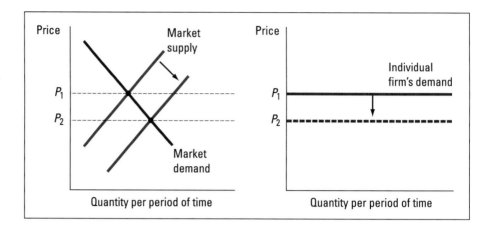

a revenue represented by the rectangle $0Q_pAP_p$ at a cost represented by the rectangle $0Q_pCP_c$, thus generating an economic profit represented by the rectangle P_pCAP_p.

The firm is earning a positive economic profit, which means that all opportunity costs are being paid and investors are getting more than their opportunity costs in return. Other investors want to get in on the profit and so organize firms to enter and compete. What does the entrance of new firms do? It increases market supply, lowers market price, and thus shifts the demand for the individual firm down, as shown in Figure 6.4.

For the individual firm, the lower demand means less profit. Entry occurs until profit is driven to zero. This occurs when the demand = marginal revenue line is just touching the minimum of the average total cost curve and is equal to the marginal cost, as shown in Figure 6.5

It is this process of new firms entering the market, increasing market supply, and forcing each individual firm to lower price until earning zero economic profit

Figure 6.5

**ZERO ECONOMIC PROFIT
FOR THE PERFECTLY
COMPETITIVE FIRM**

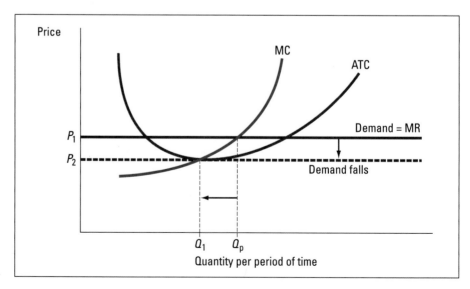

that people are alluding to when they indicate that they are getting out of a market because it is becoming a commodity market. This is what Intel did when it moved from DRAM (dynamic random access memory) production to microchips and then from microchips into another technology. This is what Motorola experienced with cellular phones in the late 1990s and early 2000s.

Positive economic profit attracts competitors who increase supply, lower price, and force all firms to the point where economic profit is zero.

Monopoly

Entry and competition drive economic profit toward zero. Of course, this occurs when entry can occur. To illustrate what occurs when entry cannot occur, economists have devised the model of monopoly—the extreme situation when only one firm exists in the market and no other firm can enter that market to compete with the monopolist.

With a **monopoly**, the single firm is the entire market. There is still a market demand consisting of the sums of the demands of all individual consumers. But, since the single firm is the only supplier, the market supply is what that single firm chooses to supply at each price. Monopoly is a market structure in which there is just one firm and entry by other firms is not possible. Consumers have only one place to buy the good, and there are no substitutes. Since entry by other firms is impossible, the monopolist may earn positive economic profit for as long as it has a monopoly.

The primary reason a monopoly exists is the government; most monopolies are government created. In the fifteenth through the seventeenth centuries, governments raised revenue by granting monopolies to special-interest groups in return for some of their profits. Christopher Columbus was granted a monopoly from Queen Isabella of Spain; the Hudson Bay Company was granted a monopoly by the English monarchy; most of the explorers and trading ships of the time had been granted monopoly charters. Today, government granted monopolies include the U.S. Postal Service—a monopoly supplier of first-class mail delivery, the Federal Reserve Bank—a monopoly supplier of U.S. currency. In addition, patents can provide a government-created monopoly. Glaxo-Wellcome, for example, was granted a patent on AZT and thus was, by law, the only supplier of the drug for a period of seventeen years. Licensing provisions and permits may create monopolies such as taxi service at an airport or vendor sales outside ballparks.

Theoretically, a monopoly could arise because of cost conditions rather than through government actions. If economies of scale exist throughout the market, a large firm can supply the product at a lower cost per unit than a smaller firm could. As a result, the larger firm can underprice smaller firms and force them out of the market. The large firm then becomes the only supplier. A monopoly that would emerge because of economies of scale is called a natural monopoly. Electric utilities used to be thought of as natural monopolies because of the economies of scale that existed in the generation and transmission of electricity. That view has changed in recent years as technology has altered the benefits that large scale provides.

People may refer to a business as being a monopoly even though many firms nationwide or worldwide supply the product. Universities, hotels, cable TV companies, newspapers, and electric utilities have all been called monopolies at one time or another. They are not monopolies according to the strict definition of

Table 6.3

DEMAND AND MARGINAL REVENUE FOR THE MONOPOLIST

Price	Quantity Purchased	Total Revenue	Marginal Revenue
$20	1	$20	$ 20
$15	2	$30	$ 10
$10	3	$30	$ 0
$ 5	4	$20	$–10

being the only firm providing a good or service, but they may have considerable market power in a limited geographical area. A hotel may be the only one in the center of the city, and entry by others may be virtually impossible. There may be only one major newspaper in a city. One cable TV company may be the only supplier in a city or a portion of a city.

Profit Maximization for the Monopoly Consumers may not have any real close substitutes for some good or service but that does not mean they will pay any price to purchase the product from the monopolist. If the price rises, fewer units of the good or service will be sold. For instance, when the price of electricity rises, people cut back on their use, even if they cannot switch to another supplier. So the demand for a good or service supplied by a monopolist is a downward-sloping curve. With that demand, there is an associated marginal revenue; the marginal revenue curve lies below the demand curve. Suppose demand and price are as listed in Table 6.3. You can see that when price is lowered to sell additional units, the marginal revenue declines and is less than the price. The question for the monopolist is what price to charge and how many units to offer for sale. The answer is the same as it is for all profit-maximizing firms—find the quantity where $MR = MC$ and set a price according to demand.

Suppose that at the profit-maximizing quantity, the monopolist is earning a positive economic profit. Although others would like to enter and compete, they can't—entry is not possible. As a result, the monopolist can continue to earn that positive economic profit for as long as entry is impossible.

Comparing the extremes of perfect competition and monopoly illustrates the important role of free entry and the creation of barriers to entry. As long as entry is possible, competition will drive prices to their lowest possible level and economic profits to zero. When entry is impeded or made more difficult, economic profit can remain positive until entry does occur.

Temporary Closures Can a monopolist earn negative economic profit? Yes—just consider the U.S. Postal Service. Throughout its history, it has seldom earned positive economic profit. What occurs when a monopolist earns a negative economic profit? It depends: The government may step in to subsidize the monopolist or the monopolist may shut down temporarily or go out of business entirely. In the latter instance, the monopolist is no different from any other firm. Whether a firm closes its doors temporarily or gets out of business altogether depends on a couple of factors, and these factors apply whether the firm is a perfect competitor, monopolist, or anything else.

Consider three firms having the fixed and variable costs and revenues shown in Table 6.4. Although all three firms are making losses of $300, they make very different decisions. The first firm decides to continue producing and selling its

Table 6.4

TEMPORARY CLOSURES

Fixed Costs	Variable Costs	Revenue	Profit (loss)	Decision
$1000	$ 100	$800	($300)	Continue
$ 100	$1000	$800	($300)	Discontinue
$ 600	$ 500	$800	($300)	Quit

products. The second decides to discontinue operations for a while. The third gets out of business as soon as it can. The difference is that the first firm is earning sufficient revenues to pay for its variable costs. If it discontinued operations, its losses would be much larger—$1,100 as opposed to $300. The second firm is in a different situation because it is not able to pay its variable costs. If it shuts down operations, its losses are only $100 as opposed to its operating losses of $300. The third firm earns sufficient revenue to cover variable costs, but the firm's outlook for the future is nothing but losses. It will continue operating until it can liquidate and get out of the business. In the cases of the first two firms, the long-term outlook must be for improvements or they, too, would be looking to get out of business.

Comparing Monopoly and Perfect Competition

Comparisons between monopoly and perfect competition have important implications for public policy and for understanding some business behaviors. Consider the market represented by the graph on the left in Figure 6.6. In the perfectly competitive market, price is P_{pc}. This means consumers who are willing and able to pay any amount equal to or greater than P_{pc} have to pay only P_{pc}. As a whole, the consumers get a bonus of the amount below demand and above price: This bonus is called **consumer surplus**. Similarly, producers who are willing and able to supply the product for any price equal to or less than P_{pc} get a bonus, since they can sell the product at the market price. As a whole, producers get a bonus of the amount below the market price, P_{pc}, and above the supply curve. This is called **producer surplus**.

For analysis of monopoly and government regulations see
http://www.lawguru.com/ilawlib/315.htm

Figure 6.6

COMPARING PERFECT COMPETITION AND MONOPOLY

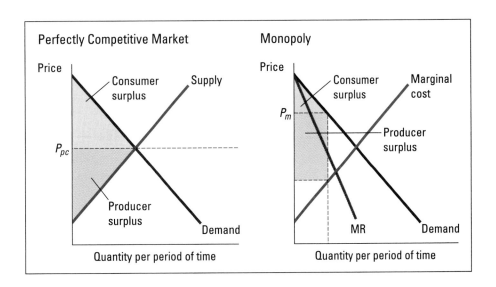

If the perfectly competitive market on the left and the monopoly market shown on the right in Figure 6.6 are identical except for the number of firms supplying the product, then the consumer surplus is smaller and the producer surplus larger in the monopoly case than in the perfectly competitive case.

Monopolistic Competition and Oligopoly

Perfect competition and monopoly are bookends to much of what goes on in the real world. They are not so much descriptions of reality as they are illustrations of possible tendencies in the real world. In most markets, products are not identical. Most are at least slightly different either because the firms supplying the products do something different or because brand name, packaging, placement in the store, or some other aspect creates a difference among substitutes. Yet competition occurs, entry is possible, and economic profit is driven toward zero. In most markets, there are not an infinite number of firms nor is there just one. To capture more realistic situations in business, economists have devised two market-structure models that have elements of both monopoly and perfect competition. The two market structures that better represent the real world are monopolistic competition and oligopoly.

Monopolistic Competition **Monopolistic competition** is characterized by a large number of firms, easy entry, and differentiated products. Each product is to some degree different from the others. Different products or firms that are close substitutes would be represented by McDonalds and Jack-in-the-Box, Coke and Pepsi, Cheerios and Wheaties, Sam Adams beer and Budweiser beer, and Tide, All, Clorox, and Fab detergents.

Product differentiation distinguishes a perfectly competitive market from a monopolistically competitive one. When a new firm enters a perfectly competitive market, it produces an identical product—more scrap metal or more wheat, for example. When a new firm enters a monopolistically competitive market, it produces a slightly different product—a different color or a different combination of sandwich materials, for instance.

Monopolistic competition is a mixture of monopoly—since each firm has a unique product—and perfect competition—since there are many firms, easy entry, and the products are close substitutes. In monopolistic competition, firms earn only zero economic profit in the long run due to free entry; but because demand is downward sloping, monopolistic competitors do not operate at the minimum of their average total costs. Competition among firms operating in a monopolistically competitive market takes place primarily through product differentiation. Advertising, promotions, packaging, and placement are perhaps more often used as a means of competition than is price.

Oligopoly **Oligopoly** is a market structure that captures most of what goes on in business; it is a structure in which there are few enough firms that each has to be concerned with what others are doing. Entry into an oligopoly is not free and easy but is not impossible. The slower entry is when a firm is earning positive economic profit, the longer that firm can sustain its profit.

The products offered by the firms in an oligopoly may be differentiated (as with monopolistic competition) or nondifferentiated (as in perfect competition). Buicks differ from Fords and Nissans. However, the steel produced by USX is no different from the steel produced by Bethlehem Steel. Automakers constitute one oligopoly, steelmakers another. Entry into an oligopoly is more difficult than entry into a perfectly competitive or monopolistically competitive market, but, in contrast to monopoly, entry can occur.

Because an oligopoly consists of just a few firms, each firm, or oligopolist, must take the actions of the others into account. For instance, an oligopolist that is trying to decide whether to lower the price of its product must consider whether its competitors will follow suit. If one firm lowers its price and the competitors follow suit, none of the firms in the oligopoly will be able to increase their sales much. However, if the competitors do not follow suit, the sales of the now-lower-priced firm may rise substantially. This type of interaction among oligopolists can be illustrated by what is known as the kinked demand curve.

Example of Strategic Behavior: The Kinked Demand Curve   Managers know from the law of demand that if they lower the price of the product their firm sells, more will be sold. But the firms in an oligopoly may not know the shape of the demand curve for their product because the shape depends on how the rivals react to one another. They have to predict how their competitors will respond to a price change in order to know what their demand curve looks like.

Let's consider the auto industry as an example. Suppose General Motors' costs have fallen (its marginal cost curve has shifted downward) and the company is deciding whether to lower the prices on its cars. If GM did not have to consider how the other car companies would respond, it would simply lower the price in order to be sure that the new MC curve intersected the MR curve, as illustrated by the move from P_1 to P_2 and Q_1 to Q_3 in Figure 6.7. But GM suspects that the demand and marginal revenue curves in Figure 6.7 do not represent its true market situation. GM believes that if it lowers the prices on its cars from the current level of P_1, the other auto companies will follow suit. If the other companies also lower the prices on their cars, sales of GM cars might increase a little but not because the lower price is attracting Toyota buyers or Ford buyers. GM does not capture the market, as indicated in Figure 6.7 by point A and Q_3 but instead gets

Figure 6.7

THE KINKED DEMAND CURVE

The kinked demand curve illustrates one type of interaction among firms. The firm has rivals that follow a price cut but not a price increase from the current price P_1.

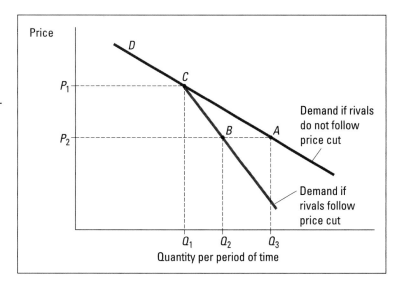

only a slight increase, shown by point *B* and Q_2. If rivals follow the price decrease, then the demand curve for GM is the kinked curve, *BCD*, rather than the straight line, *ACD*.

The kinked demand curve is a very simple illustration of strategic behavior. Most economists dismiss it as being unrealistic, but it has some value in that it illustrates that interaction among firms means that each firm's demand curve will be affected by what other firms do. In an oligopoly we do find competition taking place on the basis of price; more often, competition occurs through differentiating products or through innovation, technological changes, research and development, and other nonprice aspect of business.[1] It is also in the oligopoly that we find cases where it is in the firm's best interest to cooperate with rivals rather than compete with them. We discuss these behaviors in some detail in Chapters 8, 9 and 11. But just to illustrate the type of situation one might find with oligopolistic firms, consider a problem known as the prisoner's dilemma.

Example of Strategic Behavior: Prisoner's Dilemma   Another way that economists illustrate and examine the interaction among firms is to represent the interaction as a "game." Game theory is the name given to mathematical representations of strategic behavior. It is, as it sounds, the theory of games—specifically, poker. It was devised by John Von Neuman, a mathematician. Von Neuman created mathematical models to illustrate the possible strategies and actions that poker players might undertake. He then applied these concepts to political situations such as the cold war.[2] These models have been adopted by economists to help them understand the behavior of firms in oligopolies. The games range from very simple to very complex mathematical models. One of the simpler games and yet one that is found to occur quite often in business is called the prisoner's dilemma. In the prisoner's dilemma two firms are devising strategy simultaneously, having to forecast what the other will do. For instance, consider the situation in which firms are trying to determine whether to devote more resources to advertising. When a firm advertises its product, its demand may increase for two reasons. First, people who had not used that type of product before learn about it, and some will buy it. Second, other people who already consume a different brand of the same product may switch brands. The first effect boosts sales for the industry as a whole, while the second redistributes existing sales within the industry.

Suppose that individual firms in the cigarette industry are examining the potential payoffs to an increase in advertising. The payoffs are shown in Figure 6.8. The top left rectangle represents the payoffs when both firms A and B advertise; the bottom left represents the payoffs when A advertises but B does not; the top right represents the payoffs when B advertises but A does not; and the bottom right represents the payoffs if neither advertises. Firm A compares the left side of the matrix to the right side and sees that it earns more by advertising no matter what firm B does. If B advertises and A advertises, then A earns 70; but if A does not advertise, then it earns only 40. If B does not advertise and A advertises, then A earns 100; but if A does not advertise, then it earns only 80. Firm A will advertise. Similarly, firm B figures that firm A will advertise, so it must advertise as well. The result is that both firms advertise; and because advertising costs rise, each firm earns less than it would if both did not advertise. The firms are in a dilemma. We'll discuss how they resolve the dilemma in Chapter 11.

The interaction among the firms illustrates the environment we find in oligopolies. Each firm undertakes its strategy by examining what its rivals are doing

Figure 6.8

PRISONER'S DILEMMA

The options available to each firm are to advertise or not advertise. In this case, the firms both advertise even though both would be better off not advertising.

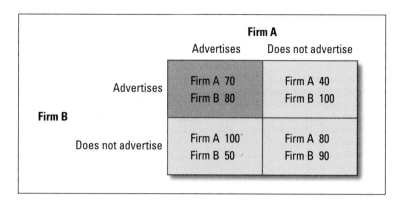

	Firm A	
	Advertises	Does not advertise
Firm B Advertises	Firm A 70 Firm B 80	Firm A 40 Firm B 100
Does not advertise	Firm A 100 Firm B 50	Firm A 80 Firm B 90

and how they will react to the firm's strategy. Unlike a firm in perfect competition or even monopolistic competition, the oligopolist has to take into account the actions and reactions of its rivals.

The kinked demand curve and the prisoner's dilemma are just two examples of the type of interaction that characterizes oligopoly. The purpose of discussing these two was to introduce the idea of **strategic behavior**—where what you do affects me and what I do affects you, so that we both have to take into consideration the responses of each other to our actions. This is what much of business is about and what we discuss in the coming chapters.

Sustaining Economic Profit

When a firm is making a positive economic profit, its revenue is sufficient to pay all costs including the opportunity costs of the investor's (owner's) capital. Other investors who see the positive economic profit want to get in on it. Whether they can or not depends on the market structure. If entry is possible—such as in the case in perfect or monopolistic competition or, with more difficulty, in oligopoly—then investors either organize firms to compete with the profitable firm or invest in the profitable firm. When a new firm begins competing with the incumbent firm, the new firm takes some business away from the incumbent. This causes the demand for the incumbent firm's products to decline. In addition, as new firms enter the market, the market supply rises, lowering the market price. Eventually, profit is driven down to the point where only a normal accounting profit (zero economic profit) is earned. With a zero economic profit, there is no incentive for additional firms to enter.

Economic profit arises from a distinctive capability—something that is unique and cannot be imitated. Distinctive capabilities enable companies to produce at lower cost than their competitors can or to enhance the value of their products in ways that put them ahead of their rivals. The primary lesson in this discussion of market structures is that profit cannot be obtained on a sustained basis simply by doing the same thing other people do, even if one does it better than others. Over time, the only way that positive economic profit will continue to be earned is if others cannot copy the unique activity or product that creates the profit. In business jargon, **sustained competitive advantage** is acquired through the ability to protect an innovation, to keep others from imitating it—that is, *to* *create barriers to entry*. This is what entrepreneurs seek and what managers attempt to create for their firms. In the next chapter, we'll examine ways in which managers attempt to sustain profits.

Profit Maximization over Time: Present Value

Managers must think in terms of many years, not just the current moment. Shareholders value the firm on the basis of expected performance, not just today's performance. Profit is created not from just this moment's action but from decisions made in many time periods. The value today of an amount to be paid or received in the future is called the **present value**. A sum of money to be received a year from now is not worth as much as if that sum was received today. A manager wants not just profit today but profit in the future as well and resources present costs not just today but costs in the future. To make proper decisions, it has to be recognized that all values are in present value terms.

> Many online calculators of present value are available at
> http://www.arachnoid.com/lutusp/finance_old.html
> http://www.1040tools.com/html/tax_calculators.htm

Consider, for example, the decision to purchase a machine that will create products and thus cash for several years. To know whether to purchase the machine it is necessary to compare two values: a purchase price today and the value in today's terms of a return that occurs over several years. To make this comparison, it is necessary to take into account that people prefer to consume today instead of waiting until tomorrow and that there is a risk that future payoffs will not be made or that money in the future will not purchase as much as it does today.

If you have $100,000 today, you can deposit that $100,000 into an account that will yield the principal (the original amount, $100,000) plus the interest after some period of time. If the interest rate is 9 percent per year, you will get interest earnings of $9,000 after one year. Thus, $109,000 one year in the future is the future value of $100,000 today at an interest rate of 9 percent, or $100,000 today is the present value of $109,000 one year in the future at a 9 percent interest rate. Let's express "one year in the future" as *FV* (future value) and "today" as *PV* (present value). Then we can write

$$FV = PV \, (1 + \text{interest rate})$$

If we divide both sides by (1 + interest rate), we have

$$PV = FV/(1 + \text{interest rate}).$$

Thus, the present value is $PV = \$109,000/(1.09) = \$100,000$.

The interest rate in this case is called the discount rate – it is the rate at which future values are reduced to be equivalent to values in today's terms.

Valuing a Stream of Payments

Calculating present and future values is simple when you are looking only one year into the future. The calculations become more complicated when you are looking ahead several years. If there is a stream of values, such as with a machine generating a constant stream of cash flows for twenty years, you could calculate the present value of each payment and sum all the values to get the present value of the entire stream. Or you could use tables that have been constructed to show the present value of some future amount.

Table 6.5 provides the present value of an annuity paying $1 each period for various years into the future. To calculate the present value of $100,000 per year over twenty years at a specific rate of interest, find the row for twenty periods and then read across the columns until you reach the appropriate interest rate. For instance, at an 8 percent rate of interest, the number indicated is 9.8181. This number is the present value of payments of $1 per period for twenty periods at 8 percent. To get the present value of a stream of payments of $100,000 per year for twenty years at 8 percent, multiply $100,000 times 9.8181. The result is $981,810. You can see from the table that as the interest rate increases, the present value of the money to be received in the future declines. Look at a 10 percent rate of interest and twenty periods in the table; the value indicated is 8.5136, so $100,000 each year for twenty years is worth $851,360 today at a 10 percent rate of interest.

Now let's put this in the context of a firm that is deciding whether to purchase a unit of capital. Suppose an airline is contemplating the purchase of a new wide-body plane that will yield a cash flow of $100,000 per year for twenty years. The present value of the cash flow from the plane is $981,810 at an 8 percent interest rate. If the price of the plane is $900,000, the firm will buy the plane. As the interest rate rises, the present value of the plane's cash flow declines. At a 10 percent interest rate, the present value of the cash flow is $851,360. The airline will not purchase the plane in this case.

Suppose that you want to calculate the present value of an income stream that is $3,000 at the end of year 1, $2,000 at the end of year 2, and $4,000 at the end of year 5, at an interest rate of 10 percent. To see how questions of this sort can be answered, it is convenient to begin by considering the simple case where you receive $1 per year for n years, the interest rate being r. The present value of this stream of $1 receipts is

$$\frac{1}{1+r} + \frac{1}{(1+r)^2} + \frac{1}{(1+r)^3} + \ldots + \frac{1}{(1+r)^n}$$

The $2,000 payment one year from now has a present value of

$$\frac{1}{(1+0.1)}(\$2,000) = \$2,000(0.90909)$$

The payment of $1,000 two years out is a present value of

$$\frac{1}{(1+0.1)^2}(\$1,000) = \$1,000(0.82645)$$

And the payment of $4,000 five years in the future is a present value of

$$\frac{1}{(1+0.1)^5}(\$4,000) = \$4,000(0.62092)$$

Thus, the present value of the income stream is given by summing the terms

$$\$2,000(.90909) + \$1,000(0.82645) + \$4,000(0.62092) = \$5128.31.$$

The present value of a sum of money to be received in the future rises as the length of time in the future the money is to be received declines and/or as the interest rate or discount rate declines. So, if the risk associated with the payment of a sum of money in the future rises—for instance, if your expectation that you

Table 6.5

PRESENT VALUE OF AN ANNUITY OF $1.00 PER PERIOD INTEREST (DISCOUNT) RATE

Period	1%	2%	3%	4%	5%	6%	7%	8%	9%	10%	12%	14%	15%	16%	18%	20%	24%	28%	32%
1	0.9901	0.9804	0.9709	0.9615	0.9524	0.9434	0.9346	0.9259	0.9174	0.9091	0.8929	0.8772	0.8696	0.8621	0.8475	0.8333	0.8065	0.7813	0.7576
2	1.9704	1.9416	1.9135	1.8861	1.8594	1.8334	1.8080	1.7833	1.7591	1.7355	1.6901	1.6467	1.6257	1.6052	1.5656	1.5278	1.4568	1.3916	1.3315
3	2.9410	2.8839	2.8286	2.7751	2.7232	2.6730	2.6243	2.5771	2.5313	2.4869	2.4018	2.3216	2.2832	2.2459	2.1743	2.1065	1.9813	1.8684	1.7663
4	3.9020	3.8077	3.7171	3.6299	3.5460	3.4651	3.3872	3.3121	3.2397	3.1699	3.0373	2.9137	2.8550	2.7982	2.6901	2.5887	2.4043	2.2410	2.0957
5	4.8534	4.7135	4.5797	4.4518	4.3295	4.2124	4.1002	3.9927	3.8897	3.7908	3.6048	3.4331	3.3522	3.2743	3.1272	2.9906	2.7454	2.5320	2.3452
6	5.7955	5.6014	5.4172	5.2421	5.0757	4.9173	4.7665	4.6229	4.4859	4.3553	4.1114	3.8887	3.7845	3.6847	3.4976	3.3255	3.0205	2.7594	2.5342
7	6.7282	6.4720	6.2303	6.0021	5.7864	5.5824	5.3893	5.2064	5.0330	4.8684	4.5638	4.2883	4.1604	4.0386	3.8115	3.6046	3.2423	2.9370	2.6775
8	7.6517	7.3255	7.0197	6.7327	6.4632	6.2098	5.9713	5.7466	5.5348	5.3349	4.9676	4.6389	4.4873	4.3436	4.0776	3.8372	3.4212	3.0758	2.7860
9	8.5660	8.1622	7.7861	7.4353	7.1078	6.8017	6.5152	6.2469	5.9952	5.7590	5.3282	4.9464	4.7716	4.6065	4.3030	4.0310	3.5655	3.1842	2.8681
10	9.4713	8.9826	8.5302	8.1109	7.7217	7.3601	7.0236	6.7101	6.4177	6.1446	5.6502	5.2161	5.0188	4.8332	4.4941	4.1925	3.6819	3.2689	2.9304
11	10.3676	9.7868	9.2526	8.7605	8.3064	7.8869	7.4987	7.1390	6.8052	6.4951	5.9377	5.4527	5.2337	5.0286	4.6560	4.3271	3.7757	3.3351	2.9776
12	11.2551	10.5753	9.9540	9.3851	8.8633	8.3838	7.9427	7.5361	7.1607	6.8137	6.1944	5.6603	5.4206	5.1971	4.7932	4.4392	3.8514	3.3868	3.0133
13	12.1337	11.3484	10.6350	9.9856	9.3936	8.8527	8.3577	7.9038	7.4869	7.1034	6.4235	5.8424	5.5831	5.3423	4.9095	4.5327	3.9124	3.4272	3.0404
14	13.0037	12.1062	11.2961	10.5631	9.8986	9.2950	8.7455	8.2442	7.7862	7.3667	6.6282	6.0021	5.7245	5.4675	5.0081	4.6106	3.9616	3.4587	3.0609
15	13.8651	12.8493	11.9379	11.1184	10.3797	9.7122	9.1079	8.5595	8.0607	7.6061	6.8109	6.1422	5.8474	5.5755	5.0916	4.6755	4.0013	3.4834	3.0764
16	14.7179	13.5777	12.5611	11.6523	10.8378	10.1059	9.4466	8.8514	8.3120	7.8237	6.9740	6.2651	5.9542	5.6685	5.1624	4.7296	4.0333	3.5026	3.0882
17	15.5623	14.2919	13.1661	12.1657	11.2741	10.4773	9.7632	9.1216	8.5436	8.0216	7.1196	6.3729	6.0472	5.7487	5.2223	4.7746	4.0591	3.5177	3.0971
18	16.3983	14.9920	13.7535	12.6593	11.6896	10.8276	10.0591	9.3719	8.7556	8.2014	7.2497	6.4674	6.1280	5.8178	5.2732	4.8122	4.0799	3.5294	3.1039
19	17.2260	15.6785	14.3238	13.1339	12.0853	11.1581	10.3356	9.6036	8.9501	8.3649	7.3658	6.5504	6.1982	5.8775	5.3162	4.8435	4.0967	3.5386	3.1090
20	18.0456	16.3514	14.8775	13.5903	12.4622	11.4699	10.5940	9.8181	9.1285	8.5136	7.4694	6.6231	6.2593	5.9288	5.3527	4.8696	4.1103	3.5458	3.1129
21	18.8570	17.0112	15.4150	14.0292	12.8212	11.7641	10.8355	10.0168	9.2922	8.6487	7.5620	6.6870	6.3125	5.9731	5.3837	4.8913	4.1212	3.5514	3.1158
22	19.6604	17.6580	15.9369	14.4511	13.1630	12.0416	11.0612	10.2007	9.4424	8.7715	7.6446	6.7429	6.3587	6.0113	5.4099	4.9094	4.1300	3.5558	3.1180
23	20.4558	18.2922	16.4436	14.8568	13.4886	12.3034	11.2722	10.3711	9.5802	8.8832	7.7184	6.7921	6.3988	6.0442	5.4321	4.9245	4.1371	3.5592	3.1197

might not receive the money rises—what happens to the present value? Yes, it declines. The discount rate, that rate at which future values are decreased in order to make them equivalent to today's values, must rise to account for the increased risk.

In examining business and firm behavior, we are really comparing the present values of various actions. A firm desires to maximize shareholder return or profits not just today, but over several months, quarters, or years. A firm's allocation of its capital has to involve the comparison of the present value of potential income streams and the present value of various expenditure streams. Thus, keep in mind that we are really referring to present value when we discuss revenue, costs, and profit, although it is easier to discuss these concepts by treating them as if they covered only one period.

CASE REVIEW *Kmart*

Will Kmart survive? In analyzing the facts of this case, you may find that you bump up against many of the topics discussed in this chapter: seeking competitive advantage, pricing, market structure, present value, and creating distinctive capability. Kmart, at one time, had a competitive advantage. Initially it was Sears that dominated the department store market. By the 1960s, Sears department stores were in every large city and its catalogs took its merchandise to every small town in the United States. Kmart began taking significant chunks of business away from Sears as Kmart established stores on the outskirts of towns and sold branded merchandise at discounted prices. But then Wal-Mart, offering a friendlier store layout and replacing Kmart's "Blue Light Special" promotions with "everyday low prices," took business away from Kmart. Kmart attempted to compete by cutting its prices, but business still did not improve and the lower prices meant even smaller margins and, in many cases, sales at prices that were less than costs. A competitive advantage cannot retain value when market entry is relatively easy. Sears lost its competitive advantage when Kmart entered and Kmart lost its when Wal-Mart entered. The three firms are broadly in a monopolistically competitive market—easy entry and differentiated products. In monopolistic competition, competition is based more on differentiation than on price. Wal-Mart differentiated itself with its store layout and everyday low prices. As we'll discuss later, Wal-Mart was able to support the lower prices because of its more efficient inventory control system. Wal-Mart began offering supercenters, which sell groceries in addition to its department store products, in an attempt to sustain growth and increase profit margins. Kmart followed suit; but, again, Kmart could not meet the everyday low prices of Wal-Mart.

Will Kmart survive? It has been able to lighten its debt-load by declaring bankruptcy, which has enabled the firm to almost start over. Many of its creditors have agreed to accept reduced payments, while other debts have simply been discarded. Nevertheless, without a competitive advantage, it cannot create profit. What is its competitive advantage?

SUMMARY

1. The supply rule for all firms is to supply the quantity at which the firm's marginal revenue and marginal cost are equal. This is the profit-maximizing point.
2. In order for a firm to create a profit, it must have distinct advantages – competitive advantages.
3. Market structures or selling environments are theoretical models describing possible behaviors by firms.
4. Perfect competition exists when there are many firms, each selling an identical product, and market entry is easy.
5. Monopoly exists when only one firm sells the product. Market entry is impossible.
6. Monopolistic competition exists when there are many firms, each selling a slightly different product, and market entry is easy.
7. Oligopoly exists when a few firms are interdependent. What one firm does affects rivals; thus, what one firm will choose to do depends on what it expects rivals to do. This is called strategic behavior.

KEY TERMS

market structures   commodity market   oligopoly
differentiated products   monopoly   strategic behavior
standardized products   consumer surplus   sustained competitive advantage
perfect competition   producer surplus   present value
price taker   monopolistic competition

EXERCISES

1. What does a very large number of firms mean for competition?

2. Draw a perfectly elastic demand curve on top of a standard U-shaped average total cost curve. Now add in the marginal cost and marginal revenue curves. Find the profit-maximizing point, $MR = MC$. Indicate the firm's total revenues and total cost.

3. Describe profit maximization in terms of marginal revenue and marginal cost.

4. Use the information below to calculate total revenue, marginal revenue, and marginal cost. Indicate the profit-maximizing level of output. If the price was $3 and fixed costs were $5, what would variable costs be? At what level of output would the firm produce?

Output	Price	Total Costs	Total Revenue ($P \times Q$)
1	$5	$10	
2	5	12	
3	5	15	
4	5	19	
5	5	24	
6	5	30	
7	5	45	

5. "Ben and Jerry's Ice Cream scorns profits. This company cares more about the environment and the health and safety of its employees than it does about profit." Explain whether this statement makes sense.

6. Draw two sets of cost curves. For the first set, assume fixed costs are huge and there are large economies of scale. For the second set, assume

	Firm A	
	Lower price	Retain price
Lower price (Firm B)	Firm A 70 Firm B 80	Firm A 40 Firm B 100
Retain price (Firm B)	Firm A 100 Firm B 50	Firm A 80 Firm B 90

fixed costs are small and the economies of scale are small. Now, on each set of cost curves place a downward-sloping demand curve. Find the profit-maximizing point in each case.

7. Two firms face the payoffs given in the figure above for reducing the price of a product each sells. Decide what policies the two will follow.

8. Assume that the structure of the airline industry is characterized as an oligopoly. Airline A observes that if it raises its price, the other airlines do not follow the change, but if it lowers its price, the other airlines always follow the change. Describe the shape of airline A's demand curve. Describe how airline A might change that shape to its own benefit.

9. Explain why the present value of the cash flow expected to be created by the acquisition of a business will decline as the risk of that acquisition rises.

10. Explain why an investment today depends on comparing the costs of the investment to the returns on the investment in present value terms.

11. Two firms have decided to cooperate in order to increase profits. If both firms abide by their agreement, each will earn $100,000 in profits. If both firms cheat on the agreement, then each will earn $25,000 in profits. If one firm cheats while the other firm abides by the agreement, the firm that cheats earns $150,000 in profits while the firm than abides by the agreement earns $125,000 in losses.

   a. Construct the payoff matrix for this problem and describe the result.

   b. Assume that the two firms must confront each other in this way for many time periods. Does this alter the result? Explain.

c. Assume that the two firms must confront each other in this way for many time periods. Assume that one firm must always make its decision before the second firm does. Will this alter the result? Explain.

12. A firm's profits are the difference between its revenues and costs as represented by the function

$$\pi = P(Q)Q - C(Q)$$

where π represents profit; P is price, which depends on the output to be sold, $P(Q)$; Q is output; and C is costs, which depend on how much output is produced, $C(Q)$.

   The quantity of output at which profit is maximized is found by taking the derivative of profit with respect to output and setting it equal to zero

$$\partial\pi/\partial Q = \partial P(Q)Q/\partial Q - \partial C(Q)/\partial Q = 0$$

   a. Demonstrate that this is the golden rule of economics, $MR = MC$.

   b. Derive the relationship between marginal revenue and the price elasticity of demand, and show that the profit-maximizing price and quantity will never be the unit-elastic point on the demand curve.

   c. Using the information in part b, demonstrate that the profit-maximizing price and quantity will never be in the inelastic portion of the demand curve.

13. Calculate the present values of the following:

   a. An annual payment of $10,000 for a period of ten years with an interest rate of (i) 5 percent; (ii) 10 percent

   b. A payment schedule of $10,000 in year 1, $20,000 in year 2, $30,000 in year 3, and

$40,000 in year 4 with an interest rate of 5 percent

c. A payment schedule of $40,000 in year 1, $30,000 in year 2, $20,000 in year 3, and $10,000 in year 4 with an interest rate of 5 percent

d. A payment schedule of $10,000 in year 1, $40,000 in year 2, $20,000 in year 3, and $30,000 in year 4 with an interest rate of 5 percent.

Compare your answers to parts b, c, and d. Which is larger? Why?

CHAPTER NOTES

1. For a description of oligopolistic rivalry and the role of innovation in this rivalry, see William J. Baumol, *The Free Market Innovation Machine* (Princeton, N.J.: Princeton University Press, 2002).
2. For more on Von Neuman's role in the cold war, see Paul Strathern, *A Brief History of Economic Genius* (New York: Texere Publishing, 2002).

CHAPTER 6 APPENDIX
Profit Maximization

Profit maximization is the process of finding the price and quantity that yield the greatest difference between total revenue and total costs. It does not matter whether the firm is a perfect competitor, monopoly, monopolistic competitor, or oligopolist—the process of maximizing profit is the same. In this appendix we demonstrate how profit maximization is carried out using calculus.

Let's symbolize profit as π. Then

$$\pi = TR - TC = PQ - C(Q)$$

To find the profit-maximizing quantity, we set the derivative of profit with respect to quantity equal to zero:

$$\frac{\partial \pi}{\partial Q} = \frac{\partial PQ}{\partial Q} - \frac{\partial C(Q)}{\partial Q} = 0 \qquad (1)$$

$\partial PQ/\partial Q$ is the marginal revenue and $\partial C(Q)/\partial Q$ is the marginal cost. Equation (1) just tells us that to maximize profit, we set marginal revenue equal to marginal cost.

If the price does not depend on the quantity (that is, if we are calculating marginal revenue for a perfectly competitive firm), then

$$\frac{\partial PQ}{\partial Q} = P = \frac{\partial C(Q)}{\partial Q}$$

The perfectly competitive firm maximizes profit where price equals marginal cost.

If the price does depend on the quantity ($P = P(Q)$), as is the case for all firms not in a perfectly competitive market,

$$\frac{\partial PQ}{\partial Q} = P + Q\frac{\partial P}{\partial Q} = \frac{\partial C(Q)}{\partial Q}$$

Marginal revenue equals marginal cost, but the marginal revenue of the firm that is not perfectly competitive consists of two parts, the price of the additional unit sold, *P*, and the effect on revenue from lowering the price on all goods sold, $Q[\partial P/\partial Q]$.

Sustaining Competitive Advantage

Once a firm has created a competitive advantage, it must find a way to sustain that advantage. Part III deals with strategies firms employ to sustain competitive advantage, strategies economists refer to as "creating barriers to entry."

Chapter 7 deals with nonprice strategies. Can a firm essentially ignore its price and focus on other aspects of its product and still be successful? In Chapter 7 we discover the situations in which price competition is not productive or profitable and discuss various strategies that take attention away from price.

Chapter 8 focuses on price. The pricing strategies firms can employ to increase profits and enhance the value of the firm are discussed.

Chapter 9 deals with the New Economy and a firm's use of research, development, and innovation. Is strategy in the New Economy different from strategy in the old economy? This question is examined, and the answer provided is "not really." Chapter 10 looks at the firm's internal structure, its organization, and its culture as a means of sustaining competitive advantage. Some firms are able to attract the best people because of the environment in which these people work. Some firms are able to pass information along more efficiently because of the organization of the firm. How are they able to do these things? We'll answer this question.

Chapter 11 deals with a firm's people—it's employees. A firm may find that it has to attract and retain high-quality people in order to sustain its competitive advantage. A firm may want to create a pay structure that enhances self-reliance or one that ensures teamwork. Which it chooses crucially influences how successful the firm will be.

CHAPTER 7

Creating Barriers to Entry

CASE *Wal-Mart*

In 1987, Wal-Mart had a market share of just 9 percent. By 1995, it commanded a market share of 27 percent. Wal-Mart created the large-scale, or "big-box," format; "everyday low prices"; electronic data interchange (EDI) with suppliers; and the strategy of expanding around central distribution centers. These innovations

allowed the company to pass its savings on to customers. Competitors began to adopt Wal-Mart's innovations in earnest in the mid-1990s. Sears launched a major turnaround effort in 1994. Target considered itself the world's best student of Wal-Mart. Smaller general merchandisers, such as Family Dollar and Tuesday Morning, adopted the big-box format. As a result, competitors managed to increase their productivity by 28 percent from 1995 to 1999. A major part of Wal-Mart's success stems from managerial innovations that improve the efficiency of stores and have nothing to do with information technology (IT); employees who have been cross-trained, for instance, can function effectively in more than one department at a time. Better training of cashiers and monitoring of utilization can increase productivity rates at checkout counters by 10 to 20 percent. Even so, IT was a necessary if not a sufficient part of Wal-Mart's success. The company invested in retail IT systems earlier and more aggressively than did its competitors: It was among the first retailers to use computers to track inventory (1969), just as it was one of the first to adopt bar codes (1980), EDI for better coordination with suppliers (1985), and wireless scanning guns (late 1980s). These investments, which allowed Wal-Mart to reduce its inventory significantly, boosted its capital and labor productivity. If others are studying Wal-Mart and mimicking it, how is Wal-Mart able to sustain its economic profits?

Sustaining Profit with Size

Economic profit arises from a distinctive capability, something that enables companies to produce at lower cost than their competitors can or enhances the value of their products in ways that put them ahead of their rivals. Profit cannot be obtained on a sustained basis unless these advantages remain unique. Sustained competitive advantage is acquired through the ability to protect an innovation, to keep others from imitating it—that is, to create barriers to entry. What factors can serve as barriers to entry?

Economies of Scale as a Barrier to Entry

The size of the firm relative to the market can be an important barrier to entry. If a firm must be large in order to enter an industry and begin offering a good or service, then entry might be very difficult if not impossible. In this case, the incumbent firm may be able to earn and sustain positive economic profits. Economies of scale mean that as the size of a firm increases (all of its resources are increased), its per-unit costs decline. If economies of scale exist, a larger firm can produce a product at a lower per-unit cost than can a smaller firm. Thus, a new entrant would have to enter as a large firm in order to compete with existing firms.

In those cases where economies of scale are followed by diseconomies of scale as the firm size increases, the long-run average total cost curve will be U-shaped, as shown in Figure 7.1. When long-run costs are characterized by economies of scale for smaller levels of output and then by diseconomies of scale for larger levels of output, the larger firm may or may not have a cost advantage over the smaller one. For instance, if demand intersects the LRAC curve at a quantity that is greater than the minimum point of the LRAC curve, like Demand$_1$ in Figure 7.1, then the firm that is able to produce at the minimum point, Q_m, has an advantage over smaller firms. But that firm has an advantage over larger firms as well. If a firm tried to produce quantity Q_n, it would have higher per-unit costs than the firm producing a quantity between Q_s and Q_n. If demand is like Demand$_2$ and intersects the LRAC curve at a quantity less than the minimum point

Figure 7.1

ECONOMIES AND DISECONOMIES OF SCALE

If the firm produces Q_m, its per-unit cost is lower than if it produces less, Q_1, or more, such as Q_n.

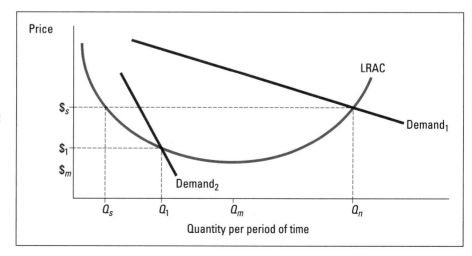

of the cost curve, then the firm operating at Q_m would have an advantage over smaller firms. If demand is just Demand$_2$, then the size Q_1 is the best size. At Q_1, per-unit costs are \$1, so the firm producing Q_1 can price below the costs of any smaller firm.

How does a firm become large? One method is to acquire other firms in the same line of business. For instance, in the past couple of years, Computer Associates acquired Platinum Software; both are software firms. Accounting firm Ernst & Young Malaysia merged with accounting firm Andersen Malaysia in 2002; both firms provide accounting and consulting services. In 2002, Comcast Corp. proposed a \$72 billion purchase of AT&T Corp.'s cable television business. DirecTV and Dish Network announced a \$25 billion plan to merge in October 2001.

Capital Requirements

When Folgers decided to move from being a regional coffee retailer to a national one, Maxwell House responded by substantially increasing its advertising and its production facilities. Maxwell House also announced that its advertising budget would be 50 percent more than Folgers' budget. If Folgers increased its advertising, so would Maxwell House. These expenditures raise the costs to firms entering the market. Potential entrants have to consider undertaking expenditures that are even more than those made by existing firms. If those expenditures are sunk, then the barrier to entry is even higher. A **sunk cost** is an expenditure on an asset that has no liquidation value. For instance, expenditures on advertising by one firm can't be sold to another firm. A firm that purchases a sign advertising the firm's name or product can not then sell that sign to another firm. Sunk costs can serve as effective barriers to entry since they tell a potential new firm that it has to throw just as much money away on similar sunk expenditures if it is going to compete.

Advertising expenditures may be the most significant sunk costs of competition. When a firm advertises, it is saying, "We have just spent millions of dollars drawing your attention to our product. If we intended to disappoint your expectations, to withdraw from the market, or to produce a poor-quality product, spending that money would be a foolish thing for us to have done." The advertisement assures the reader that the product is good, but not because it says that the product is good. Rather, the assurance that the product is good comes from the mere fact that the firm has incurred the sunk costs of advertising.

Consider the case of sidewalk vendors who sell neckties on the streets of a large city. If such a "firm" tells customers that it will guarantee the quality of its ties, customers will certainly question the validity of the guarantee since if the firm decides to go out of business, it can do so instantaneously. It has no headquarters, no brand name, no costly capital equipment, no loyal customers to worry about—indeed, no sunk, or unrecoverable, costs of any kind. It could come or go at a moment's notice.

The incentives are different for a firm that has devoted significant resources to items that have no liquidation value. These firms are not likely to pick up and leave at a moment's notice. Buyers, knowing that, can place greater trust in the promise of a high-quality product. And potential entrants know they, too, must devote resources to these activities and that once the expenditures are undertaken, there is no way to recoup them. These sunk costs could deter entry.

Access to Distribution Channels

A firm with an established distribution channel that is not easily replicable has an advantage over potential rivals. The auto industry is a good example. The dealer network is extensive and very costly to establish. Kodak's distribution network was well established by the time Fuji attempted to enter the film market in the 1970s. Fuji attempted to use Kodak's suppliers, offering to sell them Fuji materials at a fraction of the cost of Kodak products. Kodak responded with ultimatums to distributors that they sell only Kodak or they would not get Kodak products.

Differentiation

Every firm—producer, fabricator, seller, broker, agent, merchant—tries to distinguish its offering from all others. This is true even of those who produce and deal in so-called commodities, or products that are not differentiable, such as primary metals, grains, chemicals, plastics, and money. In the case of the commodity, it is the entire firm—sales, service, personnel, and appearances of offices and personnel—that matters. The reason firms try to differentiate themselves or their products is to make it more difficult for competitors to take away business.

Successful differentiation reduces the price elasticity of demand. What does this mean for a firm? It means the firm can raise the price without incurring the

Products may be differentiated on the basis of packaging. For instance, The Coca-Cola Company has introduced the Fridge Pack, which stacks a 12-pack of soft drink cans into a long, narrow package with an opening that dispenses individual cans. This is in contrast with the bulky, suitcase package used by most beverage companies. The pack is the result of joint work by Alcoa, one of the world's largest manufacturers of the aluminum used to make cans, Coca-Cola, and other packaging suppliers. It was found that the suitcase package was actually hindering the use of cans. People tended to put several cans in the refrigerator and placed the rest of the suitcase in a cabinet. When all the refrigerated cans were used, people would select another drink from the refrigerator instead of retrieving a can from the package. Coca-Cola Consolidated has eliminated the suitcase 12-packs, spending over $500,000 to convert the equipment in each of its plants to accommodate the new size.

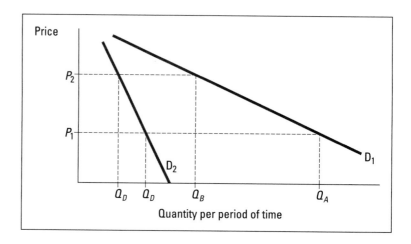

Figure 7.2

CHANGING THE PRICE ELASTICITY

loss of revenue that would come if the elasticity was higher. Consider an increase in price from P_1 to P_2 in Figure 7.2. For demand curve D_1, the price change leads to a large change in quantity demanded, from Q_A to Q_B. But for demand curve D_2, the price change leads to a much smaller change in quantity demanded, from Q_A to Q_C. The price increase leads to a total revenue increase in the case of demand curve D_2 but a total revenue decrease in the case of demand curve D_1. For years Intel was able to charge more for its microchips than competitors could for essentially the same microchip. Intel was able to do that because of its successful campaign to differentiate itself —"Intel Inside." Intel was able to shift the demand curve for its products out and make it more inelastic.

Reputation and Brand Name

A brand name differentiates a product from other products. Generic products or commodities are not so differentiated. Is the creation of a brand name important? A study by McKinsey and Associates found it was.[1] Based on more than five thousand customer interviews in the United States, Europe, and Asia, it was revealed that in both consumer and business-to-business markets, brand was a key factor behind the decision to purchase. On average, the brand was responsible for 18 percent of the total purchase decision. Moreover, prices of the strongest brands (in terms of the brand's importance in the decision to buy) were, on average, 19 percent higher than those of the weakest brands. Where does a brand name come from? How is it created?

Most goods have many different attributes—look, feel, taste, sensation, reliability, performance, and so on. Some of these attributes are revealed by search, some emerge immediately upon consumption, others are discovered through long-term experience, and some are never ascertained at all. If a business can provide information about the attributes at a lower price than can be obtained elsewhere, that business can make a profit providing that information. Similarly, if a firm can provide better or less costly information about its product than its competitors can about theirs, then that firm will have an advantage.

When people do not have complete and perfect information, economists say that information is costly or that consumers have to search for information, by perusing magazines or going from store to store to compare products, try out certain types of products, or purchase the advice of experts. Each of these activities takes time and, in some cases, money. Firms, realizing that search is costly for consumers, have an opportunity to increase business and differentiate their product by providing information and increasing familiarity with their product. This can be through promotion, placement, and packaging—marketing. It can also be done by devoting resources to portraying an image or creating a brand name. For instance, a firm that wants the public to realize it is stable and likely to be around for some time may devote resources to a large building or beautiful offices or large billboards. A clothing store in a mall is more stable than a vendor on the street corner, even though the mall location is just being rented. Harrod's massive building on Knight's Bridge and Kensington High Street in London is so well known that it is a tourist attraction. For some products, an important signal that the product is of high quality is a guarantee or warranty.

The information a firm provides depends on how the consumer acquires information about a product. You cannot learn much about the taste of the soup in a can or the flavor of a beer before you buy them, but you do discover these things almost as soon as you consume them. These types of goods are called **experience goods.**

With an experience good, the firm has to get the consumer to try the good, to experience it. What is sold is often a promise that it "tastes great" or "refreshes you." Goods are advertised by showing groups of people having fun on a beach or in the mountains—such as with Coors beer. The goods may be placed in a wealthy or upper-class setting—Grey Poupon mustard being requested by a passenger in a limousine, for instance. Gatorade is shown being guzzled by a person seeking nourishment and refreshment after extensive exercising.

Reliability is a key to the experience item. Reliability may be represented by the consistent flavor of a McDonald's hamburger, the infrequency with which a machine breaks down, or the soundness of the opinions of a professional adviser. The consumer has to experience these products and services over a relatively long period of time before reliability is established. Thus, firms want to increase customer loyalty and ensure the customers continue purchasing from them. To induce consumers to purchase the product initially, a firm has to provide consumers information regarding reliability. The uniformity of buildings for McDonald's implies uniformity of food, and a wood-paneled, rich-looking office implies a successful adviser.

Once a consumer has gained experience with a good, the price elasticity of demand for that good decreases—the consumer becomes loyal to the product. Coke and Pepsi drinkers are usually loyal to one or the other. This is why Coca-Cola and Pepsi conduct taste tests. Pepsi will set up a booth at a supermarket and ask customers whether they prefer Coke or Pepsi. If they say Coke, then they are asked to take a blind test. Coke does the same thing for Pepsi drinkers. With the result, the companies will advertise that some 60 percent of Pepsi drinkers prefer Coke or 60 percent of Coke drinkers prefer Pepsi. The belief is that if 60 percent of Pepsi drinkers actually favor Coke or vice versa, perhaps the public will rely on the tastes of others in choosing Coke or Pepsi.

Experience is useful if goods are purchased quite often but less useful if purchases are infrequent. By the time a consumer is ready to purchase a dishwasher or an automobile, the experience he had with the previous one he owned may mean little. To learn about these products requires some investigation—a look at *Consumer Reports,* asking around, or visiting stores. These goods are called **search goods.**

A search good is typically a large-budget item that is consumed on an irregular basis. Automobiles and household appliances are examples of search goods. The consumer is more willing to expend resources—time and money—to seek out information about the product than is the case with experience-type goods. Previous experience may generate some information—reliability of the car or appliance, quality of services associated with the product, and so on—but often that information is outdated at the time the consumer wants to purchase a new version. Thus, the price elasticity of demand is usually very high for search goods.

Often search involves a "reservation" price or quality characteristic. Prospective buyers get in mind the maximum price they will pay and/or the minimum quality they will accept. Then they go about searching—comparing prices and products. Once a product matches those reservation characteristics, no further search will take place.

A firm wants the consumer's search to stop with its product. The firm has to demonstrate that its product meets the customer's reservation characteristics. How do firms discover the reservation characteristic? They might ask customers by means of a survey or focus group. For instance, such consumer groups may have indicated that the most important thing they desire in a dishwasher is a lack of noise. The various manufacturers have carried out their own tests on noise levels and have had consumer focus groups examine the machines. When the consumer focus groups indicate that they prefer machine A over machine B for quietness, this becomes part of the information provided to consumers. For some consumers, such information may be sufficient for them to stop the search. For others, it is not sufficient; their search continues. Once a customer enters a firm's place of business, the firm wants the search to stop. Practices such as a guarantee of low price and product warrantees are attempts to assure the customer that continuing their search would be fruitless. And, of course, the role of the salesperson is important in closing the deal and stopping further search.

Doctors, lawyers, plumbers, teachers, electricians, bank tellers, clerks in a retail store, and many others offer a product known as a **service**. A service is usually something that is consumed immediately; it is an intangible product involving a deed, a performance, or an effort that cannot be physically possessed. There may be elements of search and experience with services, but the predominant aspect of services is that the item is usually consumed at the time it is rendered.

It is difficult for consumers to evaluate services prior to use because of their intangibility—the service cannot be seen, touched, tasted, or smelled and cannot be physically possessed. You are unable to evaluate the haircut you are to receive prior to receiving it. Often converting the service to something more tangible, such as reliability, is the key. In this way, the service becomes more like an experience good. Prudential Insurance shows "the rock" and Allstate shows the "good hands" to illustrate their reliability. While these symbols have nothing to do with the actual service, they display an aspect that consumers find valuable—that the service will be offered in the future, so that an experience now might be used to evaluate the service in the future.

Lawyers and financial advisers need to present an image of success. Who wants to use an unsuccessful attorney or financial adviser? Thus, attorneys and financial advisers typically have richly appointed offices located in large central-city buildings. They dress in expensive clothes and carry expensive briefcases. Consider the effect of a senior partner in a well-known brokerage firm who appears at a New York City bank in casual clothes to solicit business in financial instrument futures. Clearly the executive has differentiated (although demeaned the image of) his firm's product. There is no way the bank officials would trust the decision of someone who was not serious. No wonder that in the early years of IBM Thomas Watson insisted that his salesmen dress in what became known as the IBM uniform—white shirt, dark tie, and dark suit.

Firms convey information about their products to their customers through advertising and branding. In some markets in which quality standards are variable, names, such as Hertz and Avis, command large price premiums. When customers have difficulty assessing the quality of a product or service in advance, brand name becomes important, and firms with strong brand names have come to dominate these markets.

Reputation or brand name is valuable in the market when customers cannot easily monitor attributes of product quality. If consumers had perfect information, producers would have no incentive to create brand names or to differentiate products other than by actual physical characteristics. Aspirin would simply be aspirin, not Bayer. The brand name provides information to consumers; it is a signal of quality or reliability.

Many people claim that marketing and advertising create phony or artificial distinctions among products and that the benefits conferred by brand names are illusory. These critics note that there may be no difference between Tide laundry detergent and the generic detergent sold under the grocery store's label, that Ralph Lauren's Polo-brand shirts may be constructed of exactly the same fabric and knit design as several less expensive brands, and that aspirin is aspirin whether or not it is Bayer. Consumers are nonetheless often willing to pay a higher price for a brand-name product than for a similar product without a brand name. Why? Because the brand name signals something valuable. Consumers who purchase brand-name pharmaceuticals because they believe the brand name has some value may be right even if a brand-name pharmaceutical and a generic product are chemically identical. Drug companies that spend a great deal of money to create brand names may be less likely to create shoddy or dangerous products than firms that do not offer brand names.

The objective of creating a brand name is to increase consumer loyalty and thus reduce the price elasticity of demand. The greater the consumer's reluctance to shift brands, the lower the price elasticity of demand. Consumers loyal to a brand or to a firm will purchase that brand or purchase from that firm even if the prices are above those of competing brands.

Typically, brand names are costly to create and take a long time to establish. Because of this, incumbent firms are often reluctant to alter products or enter new markets for fear of damaging their brand name. The liquid soap market is a good illustration. In 1964 Robert Taylor took $3,000 and founded Minnetonka. Over the following two decades, Taylor took the company from being a niche producer of novelty toiletries to being an important player in the soap, toothpaste, and personal fragrance businesses. In 1977 Minnetonka came up with the Incredible Soap Machine, which dispensed liquid soap from a plastic pump bottle. The Incredible Soap Machine was renamed Softsoap, and sales began to take off. In test markets, Softsoap captured between 5 and 9 percent of total bar-soap sales. Softsoap reached nearly $40 million in sales in 1981 and was still growing when the big established companies—Armour-Dial, Procter & Gamble, Lever Brothers, and Colgate-Palmolive—finally entered the market. Although Procter & Gamble had the long-established name of Ivory soap, its entry was with a soft soap it named Rejoice. It wasn't until 1983 that P&G finally introduced its Ivory-brand liquid soap. Following that, Jergens entered and became third in the market. Two years later Colgate-Palmolive played catch-up by buying Softsoap for $60 million.

Why the delay by the big companies? The reason was protection of their brand names. P&G tried the name Rejoice simply to keep any failures from tarnishing the name of Ivory. Once the product looked to be a success, the extension of brand name from Ivory bar soap to Ivory soft soap made sense. Ivory soft soap moved almost immediately to a 36 percent market share.

The value of reputation depends on the likelihood of repeat purchase. In the long run, reputation can only be based on the provision of high quality in repeated trials. Because it takes a long time to establish such a reputation, some firms attempt to rent an established reputation in one market to use in a new market. Endorsement by famous personalities is a clear example. Everyone knows that celebrities give their endorsement not because they have scoured the market for the best product but because they have canvassed potential sponsors for the highest fee. So why are consumers influenced by the endorsement? The endorser is, to some degree, putting his or her reputation at risk. If the product is of low quality, the celebrity's reputation and value to other sponsors can be damaged. For the manufacturer, payment of the endorsement fee is a demonstration of its commitment to the market. Willingness to pay the endorsement fee is therefore actually a measure of product quality.

Firms will sometimes use their established reputation in one market to enter a new market, although, as demonstrated in the soft-soap case, this strategy has significant risks. BMW's reputation for producing cars reinforces its reputation for producing motor bikes and vice versa. BMW also endorses a range of "Active Line" sportswear. Caterpillar has a line of clothing—"CAT"—that provides the image of tough, no-nonsense fashions. There is small reason to believe that the capabilities that distinguish BMW cars or Caterpillar equipment are applicable to the manufacture of clothes. But it would clearly be foolish for the companies to attach their name to poor-quality clothes.

Guarantees

Guarantees and warranties can serve as barriers to entry. When Japanese automobile companies first entered the U.S. market in the 1960s, they faced the difficulty of convincing consumers of the quality of the cars. Although the manufacturers knew that their products were of high quality, their potential customers did not. In fact, many believed that Japanese goods were shoddy imitations of Western products. "Made in Japan" had become synonymous with cheap and crummy. Accordingly, Japanese manufacturers offered more extensive warranties than had been usual in the market.

Guarantees are difficult to fake. A low-quality product would break down frequently, making the guarantee quite costly for the firm. Thus, the higher the quality of the product, the better the guarantee offered by the firm.

If a firm establishes a warranty policy, then other firms either have to follow or must admit to having a lower-quality product. If a potential rival is unable to imitate the warranties of existing firms, it may decide not to enter the market in the first place. If the firm can match the warranty and beat it, then when the firm enters the market it will offer a *better* warranty. This is what the Japanese auto producers did to the U.S. auto producers in the 1970s. U.S. auto producers did not offer warranties as extensive as those now offered by the Japanese. As a result, customers soon came to see that "Made in Japan" meant quality. A similar event has been occurring in the late 1990s and early 2000s with respect to the Korean-manufactured Hyundai. Hyundai offered a 100,000-mile full warranty at a time when other manufacturers were offering 36,000-mile warranties.

Other Strategies to Deter Entry

Size and differentiation are not the only strategies firms have to deter entry. They may seek restrictions imposed by law, acquire unique resources, and even use prices to deter entry.

Government as a Source of Strategic Advantage

Visit the Federal Trade
Commission's website at
www.ftc.gov/opp/ecommerce/
anticompetitive

Seeking strategic advantages through the government is a commonly used business strategy—it is referred to as **rent seeking.** Businesses seek government restrictions on imports and on the entry of new firms, they seek subsidies for production, they look to the imposition of costs on rivals, and they devote resources to obtaining many other benefits.

A patent restricts entry for several years. A license to operate, to carry out business at a particular location, or to perform certain activities is a government-provided strategic advantage. Until the mid-1980s in the United States, banks could not operate in more than one state; interstate banking was prohibited. In some states banks could not have branches. These restrictions provided banks that already were in operation an advantage. The regulation of aviation made route licenses valuable. To be allowed to fly between major cities such as Los Angeles and New York was a definite advantage. When the number of taxis permitted to operate in New York City was strictly regulated, the value of a license to operate—a medallion—became very high.

Visit the U.S. patent office
website at
http://www.uspto.gov/

Harley-Davidson was able to get the government to protect it from competition by Japanese firms. Japanese firms were allowed to sell only small motorcycles, leaving the large machines for Harley-Davidson. The Bush administration imposed tariffs on imported steel in 2002 in order to protect U.S. steel producers from foreign competition.

The government often provides monopolies to companies. Cable TV is a series of local monopolies whereby a single firm is allowed to offer services in each region. Radio stations are assigned unique broadcast airwaves. Airlines are assigned routes. Taxi-cab companies may be assigned exclusive territories.

Smaller companies often turn to the government to restrict the behavior of the dominant firms. This was the case with IBM in the 1960s. Several companies developed tape and disk drives that were compatible with IBM machines, which allowed the companies to sell the peripherals in direct competition with IBM. IBM's ability to control price and output in the peripherals market was reduced, but because the peripheral companies could not produce a compatible central processing unit, IBM retained the ability to control price and output in the systems market. IBM dropped the price of its peripherals to a point where the other firms could not compete and retained its higher price on the central processing unit. IBM was taken to court for its actions by the competitors.

Microsoft was found guilty of anticompetitive behavior with respect to its

Internet browser. This lawsuit was filed by competitor Netscape and by the government. Microsoft was sued again by AOL over its Internet service provider—Microsoft is pushing its MSN in competition with AOL. Overall, Microsoft has been sued by the federal Justice Department, state attorneys general, and several private firms—Netscape, Sun, AOL, and RealNetwork—for unfair practices. U.S. Air and United Airlines agreed to a merger but could not proceed until the government was satisfied it would not be anticompetitive. The competitors of the merged airline lobbied the U.S. government to overthrow the merger.

The Department of Justice website and links to worldwide antitrust actions can be found at
http://www.usdoj.gov/atr/pubdocs.html

Unique Resources

If all firms in a market have the same resources and capabilities, no strategy for earning economic profit is available to one firm that would not also be available to all other firms. Any strategy that confers advantage could be immediately imitated by any other firm. However, if a firm has a unique resource, that resource may serve as a barrier to entry.

A single family owned the only mine producing desiccant clay, an important ingredient in inhibiting humidity in packaging. For years, this clay was the only material that could meet certain necessary standards for inhibiting the accumulation of humidity in packaging. A synthetic clay was eventually introduced and the value of the desiccant clay dropped.

DeBeers controlled about 80 percent of the non-Russian diamonds offered for sale in the world at the time the Soviet economy was tightly controlled by the government. Russia has about 40 percent of all diamond deposits in the world but had kept those diamonds from being sold and distributed outside the country. DeBeers therefore had a unique resource—acquisition and distribution of the non-Russian diamonds. With the breakdown of the Soviet Union, DeBeers has had to fear a flood of diamonds. It has been attempting to extend its uniqueness by stamping each of its diamonds with a certificate of quality and authenticity, hoping to ensure that diamond brokers will have to have such a stamp of approval in order to sell the diamonds.

Technological change often allows competitors to overcome resource constraints or unique resources. For example, Xerox's advantage in the plain paper copier market in the 1970s was built on superior servicing capabilities backed by an extensive network of dealers who provided on-site service calls. Canon successfully challenged Xerox in the market by building highly reliable machines that rarely broke down and did not have to be serviced as often as Xerox's. Canon's superior product design neutralized Xerox's advantage and reduced the value of Xerox's servicing capabilities and its dealer network. The unique resource Xerox had in terms of superior service and a dealer network was not imitated by Canon; instead, Canon used a technological improvement to "leapfrog" the unique resource.

Internal Strategic Assets

Measures of barriers to entry can be found at
http://www.census.gov/epcd/www/concentration.html

Anything that gives a firm an advantage and is not easily imitated serves as a **strategic asset**—an asset that restricts entry. All the things discussed above can be strategic assets—patents, licenses, brand names, and so on. Internal organization and structure can be a strategic asset for some firms. Hewlett-Packard's loose-knit structure has served the company well. The informality of Microsoft has helped foster creativity. Even company culture may be a strategic asset. Southwest Airlines has outperformed rivals partly due to its corporate culture. Compensation structures may also be a strategic asset. Lincoln Electric has been a highly successful small motor manufacturer for decades due to its unique compensation structure. We'll discuss all these issues in detail in later chapters.

CASE REVIEW *Wal-Mart*

How is Wal-Mart able to sustain its economic profit in the face of intense competition? Barriers to entry are created with the idea that other firms will not be able to readily copy the success of an incumbent firm, and thus the incumbent firm will be able to earn positive economic profits for a longer period of time. But when positive economic profit exists, others want to get in on the success. Entrepreneurs will seek ways to break down the barriers. If economies of scale lead to a barrier to entry, then new firms will attempt to become large or to redefine the market so as to change the economies of scale or develop technologies that will minimize the role of economies of scale. If a brand name serves as a barrier to entry, others will attempt to demean that brand or create brands that can compete with the incumbent brand. Resources flow to where they are most highly valued.

In the case of Wal-Mart, one success was not relied on. Wal-Mart's inventory control became legendary; others copied it and Wal-Mart's advantage dissipated. Wal-Mart's big-box strategy was a huge success; others copied it and Wal-Mart's advantage dissipated. Wal-Mart has had to continually innovate in order to maintain its advantages. Its innovations have taken place in managerial functions as well as IT functions. In creating and implementing these innovations, Wal-Mart has created a valuable brand name. That brand name has not been easy to copy. Other firms have not had the continuous innovations leading to everyday low prices as Wal-Mart has. But everyday low pricing has become quite widespread in retailing. Competitors will continue to seek those cracks in Wal-Mart's barriers to entry.

SUMMARY

1. Sustaining competitive advantage means creating barriers to entry—that is, doing something that others can't do.
2. Size can be a barrier to entry when there are economies of scale. Capital requirements can serve as a barrier to entry. Sunk costs may be a barrier to entry. Limited access to distribution channels can be a barrier to entry.
3. Brand names and reputation may serve as a barrier to entry.
4. Product differentiation may serve as a barrier to entry. The way goods and services are differentiated depends on the type of good or service being marketed. There are three very general types of products—experience goods, search goods, and services.
5. Experience goods are products that the consumer must try in order to evaluate. The price elasticity of demand for experience goods can be reduced by providing information about the experience to be obtained—using the experiences of others, for instance.

6. Search goods are products that can be evaluated prior to consumption. The consumer can learn about the good without trying it—by acquiring information from others, from independent agencies, and from the manufacturer. The search process is one of comparing costs and benefits and continuing to search until additional time and expenditure are perceived to cost more than they would benefit. The firm wants to reduce the inclination to search.

7. Services are products that are usually consumed immediately, are intangible, and are not physically possessed.

8. A strategic asset is not easily imitated and enables the firm to sustain profits—to create a barrier to entry.

KEY TERMS

sunk cost   search goods   rent seeking
experience goods   services   strategic asset

EXERCISES

1. Electricity producers in the United States are undergoing radical changes. The technology exists for a consumer to be able to purchase electricity from any producer. In fact, a computer could be installed in a consumer's electrical box so that electricity would be acquired automatically from wherever it is least expensive. What does this mean for an electrical producer?

2. What types of products are phone service and electricity?

3. *Services marketing* is a current business buzzword. It is a branch of marketing that focuses on services. Why would it be different from the marketing of goods?

4. Why does a firm spend an enormous amount on advertising when the ads provide consumers virtually no information? For instance, what does the advertisement showing the Rock of Gilbraltar and suggesting that we should "own a piece of the rock" tell us?

5. Why do firms build enormous buildings or skyscrapers when they could rent a less pretentious structure for a lot less money?

6. Why do consumers pay twice as much for Bayer aspirin than for generic aspirin when they know that the two are chemically identical?

7. Why do firms hire celebrities to advertise their products—why care whether Shaquille O'Neal (basketball player) eats at Taco Bell or whether Tiger Woods (golfer) wears Nike shoes?

8. Under what conditions is size a barrier to entry?

9. The following advertisement appeared in a recent newspaper:

We'll meet or beat the competition or double the difference! If our price does not beat the competition's advertised price on the identical item, we will meet it. If you find a lower competitor's advertised price within 30 days after the purchase, we'll double the difference.

What does this low price guarantee mean for the use of nonprice strategies? Is such a guarantee a barrier to entry?

10. A firm is considering moving its headquarters. Last year it paid $500,000 for an option to buy a building. The option gives the firm the right to buy the building at a cost of $5 million. Now it finds that a comparable building has become available at a price of $5.2 million. Which building should it purchase? Explain.

11. In 1972 DuPont and National Lead each accounted for a third of the U.S. market for titanium dioxide, a whitener used in paints, paper, and other products; another seven firms produced the remainder. DuPont was thinking about investing nearly $400 million in increased production capacity to try to capture 64 percent of the market within a few years. The market was changing because the government was imposing new environmental regulations and prices of raw material used to make titanium dioxide were rising. DuPont's

investment would mean that the production capacity that would be available would be much more than what would actually be needed. Explain the conditions that would make DuPont's strategy a profitable one.

12. Airbus began exploring the possibility of creating a jumbo jet in 1990. Initially, Boeing and Airbus collaborated on a feasibility study for the plane, but Boeing withdrew in 1995 because the project was too expensive and too risky given the uncertainty in demand. Airbus kept at it and finally emerged with a design in 1999. Management believed the company would break even on an undiscounted cash flow basis with sales of 250 planes. Airbus did not have a product to compete with Boeing's 747 in the VLA (very large aircraft) market. Suppose the situation of Boeing and Airbus, prior to Boeing's 747, is shown in the following payoff matrix. Airbus payoff is the first number presented and Boeing is the second.

| | Airbus | |
	Produce	Don't Produce
Produce	−10, −10	0, 100
Boeing		
Don't Produce	100, 0	0, 0

a. What would the two firms do?

b. How would the existence of the 747 alter this payoff matrix?

c. How might Boeing deter Airbus from entering the market?

13. Wal-Mart has had to make many decisions about whether to enter a new market or not. Suppose that Wal-Mart and Kmart are each deciding whether to enter a specific market. The payoff to each of the stores is shown in the following matrix, where Wal-Mart's payoff is listed first and Kmart's second.

| | Kmart | |
	Enter	Don't Enter
Enter	−10, −10	0, 20
Wal-Mart		
Don't Enter	20, 0	0, 0

a. Given this payoff matrix, what is the outcome if both companies move simultaneously?

b. How could Wal-Mart preempt Kmart? In other words, what could Wal-Mart do to ensure that Wal-Mart would get the greatest payoff?

14. Market demand in a particular market with two firms is given by

$$P = 1000 - 50Q$$

Firm A's cost function is given by

$$C = 20000 + 1Q$$

Firm B's cost function is given by

$$C = 20000 + 20Q$$

a. How can firm A drive firm B out of business?

b. How can firm B drive firm A out of business?

CHAPTER NOTE

1. Stephanie Coyles and Timothy C. Gokey, "Customer Retention Is Not Enough," *The McKinsey Quarterly*, 2002, Number 2 (http://www.mckinseyquarterly.com/search_result.asp); December 18, 2002.

CHAPTER 8

Price Strategies

Pricing Chips

A Phoenix tortilla chip producer enjoyed a competitive advantage over the national brand Frito-Lay. Its price was lower and quality higher than the Tostitos chip. Nevertheless, the local chip maker watched Frito-Lay very carefully because of its huge size relative to the local firm. Thus, when Frito-Lay upgraded its Tos-

titos chip, the Phoenix firm believed it had to respond in some way. It chose to reduce the quality so that its costs would be lower. It believed that in this way it could maintain its price advantage. The local company went out of business within a year. Consultants said the problem was the lower price on the locally made chips.

Several years ago, a specific size of a national brand's potato chips was priced at $1.59 while a comparable size of the local brand was $1.29, a difference of 30 cents. Over time, the price of the national brand increased several times until it was being retailed at $1.89. Following the lead of the national brand, the local brand's price increased to $1.59. However, even though the local brand was maintaining a 30 cent price differential, the national brand gained market share.

How is it possible for a firm to have a lower price on its good relative to a competitive good and still lose out to the rival? Why would equal price increases on two products lead consumers to purchase more of the higher-priced product and less of a relatively lower-priced product?

What Price?

The business strategies that get the most press involve cutting costs, introducing new products, and divesting or merging. But perhaps the most important strategy for a firm is its price strategy. Figure 8.1 presents the responses of a survey of managers from a broad range of industries to the question of what marketing issues are most important (5 is very important; 0 is not important).[1]

Although pricing is perceived by managers to be extremely important, only about 8 to 12 percent of firms do any serious pricing research, and one-third of these don't know what to do with the results once they have them.[2,3] As a result, many firms abrogate pricing responsibility—"The market sets the price" or "We have to match our competitor" or "It is determined by our costs." What factors does a manager think about when determining the price of a good? Most consider costs and competitors' prices, but few know anything about price elasticity. As illustrated in Figure 8.2, about 80 percent of managers think they are well informed on variable and fixed costs and about 75 percent on competitors' prices, but a much lower percentage feel they know anything about customers' response to price.[4]

How do businesses set their prices if they don't know much about these things?

The Internet, Auctions, and Pricing

The Internet has enabled firms and individuals to buy and sell via auctions. Have Internet auctions turned all businesses into price takers and all products into commodities? Is pricing even an issue anymore? The answer to the first question is no and that to the second is yes. The online auction is resulting in substantial changes to the pricing process but has not turned everyone into a price taker and every product into a commodity.

Figure 8.1

MOST IMPORTANT MARKETING ISSUES

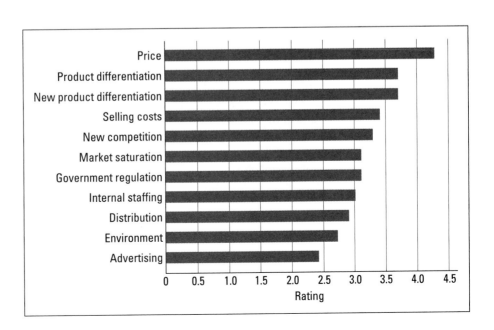

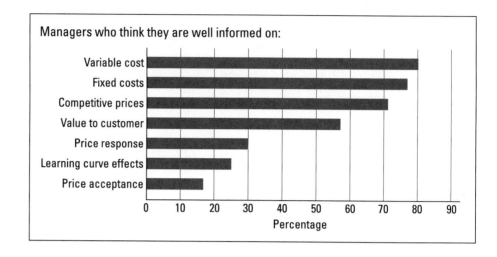

Shopping on the internet and price elasticity are discussed at http://ecommerce.internet.com/ news/insights/ebiz/article/ 0,3371,10379_759511,00.html

Figure 8.2
MANAGEMENT KNOWLEDGE

Farmers have to be on the lookout for ways to cut costs; in recent years they have turned to the Internet. Online exchanges for farmers are cutting costs for seed, feed, and chemicals while boosting prices for products. The Web also gives farmers a global marketplace in which to sell their products. Instead of driving to a sales location sometimes two or three states away—spending money on motels and restaurants and missing a day or two of work in the fields—farmers can go online and undertake sales from the desk chair in their home office.

Ford, GM, and Daimler-Chrysler have created an exchange to buy huge quantities of parts; retailers have created the WorldWide Retail Exchange and Global Net Xchange; and dozens of similar services are running or in the works. FreeMarkets has quickly moved beyond selling metal and plastic parts and is auctioning tax-preparation services, relocation services, temporary help, and other services. Sears, Roebuck and Co., the second-largest retailer in the United States, and Carrefour SA of France, the second-largest retailer in the world, cut the cost of the goods they buy from nearly fifty thousand suppliers worldwide—an $80-billion-a-year market—by using the Internet.

An increasing number of business-to-business exchanges are taking place through Internet auctions, of which there are a variety of types. In a bid/ask scheme, the seller sets an asking price and buyers try to outbid each other. Once the asking price and the current bid match, the product is sold. A straight consumer auction has a specified time period during which the market will be open and at the end of this time period, the highest bid wins. Some sites feature a name-your-price option similar to that offered by Priceline.com. Buyers post what they are willing to pay. Sellers then view the postings and decide if they want to meet the desired price.

Sellers' auctions, or reverse auctions, are very popular in business-to-business exchanges. If a firm wants to buy a million injection-molded plastic parts, it tells suppliers exactly what it wants. It then tells the suppliers that they can go online on, say, Tuesday at 2:00 P.M. and offer bids for twenty minutes. When the time is over, the low bid gets the business. Lots of companies are saving billions of dollars buying goods and services in this way. Of course, if you look at it from the seller's perspective in these reverse auctions, either the business the seller had prior to the creation of an auction has been lost or the profit margins the sellers receive on the sold items have been driven down. If the buyers are able to drive the prices down because sellers compete to sell the product, then the sellers lose relative to the situation where they did not have to compete for the buyer's business.

Business-to-business transactions are not the only type of online auctions. Consumers are increasingly using auctions to purchase everything from fish sticks to plastic surgery to kidneys. If you're thinking about a face-lift or if you want your eyes lasered, MedicineOnline.com will get a bunch of doctors to bid for your business. Supermarket clerks certainly couldn't allow the customers to haggle over every item in their shopping basket, but these days, you could haggle online for virtually any item you wanted to purchase.

How are prices set if the goods and services are traded via an auction? In many ways the auction is analogous to the perfectly competitive market where there are many buyers and many sellers all transacting over an identical good or service. Buyers and sellers bid for a product—if more buyers are willing and able to pay the price than there are quantities available at that price, the sellers will raise the price and produce more or offer more for sale. Conversely, if less is demanded than is offered at a price, the price will decrease and suppliers will offer fewer quantities for sale. The price is determined at the market-clearing level—where quantities demanded and supplied are the same. The market is a commodity market—for the individual seller, it means that $P = MR = MC$ and only normal profits are obtained.

On the surface, it would seem that the increased ability of customers to obtain information about prices and to be guaranteed "the lowest possible price" online would turn all markets into commodity markets—perfectly competitive markets. And there is no doubt that some markets have and will become commoditized. But in most markets the increased information and the existence of auctions puts an increased premium on differentiation. Consumers are willing to pay for service, delivery, and other amenities. For instance, while the average price online is about 10 percent less than for comparable offline products, the disparity of prices online is substantial. Products and services online are not any more identical than those offline; simply carrying out business online does not mean that the good or service becomes a commodity. In most cases, price will exceed marginal revenue and marginal cost ($P > MR = MC$) because of differentiation of goods and services and a positive economic profit is possible. In commodity or perfectly competitive markets, $P = MR = MC$ and economic profit is zero. As we'll discover in Chapter 9, there are just as many strategies for differentiation and pricing in the Internet economy as there were in the pre-Internet economy.

Pricing, whether online or offline, seems easy enough, doesn't it? Just find the quantity where marginal revenue equals marginal cost and set price according to demand at that quantity. Although this is the fundamental approach to pricing, there are many complications: The firm may offer more than one product; the firm may have different customer niches it tries to market to; the firm may have to consider what rivals will do if it raises or lowers price; the firm may have to consider what a high or low price means for the perception of the quality of the product; the firm might have to consider whether a high price will attract low-priced competitors; a firm has to determine whether a lower price will suggest that the product is low quality; and on and on. In fact, all these and other complications do come into play, which means that it is very difficult for managers to keep all the factors in mind when determining the price to set. Many firms are turning to software to handle these complications for them.

For instance, petroleum retailers are using technology to help them set prices. Some retailers price higher on the strengths of their brands while others aim to be known as offering the lowest prices. But in general, most retailers simply try to price slightly lower than their competition, with price increases or decreases being fairly uniform across all grades of fuel. "Pricing has been looked at as an art in the petroleum industry, something you determine by gut feel, reacting to what everybody else is doing," said Don Spears, managing director of pricing systems and consulting for MPSI Systems Inc.[5]

The "gut feel" approach is no longer necessary, and its use means retail petroleum operations are leaving money on the table. Computer technology now allows retailers to calculate price elasticity. The process starts by entering historical price, volume, and competitive data, with continual fine-tuning accomplished through daily data updates. The expected volume, the impact of a price change on volume, and the impact of a competitor's price change can all be calculated. The technology allows gas stations to change prices five times a day or more. During the two daily rush hours, commuters will be less cost-conscious and more convenience-oriented. These customers can be charged more because they are less likely to shop around. In between the rush hours, the stay-at-home population is less rushed and more price-conscious. After normal business hours—say 3:00 A.M., when the gas station is the only one open for miles—the price can be much higher.

It isn't just the petroleum retailers who are adopting the technology of pricing. In October 1999, executives of Coca-Cola were considering deploying a vending machine that adjusted the price for soft drinks based on outside temperature—the hotter the day, the higher the price. Supermarkets are turning to pricing-software analyses as well. The job of pricing the thirty-thousand-plus items in a typical supermarket seems virtually impossible. No one individual could keep track of each item and ensure that *MR* and *MC* are equal. Computerized software enables firms to set prices by tracking elasticities and customer retention.

The managers of the gas station or the supermarket or even Coca-Cola might not recognize that what the pricing technology is enabling them to do is find the profit-maximizing price level. But that is exactly what is occurring. For each product, the price is set by finding the quantity where marginal revenue is equal to marginal cost.

Personalized Pricing

Technology is enabling firms to be much more precise about their pricing. In many cases, they can personalize price to each customer and according to the time of day, or the intensity of the heat, or some other variable.

Catalog retailers have been able to use **personalized pricing** even without the technology. They send out catalogs that sell identical goods except at different prices. The unlucky consumers who live in a more free-spending ZIP code may see only the higher prices. Victoria's Secret and Staples have used these tactics for years. This approach to mailing lists is being replaced with computer analysis. Data on individual customers are collected as the customers make their purchases over the Internet or at the cash register with credit cards or membership cards.

Websites are programmed to recognize individual consumers, remember what they paid for items in the past, and charge them a **customized** price based on that history. When a customer purchases at Amazon.com, the customer's tastes in books or music are filed and suggested complementary or substitute products offered the next time the customer logs in. For a brief period of time, Amazon.com experimented with quoting each customer a different price based on that customer's price elasticity of demand. Amazon abandoned that practice when it received negative publicity. At Peapod.com, customers may order groceries over the

Internet; Peapod provides price per unit, ingredients, and nutritional information, thus giving customers a means of comparison shopping. As the customer clicks on and thus considers the prices, the nutritional information, or other aspects of the product, the time spent on each item is recorded. Marketers can then use the information to design ways to appeal to that customer. The customer becomes an individual entity rather than a member of a group of customers.

With each customer dealing with the firm online—"one-to-one marketing"—in business jargon, the firm is able to personalize the price. In essence, what the firm does is find out how much any given customer is willing and able to pay and attempt to set the price at that point for each customer.[6] If each customer is sold the product at a different price, **perfect price discrimination** occurs. If there are groups of customers with similar price elasticities of demand and the groups each pay a different price for the identical product, the price discrimination is referred to as **third-degree price discrimination. Second-degree price discrimination** occurs when the firm is not able to identify the value each consumer places on each unit of the good. Instead the firm is able to group multiple units of the good and to charge different prices for the different groups. Quantity discounts fall under the category of second-degree price discrimination; a consumer pays a high price for a small number of units, a lower price for a larger number of units, and a still lower price for an even larger number of units.

A firm is able to earn, or "appropriate," an economic profit when it provides a good or service at a price that exceeds all of its costs. In order to maximize profit, a firm will set a price and sell a quantity determined by equating marginal revenue

Tom Thumb is owned by supermarket giant Safeway and operates in the Dallas/Fort Worth metro area. Notice the listed price posted visibly on a large billboard, something most gasoline stations do. What other business posts its prices in such a prominent manner? Stations are required to post their prices, but there's no law requiring them to be blared from a billboard. The prices have to be present on the pump for consumers to see, but they need not make them visible to passing traffic. However, if stations post prices for one grade of gas, they have to post it for all grades (typically three) offered.

Consideration of pricing rules
in telecommunications is
discussed in

http://www.firstmonday.dk/
issues/issue2/different

and marginal cost. When every customer pays the same price, the price strategy is referred to as a single or uniform price.

When the price elasticities of demand are different for two identifiable market segments, then charging both segments the same price would be "leaving money on the table." Profit could be increased by raising the price for the market segment with the lower price elasticity of demand relative to the price charged the segment with the higher price elasticity of demand.

If two classes are better than one for an airline, are three better than two? Are four better than three? Is a different price for each customer better than a different price for groups of customers? The answer to all these is yes, as long as the firm can effectively build fences to separate the market segments. In other words, the seller must be sure that the market segments can not transact with each other and essentially skip the seller. If, for instance, Circuit City offered computers to senior citizens for half price, no one other than a senior citizen would purchase the computer since each potential customer who is not a senior citizen would enlist a senior citizen to purchase the machine.

Self-Selection: Product-Line Extension

Proctor-Silex sells its top-of-the-line iron for $54.95 while its next-best iron is priced at $49.95. The manufacturing cost difference between the two is less than a $1, as the top model adds only a small light to signal that the iron is ready for use. According to Proctor-Silex's marketing manager, this product-line extension allows the company to improve margins because there is a segment of the market that wants to "buy the best." How does Proctor-Silex find these people and separate them from the other customers? It doesn't. It allows the customers to self-select.

When Ford introduced the newly designed Taurus in two models, the basic GL and the more upscale LX, some customers complained that the price of the GL was too high for Taurus' traditional customers. Ford responded to the price-sensitive customers not by dropping the GL price but by announcing the introduction of a new lower-priced version of the car, the G.

Kodak markets three grades of film, with Royal Gold being the top of the line at a 20 percent premium over Gold Plus. Publishers offer the first-line copy of a book in hardback, with later versions offered in paperback. These are all called **product-line extensions.** The product-line extension is similar to price discrimination. But since the firm is not able to easily distinguish the customers, a new product is introduced so as to induce the customers to self-select, to separate themselves, and thereby to pay different prices for essentially the same product.

You might say that product-line extension is not the process of setting price where $MR = MC$. But it is. Profit is maximized by setting the price of the product and the product-line extension so that the marginal revenue of each of the products equals the marginal cost of producing each product.

$$MR_1 = MC_1$$
$$MR_2 = MC_2$$

Peak-Load Pricing

Executives of Coca-Cola let it slip that they were considering introducing a computer chip in vending machines that would raise the price of the soda as the temperature rose. Although the negative outcry that followed forced Coke to back away from the strategy, it is not uncommon for firms to use what is called a **peak-load pricing** strategy. A firm that uses the same plant or facility to supply a good or service whose demand varies at different points in time can increase profit by the use of peak-load pricing. Peak-load pricing is a form of price discrimination whereby customers purchasing the product at peak times pay a higher price than customers purchasing the product at off-peak times.

The pricing of long-distance telephone calls is a good example of peak-load pricing. Most long-distance calls are placed on weekday afternoons. The telephone company has to have the facilities to meet this demand, but this means that much of the firm's capacity sits idle during off-peak times. The telephone company would prefer to have demand be at a more even level so that its facilities could be more uniformly used throughout the week.

If phone calls could be stored at negligible cost for later use, then the phone company could build facilities for the "average" use rather than the peak use. In such a case, the marginal cost of providing phone calls would be no different whether it was a peak or off-peak time. The problem is that most calls at peak times are made for business purposes and few people would be willing to substitute a recorded call from a business associate during off-peak hours for a call during peak hours.

Cost-Plus Pricing

Consider the following statements: (1) "Products must be sold for about two and a half times what they cost to make." (2) "In a restaurant, food is marked up three times direct cost, beer four times, and liquor six times."[7] These remarks represent the approach a large proportion of businesses take to pricing. It is called **cost-plus pricing** (also called **full-cost pricing** or *markup pricing*). There are many forms of cost-plus pricing, but all basically involve two steps. First, the firm estimates the per-unit cost of producing and selling the product. Second, the firm adds a markup to the estimated cost. The markup is meant to include certain costs that cannot be attributed to any specific product and to provide a return to the firm's investment. Intel forecasts what demand for its microchips will be and then determines costs of production and finally sets a price based on the forecasts and costs, being sensitive to what its chief rival AMD is doing. John Deere determines costs of production and sets a Moline price – the price provided dealers. The dealers then have discretion to change price for their particular market situation. Chevron/Texaco sets a retail price for its gasoline based on crude oil prices, the costs of the additives in refining, and the prices charged by other retail operations.

When a firm uses a cost-plus pricing strategy, price is typically given by

$$P = (\text{average cost})(1 + \text{markup})$$

where markup is a percentage. For example, the markup might represent a predetermined profit margin or a target return on investment.

Does cost-plus pricing maximize profit? Not in most cases. The markup must be a very specific number to have the price resulting from a cost markup equal the price determined by setting marginal revenue equal to marginal cost. The cost-plus pricing rule will be the profit-maximizing strategy only if marginal cost rather than average cost is used and if the markup equals[8]

$$[1/(1 - 1/e)] - 1$$

How likely is it that a manager of a firm would realize that it must set this particular markup? Very unlikely. Nevertheless, the end result would not be all that different if the manager is at all sensitive to customer demands. As demand becomes less elastic, the markup increases, so the price is higher. Conversely, the more elastic the demand, the lower the markup and, thus, the lower is price.

Framing

In 1987, Burroughs-Wellcome (now Glaxo-Wellcome) introduced its anti-AIDS drug AZT to a hostile market reception. As a pioneering medical breakthrough, AZT gave AIDS victims and doctors the first medical hope of extending life. The introductory price for AZT was $12,000 annually. Although Burroughs-Wellcome's marketing department developed a very substantial publicity campaign that justified the price—due to the significant research costs needed to discover and develop AZT—the intensely negative public reaction nonetheless threatened the product and even the company itself. In 1991, Bristol Myers Squibb introduced a similar anti-AIDS drug, under the brand name Videx. It was not as effective as AZT and had a price tag of $150 per month, or $1,800 annually, but public reaction was overwhelmingly positive. Gay rights groups praised Bristol's actions as exemplary.

Why the difference? Videx enjoyed a significant perceptual advantage relative to AZT. People had something to compare Videx's price to, something they could not do with AZT when it came on the market. The context in which a choice is presented is important to the decision maker. The context will affect the price elasticity of demand. In short, perceptions matter.

For instance, when a customer calls a hotel regarding a reservation, the hotel reservationist generally quotes the highest rates charged during peak demand periods and then discounts those rates. This is an attempt to create a high reference price for the consumer. If the initially stated high price is the buyer's reference, then the buyer looks upon the price actually paid as a gain. Similarly, airline reservationists initially note the highest fare on a route before quoting discounts and associated travel restrictions. In written advertisements or on radio and TV advertisements, both hotels and airlines provide the lowest price as well as a reference to which they want consumers to compare the stated price. "This fare is 50 percent below previous fares" and "Friends fly free," suggesting a 50 percent discount, are common advertisements.

People generally want more for less. However, there are situations where how the "more" and "less" are presented makes a difference. Consider how people respond to the following situation.

Who is happier—person A, who wins the office football pool for $100 on the same day she ruins the carpet in her apartment and must pay the landlord $75, or person B, who wins the office football pool for $25?

Most people believe person A is happier even though both A and B end up with the same $25 gain. Consider the same problem with a slight revision.

Who is happier—person A, who ruins the carpet in her apartment and must pay the landlord $100, or person B, who wins the office football pool for $25 but also ruins the carpet in his apartment and must pay the landlord $125?

In this case, most people believe person B is happier even though A and B must pay the same amount, $100. In these situations, the individual market baskets being compared include the presentation of the goods in the baskets. If the market basket involves a gain, people prefer to have the results of the actions presented separately so that the gain seems larger—a $100 gain and a $25 loss rather than a $75 gain. But if the market basket involves losses, people prefer to have the losses integrated or shown just once.

In the June 29, 2001, issue of *USA Today,* there was an article titled "Energy Fees Leave Hotel Guests Hot Under the Collar." The article noted that hotels were imposing "energy fees" of $1.50 to $7 per night because energy costs had risen and the hotels were simply passing these along to the consumer. The hotels thought they would be able to raise the price of their rooms without having to take the blame for the price increase. Consumers did not react positively. According to the idea that people prefer getting bad news all at once, this pricing strategy is very poor. Hoteliers should be lumping the entire fees together into one amount. They mistakenly believed that consumers would blame the energy charges on something other than the hotel.

Odd pricing is the practice of specifying the rightmost digits in the price in amounts that are less than the higher even price. For instance, $2.98 as compared to $3.00 or $499 as compared to $500 are odd prices. The use of odd pricing is based on reference prices. The advertised price of $499 allows the consumer to realize there is a gain relative to $500, the reference price. Moreover, because a loss means more than an equal gain, we don't see odd prices above the even reference price.[9]

It is more painful to consumers to give up an asset that they possess than it is pleasurable to acquire an asset they don't possess. Buyers want to retain the status quo, to keep the assets they already own. This means that the price elasticity of demand can be changed—made less elastic—if consumers feel like they own the product. Thus, the purchase decision can be influenced by having the buyers assume ownership, even temporarily, prior to purchase. If buyers can be persuaded to take the product home to try it out, they will adjust their reference point to include the new asset. They will then be reluctant to return the product when payment is due, since they would be giving up something they now feel like they own. A frequent tactic of home decorator and furniture stores is to encourage customers to take a piece of furniture or a carpet home to "see how it looks." This is also the approach of buy-now, pay-later plans. During holidays, for example, retailers frequently offer installment plans that delay payment for 90 days so that buyers can integrate the new purchases into their reference points. Health clubs, fitness centers, and weight-loss clinics often offer an initial trial membership either free or at nominal rates.

Publisher's Clearinghouse addresses individuals who receive their direct-mail promotion as "finalists" and warns them that they are about to lose millions of dollars if the entry form is not returned. Publisher's Clearinghouse is attempting to give consumers the impression that they possess an asset that they will have to give up if they don't submit the entry form.

Pricing to Deter Entry

A firm may be able to use prices to deter market entry by potential rivals. A price that discourages or prevents entry is called a **limit price**. A limit price is one that will keep potential entrants from entering the market and yet allow the incumbent firm some profits. How can a limit price work? It can only work if the incumbent has lower costs than potential entrants.

Suppose that the Middle Company is a very-low-cost producer of plumbing products. If potential entrants knew how low its costs really are, they would not be foolish enough to enter the industry because they would recognize that they have no chance to survive. But they have no reliable way of telling what Middle Company's costs are because plumbing is just one of its products. To signal potential entrants that it is a very-low-cost producer, Middle Company may find it worthwhile to set a relatively low price. This will lower Middle Company's profits in the short run, but it may result in bigger profits over the long run because of the reduced likelihood that Middle Company will have to compete with entrants to the market. Why can't Middle Company simply announce that its costs are very low? Because potential entrants would be suspicious enough to recognize that such announcements may be lies aimed at discouraging entry.

While limit pricing would seem to be a potential deterrent to entry, it could be very costly for a firm to employ the strategy. The revenue lost during the period the firm charges the low price may never be recouped or the low price may become the company's standard—it may not be able to increase prices in the future without losing customers.

An interesting article on Microsoft and predatory pricing is available at
www.businessweek.com/ magazine/content/1998/47/ b3605129.htm

Predatory pricing is discussed in www.businessweek.com/ magazine/content/01_20/ b3732075.htm

Limit pricing is sometimes referred to as **predatory pricing.** Predatory pricing is setting a very low price (a price that is below average variable cost) in order to drive competitors out of business and then increasing price to recoup the lost revenue. Could a business do such a thing? Could it set prices below its costs in order to drive competitors out of business and then increase prices once the competitors have left the market? Wouldn't the higher price just entice new startups in and force the dominant incumbent to lower price again, and then again, and basically forever?

According to one study, airlines that have near-monopoly status at hub airports can use their size to drive low-cost carriers from their markets.[10] For instance, in 1995 Spirit Airlines entered the Detroit–Philadelphia market, which was dominated by Northwest Airlines. Spirit started by offering one round-trip flight daily, with fares ranging from $49 to $139. Northwest struck back by matching Spirit's fare. The result: Northwest's revenue plunged, but regained its entire market. In late 1996, Spirit gave up. A few months later, Northwest eliminated virtually all low-cost fares on the route, and its revenue returned to precompetition levels. This same study cited twelve cases where the upstart carrier offered initial fares at half the price of the market's dominant incumbent—and the threatened major airline responded with price cuts. Within two years, half the new carriers had exited the market because they were unable to make a profit and most of the incumbent firms had recouped their losses.

So why didn't other startup airlines enter once the incumbent firm increased fares, or why didn't the fear of new entries keep the incumbent from raising fares? One reason cited was the dismal performance of the startups; investors would not provide funds for an airline to get started. Knowing the incumbent has deep pockets and can afford losses for a while if they can be recouped later, investors decline to get embroiled in a battle with the incumbent. But the real problem is that access to airports is tightly controlled by the federal government and airport officials; the incumbent firms have near-monopolies. Few if any startups can gain access to a landing gate in order to enter the business.[11] Unless entry is very difficult, predatory pricing cannot work; the incumbent firm can not recoup losses even if it drives the rivals out of the market. Once the incumbent firm increases price, new rivals would enter.

Are airlines the only industry in which predatory pricing occurs? As we'll see in the next chapter, predatory pricing seems to occur more regularly in the New Economy than it used to in the old economy.

More Complexities

What we have discussed to this point is the situation in which the firm has a single product to sell and a single price to determine. Let's now consider more complex situations.

Bundling

Cable television providers have a difficult pricing situation. They have several channels to sell (several products), and customers differ distinctly in the channels that are of interest to them. To illustrate, suppose that Cox Cable has just two channels, 1 and 2. Also, suppose there are just two segments among the viewer population: A and B. The A segment gets much more value out of channel 1 than does segment B, and segment B likes channel 2 more than does segment A.

Suppose that members of segment B would be willing to pay no more than $12 a month for channel 1 and no more than $12 a month for channel 2. Members of segment A would be willing to pay no more than $20 a month for channel 1 but only no more than $4 a month for channel 2.

If the channels are sold separately, the most Cox Cable could get for the channels would be the sum of the prices each segment was willing to pay. If Cox set a price of $20 for channel 1, it would sell only to segment A. To get segment B to purchase channel 1, Cox has to set a price of no more than $12. Since Cox is not able to distinguish between segments A and B, it has to set the same price for all customers. Thus, total revenue from channel 1 is

$$TR = (Q_A + Q_B)\$12$$

where Q_A is the number of people in segment A and Q_B is the number of people in segment B.

Similarly, Cox can charge only $4 to get segment A to purchase channel 2, so it cannot charge more than $4 for channel 2. The total revenue from channel 2 is

$$TR = (Q_A + Q_B)\$4$$

Now, consider what would happen if Cox sold the two channels as a package—bundled the two channels together. Cox could set a price of $24, the lowest price that would attract the two groups to the bundle of channels 1 and 2. In the bundling case, $TR = (Q_A + Q_B)\$24$. This is called **pure bundling** since the only way the channels can be purchased is as a package. Pure bundling does not discriminate among the customer segments—all customers pay the same price.

Mixed Bundling In the preceding example, the seller, Cox Cable, offered the channels only as a bundle. Often, the seller can make a larger profit by allowing buyers a choice between the bundle and the individual products. To illustrate, suppose that Cox Cable incurs a marginal cost of $5 per month per channel for each customer. The marginal cost of $5 is more than segment A would pay for channel 2. It wouldn't make sense to sell channel 2 to segment A at a price that is less than marginal cost. Since segment A is willing to purchase channel 1 at a price of $20 or less, it would make sense to offer channel 1 at a price of $20. Segment B would not pay more than $12 for channel 1 alone but would pay up to $24 for the two channels together. If the price of channel 1 alone is set at $20 and the bundle of channels 1 and 2 at $24, total revenue would be $TR = Q_A(\$20) + Q_B(\$24)$ and profit would be $Q_A(\$20 - \$5) + Q_B(\$24 - \$10)$.

Compare this to offering only the bundle at a price of $24. Total profit with pure bundling and a marginal cost of $5 for each channel is

$$TR = Q_A(\$24 - \$10) + Q_B(\$24 - \$10)$$

Cox's profit is higher by offering the **mixed bundle** than it is by offering a pure bundle.

Bundling is, in fact, a rather common pricing strategy. In the travel business, a package consisting of airline travel and rooms in a beach resort will be relatively more attractive to vacationers than to business travelers. Given a choice of airline travel and a package holiday at a somewhat higher price, business travelers are relatively more likely to choose the separate airline travel. Vacationers will prefer the package. Cable television does a great deal of bundling. It offers a "basic" package, which is a bundle of channels, then different packages at additional prices. Procter & Gamble, Gillette, Schick, and other firms bundle products quite regularly. A razor is packaged with shaving cream, laundry detergent with hand soap, and so on. Microsoft's Office bundle contains several programs—Word, Excel, and PowerPoint—as well as an Internet browser. Each could be purchased individually. McDonald's and other fast-food outlets offer different bundles, such as food items and a beverage, for a price that is less than would be the case if the items were purchased separately.

Tying Tying is a form of bundling. *Tying* is a general term referring to any requirement that products be bought or sold in some combination. The buyer of the main product (tying good) agrees to buy one or several complementary goods (tied goods) that are necessary to use the tying good. Often the tying good is a durable, such as a copier, while the tied goods are nondurables, such as toner or paper. Cellular phone companies tie their goods and services—a phone, activation, and the calling service.

Knowing which elements customers focus on can be critical in constructing the right ties among goods and pricing the tied products correctly. If the customer is more price-sensitive to one aspect of the bundle than another, then the firm will want to price accordingly. It will want to attract the buyers to the good to which they are price-sensitive by making that good appear to have a low price.

Cannibalization When a firm produces or offers for sale more than one good or service, it must set the price and the quantity it produces and/or offers for sale of each good or service by taking into account the effects of the price and quantity on all of its goods and services. Consider the case of a firm that produces two interdependent products, A and B; sales of one affect sales of the other. The marginal revenue associated with a change in the quantity sold of product A is composed of two parts: the change in total revenue for product A associated with a marginal increase (or decrease) in the quantity sold of product A and the change in total revenue for product B associated with a marginal increase (or decrease) in the quantity sold of product A. Similarly, the marginal revenue for product B consists of two parts. The interdependency between A and B can be positive, negative, or zero. If the two products under consideration are complements, then an increase in the quantity sold of one product will result in an increase in total revenue for the other product. If the products are substitutes, then an increase in the quantity sold of one product will result in a decrease in total revenue for the other product.

As an illustration, suppose Procter & Gamble (P&G) has identified two segments in the market for its laundry detergent, single people and families. Suppose that P&G produces two different-sized packages of detergent, 5 ounce and 10 ounce. Let's also assume that the marginal cost of laundry detergent is constant at 10 cents per ounce and that there are no other costs.

If P&G did something like set the price of the 5-ounce bottle at $2.50 and the 10-ounce bottle at $6, a family would substitute the smaller bottles for the larger one. In marketing language, the small bottle would *cannibalize* the demand for the large bottle. **Cannibalization** occurs when sales of one product produced by a firm reduce the demand for another product produced by that same firm.

The reason that cannibalization occurs is that P&G has no way to separate the two market segments—that is, to distinguish families from singles. Accordingly, P&G must design and price the two bottles so that families voluntarily choose the large bottle. P&G sets its quantities and prices where $MR_A = MC = MR_B$. The complication is that the two products are interdependent. This means that sales of the small bottle affect the large bottle and vice versa. The marginal revenue equals marginal cost rule thus takes the form:

$$MR_A + MR_{AB} = MC = MR_B + MR_{BA}$$

where MR_{AB} represents the effect of sales of product B on the marginal revenue of product A and vice versa for MR_{BA}.

As another example, consider the Gillette Company, which sells razors, razor blades, toiletries, cosmetics, stationery products, Braun personal care appliance products, Braun household appliances, and Oral-B preventive dentistry products. Its razors and blades include Sensor, Altra, Trac II, Good News, and Daisy Plus, and each of the other divisions includes several different brands. There is probably no interdependence between pens and electric shavers, but there is between the Altra and Trac II razors. In fact, when Gillette introduced the Sensor in the United States in 1990, sales of the Trac II razor declined. Gillette had to take the cannibalization effect into consideration when deciding how to price its new Trac II razors.

Multiple Products The profit-maximizing strategy for firms with multiple products is quite straightforward—find the point where $MR_i = MC$ for all *i*; that is, for each product, set the price where the product's marginal revenue is equal to the firm's marginal cost.

Supermarkets illustrate this strategy quite well. Shelf space can be allocated among a wide variety of product categories, such as meat, dairy products, canned goods, frozen foods, and produce. The supermarket is obviously providing multiple products. It maximizes profit by setting $MR = MC$ for each product. Suppose that for one product marginal revenue is less than the marginal cost and for another marginal revenue is greater than the marginal cost. Clearly, it would make sense to increase the production of the second at the expense of the first. This is what supermarkets have done by adding higher-profit-margin categories such as delicatessens, in-store bakeries, and floral departments and reducing the shelf space assigned to lower-profit-margin items.

Joint Products

Rather than producing several alternative products, firms often produce joint products—products that are interdependent in the production process instead of at the consumer level. A change in the production of one causes a change in the cost or availability of the other. Examples include the production of liquid oxygen and nitrogen from air, beef and hides from steers, and gasoline and fuel oil from crude oil.

When joint products are produced in fixed proportions, they should be analyzed as a product package. In such a case, the costs incurred in production of the package of goods can not be assigned to the individual products. This means that the quantity of output and the price is determined by setting marginal revenue equal to marginal cost rather than finding the individual product marginal revenues and marginal costs and setting these equal.

Profit Centers and Transfer Prices

Firms are often organized in terms of profit centers. Each profit center will make the decisions that maximize the profits of that part of the firm. One difficulty with this organizational form occurs when goods or services are transferred from one profit center to another. Let's consider the case of one division selling to another. At Chevron/Texaco, the procurement division, called Supplier Management & Integration (SM&I) provides services to the other divisions—it handles purchases of supplies for each of the divisions. What price does the SM&I division sell its services to the other divisions for? At Intel, the commodity management division is the middleman between the factory and the buyer, the original equipment manufacturer or OEM. What price does the division charge for its service of managing the distribution and inventory of Intel products? A transfer price must be determined—the price at which one product or service is transferred from one profit center to another.

If the goods or services offered by SM&I at Chevron/Texaco or Commodity Management at Intel could also be offered to any firm, then we say there is an external market for the service. If the companies restrict the goods or services to be utilized only by other divisions in the firm, we say there is only an internal market. If there is an external market, the transfer price is easy to determine; it is the same price as the profit-maximizing price in the external market. But if there is no external market for the intermediate product—what one division sells to another cannot be sold to other firms—then what is the transfer price?

The transfer price is determined by setting the marginal cost to the firms of producing and selling the product equal to the marginal revenue. Suppose there are two divisions and one supplies an intermediate product to the other. Then the marginal cost to the firm is the sum of the marginal costs in each division. By equating the sum of the marginal costs to marginal revenue, the firm's profit-maximizing prices and quantities are determined. In both Chevron/Texaco and Intel, the division services are sold only in the internal market and in both cases a fixed annual fee is charged for the services. The problem with this arrangement is that if the downstream divisions determine that the fee they pay is too costly, they may choose to forego the service by using a less efficient method of obtaining the service. What the companies need to do is find the marginal cost of each division and set it to the marginal revenue. So if SM&I has a marginal cost for each transaction, then the company should sum that marginal cost along with the marginal costs of the downstream division's activities to the firm's marginal revenue to determine the efficient price.

Interdependencies Among Firms

What we have discussed to this point are situations in which a firm is defining its price strategy independent of what other firms do. In most markets, firms can't act so independently. This is what the oligopoly market structure represents: What one firm does affects how others behave. In these situations we say that the firms are interdependent and that they undertake strategic decision making.

As you might suspect, determining an equilibrium price and quantity is not always easy when firms are interdependent. The final equilibrium price and quantity will depend on the number of firms in the market, the information available to each firm, the payoffs, the strategies selected by each rival, and whether or not owners of firms act independently or cooperate.

In introducing oligopoly in Chapter 6, we presented two illustrations of interdependence—the kinked demand curve and the prisoner's dilemma. The kinked demand curve illustrates what could happen when rival firms follow price decreases but not price increases. The prisoner's dilemma illustrates a more complex interdependency—firms undertake their actions after predicting the actions of rivals.

Let's consider a potential price war between two office supply superstores, Staples and Office Max. Each store has a core of loyal customers, but there is also a group that is price-sensitive. The firms are considering how to set the price of a popular item. Through market research, the companies know how they will do if they respond to the other's pricing in a certain way. But each must set the price now and advertise the price without knowing what the other company will do. Depending on what both firms do, they will earn more or less profit. The results are shown in Figure 8.3.

If Staples selects a lower price and so does Office Max, then Office Max earns 70 and Staples, 80. (We don't specify what 70 or 80 mean, just that more is better than less.) If Staples selects the lower price and Office Max the higher price, then Staples earns 100 and Office Max only 40. If Staples sets the higher price while Office Max sets the lower, then Office Max gains the most. If both stores select the higher price, then both do well. Clearly, they would be better off if they would each select the higher price. But, not knowing what the other will do, neither wants to be the higher-price store while the other takes the major portion of the market. Thus, each looks at the payoffs and decides the other is likely to select the lower price. Choosing lower yields a better result in each case than choosing higher, assuming the other store also chooses low.

Figure 8.3

PRICE WAR

Office Max finds that a lower price is its best choice no matter what Staples does. Staples similarly finds that the lower price is its best choice as well.

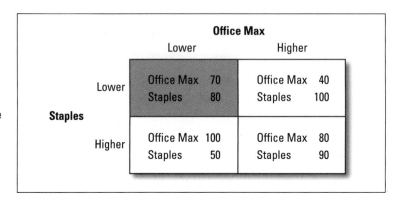

The solution in the upper left portion of the matrix indicates that each firm gains less revenue than if the two each set a higher price. The firms are caught in what is called a dilemma.

The firms could get out of this dilemma and increase profits by cooperating. For instance, they might agree to set the higher prices, that is, to "fix" prices. The problem is that in the United States and in most of the industrial nations it is illegal to fix prices. Thus, the firms must figure out a way to create the same result but not by explicit price fixing.

One way to "implicitly" fix prices is to set up a **meet-the-competition clause,** a situation where the company has the option to meet any offer the customer receives from a rival firm. This reduces the incentive for one firm to attempt to steal customers from another. The meet-the-competition clause is seen in such phrases as "We can't be undersold" and "Low price guarantee." The firm tells the customers that if they find a price that is lower at any other store, the firm will match the price. Rivals, knowing that each will match the prices of the other, have no incentive to offer a lower price; and since offering a higher price will result in loss of sales, the firms tend to keep the same prices.

Another method to avoid price fixing and still end up with a fixed price is called a **most-favored-customer clause.** This ensures the customer that it will get the best price the company gives to anyone. If another customer receives a lower price, then all most-favored customers will get the lower price as well. When the firm has a most-favored customer policy, it is better able to withstand pressure to lower prices. The firm informs the customer that "I'd really like to give you a lower price, but I can't. If I do, I have to give everyone the lower price."

How do firms change prices when they are implicitly fixing prices? Sometimes firm rivalry evolves to a situation in which one firm becomes the price leader. What that firm does is then followed by others in the industry. In the Staples and Office Max example, if Office Max was the price leader, it would set the higher price, which would then be matched by Staples. Each would be better off by cooperating in this way than by indulging in a price war. The leaders in cases of price leadership vary. In the airline industry, leaders are often the largest companies, but in some cases they are the new upstart firms. Often you will observe one airline testing the waters to see if it could be the leader; it raises price and if others don't follow it lowers price back to the original level.

CASE REVIEW *Pricing Chips*

How is it possible for a lower price to be a problem for a firm, even to be the cause of the firm's failure? Why did the consultants determine that the problem with the local tortilla chip firm was its low price? The Phoenix tortilla chip maker altered its product, lowering quality. In essence, this act had the effect of actually increasing the cost to the consumer. Even though the price did not change, the quality of the chip did. A constant price for a lower-quality product is, in essence, a higher price. If consumer demand is price-elastic, the higher real price means lower sales and lower revenue. Had the Phoenix chip maker been able to maintain both its quality and its price, it would not have had the problem competing with Frito-Lay that it did. One strategy the Phoenix chip maker might have taken would have been to separate the market into different price elasticities of demand by positioning its chips as the high-quality chip. This less elastic niche might have enabled the Phoenix firm to maintain profitability. Another strategy might have been to offer two chips, one a lower-quality chip and one a high-quality chip, thereby appealing to both sets of customers.

Why would equal price increases on two products lead consumers to purchase more of the higher-priced product and less of the relatively lower-priced product? The national brand increased its price 30 cents, from $1.59 to $1.89, while the local company also increased its price 30 cents, from $1.29 to $1.59. The difference is that the price increase from $1.59 to $1.89 is a 19 percent increase whereas from $1.29 to $1.59 it is a 23 percent increase. The larger percentage increase means a larger percentage change in quantity demanded. The higher-priced firm increased prices relatively less than the lower-priced firm and thereby took market share from the lower-priced firm.

SUMMARY

1. When a firm sells just one product, it will maximize profit by setting a single or uniform price where marginal revenue equals marginal cost as long as customers cannot be separated according to price sensitivity.
2. When customers or customer segments can be separated by price elasticity of demand and when resale between and among customers can be avoided, the firm can increase profit by price discrimination, which is often called price customization or personalized pricing.
3. The auction has become a much more prevalent mechanism for exchanging goods and services as a result of the Internet. While the Internet has changed most businesses, the prevalence of auctions has not turned every market into a perfectly competitive one. The importance of differentiation has become more evident as firms look to ways to get greater control over price.
4. The Internet has made personalized pricing much more prevalent because firms are able to learn more about customers and their likes and dislikes.
5. There are various forms of price discrimination. Third-degree price discrimination essentially separates customers into two groups. Perfect price discrimination personalizes price to the extent that each customer pays a different price. Second degree price discrimination sets different prices on different quantities of a good or service.

6. The profit-maximizing rule for price discrimination is to set a price at which the marginal revenues for the market segments are equal and are also equal to marginal cost.
7. Product-line extension is a form of discrimination—providing a slightly different version of the same product at a different price. The profit-maximizing rule is to set the price where the marginal revenue of each product equals the marginal cost of each.
8. Peak-load pricing is a form of price discrimination whereby different prices exist for different times of the day or different periods of time. The profit-maximizing rule for peak-load pricing is to set the price where the marginal revenue of each time period equals the marginal cost of each time period.
9. Cost-plus pricing is the practice of setting a price based on a markup above costs. The cost-plus pricing strategy is a profit-maximizing strategy if the markup is equal to $[1/(1 - 1/e)] - 1$ and is based on the marginal cost.
10. Bundling is the practice of offering more than one good or service in a package for a single price.
11. Pure bundling is the practice of offering only the package of bundled goods for purchase. Mixed bundling is the practice of offering both of the bundled products in one package and at least some of the products in the bundle individually.
12. *Tying* is a general term referring to the practice of pricing and selling combinations of complementary products.
13. Cannibalization occurs when sales of one product offered by a firm reduce the sales of another product offered by that same firm.
14. Pricing strategies become more complex when there are interdependencies among firms.
15. Pricing interdependencies can be illustrated quite well by the prisoner's dilemma. In a prisoner's dilemma, players become trapped in a second-best solution. The only way to get out of the dilemma is to have repeated interactions and/or to change the payoff.
16. A price war may result if the cooperative arrangements arrived at in order to get out of a dilemma break down as one party attempts to cheat on the others.
17. Joint products refer to the production process: Production of one product also results in production of other products.
18. A transfer price is the price at which one division in a firm provides a good or service to another division in that same firm. The optimal transfer price is determined by equating the external marginal revenue to the divisions' marginal costs.
19. In every case, the profit-maximizing strategy is to set marginal revenue equal to marginal cost. The trick is to appropriately define the marginal revenue and marginal costs of different products, combinations of products, or production processes.

KEY TERMS

personalized pricing
customized
perfect price discrimination
second- or third-degree price discrimination
product-line extension

peak-load pricing
cost-plus pricing
full-cost pricing
limit price
predatory pricing
pure bundling

mixed bundle
tying
cannibalization
meet-the-competition clause
most-favored-customer clause

EXERCISES

1. Explain why marginal revenue is less than or equal to price. How does the difference between price and marginal revenue depend on the price elasticity of demand?

2. Why would a firm not want to price at the point where marginal revenue is greater than marginal cost?

3. Many supermarkets sell both branded and private-label goods. Suppose that a supermarket estimates that the demand for its private-label cola is less elastic than the demand for Coca-Cola. How should it price its private-label cola?

4. An engineer has discovered a way to improve the production of a microchip to reduce its marginal cost from $1 to $0.80. Should the firm reduce the selling price of the microchip by $0.20?

5. Magazines are sold both on newsstands and by subscription. Advertising accounts for up to one-half of the revenues of magazines such as *Time* and *Sports Illustrated* and advertising depends on the number of subscriptions. How should a publisher determine the subscription price relative to newsstand price?

6. Some personal computer software is sold at special discounts to students. Other software is provided in a less powerful version for students. Why do publishers offer discounts to students? What is the purpose of developing less powerful editions?

7. Using the kinked demand model, explain why a decrease in costs might not lead to a change in price or output.

8. At one time a major U.S. airline proposed that all airlines adopt a uniform fare schedule based on mileage. Doing so would have eliminated the many different fares that were available at the time. Most major airlines applauded the suggestion and began to adopt the plan. Soon, however, various airlines began cutting fares. Explain this occurrence using the prisoner's dilemma.

9. When one airline announced a substantial reduction in domestic airfares, within a day, other airlines announced similar price cuts. What would you expect the outcome of this price war to be?

10. Stargazer Recordings sells compact discs in two markets. The marginal cost of each disc is $2. Demand in each market is given by $Q_1 = 40 - 10P_1$ and $Q_2 = 40 - 2P_2$ where Q is thousands of compact discs.

   a. If the firm uses price discrimination, how much output should it produce and what price should

it charge? What is its profit? What type of price discrimination is it using?

   b. If the firm cannot prevent resale of compact discs, what will its profit be?

11. A major airline estimates that the demand and marginal revenue functions for first-class and excursion fares from New York to Paris are:

   First class: $P = 4,200 - 2Q$ $MR = 4,200 - 4Q$

   Excursion: $P = 2,200 - 0.25Q$ $MR = 2,200 - 0.5Q$

   If the marginal cost of flying is $200 per passenger, what fare and what number of passengers will maximize profit? Show that profit is greater than if the airline used a single or uniform price.

12. Airline pricing is a good example of price discrimination. Airlines set different prices for first class and excursion. Suppose the economics division of a major airline company estimates that the demand and marginal revenue functions for first-class and excursion fares from Los Angeles to Beijing are:

   First Class   **Excursion**

   $Q_A = 2,100 - 0.5P_A$ $Q_B = 8,800 - 4P_B$
   $MR_A = 4,200 - 4Q_A$ $MR_B = 2,200 - 0.5Q_B$

   a. If the marginal cost of production is $200 per passenger, what fare and what number of passengers will maximize profit? (Profit is maximized by setting prices such that $MR_A = MR_B = MC$.)

   b. Would the airline make more profit by charging a single price? (If a single price is to be set, the demand equations from each market segment have to be combined.)

13. A health club where most people want to work out before 8:00 A.M. and after 4:00 P.M. must determine its pricing structure. As the manager, you have to set membership prices so as to best utilize your facilities and maximize profit. Demand varies throughout the day and, according to your best estimate, is as follows:

   Monday–Friday, 6:00 A.M. – 8:00 A.M.; 4:00 P.M. – 9:00 P.M.

   $$Q_1 = 1000 - 10,000P_1$$

   All other days and times

   $$Q_2 = 1000 - 20,000P_2$$

   where Q is minutes and P is the price per minute. So, considering the weekday schedule, how many hours should be peak and how many off-peak and what price should be charged for each? If the marginal cost of providing facilities is given by

$$MC = 0.02 + 0.0001Q$$

what are the profit-maximizing prices to charge?

14. Suppose that a single firm producing and then selling a product has decided it must enable the divisions to be profit centers. This means that a price must be determined for the product when it is transferred from the production division to the marketing division. The marketing division's total cost function is

$$C_m = 300,000 + 10Q_m$$

The production division's total cost function is

$$C_p = 500,000 + 15Q_p + 0.005Q_p^2$$

where Q_p is the quantity produced and sold. The marginal cost per unit to the firm, MC, is equal to the sum of the marginal costs of production, MC_p, and marketing, MC_m. The marginal cost of production is

$$MC_p = 15 + 0.01Q_p$$

The marginal cost of marketing is

$$MC_m = 10$$

Combining these gives the marginal cost of producing and then marketing a product: $MC = 25 + .01Q_m$. The marketing division's marginal revenue is

$$MR = 100 - .002Q_m$$

Find the transfer price that will maximize overall firm profit.

CHAPTER NOTES

1. Robert J. Dolan and Hermann Simon, *Power Pricing* (New York: Free Press, 1996), p. 5.
2. "Pricing Society Survey Reveals That Price Setting Is Driven by Increased Competition and Customer Haggling," *PR Newswire*, March 12, 2002; "Transfer Pricing Still Ranks as Most Important International Tax Issue According to New Ernst & Young Survey," *Business Wire*, November 28, 2001; Garret Van Ryzin, "Survey-Mastering Management: The Brave New World of Pricing," *Financial Times* (London), October 16, 2000, Monday Surveys MMC1 Pg. 6.
3. K. Clancy and R. Shulman, *Marketing Myths That Are Killing Businesses: The Cure for Death Wish Marketing* (New York: McGraw-Hill, 1994).
4. Ibid., p. 46
5. Quoted in Keith Reid, "The Science of Pricing," *NPN International* 5, no. 2 (March 2000): 33–35.
6. The firm is attempting to collect the consumer surplus.
7. S. Godin and C. Conley, *Business Rules of Thumb* (New York: Warner Books, 1987), p. 58; and Dolan and Simon, *Power Pricing*.
8. Profit is maximized by setting marginal revenue equal to marginal cost. Marginal revenue is given by $MR = P(1 - 1/e)$, where e is the price elasticity of demand [if the absolute value of e is used, then the term in parentheses is $(1+1/e)$]. So, $MR = MC$ is
    $$P(1 - 1/e) = MC$$
    Solving for P gives us a cost-plus pricing rule that is in fact based on profit maximization:
    $$P = MC[1/(1 - 1/e)].$$
    The cost plus markup pricing rule is
    $$P = MC(1 + markup)$$
9. Interestingly, odd pricing is often thought to be not an application of framing but rather an attempt to trick consumers or to control employee theft. A best-selling marketing textbook, *Marketing: Concepts and Strategies* by William M. Pride and O. C. Ferrell (Boston: Houghton Mifflin, 1995), p. 649, notes that "Odd pricing assumes that more of a product will be sold at $99.99 than at $100. Supposedly, customers will think, or at least tell friends, that the product is a bargain—not $100 but $99, plus a few insignificant pennies." Odd pricing is also explained as an attempt to exploit a psychological bias in T. T. Nagle and R. K. Holden, (New York: Prentice Hall, 1995), p. 300: "The belief is that buyers perceive the odd-numbers as significantly lower than the slightly higher round numbers that they approximate." While this rationale seems appealing, it assumes that consumers are pretty dense—that they do not learn from mistakes. Perhaps seeing an odd price once might induce consumers to think that the price was actually a lower number, but wouldn't they eventually learn?

    The second rationale of odd pricing—more folktale than academic explanation—is that odd pricing is used to minimize employee thefts. The origination of odd pricing is attributed to Macy's around 1862. Early corporate historians stated that the reason Macy's used odd pricing was to control theft by clerks. When a customer gave a clerk an even amount of currency in payment for an item with an odd price, the clerk would have to make change at the cashier's desk, thus reducing the opportunity of pocketing funds.

10. Clinton V. Oster Jr. and John S. Strong, "Predatory Practices in the U.S. Airline Industry," (January 2001), (ostpxweb.dot.gov/aviation/domestic-competition/predpractices.pdf), and U.S. Department of Transportation, Domestic Competition Series, "Dominated Hub Fares," January 2001. Washington D.C.: Government Printing Office(ostpxweb.dot.gov/aviation/domestic-competition/hubpaper.pdf)

11. Predatory pricing could be the basis for antitrust action. In 1999, the Department of Justice's antitrust division filed suit against American Airlines for predatory pricing at its Dallas–Fort Worth hub, where it carried 77 percent of all nonstop passengers at the time the suit was filed. During the 1990s, new airlines such as Vanguard, Sun Jet, and Western Pacific occasionally offered stiff competition on flights to second-tier cities such as Wichita, Kansas City, and Colorado Springs. In each case, American responded by drastically cutting its fares until the fledgling was driven from the route. Then American raised fares and reduced service to accommodate the declining number of passengers. The suit was dismissed by the judge because it was not proven that American was selling below average variable cost.

Inverse Demand and Marginal Revenue

Often, profit maximization requires us to use the inverse demand function in order to derive marginal revenue. If the demand function is written $Q = f(P)$, the inverse demand function is $P = g(Q)$. Then total revenue is $PQ = g(Q)Q$, which allows us to find marginal revenue $\partial TR/\partial Q$. We have to use the inverse demand function since marginal revenue is $\partial TR/\partial Q$, not $\partial TR/\partial P$; in other words, we have to have demand defined in terms of Q.

Suppose that demand is $Q = 40 - 10P$. The inverse demand function is $P = 4 - 0.1Q$. Total revenue is found by multiplying the inverse demand by Q:

$$PQ = 4Q - 0.1Q^2$$

Now we can derive marginal revenue, $\partial TR/\partial Q$:

$$MR = 4 - 0.2Q$$

Just for completeness, let's assume that marginal cost is \$2 and then solve for the profit maximizing quantity and price. Setting $4 - 0.2Q = \$2$ yields $0.2Q_1 = 2$, so that $Q = 10$. Substitute $Q = 10$ into the demand equation:

$$10 = 40 - 10P$$
$$P = \$3$$

Let's consider some examples of pricing problems using the inverse demand function.

Price Discrimination

Airline pricing is a good example of third-degree price discrimination. Airlines set different prices for first-class and excursion fares. Suppose the economics division of a major airline company estimates that the demand and marginal revenue functions for first-class and excursion fares from Los Angeles to Beijing are as follows.

First Class	**Excursion**
$Q_A = 2,100 - 0.5P_A$	$Q_B = 8,800 - 4P_B$
$MR_A = 4,200 - 4Q_A$	$MR_B = 2,200 - 0.5Q_B$

If the marginal cost of production is \$200 per passenger, what fare and what number of passengers will maximize profit?

Profit is maximized by setting prices such that $MR_A = MR_B = MC$.

$$MR_A = 4,200 - 4Q_A = 200$$

which implies that $Q_A = 1,000$.

$$MR_B = 2,200 - 0.5Q_B = 200$$

which implies that $Q_B = 4,000$.

Prices are obtained by substituting the profit-maximizing quantities into the demand equations. This gives $P_A = \$2,200$ per passenger and $P_B = \$1,200$ per passenger.

This is the price-discriminating result. It requires that the airline can segment the market into the two groups and that the two customer segments cannot exchange with each other—in other words, that arbitrage cannot occur. Does price discrimination generate more profit than a single uniform price?

If a single price is to be set, the demand equations from each market segment have to be combined. Expressing the demand in terms of Q and then adding the two together yields $Q = 10,900 - 4.5P$. Marginal revenue is $(10,900/4.5) - (2/4.5)Q$. Equating marginal revenue and marginal cost gives $Q = 5,000$ passengers. Substituting this into the total demand function yields $P = 5900/4.5 = \$1,311$. Thus if a single uniform price of $1,311 is charged, profit is $\$6,555,556 - \$1,000,000 = \$5,555,556$, which is less than the $6 million obtained under price discrimination.

The approach of solving for the inverse demand function and then total revenue is used to solve most pricing problems, including all forms of price discrimination and transfer pricing.

Transfer Pricing

Suppose that for a single firm, the sales division's total cost function is

$$C_s = 150,000 + 20Q_s$$

and the manufacturing division's total cost function is

$$C_m = 100,000 + 25Q_m + 0.01Q_m^2$$

where Q_s is the quantity produced and sold. The marginal cost per unit to the firm, MC, is equal to the sum of the marginal costs of manufacturing, MC_m, and sales, MC_s. The marginal cost of manufacturing is

$$MC_m = 25 + 0.02Q_m$$

and the marginal cost of sales is

$$MC_m = 20$$

Combining these gives the marginal cost of manufacturing and then selling the product:

$$MC = 45 + 0.02Q_m$$

Suppose the sales division's marginal revenue is

$$MR = 200 - 0.002Q_s$$

Setting MC equal to MR, we obtain

$$45 + 0.02Q_s = 200 - 0.002Q_s$$

Solving, we obtain $Q_s = 7,045$ units. Because $Q_m = Q_s$, the output for the manufacturing division is also 7,045 units. Therefore the optimal transfer price is equal to the marginal manufacturing cost at the output level of 7,045 units, or

$$P = MC_m = 25 + 0.02(7,045) = \$161 \text{ per unit}$$

If there is a market outside the firm for the product that is transferred from one division to another, the output levels of the divisions do not have to be the same. Consider a firm with an extraction division (mining or oil extraction) that provides product to the manufacturing division. Then, if the manufacturing division wants more of the product provided by the extraction division than it is allocated internally, it can purchase some from the external market; if the manufacturing division has more of the extraction material than it wants, it can sell it to other firms.

Suppose the demand for the manufactured product is:

$$P_m = 200 - 0.5Q_m$$

and the total cost, excluding the cost of the extracted product, is

$$TC_m = 400 + 10Q_m$$

The extraction division's total cost is

$$TC_e = 40 + 8Q_e + 0.2Q_e^2$$

Now let's assume there is a perfectly competitive market for the extracted product and that the market price is \$30. The extraction division can sell all of the extracted product for \$30. Thus, its marginal revenue is \$30. Since its marginal cost is

$$MC = 8 + 0.4Q_e$$

we can set $MC = MR$

$$30 = 8 + 0.4Q_e$$

which means that $Q_e = 55$. Thus the extraction division should extract 55 units. The transfer price is found by equating the manufacturing division's marginal cost to the marginal revenue. The marginal cost of the manufacturing division is the sum of its marginal cost excluding the cost of the extracted product and the marginal cost of the extracted product, \$30:

$$MC_m = 10 + 30 = 40$$

The marginal revenue is derived from the demand function:

$$P_m = 50 - 0.5Q_m$$

Since total revenue is $P_m Q_m = 50Q_m - 0.5Q_m^2$, marginal revenue is $50 - Q_m$. Thus, $MR_m = MC_m$ is $40 = 50 - Q_m$ and $Q_m = 10$. Thus, the manufacturing division should sell 10 units. The extraction division should extract 55 units, selling 10 to the manufacturing division and the remainder in the external market. All product should be sold at the same price, \$30.

Peak Load Pricing

A peak load problem is a form of price discrimination—charging a different price for the same product when that product is sold at different times. For instance, suppose a firm's IT director must allocate computer time, CPUs, in the most efficient manner. The firm has been experiencing problems because during certain times of the day, the system is more than fully utilized and often crashes. But at other times, mostly evenings, there is excess capacity. The director has chosen to allow use prices to allocate the scarce computer time. Demand for CPU time is as follows:

Nights after 9:00 P.M.: $P_n = 0.2 - 0.0005Q_n$
Days: $P_d = 0.8 - 0.0005Q_d$

The marginal cost of providing the computer time is given by $MC = 0.02 + 0.0001Q$, and this does not vary according to time of day.

The profit-maximizing prices and quantities are found by setting $MR = MC$ for each period. For days, total revenue is

$$P_dQ_d = 0.8Q_n - 0.0005Q_d^2$$

Marginal revenue is

$$MR_d = 0.8 - 0.001Q_d$$

Profit maximization is found where $MR = MC$:

$$0.8 - 0.001Q_d = 0.02 + .0001Q_d$$

Since $Q_d = 0.78/0.0011$, the price is

$$P_d = 0.8 - 0.0005(709) = 0.55$$

For nights, total revenue is

$$P_nQ_n = 0.2Q_n - 0.0005Q_n^2$$

Marginal revenue is

$$MR_n = 0.2 - 0.0002Q_n$$

Setting $MR_n = MC$,

$$0.2 - 0.002Q_n = 0.02 + .0001Q_n$$
$$Q_n = 0.18/0.0021$$

Substituting into demand, we find the price:

$$P_n = 0.2 - 0.0005(85.7) = 0.16$$

So, the answer is to charge $0.16 per unit at night and $0.55 per unit during the day.

CHAPTER 9

The New Economy:
Technological Change and Innovation

CASE *Winner-Takes-All*

About 35 percent of US households and 17 percent of European ones are active Internet users. In the United States, two main broadband technologies, digital subscriber line (DSL) and cable, which deliver applications such as teleconferencing, interactive entertainment, and distance learning, are being adopted in households and businesses around the country. Both technologies rely on wires originally laid down for other purposes. DSL travels over ordinary copper telephone lines, which span the "last mile" from a telephone company's local service office to the home. Cable runs through coaxial cables, which have delivered pay television to many U.S. homes for at least three decades.

Although both technologies will probably claim meaningful market share eventually, the question of which will take the lead—especially in higher-margin market segments—is of no small concern to the companies that have staked large bets on the outcome. AT&T, for example, spent tens of billions of dollars to acquire cable systems across the United States, while incumbent telephone companies such as SBC Communications have invested heavily in upgrading their networks to accommodate DSL. In Europe, fewer households have access to the Internet, so many homes not yet connected to it will move straight to broadband. And because cable television in Europe has never approached the popularity that it enjoys in the United States, Europe lacks an extensive cable network. Where cable systems do exist, they are often owned by the very telephone companies that control the only other wire into the home. This monopoly has made it possible for such companies to delay carrying out the upgrade required for broadband access through either medium, thus allowing other technologies—particularly satellites and ground-based microwave receivers—to become serious contenders.

What will be the end result? Will one technology dominate, become a winner-takes-all, or will a patchwork of different technologies emerge?

What Is the *New* Economy

Phrases such as *the New Economy, e-commerce, e-business,* and other *e*-words suggest that something major has been going on. For many, whatever has been happening is earth-shattering. Business gurus have told us that the *New Economy* means that nothing we are used to will remain in the future. A headline in the *Wall Street Journal* on January 1, 2000, announced: SO LONG SUPPLY AND DEMAND. In that same issue of the *Wall Street Journal,* others declared that "conventional economics is dead." The management guru Peter Drucker stated that "the axiom of scarcity does not apply to information." The novelist Saul Bellow said that ". . . mankind has been fighting scarcity since the beginning of time. There does seem to be some possibility that the war with scarcity is tapering off. There will be enough for everyone." The editors of the *Wall Street Journal* also noted that "products used in networks increase in value as supply rises, thereby contradicting the old economics of supply and demand."

The **New Economy** refers to the technological changes that have occurred in information processing and management. As has always been the case, technological change alters the face of business but does not change human nature. *Scarcity is and always will be with us—it is simply part of the human spirit to want more than is available.* This means that the laws of economics also will always be applicable. How they apply may vary over time, but they will apply.

Notwithstanding this point, it does appear that something was different in the 1990s. Firms that had never made a profit were valued very highly on Wall Street. Firms not in existence prior to 1990 were more valuable than firms that were once referred to as the stalwarts of the economy. The five best stock market performers in the 1980s are listed below, along with the percentage change in the price of their stocks over the decade. Following that list is a list of the top five performers for the decade of the 1990s.

1980s Top Performers

Company	% Change
1. Circuit City	8,252
2. Limited	6,100
3. Hasbro	5,582
4. Home Depot	4,997
5. Wal-Mart	4,032

1990s Top Performers

Company	% Change
1. AOL	79,630
2. Dell	72,445
3. EMC	69,638
4. Cisco	64,498
5. CMGI	61,187

The difference in percentage changes is staggering: 8,000 versus 80,000. The top businesses in the 1980s were retailers that were innovative in store design, inventory control, pricing, or styles, while the top performers in the 1990s were firms involved with computers and the Internet.

Technological Changes and the Supply Chain

The technological changes in information processing that occurred in the 1990s have altered the business landscape in two ways. First, the supply chains of many businesses were destroyed or decomposed. Look at encyclopedias, for instance. The *Encyclopaedia Britannica* went from a 1989 peak of $650 million in revenue and a sales force of 2,300 to a point where it won't release financial figures and has only about 300 employees. What happened? Technological change totally altered the encyclopedia business. The content of encyclopedias is provided online, making the door-to-door sales force obsolete. And encyclopedias are not alone; virtually every supply chain has been and is being affected by the technological changes occurring in information processing and communication.

Consider Figure 9.1, showing part of the supply chain of a newspaper. Journalists and advertisers sent their articles and advertisements to copyeditors and then to the editors, to the printing press, to delivery, and finally to the customer. But in the wake of technological changes, the supply chain may change. Many newspapers and magazines offer online versions so that readers can forego the hard copy of the material.

Prior to the 1990s, a sales force, a system of branches, a printing press, a chain of stores, or a delivery fleet could serve as strategic assets in creating barriers to entry. In the New Economy, these often became liabilities. For example, in banking, people used to have to go to the bank building to conduct business. With the advent of automated teller machines (ATMs), people were provided the opportunity not to have to wait in line for a teller to provide service. Now ATMs are also located independently of bank buildings so that consumers can do banking business without even visiting the bank building. Now banking on the Internet is becoming popular. Several firms have created online banks that have no building at all. Today, people can do all their banking from home via the Internet.

Many different types of businesses have been or are being fundamentally altered by these informational changes. Consider the selling of automobiles. Currently, dealerships provide information in showrooms and test drives; they hold inventory and distribute cars; they broker financing; they make a market in secondhand cars; they operate maintenance and repair services. In the New Economy, each of these might be a separate business. Some businesses might specialize in test drives, providing those autos a customer has specified. Distributors might

Figure 9.1

PARTIAL SUPPLY CHAIN FOR A NEWSPAPER

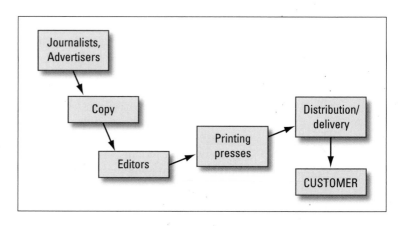

Technological change in the past twenty years has dramatically altered some supply chains. Prior to the advent of wireless communication devices, the purchasing of materials used to require contact with a telephone and fax machine or even hand-to-hand connections between buyer and seller. With wireless communication devices a purchasing agent can fill inventories of stores on the mainland while examining the ocean floors.

have a single warehouse from which the desired car would be shipped. Car purchasers could obtain financing via an auction on an electronic bulletin board. Another approach might be what is called the Dell business model where consumers create the product they desire online. The company then manufactures the product and ships it directly to the consumer.

When the information content of a product can be separated from the physical product, the business will be fundamentally altered by the technological changes. When this occurs, the supply chain is said to have been *decomposed*. The information content of a newspaper no longer has to be tied to the actual physical newspaper; the information content of an automobile purchase does not have to be tied to an auto dealership; the information content of banking does not have to be tied to the physical presence of a bank.

The battles over downloading music illustrates the decomposition of a supply chain and the separation of information from physical product. Napster was a software firm that enabled people to download music for free. Prior to Napster, the supply chain of music was from musician to recording to CD to distribution and sales. The information content (the music) was attached to the physical product (the CD). That attachment is no longer necessary. Thus, the firms cut out of the supply chain believe they are losing out and are fighting that loss. The companies that created, owned, and sold the CDs filed lawsuits to stop Napster; the copyrighted material, claimed Sony and other companies, was being stolen or pirated. Napster was essentially put out of business by the legal ruling that it had to stop providing the service. But because the technology exists to download music and movies, entrepreneurs will figure out ways to provide the service and to make economic profits doing it; in fact, other upstarts took over the business. There is now a flood of downloading opportunities. Even the personal computer (PC) makers—Gateway, Dell, HP/Compaq, and others—pack their machines with software to download music and movies.

Networks

The second major characteristic of the New Economy is the importance of **networks**. What is a network? It can be an alliance of firms or it can refer to a "standard" to which several businesses comply. Examples of networks are the use of alternating current in transporting electricity, local and long-distance telephone services, high-definition television (HDTV), railroad track gauge, computer operating systems, airline routes, Internet service providers (ISPs), smart cards, and international mail. In a network, members can easily interact or communicate with each other but have a more difficult or costly time interacting with those who are not members.

When there is more than one network, then whether members of one network can interact with members of the other networks depends on whether the networks are interconnected. Are the networks mentioned above interconnected? Electricity is; telephones have not been in the sense that a phone number is not portable; rail track is now all the same size in the U.S.; HDTV is not; computer operating systems are not; airline routes are not; ISPs are in some cases (email from one system can connect with other systems, but the connection is not as easy as the communication among members of any given ISP network); smart cards are not; international mail is (you can mail a letter in any nation to someone in a different nation using the stamp of the originating nation and the mail will be delivered).

The Economics of Networks   The economics of networks centers around <u>positive feedback,</u> or what economists call **positive network externalities.** Feedback refers to the idea that the benefits to an individual on joining a network go to every member of the network, not just the member joining.

Suppose that the value of a network to each individual member rises as the number of members rises. Specifically, suppose that value is proportional to the number of users that can interconnect, so that if there are n users, the value of the membership is proportional to $n \times (n - 1) = n^2 - n$. If the value of a network to a single user is $1 for each other user on the network, then a network of size 20 has a value of $(20 \times \$20) - 20 = \$380$. If the value of a network to a single user is $1 for each other user on the network, then a network of size 200 has a value of $(200 \times \$200) - 200 = 40000 - 200 = \$39,800$.

Why would the value of a network rise as the number of members of the network rises? Consider an ISP such as AOL. Suppose AOL had 20,000 members who could communicate easily with each other but could not communicate with anyone else. The value of AOL would be quite small, since very few members would want to communicate only with other members. However, if the membership were 100 million, the value of the membership would be much higher. In a similar vein, consider HDTV. There are several competing standards for transmitting high-definition television. If you purchase a television configured for one standard and then most transmitters choose another standard, the value of your HDTV is very low. You want to be a member of the network having the greatest number of transmitters.

An overview of literature on network externalities is contained in
http://www.utdallas.edu/~liebowit/palgrave/network.html
http://economics.about.com/library/weekly/aa030198.htm

A site linking to many sources related to network economics can be found at
http://www.sims.berkeley.edu/resources/infoecon/Networks.html

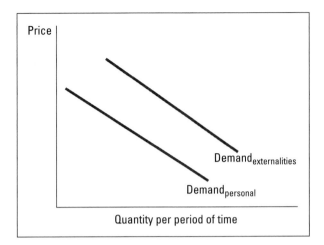

Figure 9.2

THE EXISTENCE OF POSITIVE EXTERNALITIES

The existence of positive externalities can be illustrated by Figure 9.2. Any individual's demand for the minutes of viewing using a certain type of HDTV provider is shown as $Demand_{personal}$. The existence of positive externalities means that each individual receives benefits beyond what each is willing and able to pay—thus, demand with positive externalities is $Demand_{externalities}$. Positive externalities increase the value of the output, that is, increase demand.

The effect of positive feedback in a network and the value of membership in that network as membership increases are illustrated as an outward shift of the demand curve as the network increases, as illustrated in Figure 9.3. With feedback effects, the value of the network to a member rises as the size of the network increases (output increases).

Think about what the existence of positive feedback in a network means. The more members in that network, the greater the value of membership to an additional member. Thus, if, say, an ISP can develop a large membership, it is more likely that additional members will want to join than if that ISP is just starting up or has few members. So the question for businesses in a market where competitors are networks is how to increase the membership in its network.

Figure 9.3

POSITIVE FEEDBACK EFFECTS

The demand for membership in the network or the demand for the output of the network rises as the number of members rises.

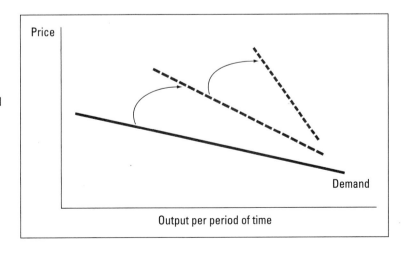

An overview of speculative bubbles, a type of epidemic, can be found at

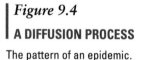

http://www.economymodels.com/bubbles.asp

Tipping: Winner-Takes-All[1] What do Hush Puppies, murders in New York City, cases of syphilis in Baltimore, and sales of electronics have in common with epidemics? They follow the same pattern. In an epidemic, the number of people who contact the disease is initially low. Then at some point the number of victims rises exponentially.

In the early 1990s, Wolverine had determined that its old-line type of shoes, Hush Puppies, had lived past its time. The company decided to discontinue the shoe. But all of a sudden, sales exploded: The company sold 430,000 pairs of the shoes in 1995, four times that in 1996, and in 1997 still more. What had happened?

Crime in New York City had been rising for years—in fact, for decades. In 1992, there were 2,154 murders in New York City and over 600,000 serious crimes. Why then did crime begin to decline; in fact, by 1997, murders had dropped 64 percent to 770 and total crimes had fallen by almost half, to 355,000.

The number of newborns in the city of Baltimore born with syphilis each year had been about the same for decades. But then, between 1995 and 1996 it rose 500 percent. What caused this massive increase?

Sharp introduced the first low-priced fax machine in 1984. It sold only about 80,000 in that first year; sales rose very slowly until in 1987 sales exploded. Radio, then black-and-white television, and then color television all followed the same pattern—being introduced and purchased only very slowly, then catching on and accelerating and finally tapering off.

The pattern followed by these events, illustrated in Figure 9.4, is the same; it is called a diffusion process. The diffusion process shows that few people have the product (or disease) initially. Then some marginal change occurs, causing the take-off. Finally, the epidemic reaches the saturation point, where enough of the potential "victims" are affected that continued rapid growth is not possible.

The emergence of fashion trends, the ebb and flow of crime, the rise of teenage smoking, the adoption of technology, sales of electronics, and many other everyday events share the basic pattern of an epidemic as described by the S-shaped diffusion process of Figure 9.4. While fashion trends and the Black Plague may not seem to have much in common, all such "epidemics" share several elements.

First, they are contagious. A few kids in Manhattan had begun wearing the Hush Puppies just because the shoes were so dated. These kids infected others

Figure 9.4
A DIFFUSION PROCESS

The pattern of an epidemic.

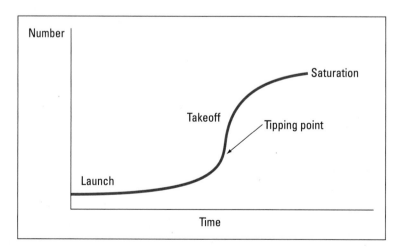

with the Hush Puppies "virus." Teenage and pre-teenage kids want to be different by looking like all the others in their peer groups.

Second, little changes have big effects. *Marginal* matters. All of the possible reasons for the drop in New York's crime rate were changes that happened at the margin; they were incremental changes. The crack trade leveled off, the population got a little older, and the police force got a little better. But the result of these marginal changes was dramatic. Similarly, the human immunodeficiency virus (HIV) had been around for a long time but did not turn into an epidemic until one individual set the epidemic off. These characteristics—contagiousness and the importance of marginal changes—are the same principles that define how measles moves through a grade school classroom, how the flu attacks every winter, and how fads such as the Pokémon cards and games spread among pre-adolescent children.

The name given to that moment in the emergence of an epidemic when the explosion of the numbers infected occurs is the **tipping point.** A situation or a market tips when the acceleration of the diffusion process occurs.

What makes things "contagious" and what situations are likely to tip? Answers to these questions are necessary if we are to understand how to manage in the New Economy.

Whether a market has the potential to tip depends on the tradeoff of positive feedback and variety. The existence of positive feedback effects means that a market could tip. The tradeoff is that when a market does tip, standardization has occurred—choices are reduced. Thus, if people have strong desires for variety, a market is less likely to tip. If a market tips, will just one firm or one network survive, that is, will there be a **winner-takes-all**? Some business gurus and economists say yes, there is a winner-takes-all and the reason is the difference between the old economy and the New Economy. They say that the old economy was driven by economies of scale while the New Economy is driven by the economics of networks.[2] In reality, these differences are much exaggerated. In both the New Economy and the old economy, economies of scale on the supply side, a sufficient size on the demand side (such as caused by positive feedback), and weak or no demand for variety are necessary for a winner-takes-all.

Figure 9.5 illustrates the point. There are economies of scale: The costs per unit of output decline as output rises from zero to output level *A*, and diseconomies of scale occur (costs per unit of output rise) as output rises beyond quantity A. Only if economies of scale persisted throughout the entire market could one firm "own" the market. General Motors experienced economies of scale at the beginning of the twentieth century, yet it was unable to take over the entire market. Why? The reason is that the economies of scale were not large enough to allow just one firm to supply the entire market. You can see in Figure 9.5 that a firm would not produce beyond point *A,* the bottom of the long-run average cost curve. Thus, some other firm or firms would have to enter the market to satisfy demand. There would be no winner-takes-all.

In the case of a network, as the size of the network increases, the demand for the output of the network increases. An online dating service illustrates this well. With just a few people subscribing, the service is not very valuable to any potential new member because it would be very unlikely any member would find a match with any other member. Thus, demand for the service is low. But as membership increases and the probability of a match rises, the value of membership rises. As a result, demand for the service increases. In the numerical example presented in the

An interview with author of *The Tipping Point* is available at http://www.cnn.com/ COMMUNITY/transcripts/ 2000/3/gladwell/

Figure 9.5

ECONOMIES OF SCALE

The firm would not produce beyond point *A*. The market thus ensures room for more than one firm.

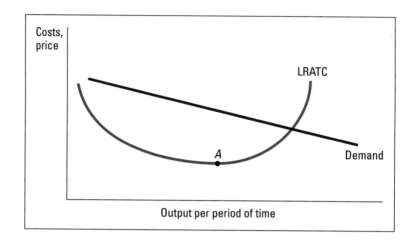

subsection "The Economics of Networks" (see p. 192), the value of the network increases exponentially as users increase linearly. If this type of feedback situation does characterize a network, it implies that it is difficult for a small network to survive. For the same cost of connection, would a user choose the smaller 20-person network or the larger 200-person network? Clearly, a new member would choose the larger network. Another aspect of a network is that it is difficult (costly) for a member to switch to another network. The larger the network, the greater the cost for any one individual user to switch to another network (the opportunity cost of not being connected to the large network). As a result, it would seem that one network would dominate—that there would be a winner-takes-all.

NAV Canada provides civil air navigation services for all of Canada. Imagine what would occur if the air traffic controllers in British Columbia could not communicate with Alberta. It is important that the network of air traffic controllers is interconnected so that one location is able to communicate with another. Thus, when a new technology is introduced in one location, it becomes the dominant technology (winner-takes-all technology), throughout the NAV Canada network.

In 2002 the Canadian Automated Air Traffic System (CAATS) was adopted for landing airplanes. The system was developed by Raytheon Canada; once Raytheon was accepted, no other system or technology was considered in any part of the system.

In Figure 9.6(a) positive feedback and economies of scale both occur. In this case, there would be a winner-takes-all—just one network would survive. But in Figure 9.6(b), the network, represented by the LRATC, does not have sufficient economies of scale to satisfy demand. Thus, several networks would be required—this market would not have a winner-takes-all.

AOL-Time Warner, the largest ISP in 2002, has to compete with MSN, among others. Why hasn't AOL taken the market completely? The primary reason is that there are not sufficient economies of scale. MSN has been able to entice people to join its network by bundling MSN with the Windows software included on virtually every personal computer. Had economies of scale enabled AOL to lower costs, lower prices, and increase the value of membership, it is likely MSN would not have been able to compete. Both economies of scale and positive feedback effects are necessary for a winner-takes-all. Feedback effects alone are not sufficient for a winner-takes-all to emerge.

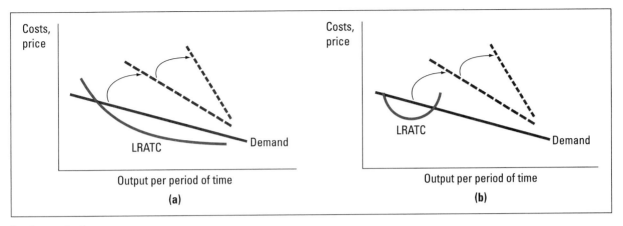

Figure 9.6

WINNER-TAKES-ALL

If demand increases, so that economies of scale persist throughout the market, then one firm or one network will survive. This is shown in (a). If economies of scale are not sufficient to meet the market, as shown in (b), then a winner-takes-all will not arise.

Lock-In, Path Dependence, and Winner-Takes-All Because information goods and information infrastructure often exhibit both demand-side positive feedback and supply-side economies of scale, many people have claimed that the New Economy is synonymous with winner-takes-all. The argument is that there is a **path dependence** to technology; that is, once some historical accident or random event favors some technology, it becomes the standard and is used thereafter even if it is not the most efficient one possible.

One example widely used to illustrate the winner-takes-all argument is the typewriter keyboard, called QWERTY for short (the first letter line on a keyboard is QWERTYUIOP). According to many economists, it is not the most efficient layout in terms of finger movement. Their argument is that manufacturers designed a layout that forced typists to work more slowly because of the tendency of keys to jam on early typewriters.[3] But several decades ago, jamming keys ceased to be a problem and it would have made sense to shift to an alternative, more efficient design. A rival layout, called the Dvořák keyboard, was available and purportedly more efficient. But the standard keyboard was a network that had become **locked-in.** People who had learned on the old keyboard were not about to change to a new one.

Other examples include VHS videotape rather than the *superior* Beta, Windows rather than the *better* Mac system, gas-powered automobiles rather than the *better* steam-powered ones, and light-water nuclear power plants rather than the *better* inert-gas version. These examples are used to support the general view that free markets cannot be relied on to select the best technology. Market winners will be the best of the available alternatives only by the sheerest of coincidences. The first technology that attracts development, the first standard that attracts adopters, or the first product that attracts consumers will tend to have an insurmountable advantage, even over superior rivals that happen to come along later. Many economists argue that in a QWERTY world, markets cannot be trusted.[4] If a product has an established network, it is almost impossible for a new product to displace it. This means that as society gets more advanced technologically, luck will play a larger and larger role and markets will be less and less efficient.

There is no doubt that historical events or accidents can be the marginal event that causes tipping. But this does not mean the epidemic is a case of "extraordinarily bad luck" or is inefficient. Producers of alternative keyboards were motivated to cash in on any successes that alternative systems could generate.[5] Other keyboards did compete with QWERTY; they just couldn't surpass QWERTY. DOS was not the first operating system, but the DOS system was more appropriate for many users given the hardware of the time and the Mac system was far more expensive than DOS. Consumers switched to DOS and then switched away from DOS when they moved to Windows.

If lock-in occurs and it is inefficient, won't entrepreneurs find ways to interconnect networks? Look at email systems. They are not compatible, but software was developed to make them compatible. Consider telephone systems. Although they are not compatible, means have been developed to ensure that a phone call can originate anywhere and go anywhere; thus, telephone mobility across networks is becoming a reality. A great deal of work is being done on a software system that will make phone numbers portable—converting a user's assigned number in one network to the user's assigned number in a different network. In fact, the more a market tips, the greater the possible returns from making the dominant network compatible with other networks. Atari has developed an adapter so that its machines can play Nintendo cartridges. Discover and American Express want to offer cards that could be used as Visa cards if a cardholder went to a merchant that did not accept Discover or American Express. In the mid-1980s, Apple had disk drives that could read floppy disks formatted on either DOS or Windows.[6]

Contagiousness One of the critical elements of an epidemic is contagiousness. Something becomes contagious when the costs of *not* being infected are greater than the costs of being infected (or, conversely, when the benefits of *not* being infected are less than the benefits of being infected). The goal of the manager attempting to create an epidemic for the firm's product is to reduce the net costs (costs-benefits) of being infected or raise the net costs of avoiding infection. To do so, the manager focuses on the margin—small, incremental changes. The approach is completely analogous to the way crime was reduced in New York City.[7]

In the mid-1980s crime on the New York City subways was at the epidemic stage. The New York Transit Authority had to find a way to reduce crime on the subways or the subway system would die. The Transit Authority focused its attention on the graffiti on the subway cars. Many critics argued that the Transit Authority should not worry about the small stuff—it should focus on the larger questions of crime and subway reliability. The Transit Authority forged ahead and began cleaning the cars. Each time a car would come out of service with graffiti, it would be cleaned immediately. It soon became clear that there was no benefit to marking the cars with graffiti. This, in turn, enticed users to the subway system because the cars and platform were cleaner and gang members were not hanging around looking to sign their graffiti on the cars. Using the same idea of focusing on a marginal change, the Transit Authority also began a program of enforcing payment for subway use. A huge police force was allocated to several main subway stations. The police would nab fare-beaters (who usually did so by jumping over the turnstiles rather than paying with a token) one by one, handcuff them, and leave them standing on the platform until several violators had been captured. The idea was to signal that the transit police were now serious about cracking down on fare-beaters.

These marginal efforts stopped the crime epidemic. In fact, it reversed the epidemic. The clean subway cars and the enforcement of fares signaled that someone was in charge and that participating in crime had become more costly and less beneficial. The main point is that, in total opposition to the old saying, "don't sweat the small stuff," you *should* sweat the small stuff. It is the margins that matter.

Although the topic of epidemics and tipping points did not arise in the old economy, focusing on the margin is not something new or unique to the New Economy. As has been demonstrated throughout this text, focusing on the margin is one key to success. Economic thinking is often called "marginal thinking." Managing in the New Economy requires the same analyses that managing in the old economy required even though some of the words and descriptions sound different. For instance, if you want to start an epidemic, you must have something that is contagious. How do you create contagiousness, that is, how do you ensure that people will like your product and will buy it in epidemic levels? You can't, you don't. The best you can do is to "know your customer," as described in Chapter 4. But in addition to knowing your customer, you must know and understand your costs (as discussed in Chapter 5): Are there economies of scale or scope, are there externalities, are products independent or are they more efficiently produced in conjunction with other products as part of an integrated supply chain?

Standards Wars In recent years we have been introduced to the idea of a standards war. When two or more incompatible technologies struggle to become a standard, they are engaged in a *standards war*. You have probably heard of the standards wars with PC modems, with video games, with VCRs, and with HDTVs. You may not have heard of the standards war involving AM stereo because there was no winner. In the 1970s several incompatible AM stereo broadcasting systems were competing for Federal Communications Commission endorsement—Magnavox, Motorola, Harris, Belar, and Kahn. The pivotal player was General Motors' Delco Electronics Division, the largest dominant manufacturer of radio receivers. Since Delco picked the Motorola system, Motorola looked like the sure winner. However, no one had asked the customer what was desired. AM stereo was estimated to add $20 to $40 to the retail price of a car radio—not much, but enough that people did not think it worth the cost. Radio stations saw little reason to invest in equipment if there weren't going to be consumers of the AM stereo. As a result, AM stereo died. All AM broadcasts today are in mono.

What does it take to win a standards war? The answer is no different from the answer to what it takes to sustain economic profits. You must have a distinct capability that has value: efficiency in manufacturing or operations, patents or other means to own intellectual property rights, first-mover advantages, brand-name reputation, or size. In other words, managers must ask, "What do we do that is unique and has value? How can we sustain that value?"

If a firm has won a standards war, how does it keep its network alive and healthy? One way is to encourage as many others as possible to tie into that firm's network. The firm wants to encourage a strong market for complements to its product. For instance, Nintendo worked aggressively to attract developers of hit games and used its popularity to gain very strong distribution. Intel invested in as many firms as it could that might extend the demand for processing capabilities.

How do you set prices in the New Economy? Exactly as you did in the old economy; you find $MR = MC$ and price according to demand. In many cases involving information, the marginal cost is extremely low, near zero. In such a case you might set the price at zero (give away the information) in order to attract purchases to complementary products. For example, AOL offers a few months of free service. Why is Internet access given away for lengthy trial periods? In order to attract users to a system that enables the Internet service providers to charge for advertisements placed on the server. In addition, once the customer is using the service, the ISP can charge a small fee, one based on marginal cost, without causing the user to switch to another service.

Technological Change

Now that we've discussed the New Economy, networks, positive feedback, winner-takes-all, and strategies for success in the New Economy, let's examine the management of technology in general. Technological change is nothing new—it has occurred since the beginning of time. Indeed, technological change and innovation are necessary—for a country they increase standards of living and for individual firms they increase shareholder wealth. They can also create distinct capabilities and barriers to entry.

Where does technological change come from? It is primarily the result of research, the R in R&D. There are two kinds of research: **basic research,** which is aimed purely at the creation of new knowledge, and **applied research,** which is expected to have a practical payoff. **Development** is the D in R&D; it is the process of turning research findings into practical applications. Some firms are involved in all three activities, some in just one, and some firms do no research or development at all. Most businesses involved in R&D are interested in applied research, since the return to the R&D expenditures is quicker there than in basic research. Most basic research occurs at academic institutions—universities. The end result of technological change is to increase the quantity of output a given quantity of resources is able to produce.

The long-run effect of the adoption of technology typically means a reduction in the long-run cost curves—more output produced per dollar of expenditure—but may also affect economies and diseconomies of scale. For instance, in Figure 9.7(a) the shape of the long-run average cost curve remains the same but shifts downward due to increased productivity. Figure 9.7(a) shows what would occur if total factor productivity rises but the scale efficiencies do not change. New methods of delivering vaccines (e.g., using fruits such as bananas to deliver vaccine) have reduced the costs of vaccination but have not changed the economies of scale. This is an example of innovating without altering scale economies. Figure 9.7(b) illustrates the case where the new technology increases the range of economies of scale. An example of this type of innovation is the basic oxygen furnace, which quadrupled the range over which economies of scale occurred in steel manufacturing. Figure 9.7(c) illustrates the case where the new technology reduces the range of economies of scale. Examples include fiber optics and satellites, which reduced the economies of scale in communication; ATM machines, which reduced the economies of scale in banking; and new power plants, which reduced the scale economies in electricity generation.

Patent Races

R&D is often referred to as a "patent race" in that firms compete to develop a new product or process and then obtain a patent on it. The first firm successfully doing this is the winner. A patent race is no different from a standards war. The objective is to reach the finish line first and become the only survivor.

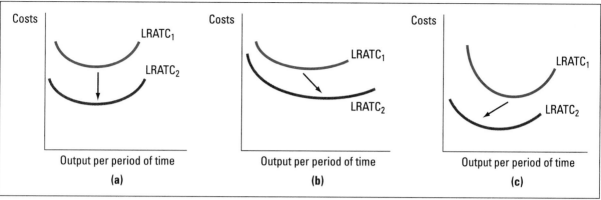

Figure 9.7

TECHNOLOGICAL CHANGE AND ECONOMIES SCALE

(a) Technological change has no effect on scale. (b) Technological change leads to an increase in economies of scale. (c) Technological change reduces economies of scale.

Patents confer a property right—a right to the exclusive ownership of the patented product or process. Gaining that property right is not necessarily gaining the profit. There is a long-standing debate as to whether or not patents secure the profits for the innovating company and, thus, whether the patent system spurs innovation or retards it. Some argue that a patent system ensures that rival firms will learn about the innovation and "reverse engineer" it—take it apart and reconstruct it—so that sales by imitators occur earlier than they would have without the patent system. The costs of duplicating a major new product are only about one-half of the original innovator's R&D costs. Even though patent protection increases imitation costs by 40 percent in pharmaceuticals, by 25 percent for typical equipment and computer products, and by an average of 17 percent for machine tools, pumps, and compressors, imitating is much less costly than being the innovator. Timely duplication of a major new patented product is reported to be impossible in only a few industries.[8] The conclusion from several surveys of executives is that patents are not as important as other incentives for innovation. For both products and processes, the advantages from being a first mover are substantially more important than the patent protection itself.[9]

The potential for a firm to earn profits from an innovation is dependent on time. A firm wants to reap as much of the profit potential as possible, but gains cannot be realized until research and development are completed and the innovation (or new product) is commercially introduced. It usually takes time to build up to the new product's full profit potential.

How much should a firm devote to R&D? That depends on how quickly the firm wants to introduce the innovation. Usually, the more expenditures on R&D, the sooner introduction occurs and the more profits that are possible. R&D costs typically accelerate as the date of introduction is moved closer to today. Thus, the firm must trade off the increased profit potential and the increased costs of R&D and choose the introduction date that will maximize the difference. If an imitator introduces a rival product, then the rival begins appropriating some of the profits the innovator would otherwise capture.[10]

The first firm to introduce the innovation will acquire revenue from being first but will also have to bear greater development costs. If a potential rival exists, delaying introduction means a loss of profits. Thus, the introduction point is usually sooner when a rival exists than it would be if no rival was in view. But there is a limit to this result. If firms do not expect to earn profits because rivals will be introducing the innovations at nearly the same time, then innovation may not oc- cur. Why devote the resources if there is no reasonable expectation to earn a re- turn? This is often the argument presented in support of patent laws—that the patent will ensure profit for the first firm and thus ensure that innovation takes place.

To the extent that a patent race is a winner-takes-all situation, what matters is to be first, not how far behind one finishes in the race. If a firm's probability of discovery per unit of time depends not on current R&D expenses but on experi- ence accumulated to date, the patent race will take on a different flavor. Consider a patent race between two firms in which both firms expect losses if neither of them drops out of the race. The first firm to drop out is the first to perceive that it has a disadvantage. It seems plausible that if the firms have access to the same R&D technology, the firm that drops out of the race would be the one with less experience. In fact, the less experienced firm might as well not even start the race. This result seems to suggest that once a firm acquires a patent or wins the race to introduce an innovation, it may have an inherent advantage over rivals in further innovations.

In industries where improvements in productivity are the result of learning and on-the-job experience that occurs as a firm produces more and more of a given item, the experience curve we discussed in Chapter 5 becomes important. To review: Holding the firm's output rate constant (for instance, a hundred per day or a hundred per month), the firm's average cost declines with increases in its cumulative total output (that is, the total number of items of this sort that the firm has produced in the past). For example, production of the first hundred machine tools of a particular type may require about 50 percent more hours of labor than production of the second hundred machine tools of this type, even though the number of machine tools produced per month remains about the same.

Figure 9.8(a) shows the learning curves for two products: a piece of optical equipment and a portable turbine. Producing more, and thus learning, results in reductions in the average costs of both products. For any cumulative amount of output produced, there is an average total cost curve. Thus, for the turbine, if a total amount Q_1 had been produced over the years, the per-unit costs of produc- ing at a certain rate for the next month or next year might be represented by ATC_1 in Figure 9.8(b). However, had the total amount produced over the years been Q_2, the costs of producing at a certain rate of output for the next month or next year would be represented by ATC_2.

As noted above, it is conceivable that when learning economies are impor- tant, the capturing of an initial advantage by some company could set in motion a process that ends with the relevant product being more or less permanently pro- vided only by the initial company.[11] The essence of the experience curve is that one learns how to reduce production costs through actual production experience so that the more a firm has produced, the lower its unit costs tend to be, all else equal. To the extent that such experience is not readily transferable to other en- terprises, the first company to enter some new product line begins with a cost ad- vantage over subsequent rivals. By the time the latter enter or consider entering, the pioneer has already progressed some distance down its learning curve. It is quite likely, however, that the firm can not keep all advantages to itself. Some of the cost-reduction benefits associated with cumulative experience will spill over to other firms as skilled employees are hired away, patents expire, and production techniques become public knowledge.

Figure 9.8
LEARNING CURVES AND AVERAGE COST CURVES

(a) Learning curves for two industries are illustrated. As more and more output is produced over time and thus as experience in producing is gained, the cost per unit of output declines. (b) The average cost curves represent the cost per unit output when output is produced at a particular rate during a particular time period. If the experience factor reduces unit costs over time, then the average cost curves would shift downward over time, as shown in the move from ATC_1 to ATC_2.

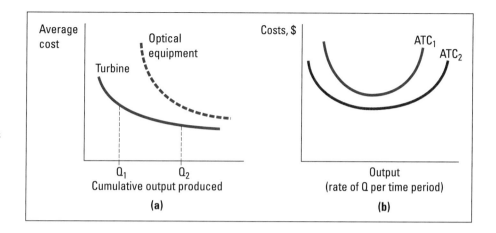

When experience or learning is important and firm-specific for at least some period of time, firms can exploit the situation. Texas Instruments, a major producer of semiconductor chips and electronic products, was able to use its experience as a strategic advantage. When the industry was young, Texas Instruments priced its product at less than its then current average costs in order to increase its output rate and thus its cumulative total output. Believing that the learning curve was relatively steep, the company hoped that this would reduce its average costs to such an extent that it would be profitable to produce and sell at this low price. The strategy was successful and Texas Instruments was able to drive rivals from the market.

On the other hand, when Douglas Aircraft planned the production of the DC-9 airframe, the company believed it would experience the learning curve effect. However, the labor market was so tight at the time of production that Douglas lost twelve thousand of the thirty-five thousand workers it had hired. The result was that the company did not experience learning and costs did not fall. Moreover, other firms were able to enter the market at virtually the same experience level as Douglas. This situation was so bad for Douglas that it was forced into a merger—resulting in McDonnell Douglas.

Firm Size

It is often pointed out that it is the new, upstart firms who are first to innovate, not the large, dominant firms.[12] Examples include Gillette's lag behind Wilkinson on stainless-steel razor blades in 1962–1963, IBM's slow start in developing its first digital computers, the introduction of granola-type cereals by small, upstart firms rather than Kellogg and General Mills, and NCR's delay in shifting from mechanical cash registers to electronic point-of-sale devices, among others.

Business history contains many instances of companies with a wealth of assets, innovative products, strong reputations, financial resources, and powerful distribution channels whose market position was eroded or overtaken by companies with seemingly much smaller resource bases. Canon, for example, entered as a small firm and took market share of copiers from Xerox, Sony followed RCA in television, and CNN was the upstart as compared to the networks in news programming. A frequent explanation for this is that small firms are more nimble and less bureaucratic than large ones. It is often said that large companies become fat and happy or they fall asleep while small companies are hungry or lean and mean.

Also, there are conspiracy theories about how dominant firms keep innovations hidden away and even buy up and hide the innovations of small upstart firms. Though superficially appealing, these arguments fail to answer a fundamental question: Why are established firms systematically less able to innovate or break with established practice than new entrants or marginal firms?

A more reasonable explanation than a conspiracy might be that by virtue of well-established reputation, distribution channels, and other attributes, dominant firms are not as afraid of losing market share as are small firms. Suppose that the dominant firm, firm A, would win 80 percent of the new product's sales and firm B only 20 percent if each rolled out the fruits of their R&D on the same day. The introduction date or adoption date could be a much later date for the dominant firm than for the smaller firm without hurting the dominant firm.

Another explanation of why dominant firms tend to lag with the introduction of innovations is called the "sunk-cost effect." The sunk-cost effect arises because a firm that has already committed to a particular technology has made investments in resources and organizational capabilities that are likely to be specific to that technology and are thus less valuable if the firm switches to another technology. In the early 1950s, steelmaking was changed by the oxygen furnace. The furnace reduced milling time to forty minutes as compared with the six to eight hours needed with the open-hearth (OH) furnace that had been the industry standard since World War I. Despite the apparent superiority of the oxygen furnace, few American steelmakers adopted it. Throughout the 1950s, U.S. steelmakers added nearly 50 million additional tons of the old furnace (OH) capacity; they did not begin to replace their OH furnaces with the new furnaces until the late 1960s. Meanwhile, steelmakers in the rest of the world were building new plants incorporating state-of-the-art technology. The cost advantage afforded by this new technology was a key reason why Japanese and Korean steelmakers were able to penetrate the American domestic market.

Why did American steelmakers continue to invest in a seemingly inefficient technology? American steel firms had developed a considerable amount of specific know-how related to the old technology, but the investment in this know-how was sunk. It should have made no difference to the decision to switch to new technology. Was the reluctance to change due to managerial ignorance—the mistake of not ignoring sunk costs? According to one study it was:

> The most likely explanation of the hesitant adoption of the Austrian converter by the large American firms is that their managements were still imbued with Andrew Carnegie's motto "invention don't pay."[13]

Actually, what is a sunk cost for the firm might not be a sunk cost for individuals involved with the firm. The CEO may have to justify costs to shareholders or the board of directors. Underlings may have vested interests in maintaining the current technology—their jobs may be based on it. Suppliers may realize that a technological change by the firm would mean a loss of business for them. There is, in such cases, a reluctance to adopt the newest technology not because of the failure to ignore sunk costs but because of the costs to individuals within the firm.

In the case of steel companies, because the new technology used relatively more pig iron than the old technology, a steel plant that was located closer to sources of pig iron would gain large operating cost reductions by adopting the new technology. A change to the new technology might require new plants to be built at different locations. This could cause a considerable loss of income for many individuals within the firm, suppliers working with the firm, and communities in which the plants were located. Thus, a great deal of pressure was placed on U.S. steel companies not to change technologies.[14] The Japanese and Korean steelmakers could adopt the newest technology because they started from scratch. There were no special-interest groups tied into the old technology.

According to one study,[15] IBM failed to develop personal computers profitably after having invented them because the "mainframe people" within IBM opposed the growth of the PC group. The mainframe group saw the PC group as a potential threat to their internal power.

This discussion is not meant to imply that the large, incumbent firms never introduce new technology first. Microsoft, Hewlett-Packard, and Intel, for example, have been innovators and first movers in their respective markets. Even though it is the dominant retailer in the United States, Wal-Mart continues to be the first mover in many innovations. The point of the above discussion is to look more carefully into the reasons that it is not always the large, dominant firm that is the first mover or innovator. On the surface, it might seem that with large market share, deep pockets, and experience, the incumbent firm would always be the innovator and would, therefore, be able to sustain its economic profit seemingly forever. But it does make sense that innovation would come from new firms. In many cases, new firms are created because of an innovation that investors believe will enable that firm to wrest profits from the incumbent firm. Positive economic profit creates an incentive for innovation; the more successful a firm is, the more likely the competition for that firm will increase.

The Old Versus the New Economy

How different are the old economy and the New Economy? Consider the following description.

> As the century closed, the world became smaller. The public rapidly gained access to new and dramatically faster communication technologies. Entrepreneurs, able to draw on unprecedented scale economies, built vast empires. Great fortunes were made. The government demanded that these powerful new monopolists be held accountable under antitrust law.[16]

This sounds like a description of the new millennium, but it is not. It is a description of the turning of the century from the 1800s to the 1900s. The point is much like Yogi Berra said: "It's déjà vu all over again." The basics of business have not changed: Economic principles continue to persist in the New Economy.

CASE REVIEW *Winner-Takes-All*

What are the business prospects for technology? Will one technology dominate, become a winner-takes-all, or will a patchwork of different technologies emerge?

A winner-takes-all requires certain conditions in the market: economies of scale, feedback effects or positive network externalities, and no strong demand for variety. Do these conditions exist in the broadband market? It appears there are economies of scale in satellite and cable broadband distribution. But does one medium have an advantage over the other? Evidence does not suggest that this is the case. Is there a demand for variety—do consumers want choices among the various media? As long as each medium can deliver the same broadband features, it would not seem to matter whether different media existed or just one. Why would it matter whether a household used copper wire or coaxial cable or satellite as long as all had the same broadband capability? Are there positive network externalities? Would an additional user of any of the systems create benefits to the existing users? Not likely. It would not appear that positive feedback exists. Since all conditions necessary for a winner-takes-all result do not exist, it is not likely that such a result will occur unless it becomes clear that one media offers better services than another.

SUMMARY

1. The New Economy is characterized by networks, positive feedback, and standards wars. The old economy is characterized by economies of scale and patent races.
2. For a winner-takes-all to arise in either the New Economy or the old economy, the market must be sufficiently large (demand must be large, perhaps as a result of feedback effects dominating customer desires for differentiation) and there must be economies of scale. If the economies of scale apply to a single firm, then that firm will be the dominant one. If the economies of scale apply to a single network, then that network will be the dominant one.
3. In both the New Economy and the old economy, there are often first-mover advantages. The first firm to obtain a patent might be able to restrict others from entering the business and might be able to dominate the market for a long time. The first network to experience positive feedback might be able to achieve economies of scale and restrict entry.
4. In both the old economy and the New Economy, the advantages of being first or even being the winner in a winner-takes-all situation will not last long. The incentives for others to take some of the economic profit from the dominant firm or network increase over time. Technological change enables new entrants to leapfrog the incumbents or to compete with the incumbents. It is only through government that the winner will remain the dominant firm or network and thus earn positive economic profits for a long time.
5. Technological change that involves the improvement of production alters the production function and thus the cost functions, typically lowering the average cost curve and altering the long-run cost curves.
6. Managing technological change involves making the R&D decision, determining how many resources to devote to R&D, determining the strategy of R&D to employ, and determining whether and when to introduce an innovation.
7. Managing technological change also involves determining whether and when to adopt a new technology.
8. Often the incumbent dominant firms are slower to innovate or introduce new technology than are new or upstart firms. One reason is called the sunk-cost effect. This means that existing, dominant firms have invested heavily in the status quo and do not want to alter it. In addition, there are many cases in which a subset of employees within the firm will be harmed by the adoption of new technology and thus work to impede its adoption.

KEY TERMS

New Economy
networks
positive feedback
positive network externalities

tipping point
winner-takes-all
path dependence
locked-in

basic research
applied research
development

EXERCISES

1. If the downsizing trend of the late 1980s and early 1990s was due to technological change, what should it mean for individual firm cost curves? If the downsizing trend was a mistake—firms cutting employees and increasing productivity in the short term only to suffer long-term reductions in productivity—what should it mean for individual firm cost curves?

2. Several cities are associated with specific industries: Akron with tires, Sunnyvale with computer chips, Orlando with tourism, Hollywood with movies. Why do such centers emerge?

3. Two networks are vying for dominance in the HDTV network, the United States and Europe. It has been said that the winner is likely to be determined by economies of scale in manufacturing televisions. Explain.

4. Amazon.com was the first mover in online book sales. It patented the one-click purchasing system. Barnes and Noble was a later entrant with BN.com. Is this a battle with a "winner-takes-all" outcome? Why or why not?

5. In early 1998, S3 was a small microchip-design firm with a big problem. The company knew that Intel's patent wall would eventually stall its high-performance graphic-microchip business. S3 hatched a plan to fix the problem. It outbid Intel to acquire the patents of bankrupt microchip maker Exponential Technologies. In doing so, S3 acquired a patent that predated Intel's. Explain why S3 spent $10 million to purchase a bankrupt firm. What is the implication for the dominance of Intel?

6. In 1994, the $3.5 billion Avery Dennison Corporation developed a new film for use in product labeling. The film unit won a contract to provide the labels for Procter & Gamble shampoo bottles and appeared to have huge growth potential. But an analysis of patent activity indicated that Dow Chemical was beginning to move into this business. Should Avery commit the huge resources needed to exploit the market opportunity for the film unit?

7. Explain why feedback effects alone are not sufficient for a winner-takes-all?

8. Explain what market tipping is. What conditions are necessary for tipping to occur?

9. Is it mere coincidence that the life cycle of consumer electronics products resembles the life cycle of an epidemic? Explain.

10. Contagiousness is one condition necessary for an epidemic. In terms of business strategy, explain the following:
    a. the creation of an epidemic
    b. the prevention of an epidemic using vaccinations

11. Using the following cost function, derive the profit-maximizing price:

$$C = 200,000 + 0.01Q$$
$$P = 500 - 0.2Q$$

    Suppose that the firm is interested in creating a very large number of users of the service—a membership in its network. How might it then price?

12. Suppose that several firms are trying to develop the same product. The first to succeed obtains a patent and thus a monopoly on the product, while the other firms get nothing. Assume all firms have the same research capabilities. If two firms spend the same amount on R&D, they will complete the project at the same time. Who will win the patent war? Demonstrate how much a firm will spend on R&D.

13. Suppose that in Exercise 12, two or more firms spend on R&D. If they spend different amounts, then the firm being outspent will lose the race for sure. How many firms will participate in R&D spending? How much will be spent?

14. Suppose that four firms are each spending $1 million on R&D. Each firm believes it has a 0.25 chance of being the first to innovate. One firm is thinking about increasing its R&D outlays by $1 million for a total of $2 million. The firm calculates that if all other firms maintain their $1 million R&D budget, its chances of winning the patent race rises to 0.32. Under what conditions is the increase in R&D budget a good strategy? Under what conditions is it a poor strategy?

CHAPTER NOTES

1. For more on tipping, see Malcolm Gladwell, *The Tipping Point: How Little Things Can Make a Big Difference* (Boston: Little, Brown, 2000).
2. Carl Shapiro and Hal R. Varian, *Information Rules* (Boston: Harvard Business Press, 1999), p. 173.
3. This question was first asked by Paul David, "Understanding the Economics of QWERTY: The Necessity of History," in W. N. Parker, ed., *Economics History and the Modern Economist* (London: Blackwell, 1986).
4. See the list of references provided in Liebowitz, Stan J. and Stephen E. Margolis, "The Economics of Qwerty: Papers by Stan Liebowitz and Stephen Margolis," ed. Peter Lewin, Macmillan/ NYU Press (in press), including Robert Frank and Philip Cook's *The Winner-Take-All Society* (New York: Penguin, 1996); and Paul Krugman's *Peddling Prosperity* (New York: W. W. Norton & Co., 1994), pp. 221–244.
5. Liebowitz, Stan J. and Stephen E. Margolis, "The Economics of Qwerty: Papers by Stan Liebowitz and Stephen Margolis," ed. Peter Lewin, Macmillan/NYU Press, forthcoming.
6. What explains the fact that if you work in the film industry, you probably live in Los Angeles; if you are involved with venture capital, you probably live near Palo Alto, California, or along Route 128 in Massachusetts; and if you are an investment banker, you probably work in New York? These are examples of lock-in but are quite different from those based on the QWERTY story. As long ago as 1900, this was explained by the economist Alfred Marshall. He noted that an industrial cluster supports a specialized labor pool and providers of specialized services. While some accident or other event may cause a particular industry to locate at a specific place, it is the external economies of scale that continue to draw firms to that location. The clusters of high-tech firms along Route 128 in Massachusetts and in Silicon Valley in California are also examples of this phenomenon. High-tech firms are located along Route 128 and in Silicon Valley because of their proximity to great universities and the trained work force and R&D that emerges from those universities. It is efficient for these industry concentrations to be located where they are.
7. Described in Gladwell, *The Tipping Point*.
8. In fewer than 10 percent of industries according to Richard C. Levin, Alvin Klevorick, Richard R. Nelson, and Sidney G. Winter, "Appropriating the Returns from Industrial Research and Development," *Brookings Papers on Economic Activity*, no.3 (1987): 80–89.
9. F. M. Scherer and David Ross *Industrial Market Structure and Economic Performance* (New York: Rand McNally & Co., 1990), p. 677.
10. In addition, all R&D must generate returns that exceed the cost of capital.
11. But this could occur only if there were economies of scale and barriers to entry—in other words, only if the learning benefits are not easily copied and technological change does not occur.
12. A. Cooper and D. Schendel, "Strategic Responses to Technological Threats," *Business Horizons* 19 (February 1976): 61–69; and Eric K. Clemins, "Technology-Driven Environmental Shifts and the Sustainable Competitive Disadvantage of Previously Dominant Companies," in George S. Day and David J. Reibsten, eds., *Wharton on Dynamic Competitive Strategy* (New York: Wiley, 1997), pp. 99–122.
13. W. Adams and H. Mueller, "The Steel Industry," in W. Adams, ed., *The Structure of American Industry*, 7th ed. (New York: Macmillan, 1986), p. 102.
14. Sharon Oster, "The Diffusion of Innovation Among Steel Firms: The Basic Oxygen Furnace," *Bell Journal of Economics* 13 (Spring 1982): 45–68.
15. P. Carrol, *Big Blues: The Unmaking of IBM* (New York: Crown, 1993).
16. Shapiro and Varian, *Information Rules*, p. 1.

CHAPTER 10

The Firm's Architecture:
Organization and Corporate Culture

CASE *Culture Clashes*

Corporate cultures, particularly strong cultures, can create additional costs for merging or combining firms. A common explanation of the failure of firms to merge successfully is that their cultures did not mesh. A *Wall Street Journal* headline declared on October 14, 1998, that CLASH OF CULTURES KILLS MONSANTO, AHP MARRIAGE. Another example is the merger of Pharmacia and Upjohn. A culture clash between the two companies was at the root of the problems, according to the February 3, 1997, issue of *Business Week*. Pharmacia was a loose patchwork of companies, while Upjohn had a more structured, paternalistic bent. To unite the two companies—which had been based in Stockholm, Sweden and Kalamazoo, Michigan—a centralized headquarters was instituted in suburban London and executives there had much of the responsibility for the financial and operating performance of the local units. The Pharmacia executives

didn't respond well to the change. Having long held sole responsibility for their units, many managers were offended. Many analysts claimed that the 2002 acquisition of Compaq by Hewlett-Packard was yet another example of clashing cultures. On May 7, 2002, the *Financial Times* noted that "JP Morgan and Chase Manhattan's banking merger is producing an intriguing culture clash. Former Chase employees, it seems, are more avant-garde than their Morgan counterparts—at least when it comes to art. As one Morgan employee says: 'We've got a pair of old grey pyjamas hanging up on our walls . . . I don't get it.'"

What is a culture clash? What is a corporate culture and what is it supposed to do?

Organizational Change

"Our organization is paralyzed by the smiling dead hand of middle management," complained the general manager. "Whenever I want to take an initiative, do something different, rock the boat, I see the smiles and nods of agreement . . . but nothing happens. What do I do?" The management consultant's answer: "Flatten the structure."[1]

This advice was rampant in the 1990s. Hierarchy had been branded as "the devil we know." Accordingly, many firms set out to obliterate hierarchy and change reporting relationships and titles. In the resulting organization, the pyramid was flattened, turned upside down, or even recast as a horizontal organization. Instead of subordinates and superiors or bosses and underlings, people referred to associates, colleagues, sponsors, or advisers. The work unit became the team, not the individual.[2]

Institutions, organizations, and organizational structures exist in the long run because they are efficient. When a firm is able to create a more efficient architecture than other firms, it has a competitive advantage over these firms. As long as it is able to sustain the advantage, it can earn above-normal profits. It is logical, then, that firms will search for competitive advantage not only in their relations with each other and vis-à-vis customers but also internally in their architecture.

The Evolution of the Firm

Before 1840, most businesses were family owned and operated. The dominance of the family-run business was a direct consequence of the limitations in transportation, communications, and finance of the time. Transportation was either by waterway or wagon; the primary mode of long-distance communication in 1840 was the public mail via pony express; and financing was local and cumbersome. Most businesses found it difficult to obtain external financing. Public ownership (shares of stock) was virtually nonexistent, and most loans were made on the basis of personal relationships.

Between 1840 and 1910, developments in transportation, communications, and finance created economies of scale. To fully exploit these, firms increasingly chose to acquire raw materials and/or distribute finished goods themselves rather than rely on independent suppliers and agents. In addition, new production technologies allowed firms to produce a wider range of products at lower costs than if they were produced separately, enabling economies of scope. The owner-operator's responsibilities in functional areas of business—purchasing, sales, distribution, and finance—rose tremendously. Because a single owner-operator could not be involved in every aspect of business, owners increasingly turned to professional managers. The professional manager created a central office or headquarters to assure that production runs went smoothly and finished goods found their way to market. As the business grew, it was organized into semi-autonomous divisions, each of which made the principal operating decisions for itself, while the separate headquarters office made decisions that affected the entire corporation. For example, the divisions of General Motors would make operating decisions for each car line, while corporate management would make decisions regarding corporate finance and research and development.

By the mid-twentieth century, continued market growth had caused many firms difficulty in coordinating production processes across different customer groups and market areas. Firms such as Dow Corning, Amoco, Citibank, and Pepsi-Co reorganized according to two or more different types of divisions—geographic and client, product groups and functional departments, or geographic and functional lines. The market growth also meant that specialization in various activities became feasible. Firms could purchase from others many activities they had previously performed in-house.

In the 1990s, firms moved to reduce, or "flatten," their hierarchical structure, to downsize, and to focus on core competencies. Firms reduced the number of managers and administrative staff; they chose to keep fewer activities in-house and thus purchased more from other firms. In the New Economy, alliances and networks often become the structure of business. Enron captured the essence of what many thought was the ideal structure in 2002 for many companies—the corporation without fixed assets. All activities requiring fixed assets were outsourced. Outside firms would then specialize in providing the services associated with a particular fixed asset, while the assetless company would focus on trading. Although the norm in the late 1990s and into 2002 was to focus on a core competency and divest other activities, many firms still believed that bigger was better; merger activity was near or at all-time highs.

The evolution of the firm is the process of defining a firm's vertical and horizontal boundaries and finding the most efficient way to perform activities within the firm. Each firm is the result of decisions regarding what the firm should do itself and what it should acquire in the market. The structure of each firm (called the firm's architecture) is the result of the search for competitive advantage and efficiency.

Vertical Boundaries

The process that begins with the acquisition of raw material and ends with the distribution and sale of finished goods is known as the value or supply chain.[3] The vertical boundaries of a firm define the activities that the firm performs itself instead of purchasing from other firms via the market. The choice of whether to carry out the activity in-house or to purchase from other firms is referred to as a make-or-buy decision.

Make or Buy?

While many firms have been successful in producing their own supportive activities or inputs, others prefer to obtain these from specialized providers in the market. When a firm buys activities or inputs from other firms, we say that it is **using the market**; when a firm carries out more than one step in the vertical chain itself, we say that it is **vertically integrated** in those activities. General Motors is a vertically integrated firm: Fisher Body is the manufacturer of automobile frames for General Motors, and Fisher Body is part of General Motors. Many manufacturing companies prefer to contract with independent sales people, called manufacturers' representatives, rather than maintaining their own sales force. These manufacturers' reps specialize in providing the products and services customers desire and typically earn a commission on sales. They are not part of the manufacturing company and don't receive insurance, retirement, or other benefits from the manufacturing company. A vertically integrated manufacturing company would include the sales force in-house.

One firm's relationship to another is often described as being **upstream** or **downstream** in the supply chain. The terms are relative—a firm may be upstream from some firms and downstream from others. Intel is downstream from Corning but upstream from PC makers such as IBM and Dell. IBM is downstream from Intel but upstream from Procter & Gamble. If Intel acquired Corning, that would be a vertical acquisition; if Intel acquired IBM or Dell, that would be a vertical acquisition.

The decision of a firm to perform an upstream or downstream activity itself or purchase it from an independent firm is called a **make-or-buy decision.** Consider the distribution of finished goods from a manufacturer to retailers. The manufacturer could distribute the goods itself or use an independent distributor. Choosing to buy rather than make does not eliminate the expenses of the activity. Suppose that it costs a distributor $100,000 to run the distribution business, for which it expects to generate $110,000 in net revenues. It appears that the distributor is realizing a profit margin of 10 percent that the manufacturer could gain for itself if it distributed the goods itself. If the manufacturer does its own distribution, it would be investing $100,000 of its own funds. The manufacturer thus faces an opportunity cost—it could use those funds elsewhere. If the manufacturer could invest the money into an equally risky venture and generate more than a 10 percent increase in net revenues, then it would lose money by tying up $100,000 in distribution. A firm must compare the costs and benefits of using the market rather than performing the activity in-house. In May 2002, Sears offered to purchase Lands' End. Sears could have simply contracted with Lands' End to provide Lands' End clothing in its stores; instead, it decided to integrate the firm into the Sears company.

Firms that use the market may be able to exploit efficiencies that they alone cannot achieve. When economies of scale are present, firms that produce more of a good or service do so at lower average costs. Firms that specialize in the production of an input can often achieve greater economies of scale, and thus lower unit costs, than can the downstream firms that use the input.

We might think of each step in the vertical chain as a distinct market. Then, in each step, whether to use the market or not depends on which is more efficient. The vertical boundary of a firm is defined by efficiency: Is it more efficient to use the market or to carry out the activities in-house?

Transactions Costs

Using the market may allow a firm to get the benefits of economies of scale and avoid the opportunity costs of tying up funds but may also create costs of carrying out transactions that would not occur if the activity was undertaken in-house. The concept of transactions costs was first described by Ronald Coase in 1937.[4] Coase raised the question of why, in light of the efficiencies of the competitive market mechanism, so much economic activity takes place inside the firm and thus outside the market or price system. Coase concluded that there have to be costs to using the market that can be eliminated by using the firm. These costs have come to be known as **transactions costs.**

Transactions costs include all costs involved in an exchange. The verification of the quality of tradable items, the delivery of the items, and the time involved in the exchange are transactions costs. Since most aspects of an exchange are specified in some form of contract, contracting costs—the time and expense of negotiating, writing, and enforcing contracts as well as of communicating and transferring information—are also transactions costs.

Contracts   Contracts arise (are used) because the costs of exchange are higher without them. Without contracts, only spot transactions would occur. A *spot* transaction is a simultaneous exchange of traded items, such as dollars for goods. While a spot economy would avoid contracting costs, it would exclude all transactions that involve a sequential exchange, such as delivery prior to payment or a period of free trial. Contracts are a key element of a private ownership economy because, in most exchanges, parties perform their obligations sequentially rather than simultaneously.

A contract has to be enforceable. An *enforceable* **contract** is an agreement that defines the conditions of exchange and for which there is some penalty that has to be borne when the conditions of the contract are not upheld. Without enforcement, the contract is not binding and any party could renege on the agreement anytime it wanted to; this is called *opportunism.*

Governmental institutions—the legal structure of a society—are typically given the role of guaranteeing enforcement of contracts and property rights. Where legal enforcement is costly and yet the gains from trade cannot be attained through spot transactions, mechanisms for assuring contracts arise that are not government-oriented. One such mechanism is referred to as a **hostage** situation.[5]

In the very earliest contracts, it was common for the contracting parties to exchange hostages to ensure contract compliance. There are hostage components to many contracts today. Hostages in modern transactions include **buybacks** and **offsets.** Buybacks are a type of joint venture in which two organizations or parties provide some inputs to a production process and the good produced is allocated to the two organizations in pre-arranged fixed proportions. An example is the case of Japan's Mitsui Corporation, which provided $1.5 billion worth of capital and technology for a fertilizer plant in Eastern Europe. Mitsui then bought a portion of the output as part of its buyback agreement. The hostage in this agreement is that part of the resulting output that is shared between the two organizations. If the fertilizer plant does not fulfill its part of the agreement, Mitsui will not buy the output. If Mitsui fails to fulfill a clause, then it won't get any of the output.

An offset is another form of hostage situation. The purpose of an offset is to compensate the buyer of a good for some of the costs of purchase through other ancillary transactions. Direct offsets involve ancillary transactions in goods related to the one purchased; for example, licensing and joint ventures of product components. Indirect offsets involve goods or services that are not directly related to the good purchased. In an offset contract, the seller incurs an obligation to generate an ancillary transaction of a certain value to offset the initial buyer's capital expenditures. In some cases, this can be over 100 percent of the original transaction. An example of an offset contract is the purchase of civilian aircraft from McDonnell Douglas by the former nation of Yugoslavia. This was offset by the purchase of that nation's ham by McDonnell Douglas. Some 30 years ago what was then the nation of Yugoslavia purchased a fleet of McDonnell Douglas DC-9s; in return, McDonnell Douglas found buyers for Yugoslavian canned hams, and, in a gesture of goodwill, bought a shipment of Yugoslavian ham to serve in its company cafeterias and executive dining rooms.[6]

Since McDonnell Douglas had to undertake expenditures to build an infrastructure for the nation prior to the sale of aircraft, and since McDonnell Douglas would have had no legal recourse if the agreement had been breached following the development of the infrastructure, the hams served as hostage. If the agreement had been breached, McDonnell Douglas would not have purchased the hams. In another case, McDonnell Douglas helped establish a Domino's Pizza franchise in Barcelona as part of a deal to sell the F/A-18 fighter plane to Spain.

Another means of assuring contractual fulfillment is the threat of loss of reputation. Japanese firms such as Toyota often share technical information with their suppliers and exchange managerial staff so as to create informal, but long-term, commitments. Reneging on contracts would lead Toyota or its contractual partner to "lose face," or tarnish its reputation. In the case of ethnic Chinese in Southeast Asia, hostages include family. A person's descendants and relatives are linked to a contract, and their reputations would be harmed if their ancestors or other family members failed to fulfill the contract; other ethnic Chinese would scorn the families and refuse to do business with them.[7] Contracts arise when transactions costs would inhibit an exchange from occurring.

Organization and Transactions Costs A contract arises when exchange is sequential and information is not perfectly known. But, the existence of a contract does not necessarily mean that the exchange is carried out efficiently. That depends on the organizational structure in which the contract is established. Organizational structure is supposed to minimize the inefficiency of exchange. There are many different organizational structures used in business today. In one structure, tasks are performed individually; members of the work group are treated as if they are independent, receiving incentives based on individual actions and outcomes. Lincoln Electric, discussed in the Chapter 1 Case, is an example of this type of structure. Another organization structure is the **team**. In this arrangement, one member of the work group specializes in monitoring and coordinating the work of the others; that person is the boss. In **self-managed teams,** there is a collection of individuals, each of whom works with others to set and pursue some common set of objectives.

For many tasks, any of these structures could be a workable way to organize. Each of them is relatively more appropriate than the others in different circumstances. For instance, each organizational form requires more or less interaction among individuals. In general, the number of potential interactions among n independent individuals is $n(n-1)/2$, since each individual must interact with the $(n-1)$ other individuals. In contrast, the number of interactions among n individuals, one of whom supervises the others, is $(n-1)$, since each of the $(n-1)$ individuals has to interact with just the one boss. Hence, as n increases, it becomes increasingly more efficient to have bosses or managers in terms of the number of interactions. An organizational form with managers, supervisors, or bosses is called a *hierarchical* form.

An organizational structure based on individuals acting almost like sole proprietors is most appropriate when tasks require neither much coordination nor many interactions among individuals. When coordination is necessary, then either a team or hierarchy is more appropriate. Complex hierarchy arises when it is efficient to organize individuals into groups and groups into larger groups. *Departmentalization* is a grouping along dimensions such as a common task or function, input, output, geographic location, or time of work. Examples of departments organized around common tasks or functions include accounting, marketing, and production. Examples of input- and output-based groupings include the Pepsi Bottling Group and Fountain Beverage Division. Examples of departments organized around location include regional sales offices of publishing companies such as Houghton Mifflin and

McGraw-Hill. An example of time-based groupings would be multiple shifts within a manufacturing firm: 8:00 A.M. to 4:00 P.M., 4:00 P.M. to midnight, and midnight to 8:00 A.M. Departmentalization is efficient when there are economies of scale in specific activities. However, departmentalization can increase transactions costs when problems arise that are not aligned with specific departments.

Horizontal Boundaries

The horizontal boundaries of the firm are the varieties of products and services that the firm produces—the scope of the firm. A horizontal boundary refers to activities carried out by the firm at one specific level on the value chain. Quaker Oats, for example, produces drinks (Snapple, Gatorade) and cereals, both of which are at the same level on the value chain. Tomorrow International Holdings, which has a core business manufacturing electronic timing and weather-monitoring devices, has been acquiring pharmaceutical projects. Microsoft has been diversifying for some time into areas such as Internet service provision, enterprise software, mobile computing, and games consoles. For decades, *diversification* was the watchword at TRW Inc. At one time, the company made parts for everything from blue jeans, refrigerators, automobiles, aircraft, and satellites to intercontinental ballistic missiles.

The standard term applied to a firm that has wide horizontal boundaries is diversification. Diversification is the opposite of a focus on one line of business. Just as with the vertical boundary, the horizontal boundary of the firm is defined by efficiency. Is it more efficient to produce multiple products in-house or to narrow production to one or a few goods and use the market for others? Rationales for horizontal expansion include economies of scope and transactions costs.

Economies of Scope

Economies of scope exist if the per-unit cost declines as a firm increases the variety of activities it performs, such as the variety of goods it produces. In business jargon, the exploitation of economies of scope is referred to as "leveraging core competencies," "competing on capabilities," and "mobilizing invisible assets."[8] Economies of scope may arise at any point in the value chain, from acquisition and use of raw materials to distribution and retailing.

An example of economies of scope in distribution arises in a number of industries in which goods and services are routed to and from several markets. In these industries, which include airlines, railroads, and telecommunications, distribution is often organized around hub-and-spoke networks. In an airline hub-and-spoke network, an airline flies passengers from a "spoke" city through a central "hub," where passengers then change planes and fly from the hub to their outbound spoke destination. Thus, a passenger flying from Indianapolis to Salt Lake City on American Airlines—whose hub is Chicago—would fly from Indianapolis to Chicago, change planes, and then fly from Chicago to Salt Lake City. American Airlines is able to offer travel to many pairs of cities less expensively by going through Chicago than by offering direct flights between them, such as Indianapolis to Salt Lake City.

Firms that sell a variety of products or that sell in many markets may enjoy scope economies in advertising. Economies of scope may also result from R&D spillovers—where ideas that arise in one research project are of help in another project.

Diversification

Beginning around 1960, many firms expanded (horizontally) beyond the boundaries of a particular business area. General Electric produces toasters and turbine generators; Morton Thiokol produces salt and aerospace equipment; Martin Marietta produces electronics and cement; TRW produces seat belts, air bags, and credit rating services; and so on. These firms are called conglomerates—firms diversified into apparently unrelated lines of business.

Rationales for diversification ranged from applying economies of scope to using cash cows to stemming the abuse of power by top management. The economies-of-scope rationale includes transactions costs, R&D spillovers, administrative spillovers, and others. In short, there are economies of scope when diversification results in lower per-unit costs of production than can be attained without diversification.

The *cash cow* rationale argues that the long-term success of a growing firm requires it to develop a portfolio of businesses that assures an adequate and stable cash flow with which to finance its activities. In addition to boosting and stabilizing cash flows, the parent firm can use profits from one business to subsidize another. Some say that this is what General Electric has done. GE Capital has provided the growth and revenue to support GE industry.[9] While portfolio strategies may smooth cash flows and may help the parent firm save troubled business lines, they do not necessarily create value for the owners of the firms. It is easier and less costly for shareholders to diversify their personal portfolios than for a firm to do so.[10]

Another common rationale for diversification is the pursuit of growth. Firms may diversify when it is easier to acquire new sales than to develop them internally.[11] Some scholars have argued that diversification for growth is pursued not because it benefits shareholders but because it benefits managers. Growth may provide increased career development opportunities for managers and employees. Unrelated acquisitions may also enhance job security.[12] The argument is that shareholders are unlikely to replace top management unless the firm performs poorly relative to the overall economy. To reduce the risk of job loss, managers must therefore reduce the risk of poor performance. One way to do this is through unrelated acquisitions. The performance of a highly diversified firm is likely to mirror the performance of the overall economy and, therefore, is less likely to lead shareholders to get rid of current management.

The problem with this argument is that it assumes that diversification will generate returns that do not vary from the other opportunities investors have. But if other firms are focused narrowly and do better as a result, shareholders of the diversified firms lose. The fourth wave of corporate acquisitions that began in the mid-1970s was based on this idea. Hostile takeovers involved corporate "raiders" such as Goldsmith, Pickens, Icahn, and Jacobs, who claimed that they were replacing entrenched, inefficient management to benefit shareholders. The raiders would dismantle the firm, selling off inefficient or unrelated lines of business and repacking the firm into one with a more narrow focus.

Relationship-Specific Assets

When the production process involves specialized assets, such as human capital, organizational routines, or other forms of proprietary organizational know-how, transactions through the market may be very difficult. In such cases, it may be more efficient to bring the activity in-house. This seems more obvious in a vertical direction than a horizontal one. Yet relationship-specific assets may raise transactions costs among horizontally related activities as well.

A *relationship-specific asset* is an investment made to support a given transaction. When a transaction involves relationship-specific assets, parties to the transaction cannot switch trading partners without cost. This is because the assets involved in the original exchange would have to be reconfigured to be valuable in the new relationship or the investments would have to be made all over again in the new relationship.

Most asset-specific relationships occur between upstream and downstream firms. An example is the relationship between International Systems and IBM. International Systems developed specific facilities in order to deliver integrated circuits to IBM. This created a mutual dependence. International Systems could not easily alter its production facilities to fit those required by another computer maker. IBM was dependent on International Systems because no other suppliers had the dedicated facilities or know-how to produce the integrated circuits IBM required.

A typical type of horizontal relationship-specific asset exists among firms that are located near one another to achieve economies of scale in input acquisition, such as with the high-technology firms in Silicon Valley, or customer attraction, such as with fast-food outlets. McDonald's, Burger King, Jack-in-the-Box, and other fast-food outlets often locate very near one another partly because together they generate more customers than each would if located separately from the others. Similarly, firms rent space in a mall because of the external economies of scale—the customers brought in by other firms may spill over to your firm.

Internal Structure

Having defined the vertical and horizontal boundaries of the firm, we now turn to the internal organization. Over time, the structures of large organizations have generally fit one of four forms: U-form, M-form, matrix, or network structure.

U-Form

In the late nineteenth century, most larger firms were characterized by loose combinations of formerly independent firms, often still run by their founders. U.S. Steel looked this way when it became the first billion-dollar firm in 1901. But at this time, developments in technology and market infrastructures created opportunities for achieving unprecedented economies of scale and scope in industries. Firms responded to these opportunities by investing in large-scale production facilities and internalizing activities, such as sales and distribution, that had previously been performed for them by independent companies. The organizational structure that evolved in these early firms was the U-form. The **U-form,** also called **unitary form** or **functional form,** refers to the case in which a single department is responsible for a single basic business function: finance, marketing, production, purchasing, and so on. This structure allowed firms to develop a specialization of labor that facilitated the achievement of economies of scale in manufacturing, marketing, and distribution. The first firms to adopt the U-form generated above-normal profits; as a result, imitation proceeded rapidly.

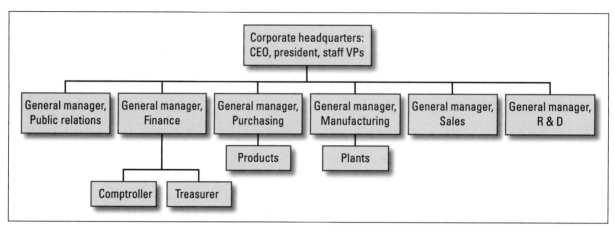

Figure 10.1

**UNITARY OR
FUNCTIONAL FORM**

The U-form organization
evolved from the owner-
operator. It involves a
headquarters to which
each division manager
reports.

An illustration of the U-form is shown in Figure 10.1. Each general manager of a department reports to the staff vice presidents in the corporate headquarters. Within each department are staff and employees.

M-Form

The firms that were the first in their industries to invest in large-scale production facilities and develop managerial hierarchies expanded rapidly and were often able to dominate their industries. But most of the early growth of these firms occurred within a single line of business or within a single market. For example, as late as 1913 only 3 percent of DuPont's sales came from outside its core business of gunpowder and nearly all of its gunpowder was sold in the United States. As markets grew, firms moved away from a focus on a single line of business or a single market to continue to exploit economies of scale and scope. Firms such as Singer and International Harvester expanded overseas. Other firms, such as DuPont and Proctor & Gamble, expanded by diversifying their product lines.

This shift in strategy from a focus on a single business or market to product-line diversification was a problem for the U-form of organization. The attempt by the top management of the firms to monitor functional departments led to administrative overload, or—to use the jargon of organizational management—to exceed the manager's "span of control."

The multidivisional structure, or M-form, that emerged in the United States after 1920 was a response to the limitations of the functional organization in diversified firms. The M-form removed top managers from involvement in the operational details of functional departments, allowing them to specialize in strategic decision making and long-range planning. Division managers would monitor the operational activities of the functional departments that reported to them and would be rewarded on the basis of divisional performance.

The **M-form,** or **multidivisional form,** involves a set of autonomous divisions led by a corporate headquarters office. The headquarters includes a corporate staff that provides information about the internal and external business environment. Rather than organizing by function or by task, a multidivisional structure organizes by product line, related business units, region, or customer type (e.g., industrial, consumer, government). Divisions are groupings of interrelated subunits.

The M-form is illustrated in Figure 10.2. Each division head reports to headquarters; within each division are necessary parts of the functional departments.

Figure 10.2

THE M-FORM

The U-form evolved into the M-form, wherein the organization retains the corporate headquarters but with many divisions.

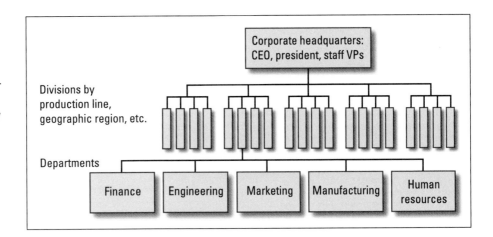

Matrix

The firms turning to the M-form were temporarily able to generate more profits than comparable firms with the U-form. But as with any imitable capability, the advantage could not be sustained. Then, as the growth of markets (both downstream and upstream) raised the transactions costs of dealing with suppliers and customers for a firm with the M-form organization, new structures evolved. For example, large regional supermarket chains often operated in territories that encompassed several different regional offices within the Pepsi Bottling Group. But Pepsi's existing M-form structure gave no one regionwide authority over pricing decisions. When faced with requests for promotion or special pricing deals by a large supermarket chain, executives at Pepsi Bottling Group had to obtain direction and decisions from the head of Pepsi USA, who was forced to become involved in regional-level pricing and promotion decisions. Not surprisingly, this impaired the speed with which Pepsi could respond and put it at a competitive disadvantage relative to those who could respond more quickly. Since Pepsi believed that national coordination of manufacturing helped achieve economies of scale in production—justifying organization along functional lines—but that regional coordination would increase its effectiveness in negotiating with large purchasers, the company organized in a dual-department structure, called a **matrix.**

The matrix structure, illustrated in Figure 10.3, can include product groups and functional departments or different types of divisions, such as ones focused on geographic regions and specific clients.

Network

Because some markets offer economies of scale in some activities and diseconomies in others, neither small nor large firms necessarily have an advantage in all activities. In such cases, the most efficient structure may be the **network**—an affiliation of independent firms that together can exploit economies of scale but separately can avoid diseconomies of scale. The high-tech firms in Silicon Valley and along Route 128 in Massachusetts are examples of networks. Together they are able to benefit from large pools of trained labor and available supplies but separately can avoid the redundancy, bureaucratic inefficiencies, and large fixed costs that would come from merging into one large firm.

Figure 10.3

THE MATRIX FORM

The matrix form allows more flexibility than the M-form.

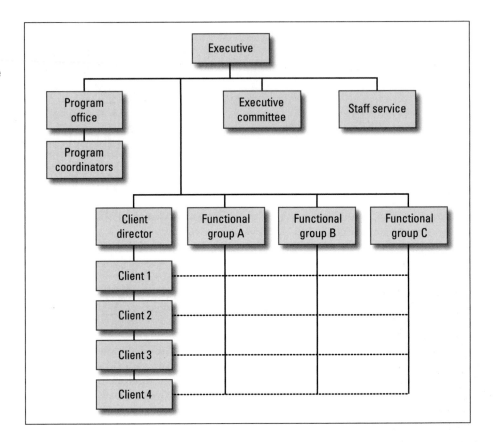

Hierarchy

The evolution of organizational form in the last seventy-five years appears to have been a move from a hierarchical to a nonhierarchical structure. This, at least, is the interpretation given by many consultants, executives, and members of the business press who attack the hierarchical structure. Peter Drucker, for instance, has argued that the modern organization should be an orchestra, in which a single conductor provides guidance to many players, each of whom is a highly skilled expert, not a complex hierarchy.[13] A form of the orchestra model that is often alluded to is "managing by walking around" (MBWA). The CEO is urged to manage by visiting the shop floor and front-line office and talking directly with lower-level employees.

Organizational form is the result of economizing—comparing costs and benefits and selecting the form that is most efficient. The criticisms leveled against hierarchy need careful scrutiny. Think about the implications of the orchestra model. It relies on the CEO's ability to directly supervise and talk to all employees. Yet research on communication does not support the idea that direct communication with the work force is preferable to communication via the hierarchy.[14] Even in the case of MBWA, a hierarchy is implied—someone, the CEO, must come down to the shop floor. The Gore Company is one of the most well-known examples of a firm without hierarchy. There are no bosses. All employees are associates. Decision making often involves a vote. The physical layout of the plant involves separate buildings for separate products. The objective is to keep the small feeling even as the firm grows. But this form works for only a very few firms.

Hierarchy is economically efficient when communication or interaction is required among employees. Having a boss or a monitor to whom employees report is more efficient than each employee communicating with each other. In a hierarchical form, meetings take place to enhance communication and interaction; divisional managers communicate with the senior manager and then, in turn, communicate with those they supervise. In a flat organization, meetings would be less structured and formal than in a hierarchical organization since employees would be interacting and communicating with each other and not with a superior.

Although downsizing had been at the center of business activity in the early 1990s, such attempts to get rid of middle managers cannot be attributed solely to improved communications and computing abilities. Computing and communications can replace management only if management is doing repetitive tasks or work that consists of processing data according to rules. Is this the only thing middle management did? Without middle managers, who interprets the data and suggests strategies? If there is no middle management to carry out these tasks, then the burden on upper management will have increased. Is this efficient?

Does hierarchy create excessive overhead costs? In other words, is a hierarchical structure inefficient?[15] Work that can be easily specified and for which people can be trained, such as the work of telephone operators, needs little supervision. When work is less routine and when learned rules or routines can't be relied on, more involvement by supervisors is needed, as in custom manufacturing. When jobs are physically separated or require intricate interactions, the supervisor becomes busy very quickly. A supervisor to supervise the supervisors is needed; that is, a hierarchy.

The downsizing, flattening, and cost cutting of the late 1980s and early 1990s was replaced by an emphasis on growth in the late 1990s. To enhance growth, a number of leading firms turned to a more hierarchical structure. Coca-Cola, for instance, used to sell beverages though independent bottlers and distributors, each carrying out its own pricing, promotion, and sales. But as buyers such as Wal-Mart and fast-food chains like Pizza Hut and McDonald's became more important to Coke's sales, the company needed to control its sales and marketing more closely. So it began acquiring distributors and combining what had been thousands of small businesses operating in a flat, nonhierarchical structure into a few large, hierarchically managed organizations.[16]

Contracting-out has become associated with a flat organization. Nike contracts out most of the manufacturing of its shoes, and McDonald's contracts out supply of and logistics regarding raw materials and packaging. Yet the activities retained in each firm are carried out within a hierarchy.

Organizational structure can be a strategic asset—if it adds value and cannot be imitated. An efficient organizational structure minimizes transactions costs. An inefficient structure will not last because it will cause a firm to lose out relative to efficiently organized firms. The first merger wave in the United States, which began after the depression of 1883, was the result of firms extending vertical boundaries and adopting the U-form organization. Merger activity peaked around 1900 and ended thereabouts. A second merger wave occurred in the early 1920s. This wave was a further extension of vertical boundaries and a reorganization to the M-form. The two merger waves, in the 1890s and 1920s, were vertical extensions—vertical integration. They were attempts to exploit economies of scale. By 1960, the next wave of merger activity had begun. This wave was primarily one of extending horizontal boundaries and brought with it organizational change, the rise of the matrix and the network. The early portions of this wave of mergers and acquisitions included unrelated diversification, most of this was due to antitrust laws—specifically, the Cellar-Haufman Act—that limited the market share a firm could attain.

The massive switch to the U-form in the late 1890s and early 1900s and from the U-form to the M-form in the 1920s occurred because previous organizational forms had become inefficient. The architecture of the firm—vertical and horizontal boundaries and internal structure—is the result of the competitive process. The efficient architecture survives, while the inefficient disappears.

Culture

Architecture refers not just to the organizational form a firm uses but also to the glue that holds the form together. Many people refer to this "glue" as corporate culture. **Corporate culture** refers to a set of collectively held values, beliefs, and norms of behavior among members of a firm that influence individual employee preferences and behaviors. Corporate culture usually encompasses the ways in which work and authority are organized, the ways in which people are rewarded and controlled, and organizational features such as customs, taboos, company slogans, heroes, and social rituals. A culture can be valuable if it reduces information-processing demands on individuals within the firm, if it reduces the costs of monitoring individuals within the firm, and if it shapes the preferences of individuals within the firm toward a common set of goals—that is, if it decreases transactions costs.

Corporate culture information is available at
http://www.companyculture.info/

Interestingly, many business problems are associated with clashes of corporate cultures. Around 1995, Arthur Andersen was the largest financial services conglomerate the world had ever seen. In 2002 the firm was imploding from scandals involving its auditing services. Some analysts attributed the problem to a clash of culture between the CEO and other executives in the company. The bitter battle between its fledgling consulting arm, Andersen Consulting (now Accenture), and the parent firm began around 1990.

In 1989, the two had reached an agreement—known as the Florida Accord—that created Andersen Consulting as a separate division. The consulting division was to pay an annual fee to Arthur Andersen in recognition of its debt to its parent firm. By 1997, the consultancy was outpacing its parent and the fee income was becoming a very important part of the revenue stream of Arthur Andersen. Thus, the parent company wanted the consultantcy to gain ever more business. As a result, potential conflicts of interest arose between the auditing division of the company and the consulting division.

Creation of Culture

The term *culture* originally comes from social anthropology. Late-nineteenth- and early-twentieth-century studies of early societies such as Eskimo, South Seas, African, and Native American, revealed ways of life that were not only different from those in the more technologically advanced parts of America and Europe but were often very different from each other.[17] These ways of life were deemed to be the culture of the society. In each society certain behaviors and organizations were passed from one generation to the next through behavior, example, stories, and myths. Corporate culture refers to the values and practices that are shared across employees and are passed from more senior employees to new ones.

Once established, organizational cultures are perpetuated in a number of ways. Potential group members may be screened according to how well their values and behavior fit in. New members may be explicitly taught the group's style through training sessions or retreats. Stories, myths, or legends may be told again and again to remind everyone of the group's values and what they mean. Within Wal-Mart, Sam Walton's legend is constantly alluded to. The "HP [Hewlett-Packard] way" and "Houghton Mifflin casual dress" are commonly referred to in these firms. People who successfully achieve the ideals inherent in the culture may be recognized and made into heroes. The natural process of younger members identifying with older members may encourage the younger members to take on the values and styles of their mentors.[18] The company's stories or legends help employees fill in the cultural rules.

Cognitive psychologists argue that the mind naturally categorizes what *people* do, rather than what *events* transpire; if this is true, then employees trying to guess what the cultural rules mean in a new setting can learn best by generalizing from the successful actions of leaders or role models in that setting. Slogans, role models, and social rituals can be viewed as methods of communicating to workers in a low-cost fashion. A slogan like "At Ford, Quality Is Job 1" emphasizes that workers are expected to focus on quality and customer service and that this focus will be rewarded by the company. Thus, employees at Ford may have a reasonably clear idea of how to respond to situations such as encounters with angry customers even without formal policies to follow.

We encounter organizational cultures all the time. Consider the following well-known vision statement:

> These are the voyages of the Starship Enterprise. Its five-year mission: To explore strange new worlds, to seek out new life and new civilizations, to boldly go where no one has gone before.

This statement tells the employees how to behave: They are to explore new worlds and seek out new life. They are even to go boldly into these activities. And this mission has been passed from one generation to another (from one generation of the TV show *Star Trek* to another.)

Performance and Culture

What is the purpose of corporate culture? It is a low-cost way to create and enforce contracts; a corporate culture can be a strategic asset if it economizes on transactions costs and is not easily copied. Managers could take the time to dictate exactly what employees should do by issuing a long book of rules and monitoring employees carefully, but the firm economizes on communication and monitoring costs if employees can accurately guess what they should do.

In 1989, about a decade after the term *corporate culture* came into general use, Time Inc. blocked a hostile bid by Paramount by arguing that its culture would be destroyed or changed by the takeover and that this would be to the detriment of its customers, shareholders, and society. The argument was accepted by the courts and the takeover voided. Is culture important? Is it a strategic asset? Does it add value?

Research does not seem to support the idea that corporate culture enhances performance. Figure 10.4 shows the relationship between the strength of corporate culture and annual growth in stock market value between 1977 and 1988. There appears to be, at most, a very modest positive relationship between the strength of a culture and the stock market performance.[19]

The pattern illustrated in Figure 10.4 is in line with most studies: Evidence does not support the idea that corporate culture serves as a strategic asset. In fact, there are anecdotes and case studies indicating that corporate culture has at times inhibited performance. IBM was a widely admired firm for its management depth and corporate culture until the mid-1980s. Then that culture became a detriment because it was seen as being too conservative and stifling creativity. Similarly, Imperial Chemical Industries, a leading British chemical manufacturer, possessed a strong and homogeneous management culture that had spanned its nearly fifty

Figure 10.4
CORPORATE CULTURE AND PERFORMANCE

The relationship between the strength of corporate culture and market value growth is illustrated.

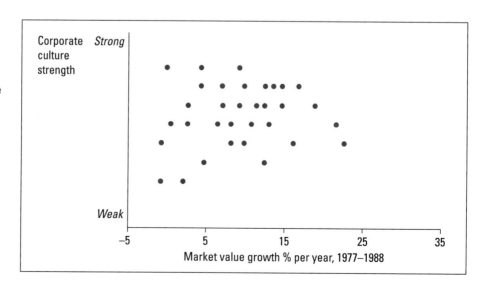

years of existence. In the 1970s, the demand for the core business declined and profitability followed suit. Calls for structural change were made but were not heeded "because of the conservative culture."[20]

If evidence does not show corporate culture adding value, why is so much attention paid to the idea of a corporate culture? The reason has to be that culture is important—is necessary for acquiring profits—but cannot sustain profits because it can be imitated. For instance, virtually identical stories are told in different organizations: IBM workers tell the story of the employee who refused to allow Chairman Thomas Watson Jr. into a restricted area without a badge; at Revlon an identical story is told about Charles Revlon. If a culture reduces transactions costs, then a firm would have to have a culture to be successful. But would it matter just what that culture was? As long as the culture serves to reduce transactions costs, it would not seem to matter exactly what that culture is. Moreover, since it is relatively easy for firms to imitate successful cultures, it would be difficult to sustain above-normal profits on the basis of corporate culture.

CASE REVIEW *Culture Clashes*

What is a culture clash? Could the "clash" of cultures doom the merging of companies like Pharmacia and Upjohn, JP Morgan and Chase Manhattan, or Compaq and Hewlett-Packard?

As we've seen in this chapter, a culture is a set of collectively held values, beliefs, and norms of behavior among members of a society that influence individual behaviors. Corporate culture refers to the values and norms of behavior among the employees of a firm. The purpose of a culture is to improve efficiency. Among societies, a culture creates behaviors that enhance the society—that reduce the costs that individual behavior might impose on society as a whole. The same thing is true for a corporation, where the corporate culture creates behaviors that enhance the operation of the corporation. A corporate culture can be valuable if it reduces information processing demands on individuals within the firm, if it reduces the costs of monitoring individuals within the firm, and if it shapes the preferences of individuals within a firm toward a common set of goals—that is—if it decreases transactions costs.

The questions posed in the case were: What is a culture clash? What is a corporate culture and what is it supposed to do? A culture clash typically refers to a situation where two firms with different cultures attempt to combine but the cultures do not mix. In such a situation, the transaction costs may rise significantly. For example, if one firm had a culture of casualness, informality, and a focus on creativity while another's culture was formal and strictly hierarchical, the two firms would find it difficult to merge. The employees of the more informal firm would feel stifled if they had to work under the more formal culture; the employees of the strictly hierarchical firm would find themselves at a loss regarding what activities they should pursue if they suddenly found themselves working in the more informal culture. An example of this was the merger of AT&T and NCR. NCR employees had a hard time melding into AT&T's highly structured system after years of working in a "fluid" entrepreneurial workplace. The same problem occurred when IBM acquired Rolm, a Silicon Valley–based maker of computerized phone systems in 1984. Rigid Big Blue and laid-back Rolm were a bad match from the start. At Rolm, the culture was one of making decisions from the hip. At IBM, decisions were made by committee.

A firm's organization is supposed to be one that increases efficiency and minimizes transaction costs. The firm's culture has to fit with that organization. A firm organized in an hierarchical form would find its organization clashing with its culture if it attempted to create an informal atmosphere wherein underlings did not report to superiors. Similarly, a firm organized into teams would find a clash with a culture designed to enhance individuality or entrepreneurship.

Pharmacia was a loose patchwork of companies while Upjohn had a structured, hierarchical structure. With their merger came a centralized headquarters where executives there had responsibility for the performance of the local units. This offended many Pharmacia managers and many left the firm. The result was that the remaining company did not have sufficient numbers of people who understood some of the pharmaceuticals in Pharmacia's pipeline—transaction costs rose. Consequently, subsequent product launches were failures. The combined company's stock did not perform well, leading Pharmacia to look to additional acquisitions as a panacea. The company acquired Monsanto Co. in 1999. Since that deal closed, the company's stock has underperformed the Standard and Poor's drug industry average.

In the case of HP and Compaq, performance has not been good since the merger took place in 2002 but it is still too soon to tell if it can earn economic profits over time. It did not earn economic profits in 2002.

SUMMARY

1. The architecture of the firm refers to the firm's organization both internally and externally.
2. Organizational form exists because it is efficient. It can serve as a strategic asset if it adds value and is temporarily, at least, not able to be imitated.
3. Organizational forms have evolved from the family-owned-and-run business, to the U-form, to the M-form, to the matrix and network as conditions have made one efficient and the former one inefficient.
4. The vertical boundaries of the firm are defined by how much of the vertical chain (value chain) is carried out in-house rather than in the market.
5. The horizontal boundaries of the firm are defined by how many different lines of business are carried out in-house rather than being purchased in the market.
6. Transactions are specified in contracts; without enforceable contracts, transactions will be spot transactions.
7. Contracts improve the efficiency of exchange and enable sequential transactions.
8. Corporate culture serves to enhance the efficiency of exchange—to enable contracts to remain general and broad without specifying every contingency.

KEY TERMS

using the market	contract	U-form, unitary form, functional
vertically integrated	hostage	form
upstream	buybacks	M-form, multidivisional form
downstream	offsets	matrix
make-or-buy decision	team	network
transactions costs	self-managed teams	corporate culture

EXERCISES

1. Explain how singing a company song at the beginning of the workday could create a corporate culture. What would the culture be?

2. Assess the relationship between corporate culture and performance. If there is no relationship, why is so much attention paid to corporate culture?

3. Is it possible for a firm to have several different cultures? If so, what does this imply about the relationship between culture and performance?

4. Why is a firm's culture difficult to change?

5. Explain why a firm might select the U-form rather than M-form organizational structure.

6. What is the advantage of the network over the M-form?

7. How could organizational form ever be a competitive advantage?

8. If it is necessary for each employee to interact with all other employees, what organizational form makes most sense? If the employees work independently, not having to interact with one another, which organizational form makes most sense?

CHAPTER NOTES

1. Quoted in Frederick G. Hilmer and Lex Donaldson, *Management Redeemed* (New York: Free Press, 1996), p. 21.
2. Eileen Shapiro, *Fad Surfing in the Boardroom* (Reading, Mass: Addison-Wesley, 1995), p. 39.
3. The term *value chain* was introduced by Michael Porter, *Competitive Advantage* (New York: Free Press, 1985).
4. Ronald Coase, "The Nature of the Firm," *Economica* 4 (1937): 386–405.
5. Oliver Williamson, "Credible Commitments: Using Hostages to Support Exchange," *American Economic Review* 73 (1983): 519–540.
6. The full article can be found at http://www.airspacemag.com/ASM/Mag/Index/1996/AS/lmad.html
7. Chong Ju Choi, "Contract Enforcement Across Cultures," *Organization Studies*, December 22, 1994, p. 673.
8. C. K. Prahalad and G. Hamel, "The Core Competence of the Corporation," *Harvard Business Review* vol. 68 (May/June 1990): 79–91; G. Stalk, P. Evans, and L. Shulman, "Competing on Capabilities: The New Rules of Corporate Strategy," *Harvard Business Review,* vol. 70 (March/April 1992): 57–69; and H. Itami, *Mobilizing Indivisible Assets* (Cambridge, Mass.: Harvard University Press, 1987).
9. "The Jack and Jeff Show Loses Its Luster," *The Economist* (U.S. edition), May 4, 2002 (www.economist.com).
10. V. Ramanujam and P. Varadarajan, "Research on Corporate Diversification: A Synthesis," *Strategic Management Journal* 10 (November/December 1989): 523–553.
11. Dennis Mueller, "A Theory of Conglomerate Mergers," *Quarterly Journal of Economics* 82 (November 1969): 643–659.
12. Y. Amihud and B. Lev, "Risk Reduction as a Managerial Mode for Conglomerate Mergers," *Bell Journal of Economics* 12 (1981): 605–617.
13. Peter Drucker, "The Coming of the New Organization," *Harvard Business Review* 66, no. 1 (January/February 1988): 45–53.
14. Hilmer and Donaldson, *Management Redeemed,* p. 25.
15. The hierarchy is called "too tall" when it is inefficient. John Child, "Parkinson's Progress: Accounting for the Number of Specialists in Organizations," *Administrative Science Quarterly* 18,

no.3 (1973): 328–348; and Lex Donaldson, *For Positivist Organization Theory: Proving the Hard Core* (London: Sage, 1996).

16. Timothy J. Muris, David T. Scheffman, and Pablo T. Spiller, "Strategy and Transaction Costs: The Organization of Distribution in the Carbonated Soft Drink Industry," *Journal of Economics and Management Strategy* 1, no.1 (1992): 83–123.

17. John P. Kotter and James L. Heskett, *Corporate Culture and Performance* (New York: Free Press, 1992).

18. See Tom Peters and R. H. Waterman, *In Search of Excellence* (New York: Harper & Row, 1982); Vijay Sathe, *Culture and Related Corporate Realities* (Homewood, Ill.: Irwin, 1985); William Ouchi, *Theory Z* (Reading, Mass.: Addison-Wesley, 1981); and Richard T. Pascale and Anthony G. Athos, *The Art of Japanese Management* (New York: Simon & Schuster, 1981).

19. John P. Kotter and James L. Heskett, *Corporate Culture and Performance.*

20. A. M. Pettigrew, *The Awakening Giant: Continuity and Change at ICI* (Oxford, UK: Blackwell, 1985), ch. 10, pp. 376–437.

Personnel and Compensation

CASE *Executive Compensation*

In the 1990s, U.S. companies fell in love with stock options as a way to reward their top leaders and to align their interests with those of shareholders. Options encourage risk taking by providing considerable upside potential while limiting losses. Options are a powerful incentive to act in ways that maximize the value of

shares and thus serve the interests of shareholders. Granting options to motivate risk taking, leadership, and hard work captured the spirit of entrepreneurship, the belief in the efficiency of the stock market, and the commitment to shareholder value that characterized American market capitalism in the 1990s. By the end of 2001, 90 percent of large U.S. companies issued stock options, more than ten million American workers received them as part of their compensation packages, and options accounted for about 60 percent of CEO pay. By 2002, in the wake of the sharp drop in the stock market and Enron's collapse, Americans were questioning the wisdom of stock options. Stories proliferated about how top management sold options at peak market values in companies that had since failed, leaving shareholders and employees empty-handed.

Stock options are supposed to align the interests of corporate managers and shareholders. Is something amiss when insiders can reap huge gains from their options while shareholders are losing their equity stakes? How can compensation be structured to create the incentives shareholders want?

Incentives Matter

There is no recipe nor is there a generic strategy for corporate success. The foundation of success is unique to each firm. That uniqueness or distinctive capability may be attributable to a product or service that cannot be imitated, a unique resource, an internal organization that cannot be imitated, or even a unique set of personnel policies. In previous chapters we examined how unique products or services and the architecture of the firm can provide competitive advantage. In this chapter we examine compensation and personnel policies that may affect the performance of the firm. The principle to keep in mind in the area of personnel is that incentives matter. It matters how, when, and how much people are paid. It matters whether people have titles. It matters who one's colleagues are, what the workplace is like, and what times one works. It matters how one perceives one is treated relative to others in the same firm and those in other firms.

A firm is a set of resources combined to generate value that exceeds what each resource alone could produce. This does not mean that the owners of the resources comprising a firm have the same interest. Owners, managers, and employees typically have different objectives. Owners may want the value of the firm to increase irrespective of what managers or employees want. Managers may want increasing compensation, benefits, and perquisites while employees want high pay and benefits, job stability, and lots of leisure time. The problem a firm has is that many of these interests are conflicting. As a result of this conflict, decisions could lead to inefficient outcomes. An important component to a firm's success may be related to how well the interests of all parties are aligned.

The Principal–Agent Relationship

Economists describe individual behavior as being rationally self-interested. The rational part of this description is that people undertake actions or make choices by comparing the costs and benefits of such actions or choices. The self-interested part of the description is that costs and benefits are subjective, defined by each individual.

Thus, whereas Michael Milken, the junk bond king of the 1980s, was self-interested in creating the junk bond financial arena and earning huge sums of money, Mother Teresa, the nun who devoted her life to helping the inhabitants of India's worst slums, was also self-interested in that she greatly enjoyed providing aid to those destitute people. Both Michael Milken and Mother Teresa were rational. Each compared what each perceived to be the costs and benefits of their actions as they made their choices.

Rational self-interest, combined with the idea that individuals prefer more over less, leads to the conclusion that people can be motivated to carry out activities by being compensated to carry out these activities. For instance, if people prefer leisure over work, then they can be induced to work by being compensated for giving up their leisure time. While economists universally agree with this proposition, some social psychologists or organizational behaviorists argue that there are other reasons that employees work. They suggest that offering explicit incentives such as compensation could actually reduce job performance and productivity by eliminating the *intrinsic* desire to carry out some activity. Their argument is based on the belief that individuals often have pride in their work and enjoy carrying out required tasks and that paying people to carry out some task reduces the intrinsic enjoyment of that task. Thus, they argue, firms should appeal to intrinsic motivation rather than compensation if they want workers to perform well.

While intrinsic motivation may be a factor in job performance, it is a very minor one. In fact, no evidence has been provided to show that it plays any kind of important role.[1] Thus, in this chapter we focus on the explicit motivations of compensation and other personnel actions.

Applying the idea of rational self-interest to behavior inside a firm, we can describe the hired manager (the CEO) as having an incentive to do the best for himself no matter what happens to the shareholder or owner. We can also assume that the owner has the incentive of wanting the value of her company to increase as much as possible no matter what happens to the CEO. These two interests may conflict. For instance, the CEO may find that his own wealth is increased by having the company undertake risky actions that could undermine the wealth of the owner, or the owner could find that the sale of her ownership is the best option for her even though it harms the CEO.

When one individual acts on behalf of another individual, a *principal–agent relationship* is said to exist. The principal is the first individual, the one wanting some task undertaken or some result carried out. The agent is the individual who carries out the action on behalf of the first individual. We can describe the CEO of a publicly held firm as the agent of the shareholders, who are the principals. The hired manager of a private firm is the agent of the owner or owners. Employees are the agents of the CEO or manager.

The problem of principal–agent relationships is that the principal and agent may have different interests. How can the principal ensure that the agent acts in the best interests of the principal? The principal must create the incentives that will align the agent's interests with his own. This is what the compensation and personnel policies within a firm are primarily about—aligning interests.

If the principal and the agent had perfect information, a contract between them could be created that would ensure the correct behaviors. But seldom, if ever, is information perfect. As a result, problems arise in the principal–agent relationship. One problem is that the incentive scheme may be incomplete or imperfect; it may align the interests of principal and agent more closely than if there was no incentive scheme, but it may not do so perfectly. For instance, using stock options to reward executives for good performance may have more closely aligned the interests of shareholder and executive, but a great deal of room remained for behavior that benefited the executive at the expense of the shareholder. Executives have an incentive to increase the value of the options even at the expense of shareholders by manipulating accounting figures, taking costs off-book, booking revenues too soon, or other activities that might increase the stock price at least temporarily.

A second problem arising in principal–agent relationships is called *moral hazard*. A moral hazard problem refers to actions taken by the agent, after an agreement between principal and agent has occurred, that are opposed to what the principal and agent agreed to. For example, an insurance company wants the drivers it insures to act responsibly and drive carefully, so it provides lower-cost insurance for those drivers who are responsible and safe. The moral hazard arises when the insured driver changes her behavior; being insured, she becomes a much less responsible and safe driver. Moral hazard may arise when the behavior of the principal or agent is difficult to observe. Consider, as another example, what could occur when the performance of employees in a certain job in the firm is very difficult for the manager to observe. The manager, aware of the problem, hires only those employees who have demonstrated high performance in the past. If,

For research on personnel, visit http://www.ssrn.com/update/ern/ern_personnel.html

once the employee lands the new job, he begins doing less work, being less productive, and devoting less efforts to the job, then a moral hazard has occurred.

The structure of contracts and compensation can be explained as ways to align the interests of principal and agent and minimize moral hazard.

Relationships Between the Firm and Its Employees

Let's begin by considering the relationship between the firm and its employees. People possess different abilities and motives, and different firms may want different types of employees. One firm might want those who are best suited to working alone. Another firm might desire those able to work in teams. If firms are not likely to know which potential employee has which characteristics, then a firm that can select or attract the appropriate personnel most efficiently may have a competitive advantage.

One approach for a firm that is unable to measure a priori (ahead of time) whether an employee fits with the firm is to create a way that individuals can sort themselves into the appropriate positions. A firm's compensation policies and other personnel policies may induce people to sort themselves into the occupations or jobs for which they have a comparative advantage. Some people may prefer to help others and be willing to accept lower pay to work at charitable institutions. Sometimes people sort themselves by skill. Firms such as Microsoft, Cray Research, and 3M are well known for attracting the brightest talent. Some of this is due to idiosyncratic factors that are hard to duplicate; for example, computer hardware designers who wanted to work with the eccentric Seymour Cray or software designers who want to work with Bill Gates and his staff. But the reward structure of the firm can also attract specific kinds of workers. For instance, paying people solely on the basis of their performance would tend to attract those who believe they can perform very well and deter those who know they cannot perform as well. Those who know they would not succeed in such a position would not even apply for it.

Employee Compensation

Efficiency Wage

Once a firm has hired the type of people it wants, it has to decide whether it wants to retain those people and for how long. If an employee can switch to another job at any time and that other job is just as desirable as the current one, then the employee doesn't care if he gets dismissed. In such a case, the employee may not contribute as much to the firm as the firm would like. The firm must make the agent want to keep the job; that is, increase the agent's opportunity cost of getting fired. One way the firm can do this is by paying an **efficiency wage**—compensating the employee more than the employee's opportunity wage or more than the existing market wage. The size of the premium the firm pays over other firms depends on the costs of monitoring the behavior of employees. The firm can take steps to reduce the efficiency wage it must pay to assure hard work, such as investing in accounting and other monitoring practices, and it can reduce the costs of working hard, for example, by offering catered lunches and dinners. The optimal efficiency wage will balance the marginal costs of monitoring activities and the marginal benefits of more productive workers.

Figure 11.1

WAGE PROFILE

Compensation rises as the years with a firm increase.

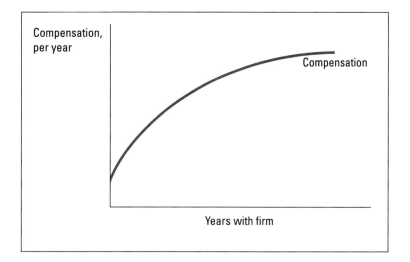

Backloaded Compensation

Another way that firms can attract and retain the personnel they desire is to structure the pay over an employee's work life in a certain way. At many firms, compensation increases with time on the job; this is called a rising wage profile and is illustrated in Figure 11.1. Why do wages tend to increase with time on the job? A simple explanation is that the rising wage profile is just a way of paying people for the value they contribute to the firm. An employee's productivity (value to the company) rises as she gains training and other skills. Medical residents, law clerks, accountants, and bank trainees, for example, earn low wages initially and then high wages as their time on the job rises.

Suppose an employee's value to the firm tends to be higher than her compensation when she is first hired. Then, as time on the job increases, compensation increases relative to the employee's value to the firm. In later years of an employee's work-life, the employee's value to the firm falls below compensation, so that the employee is getting a premium of an amount shown by the area between productivity (value to firm) and compensation in Figure 11.2.

Figure 11.2

BACKLOADED WAGES

Initially compensation is less than productivity, but eventually compensation is greater than productivity. This pattern ensures that the employee has an incentive to stay with the firm.

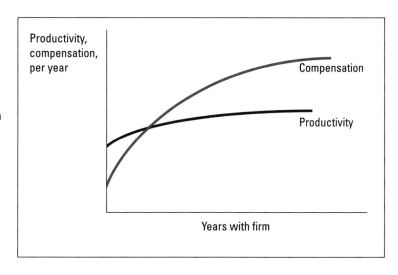

When workers are paid less than what they are worth to the firm early in their tenure and more than what they are worth late in their tenure, the pay structure is referred to as **backloaded** or *deferred* **compensation.** Why would a firm use backloaded compensation? Clearly, the longer the employee stays with the firm, the better off he is. Thus, backloaded pay creates an incentive for an employee to remain with a firm. Firms that spend significant amounts to train employees may find backloaded pay to be an efficient compensation structure. Training is costly, and the firm must tolerate low productivity by new workers until they are trained. Firms that make such investments would naturally like their workers to remain with the firm for a long time. Backloaded compensation is a means of tying the employee to the firm. It helps reduce employee turnover.

Another aspect of backloaded compensation is that it can serve as an incentive for employees to perform as they were contracted to perform. The promise of above-market wages in future years deters employees from slacking off or shirking; those who get fired lose out—they don't get to collect the "bonus" of compensation above productivity in future years.

If backloaded compensation serves as a carrot to reward hard work and investments in training, then increased labor-market turnover, such as occurs in corporate restructuring and downsizing, could have a pernicious effect on effort. Workers with little tenure may perceive that they are unlikely to keep their jobs long enough to climb up the wage–tenure profile. This might reduce incentives to work hard and undertake firm-specific training and it might keep the best people from joining the firm in the first place.

What type of firm is most likely to downsize by reducing its labor force? Everything else being the same, it would be the firm that does not have backloaded compensation and a steep wage–productivity profile. So how would a firm that has a steep wage–productivity profile and backloaded compensation lay off workers in a downsizing move? The firm would have to compare the benefits of reducing labor expenses to the costs of reducing morale and the firm's reputation. In essence, the firm would have to provide a separate package that would offset any losses of backloaded compensation; it would have to ensure that remaining employees and new hires are compensated for the additional risk of future layoffs. This indeed is what began occurring in 1997 after some large layoffs. Many companies had to face the issue of how to reestablish the loyalty or trust of employees. AT&T began giving employees more freedom to choose jobs; Xerox and many other companies instituted a program of bonuses for lower-level workers; many companies made benefits more flexible; and many others gave workers more of a say in their jobs.

Suppose a firm wants to induce turnover, to continually bring in "new blood." High-tech firms often bid for employees in other high-tech firms. This enables the companies to stay abreast of what the other companies are doing. It also enables the firm to benefit from new ideas and approaches if existing employees tend to become stale or fail to keep up with the state of the art. A relatively flat compensation profile leads to what is referred to as **wage compression.** New employees are brought in at compensation levels that nearly match or even exceed the compensation of employees who have been with the firm for a number of years. With this type of compensation scheme, the only way that an employee could receive large increases in pay would be to change companies.

People would not want to join a firm with backloaded compensation if it was known that the firm would fire them before they could acquire the backloaded benefits. As a result, a firm offering backloaded compensation would also offer guarantees for job tenure and a reputation for retaining employees. People would not invest in activities that are firm-specific if it was known that the firm did not compensate them for the investments. For instance, an employee who devotes time and money to obtain training that has value only to the current employer is at the mercy of that firm. An employee who undertakes firm-specific training would find his value to be much lower in another firm if he was fired from the position for which he obtained the training. As a result, the only way an individual will undertake such firm-specific training is if he is compensated for it.

Piece-Rate Compensation

The most simple, straightforward compensation scheme would be to pay people for the value they contribute to the firm. Lincoln Electric, as discussed in the Chapter 1 Case, pays employees on a **piecework rate** basis; that is, an employee is paid according to how much he or she produces. Employees are not paid for defective products. The piecework rates allow employees producing at a standard rate to earn a wage comparable to that for similar jobs in the local labor market. Employees can double and sometimes triple their pay by producing more. Lincoln Electric's policies prohibit piecework pay-rate changes simply because an employee is making too much money. In addition, employees cannot be dismissed for working too hard; any employee who has been at Lincoln Electric for at least two years is guaranteed employment for at least 75 percent of the standard forty-hour week. This policy of paying piece-rate has served Lincoln Electric well. It took over and dominated a market that at one time included many competitors.

A piece-rate compensation scheme attracts people who are productive, who work hard, and who enjoy working individually. People who are not productive, who do not want to work hard and put in long hours, or who enjoy working in groups or teams would not choose to work for a firm using piece-rate compensation. Thus, it would seem that a piece-rate system would lead to increased productivity in any firm, just as it did with Lincoln Electric.

Would switching workers from hourly wages to piecework rates boost productivity for any firm? Only if the costs of measuring individual output are small will piecework pay raise productivity. One firm that made the switch was Safelite Glass Corp. of Columbus, Ohio. Management changed the compensation practices, moving from hourly to piecework pay. While guaranteed a minimum wage of about $11 an hour, glass installers were offered the alternative of receiving $20 per unit installed, giving them an incentive to earn more by working faster. To keep quality from suffering, the task of replacing defectively installed windshields at no pay was assigned to the same shop. Because the names of the initial installers were known to their co-workers, employees felt strong peer pressure to improve their performance or resign. The payoff from piecework was substantial. Average productivity per worker rose 20 percent, average earnings rose by 10 percent, and overall company output surged by 36 percent. When Canadian tree planters were paid for each tree planted, the number of trees planted increased about 35 percent. When salespeople in retail department stores were paid piece-rate, store productivity rose about 10 percent.[2]

Why doesn't every firm use a piecework compensation scheme? Firms in which it is difficult to observe the productivity of individual employees would find it very inefficient to use a piecework system. There have been instances in which a piecework compensation scheme has been detrimental to firm performance. A number of retail firms that attempted to tie sales clerks' pay to the amount they sold found that this created a situation in which clerks were undermining each other and thus negatively affecting the firm's performance. When some telemarketing firms paid according to the number of calls made, the reps reduced the quality of each contact in order to increase the quantity. Revenues from calls actually declined. In 1992 Sears abolished a system of compensating mechanics in its auto repair shops on the basis of the profit from customer-authorized repairs. The mechanics had misled customers into authorizing unnecessary repairs. When computer programmers at AT&T were paid for the number of lines of code they produced, programs became much longer than was necessary.[3] A piecework pay system makes no sense if individual contributions to output cannot be measured. Such a situation exists when production is team-oriented.

Teams

In the 1990s, teams became a widely adopted management technique. The business news media were reporting that corporate America was having a love affair with teams. According to these reports, teams were instituted because of the widely held belief that when people work together the team spirit spurs individual effort and enhances the productivity of all.

When we think of teams, the first thought we often have is of sports. So to illustrate why piece-rate pay might not work in a team setting, consider professional basketball. If each player was paid solely on the basis of points scored, rebounds, and other individual measures, each would act to increase those numbers even if the number of wins declined. What would happen to diving on the floor to retrieve a ball or other elements of defense if pay was based only on the number of points one scored? How could the owner measure one player's contribution to the team? Ken O'Brien was a quarterback with the New York Jets who was prone to throwing interceptions. To try to reduce the number of times the football was caught by the opposition, the Jets gave him a contract that penalized him for the number of interceptions he threw. The contract resulted in fewer interceptions, but this was because O'Brien refused to throw the football even when he should have. The piecework pay scheme hurt team performance.

These sports examples suggest that piecework pay schemes won't work in team settings. If the best way to organize production is with teams, then a compensation scheme to encourage teamwork must be installed. What structure of compensation will enhance teamwork? We can answer this question only by knowing the incentives individuals have when they are part of a team.

The benefits of teamwork are that the whole is greater than the sum of its parts—total productivity is greater than if each individual member of the team worked alone. The costs of teamwork are that when the effort of any member of the team is not easily observed, the team members have an incentive to **free ride** on the efforts of the others. Free riding refers to the idea of doing less work because you expect others to do the work. If everyone free rides, no work gets done.

Free riding is a problem whenever output is team-oriented and an individual's contribution to that output is not easily measurable. So, if the benefits of teamwork are substantial, the firm must figure out ways to minimize free riding. One approach is to create an incentive for team members to monitor one anothers' performance. For instance, one person could be appointed the monitor. If the monitor was paid on the basis of the profits the team generated—the revenues in excess of all costs and payment to the other team members—the monitor would have an incentive to ensure that the performance was good.

But even a monitor might be unable to detect shirking if individual actions are not observable and output is team-oriented. In cases where the monitor cannot observe individual behavior but other team members can, then basing part of each team member's pay on evaluations by the other team members could help minimize shirking. Peer pressure has been found to be an important part of the team compensation process, although it does not totally solve the free-riding problem.

Many firms use profit sharing to one extent or another. In a profit-sharing scheme, employees' wages or pensions are based on the profits of the entire firm. What motivation do employees have in such cases? They have an incentive to shirk, but they also have an incentive to monitor other employees to be sure they aren't shirking. If the monitoring effect dominates the free-riding effect, then profit-sharing results in increased performance.

Subjective Evaluations

Basing at least a portion of compensation on subjective evaluations may reduce free riding. As noted above, Lincoln Electric is well known for its piecework pay system. Less well known is the fact that Lincoln Electric bases nearly half of a worker's annual compensation on the supervisor's subjective assessment of a worker's innovation, dependability, and cooperation. Why does Lincoln Electric place such an emphasis on subjective evaluations? Because the company realizes that if workers did not display these cooperative types of behavior, total productivity would decline.

While subjective evaluations may create incentives for individuals to contribute to the team, they may also result in inefficiencies. Sometimes, for example, supervisors do not sufficiently differentiate good from bad performance in their ratings. As a result, the best performers do not receive the rewards to which they are entitled, possibly causing them to become less motivated to perform well or even to leave the firm. Another possible result is that underlings spend time "sucking up" to supervisors. Economists refer to such activity as rent seeking—actions that take time or effort away from creating value for the firm. In addition, if the supervisor responds to the rent-seeking actions of employees, then inefficient promotions, bonuses, and job assignments are likely to result.

To obtain the benefits of subjective evaluations and minimize their costs, firms often implement rules or restrictions on compensation. For instance, job grades may be assigned salary ranges—minimum and maximum—that cannot be violated. The firm may then make promotion dependent on evaluations by more people than just the supervisor or may make seniority an important component in promotions and layoffs. Alternatively, positions may be constrained by minimum experience requirements—workers have to stay in a position for a certain amount of time before they can be promoted.

While rules like salary ranges and time in position may minimize rent-seeking activities, they may distort the efficient allocation of people and jobs. For instance, a worker may be promoted because of seniority even though a better candidate for the job exists. The determination of a compensation scheme and accompanying personnel policies requires a cost-benefit calculation: The benefits of the rules must be compared to the costs to determine whether the rules will lead to appropriate actions.

Risk

Firms and their employees are subject to risks. Pay may fluctuate, profits may fluctuate, people may be laid off, and firms may go bankrupt. These outcomes may be the result of actions that the individual or the firm can control as well as actions that are out of their control. Compensation schemes and personnel policies may be based on risk sharing. *Risk-sharing* occurs when the aggregate cost of bearing risk is lower when two or more individuals share that risk than when each bears the risk individually.

Insurance provides a good example of risk sharing. An insurance company that has many policyholders can spread risks widely, enabling it to reduce the risks of individual policyholders. For example, the risk that you will have an automobile accident is independent of the risk that any other person will have an accident. Thus, an insurance company can ask each policyholder to pay a price for insurance equal to the expected amount of the loss plus a margin for expenses and profit and be reasonably sure that the aggregate premium will enable it to pay whatever losses may be suffered. With the insurance, the individual policyholder is avoiding the risk—in essence sharing the risk with other policyholders and with the insurance company.

An individual would purchase insurance if he were risk-averse. He would not purchase insurance if he could tolerate risk or was risk-seeking. Insurance companies and large firms in general can tolerate risk. They are risk-neutral; that is, they are neither averse to risk nor do they seek it. When risk is shared between a risk-neutral firm and a risk-averse employee, the optimal share of the risk to be borne by the employee is zero. The risk-neutral party should bear all the risk. Thus, if firms are risk-neutral, then risk sharing would have no role in the compensation schemes and personnel policies of firms. The reason that risk sharing plays a role is because of the possibility of moral hazard. If employees can change behavior once an agreement has been reached—if once an individual has insurance, she changes the behavior that is insured—then the firm is no longer risk-neutral. It must figure out a way to ensure that the individual minimizes moral hazard behavior.

The degree to which a firm must share risk with a worker depends on the worker's attitude toward risk. Most people tend to be risk-averse. This means that most people would prefer a job where their income is assured to one that has the same expected value but where their income is at risk. For example, a risk-averse individual would prefer to get $1,000 with certainty than to have a possibility of getting either $0 or $2,000, each with a 0.5 probability. (A risk-seeking individual would prefer the chance to get $2,000—having expected value 0.5 ($0) + 0.5 ($2,000) = $1,000—to the certain $1,000.) The risk-seeking individual would require less risk sharing but more reward if the outcome is good. The risk-averse individual would require a good deal of risk sharing and a more assured reward, but not as high a reward if the outcome is good.

If a worker's income is subject to changes due to factors beyond his control, he would need to be paid more in order to accept the risk that he could work hard and produce little. As an example, consider the situation of the shift manager at a Circle K convenience store. The shift manager has very little control over demand, pricing, and other factors that affect the profits of the store during her shift. These are more affected by national-level policies governing advertising and menu composition. Paying the manager on the basis of the profitability of the store during her shift would force her to bear risks that she has no control over. Similarly, farmworkers cannot completely control the size of harvests because they do not control the weather. Paying them solely on the basis of the quantity of products they harvest would subject them to sizable risks over which they have no control.

When individuals must bear uncontrollable risk, they want some type of insurance to protect them against losses. But once they have the insurance, they may alter their behavior and become more subject to the risk. In insurance contracts, moral hazard is minimized with the use of co-payments and deductibles. Having to be responsible for some payments when insurance is used reduces the likelihood that the policyholder will act in a moral hazard manner. Similarly, firms create compensation schemes and personnel policies to provide individuals some insurance and minimize moral hazard problems.

Some firms pay workers an agreed-upon contract—an assured amount independent of the firm's performance—and then provide a bonus based on the firm's overall performance. The assured income provides the employee income without risk. The bonus adds some risk to the employee's income, but that risk is shared with all other employees of the firm. The bonus is analogous to a co-payment in an insurance contract. It creates an incentive for the employee not only to contribute to the firm above and beyond his or her job but also to monitor other employees to minimize moral hazard problems. Basing compensation or a part of compensation on relative comparisons enables the firm to share the risk with the employee. The Circle K manager's performance is compared to the performance of managers of the same shift at other stores or to the performance of other shift managers once differences between the shifts—such as the amount of walk-in traffic—are accounted for. As a result, while the manager's salary depends on her actions, it does not depend on uncontrollable risk.

Compensation schemes and personnel policies can be viewed as arrangements serving to align the interests of employees and owners of firms. They also enable the firm to risk-share with employees and to minimize potential moral hazard problems. Executive compensation policies play the same role in the relationship between the chief executive officer and the owners of the firm.

Executive Compensation

Discussing the compensation and personnel policies of a firm necessitates an examination of CEO compensation. The CEO is the most visible person associated with a firm, and the CEO's pay is often a topic of concern. The CEO is a hired manager, working as the agent of the owner. This means the interests of CEO and owner probably differ and must be aligned somehow if the firm is to be successful.

Executive pay has risen significantly since the early 1990s. Moreover, it has risen significantly more than the compensation of other employees. In 1990, the average CEO earned about 30 times more than the average employee in his or her firm; today that multiple is about 111. Why is CEO pay so high and so much higher than the pay of other employees? Is it because CEOs can do what they want and reward themselves? According to many studies, that is exactly what happens.

Michael Eisner, Chairman and CEO of Disney, receives as much as one-half billion dollars a year in compensation. In December 1997 he exercised $570 million in stock options. When Disney did poorly in 1999, Eisner was penalized with no annual bonus. Since executive bonuses in Disney are tied to the company's performance, Eisner only got an annual salary of $750,000 in 1999. In 2000, his base salary rose to $1 million, his first raise since joining the company in 1984, bringing his total compensation—an $813,462 base salary and $8.5 million bonus—to $9.3 million in 2000. Just how well did Disney do in fiscal 2000? The entertainment giant reported a profit of $1.9 billion on revenue of $25 billion.

A few studies have shown that executive pay is generally related to the size of the firm, so that executives have an incentive to pursue growth rather than profit.[4] This is what analysts say happened to Briggs & Stratton in the 1990s. The company, which produces lightweight engines such as those used in lawn mowers, was very successful from 1929 to 1989. Owners wanted continued increases in stock prices but managers directed the firm toward size. The result was poor company and stock price performance.

Some studies have pointed out that managers choose debt levels that benefit themselves more than the company's shareholders. The argument is that since their earned incomes come entirely from the firm, managers cannot diversify their income risks as easily as shareholders can. Thus, managers may choose investment projects with a risk/return combination involving lower risk or may diversify the firm. Such efforts to diversify are generally not in shareholders' interests, since shareholders are able to reap any benefits of diversification in their own portfolios. They do not need the firm to diversify for them.

It has also been argued that managers avoid returning capital to shareholders and, instead, invest that money in unproductive uses. Payment of cash to shareholders reduces the resources controlled by managers, thereby reducing their power and potentially subjecting them to the monitoring by capital markets that occurs when a firm must obtain new capital. Conflicts of interest between shareholders and managers over payout policies are especially severe when the firm generates substantial free cash flows. The oil industry's investment in exploration even after the world oil price plummeted in the 1980s is often cited as an example. Another piece of evidence of the spending of free cash is what happens when firms receive unexpected cash windfalls as legal settlements. They often proceed to borrow even more in order to make an acquisition that turns out poorly and is subsequently divested. They also use the dollars to buy out large stockholders (called blockholders).

Stock Options

Given the differing interests of owners and managers, how can the owners ensure that the manager pursues strategies that are in the owners' interests? In the 1970s and 1980s, executive pay was largely a matter of salaries and bonuses that were paid out only if financial targets were met. As studies began casting doubt on the relationship between bonuses, financial targets, and stock prices, corporate boards of directors turned their attention to shareholder value.[5] They became convinced that the surest way to align the interests of managers with those of shareholders was to make stock options a large component of executive compensation. By 2000, stock options accounted for more than half of total CEO compensation in the largest U.S. companies and about 30 percent of senior operating managers' pay.

The conventional way stock options are structured is that the exercise price (the price at which the stock can be purchased) is established at the market price on the day the options are granted and stays fixed over the entire option period, usually ten years. If the share price rises above the exercise price, the option holder can cash in on the gains. The idea was that if the CEO was able to increase stock prices above the price at which the options were granted, then the CEO would gain. This would give the CEO an incentive to increase shareholder value.

The problem firms ran into in the 1990s is that almost all stock prices rose. When the market is rising, stock options reward both superior and sub-par performance because any increase in a company's share price will reward the holder of a stock option. In the 1990s, stock options gave many managers huge compensation increases, but many of these rewards went to managers whose firms had not performed even as well as the market average.

The large rewards given to executives were not greeted well by the business press. In most magazines the issue that gained attention was executives being paid hundreds of millions of dollars while their companies were losing value in the stock market.

What is the most efficient way to create the proper incentives for CEOs to act on behalf of the shareholders? Some people have argued that the government should limit executive pay,[6] and many boards of directors have placed ceilings on CEO bonuses. A government limit on pay would have the effect of driving the best-performing CEOs out of the market. They would quit being hired managers and seek fame and fortune elsewhere. The ceilings suggested by some boards of directors can lead to perverse behavior in some circumstances. For instance, when the CEO's bonus is at its upper limit, the CEO tends to manipulate earnings downward—perhaps as a means of deferring the earnings to a later period when the bonus ceiling is not binding. When near the upper limit, a CEO may choose not to pursue a project that appears to be potentially profitable but is risky for fear that the risky venture could reduce his or rewards.[7]

Market for Corporate Control

Suppose you, as a shareholder, believe a certain CEO is running your firm into the ground. What can you do? You can sell your shares and purchase shares of companies whose CEOs are running their firms in such a way as to increase shareholder value. This action imposes some discipline on CEOs. But, as we've discussed previously, the CEO has some room between running the firm into the ground and running the firm so as not to drive all shareholders away but still create benefits for him- or herself. This room is reduced if share ownership is concentrated in the hands of a few people or institutions. Large shareholders, or blockholders, have the ability to ensure that management follows the owners' desires. CalPERS (the California state retirement system), TIAA-CREF (the largest retirement investment firm), and investment firms such as Vanguard have been involved in monitoring CEO activities to one degree or another. Increasing one's percentage of ownership in a firm is, in a sense, purchasing the right to control the corporation. Blockholders are able to exert some amount of control over the CEO's behavior by controlling a large percentage of the corporation. If the blockholder owned a majority of shares, it would own total control of the firm.

Financial innovations in the 1980s, such as junk bond financing, allowed leveraged buyouts (LBOs) and management buyouts (MBOs), which increased the ease with which an investor could take over a company. Certain investors became known as raiders or takeover experts. T. Boone Pickens and Carl Icahn, two of the best-known raiders, would purchase the majority of shares using leveraged buyouts and then often sell or dismantle the assets of the firm. To the takeover experts, the firm was worth less than the sum of its parts. Since even the largest of the *Fortune* 500 companies is potentially subject to takeover, CEOs have to maintain the value of the company. Getting taken over typically means that the CEO is out of a job. In fact, more than 50 percent of the top-level managers of target firms are gone within three years of acquisition. In general, CEO positions have become very precarious; between 1995 and 2000, the average tenure of 450 CEOs was less than three years.[8]

With a higher risk of losing his or her position, the risk-averse CEO requires some form of compensation for taking that risk. This may at least partially account for the use of stock options and the inflated rewards CEOs have obtained since the early 1990s. But irrespective of the compensation increases, a firm's executives want to make the firm immune to takeover. Many management contracts now include **golden parachutes**—severance contracts that compensate managers for the loss of their jobs in the event of a change in control—and several boards of directors have instituted greenmail, poison pills, authorized lawsuits, and the use of state anti-takeover laws. **Greenmail** occurs when target management ends a hostile takeover threat by repurchasing, at a premium, the hostile suitor's block of target stock. A **poison pill** refers to a situation in which shareholders are given the option of purchasing additional shares at a low price or selling shares at prices well above the offered acquisition price when a takeover begins. When the pill is swallowed, the acquiring firm bears the costs.

On the surface, these defense mechanisms appear to benefit the CEO at the expense of the shareholder, but it is not clear that they always harm the shareholder. The assurance of some form of compensation to the high-level manager in the event of a takeover could attract a higher quality of manager and thus cause the firm's performance to improve. Stock prices of firms that adopted severance-

For information on corporate governance, visit

http://www.oecd.org
http://www.corpgov.net/
http://www.encycogov.com/

A glossary of terms pertaining to corporate governance is available at

http://www.corp-gov.org/glossary.php3

related compensation contracts for managers in the mid-1990s rose about 3 percent when adoption of the contracts was announced. On average, however, the use of defense mechanisms has been met with negative stock price reactions.[9]

Corporate Governance

Another way to align owner and manager interests is to change corporate governance or make it more strict. Corporate governance refers to the structure of institutions that exist to watch over and direct the performance of the firm. In corporations, the board of directors is the shareholders' agent, while the CEO is the board's agent. Thus, stockholders' interests are looked after within a company by the board of directors.

Board members are directly elected by stockholders. The typical board consists of a mix of inside and outside directors. Inside directors are senior employees of the company. Their role is to provide valuable information about the company's activities—inside information that would be difficult for outsiders to obtain. Outside directors are not full-time employees of the company. These are individuals with experience at other companies or on other boards. Many of them are full-time professional directors who hold positions on the boards of several companies.

The board is responsible for hiring, firing, and compensating corporate employees, including the CEO. Some observers argue that boards are not effective stewards of the shareholders' interests because the boards are dominated by the CEO, particularly in those cases where the CEO is also chairman of the board. They point out that both inside and outside directors are often the personal nominees of the CEO. The typical inside director is subordinate to the CEO in the company's hierarchy and therefore aligned with the boss. Often the CEO nominates outside directors who are aligned with the CEO's interests rather than the shareholders'.

In the 1980s, many companies began compensating board members with stock options in order to ensure that their interests aligned with the shareholders' interests. In 1983 only about 2 percent of boards had some equity-based compensation; that number rose to about 30 percent by 2000. As with the CEO's stock options, the idea appeared to be good—to create incentives for CEOs and boards to increase the value of the firm. Obviously, the criticisms of the use of stock options to reward CEOs apply to boards of directors as well. But as we saw in the case of the CEO, the market for corporate control is a means of disciplining boards of directors; if firm value declines, a takeover could occur and the directors would lose their positions.

If a board of directors allows the CEO to manipulate earnings and inflate the stock price without increasing economic profit, then the board members are subject to legal and financial scrutiny following the collapse of the stock once the manipulations become public. The members of Enron's board of directors found themselves under intense scrutiny following the company's collapse. Many were fired from other board positions they held, and several were investigated for illegal activity.

Tournaments and Superstars

Why is CEO pay so much greater than that of other employees in the firm? One answer could be that the market for CEOs has failed—that CEOs have been able

Sustaining Competitive Advantage

to pursue their own interests at the expense of the shareholders. Another explanation could be that this structure is efficient—that it elicits the most productivity from the CEO and from other employees in the firm. There are two versions of the efficiency argument—the tournament rationale and the superstar rationale.

The tournament rationale is presented as an analogy to sporting contests. The argument notes that in most corporations, promotion and pay increases go hand in hand, so we could think of promotion as the result of a large contest pitting all employees against each other. People move up the corporate hierarchy and obtain pay raises by performing better than all the others who are also trying to move up the hierarchy. Once a person is promoted, a new tournament begins, with the winner advancing to a still higher level. The final prize is the top job, the CEO position.

If job promotion within the firm is a contest, what compensation structure will elicit the most productive behavior from participants? It has been found that in golf tournaments, the more that the first prize exceeds the payoff for second and lower finishes, the better is the average performance of the contestants; that is, the greater the payoff, the better the average performance. It has also been found that in NASCAR racing, the greater the difference between the first prize and the payoff for second and lower finishes, the faster the average track speed; again, the greater the payoff, the better the average performance. Carrying these findings over to the labor market inside the firm, economists have suggested that an extremely high pay package for the CEO relative to other employees would induce all employees (current and future) to exert extra effort on the job.

The second efficiency rationale is also explained with an analogy to sports. It is called the *superstar effect.* Consider the fact that the playing ability of the top ten tennis players or golfers is not much better than the playing ability of the players ranked between forty and fifty. Nonetheless, the compensation differences are incredibly large. The average income of the top ten tennis players and golfers is in the tens of millions, while that of the lower-ranked ten players is in the hundreds of thousands. If their performances are not that much different, why is their compensation so different? The explanation provided is that since consumers have limited time, they choose to follow the top players. A tennis match between the fortieth- and forty-first-ranked players might be nearly as good as that between the first- and second-ranked players. Yet nearly everyone would choose to watch the first- and second-ranked players. At golf tournaments, huge throngs surround the top players, while lesser-known contenders play the game without many onlookers. These differences mean that the demand for the top players is huge relative to the demand for the lesser-ranked players.

The superstar effect also occurs outside of sports. Two lawyers of relatively equal ability might earn significantly different fees, as might two economic consultants with apparently similar abilities. Consider two people who could direct the firm according to various strategies. If the choice could mean billions of dollars in firm value, even if there are very small differences between the two people, the one with the better chance of making the wealth-enhancing decision will receive a huge compensation relative to the other.

As has been stated repeatedly throughout this text, there is no recipe nor is there a generic strategy for corporate success. The foundation of success is unique to each firm. In this chapter we have discussed how firms might structure their compensation and personnel policies to develop a competitive advantage. The principle to keep in mind in the area of personnel and compensation is that incentives matter. To observe some feature of personnel or compensation and automatically claim it is unfair or incorrect is probably to miss the point: There probably is an efficiency reason the situation exists. Remember that competition and entry drive inefficiency out. If a compensation scheme were inefficient, it would not last long.

CASE REVIEW *Executive Compensation*

Is something amiss when insiders can reap huge gains from their options while shareholders are losing their equity stakes? How can compensation be structured to create the incentives shareholders want? If options are more effective than cash compensation in aligning employee and shareholder interests, then an option grant will have a greater effect on shareholder value than a cash compensation payment of the same size. The negative, or dilutive, effects of options on shareholder value will be offset in part by their positive effects on expected future earnings. The fact that options became a much more important factor in determining CEO compensation should have led to an improvement in firm performance and shareholder value. But we found that many executives were rewarded in the 1990s simply because the stock market rose so dramatically, not because their firms performed well. Options are supposed to reward business leaders for higher stock values caused not by a stock market bubble but by company actions that create the fundamentals on which sustainable shareholder value depends. The problem appears not to have been the use of options but the way in which the option payments were structured. Options could be designed to pay off only if a company's stock outperforms the overall market or a peer group of companies over some period of time. Unilever introduced a plan that embodies this approach in 2000. Boeing introduced performance units that are convertible to common stock only if Boeing stock appreciates annually for five years.

SUMMARY

1. Different people within a firm have different interests. When interests are not aligned, then the performance of the firm can be affected. Different interests on the part of employees, managers, and owners could lead to inefficiencies.

2. A means of aligning the diverse interests within a firm must be found in order for the parties to gain from working with each other (what we referred to as gains from trade in Chapter 2). An efficient resolution of the misalignment of interests could be a source of competitive advantage. Aligning the different interests is the role of personnel policies and compensation structures.

3. Efficiency wages and backloaded compensation are ways to increase efficiency. Efficiency wages is the name given to a pay scheme in which employees are paid a premium over the market in an effort to attract the best employees. Backloaded wages are deferred wages; that is, wages that are earned today but received later. A backloaded compensation scheme is one

in which employees are paid less than their value to the firm in the early years of their employment and then paid more than their value in later years. This serves to keep the employee with the firm for a period long enough to acquire the extra compensation. It also serves to minimize shirking, since employees would lose the extra compensation if they were fired.

4. Teams are used in business because they are believed to increase productivity. The primary problem with teams is free riding. Free riding occurs because individual contributions to team output cannot be measured. As a result, each member of the team has an incentive to contribute less and rely on the other members to carry the team.

5. Compensation schemes must create the incentives for employees to carry out actions that benefit owners. Compensation based on events over which the employee has no control would not do that. Compensation schemes often include some risk-sharing attributes in order to minimize the negative effects of uncontrollable risk.

6. Ownership of a firm and control of a firm are separated in the public corporation. The owners are individual shareholders who have no day-to-day stake in the firm.

7. Executive compensation is supposed to reward the executive for guiding the company to greater value, which is the desire of the owners of the company; when the value of the firm rises, the executive's compensation rises.

8. Mechanisms other than compensation that exist to ensure that executives' and owners' interests are more closely aligned include the board of directors and the market for corporate control or takeover.

9. The CEO's compensation may far exceed that of other employees. One rationale for this is that others in the firm will work harder in order to have a chance to become the CEO.

10. Golden parachutes, poison pills, and greenmail are examples of attempts by management to protect itself against hostile takeovers.

KEY TERMS

efficiency wage
backloaded compensation
wage compression

piecework rates
free ride
golden parachute

greenmail
poison pill

EXERCISES

1. Personal injury lawyers may be paid a contingency fee equal to a percentage of the amount awarded. The lawyer receives payment only if his or her client wins the case and is awarded a sum of money. Lawyers in other types of cases are often paid on an hourly basis. Use the principal–agent relationship to assess the merits and drawbacks of each type of fee arrangement from the client's (i.e., the principal's) perspective. Be sure to discuss incentive effects.

2. Suppose that an employee has two tasks to perform—assembling machinery and evaluating quality. Suppose that the supervisor can only observe how many machines have been assembled by the worker. Under what conditions should the principal closely tie pay to performance on the first task?

3. It is said that the current generation of workers will have a very small probability of being employed by the same firm throughout their work-life. In previous generations it was common for people to have just one employer. Is a more rapid turnover among employees beneficial to the firm? To the employee? Explain.

4. Many firms who use operators to assist customers evaluate the operators on the basis of how many

customers they service. Explain the results of such an evaluation system. What would you do differently? Consider the benefits and costs of any change you recommend.

5. A recent study found that workers who were laid off generally received lower wages once they found new jobs. The study noted that white-collar workers suffered relatively large declines compared to blue-collar workers. How would you explain this development?

6. The same study of laid-off workers and their new, lower-paid jobs mentioned in Exercise 5 found that workers who had been with a firm a longer period of time suffered larger declines than those who had been with a firm for a relatively short period of time. How would you explain this development?

7. Prior to about 1990, several firms instituted explicit policies never to lay off employees; that is, to create lifetime employment. What are the costs and benefits of such a policy? What types of firms might find such a policy beneficial?

8. What type of compensation policy would you expect to observe in an industry with rapidly changing technology? Explain.

9. What type of compensation policy would you expect to observe in an industry where technology changes are few and far between?

10. When Ben and Jerry decided to step down as managers of their own company, they announced that the new CEO would not earn more than ten times the lowest-paid employee. What do you think was the result of their policy?

11. The probability of a worker's being fired from or quitting a particular job in any unit of time is represented by

$$Q = a - bT - cT^2$$

where Q is the probability of leaving a job and T is the length of time the worker has held that job. Explain what this says and why it occurs.

12. An investment has returns of zero with probability one-half, $3,000 with probability one-third, and $6,000 with probability one-sixth. What is the expected value of the return?

13. If the investment described in Exercise 12 is an individual's possible weekly compensation and the individual has no control over the outcome, what effort will a risk-averse individual put in? What about a risk-seeking individual?

14. In Exercise 13, if the employee is risk-averse, what compensation scheme would elicit the greatest effort?

CHAPTER NOTES

1. Candice Pendergrast, "The Provision of Incentives in Firms," *Journal of Economic Literature*, March 1999, p. 18.
2. Pendergast, "The Provision of Incentives in Firms," pp. 7–63.
3. Ibid., p. 21.
4. These studies began with Adolf A. Berle and Gardiner C. Means, *The Modern Corporation and Private Property* (Chicago: Commerce Clearing House, 1932). More recent studies are noted in John M. Abowd and David S. Kaplan, "Executive Compensation: Six Questions That Need Answering," *Journal of Economic Perspectives* 13, no. 4 (Fall 1999). Also, Pendergrast, "The Provision of Incentives in Firms," surveys several related studies.
5. See *The Economics of Executive Compensation* (K. Murphy and K. Hallock, eds.), Boston: Edward Elgar Publishing, 1999, for several articles on the issue.
6. For a historical perspective on this issue, see Mark J. Roe, *Strong Managers, Weak Owners* (Princeton, N.J.: Princeton University Press, 1994).
7. John M. Abowd and David S. Kaplan, "Executive Compensation: Six Questions That Need Answering," *Journal of Economic Perspectives* 13, no. 4 (Fall 1999): 145-168; and Brian J. Hall and Jeffrey Liebman, "Are CEOs Really Paid Like Bureaucrats?", *Quarterly Journal of Economics*, August 1998, pp. 653–691. An interesting view of the CEO market is provided in Rakesh Khurana, *Searching for a Corporate Savior*, (Princeton NJ: Princeton University Press, 2002).
8. Roberto Newell and Gregory Wilson, "A Premium for Good Governance," *The McKinsey Quarterly*, 2002, no. 3. Retrieved September 15, 2002 at http://www.mckinsey.com/practices/CorporateGovernance/articles/index.asp.
9. Abowd and Kaplan, "Executive Compensation: Six Questions That Need Answering."

CHAPTER 11 APPENDIX
Productivity and Employee Compensation

What is the relationship between an employee's value to the firm and the compensation the employee receives? In this appendix we use calculus to examine answers.

When the quantity of one resource—say, capital—is held constant, then the hiring decision for the other—labor, in this case—is to employ additional workers until profit is at a maximum.

$$\text{Profit} = PQ - wL - \text{fixed costs}$$

So, taking the derivative of profit with respect to the variable input labor and setting equal to zero yields,

$$\frac{\partial(PQ - wL)}{\partial L} = 0$$

And since $PQ = Pf(L,K^*)$, where K^* represents the idea that capital is fixed, then

$$\frac{\partial Pf(L,K^*)}{\partial L} - \frac{\partial(wL)}{\partial L} = 0$$

and this can be written as $P(MP_L) - w = 0$ where $MP_L = \partial f(L,K^*)/\partial L$ and

$$P(MP_L) = w \tag{1}$$

Equation (1) says that a firm hires a variable resource up to the point that the marginal cost of the resource, w, equals the marginal value to the firm, $P(MP_L)$. This latter term is called the **value of the marginal product.**

When the firm is selling in a market that is not perfectly competitive, P varies as output varies; thus, the profit-maximizing result is

$$\frac{\partial(PQ - wL)}{\partial L} = 0$$

Since $PQ = P(Q)f(L,K^*)$,

$$\frac{\partial P(Q)f(L,K^*)}{\partial L} = \frac{\partial P(Q)}{\partial L}\{f(L,K^*)\} + \frac{\partial f(L,K^*)}{\partial L}P(Q)$$

This can be restructured as

$$\frac{\partial P(Q)}{\partial Q}\frac{\partial Q}{\partial L} + P(Q)/(MP_L)$$

Rewriting, we get

$$[P(Q) + Q\partial P/\partial Q](\partial Q/\partial L) = [MR](MP_L)$$

so that the profit-maximizing result is

$$[MR](MP_L) = w \tag{2}$$

248

Equation (2) tells us that the firm that is not perfectly competitive hires additional workers up to the point that the marginal cost of the worker equals the marginal value of the worker to the firm. $[MR](MP_L)$ is known as the **marginal revenue product.** It is the additional value to the firm of an additional employee (or additional hour of an employee's time).

In the chapter, a firm's compensation structure is illustrated by comparing the compensation profile to the productivity profile. As shown by equations (1) and (2), it is the not just the marginal product of the employee but, instead, the marginal value to the firm that is being compared to the marginal cost to the firm.

An efficiency wage is one where the wage paid the employee, w^e, exceeds the market wage, w. By attracting higher-quality employees or reducing turnover, an employee's marginal value to the firm is higher. Thus, the firm is still equating its marginal cost of an employee to the employee's marginal contribution to revenue in order to maximize profit even though the firm is paying the higher or efficiency wage:

$$[MR](MP_L) = w^e$$

PART IV

Analytic Problem-Solving Tools

Successful managers are often ones who appear to be able to change the way they visualize a problem or situation. They seem to see things differently, view the problem from a different direction, or, as is popular to say in business today, "think outside the box." In reality, they are just thinking, applying the tools they have at hand to examine the costs and benefits of various choices. Two of the more recently adopted tools in business decision making are real options and game theory.

In Chapter 12 we examine the process of allocating capital. We look at the conventional allocation process—called capital budgeting—and then discuss another approach known as real options. Considering potential actions as options and then using economic theory to provide a value to those options can be a useful way to examine strategies that involve different time periods and significant uncertainty. We also discuss the intuition behind real options and then demonstrate how the value of real options can be determined.

In Chapter 13, strategic behavior is discussed in the context of game theory. The chapter is not an analytically complex examination of game theory but instead focuses on how considering business situations as simple games can lead to insights. It is intended to illustrate how game theory might be a useful way to think about strategic issues. Strategic behavior refers to the idea that one business's actions will affect the actions of other businesses and thus a business's strategies must take into account the actions of other businesses. In most instances, a manager should not behave as if his or her business were totally independent of its rivals. This interdependence is what game theory attempts to describe. Game theory was developed in the 1940s but has not been fully adopted into business thinking even today. Depending on who is speaking, either managers have a lot to learn from game theory or game theory is essentially a useless toy utilized by academics. Although expressions such as *game theory, zero-sum game*, and *prisoner's dilemma* have become part of everyday language, game theory has been largely ignored by business. Yet, attempting to think about strategic issues in the framework of game theory could prove to be a competitive advantage. Game theory has managers put themselves in the shoes of competitors and requires that they focus on the competitors' probable reactions to various strategies they might undertake. This might be a valuable exercise in many situations.

CHAPTER 12

Capital Allocation:
Real Options

CASE Merck and Medco

Merck, the giant pharmaceutical company, was considering the acquisition of Medco, a company that manages prescription drug benefits for more than thirty million Americans through various employer-sponsored plans. Top management at Merck thought that the acquisition of Medco would allow Merck to provide a

coordinated approach to health care. Patients, doctors, pharmacists, pharmaceutical companies, and the plan sponsors who pay for benefits could all be linked through Medco. Some executives at Merck worried that Medco would not benefit Merck. The risk involved—an expenditure of $5 billion to $6 billion—was very high. What should Merck do?

Intertemporal Decision Making

The capital market is the channel through which producers match their future plans with their behavior today. The demand for and supply of capital determine the equilibrium quantity and cost of capital. Firms purchase capital: They buy buildings and machines that they use for several years. To decide how much capital to buy, a firm must compare the cost of the building or equipment with the additional value that capital will provide over its lifetime. *Capital budgeting* is the name traditionally given to this comparison.

The quality of investment decisions is often the single factor distinguishing winners from losers in creating shareholder value. To make good investment decisions, one must have a sound approach to evaluating potential investment projects. In all companies, someone or some committee must determine which projects to fund, which to put off until another time, and which to forget altogether. This means it is important to have some way to compare the proposal. Suppose, just for illustration, that, in one year, Intel's manufacturing engineers propose the purchase of new plant and equipment, Intel's marketing executives propose expenditures on new advertisements and marketing facilities, and Intel's research directors propose the purchase of additional instrumentation and the construction of new laboratories. Which of these investments should the company pursue?

The typical rule of operation is to accept an investment proposal if the present value of the expected future cash flows from the investment is greater than the present value of the cost of the investment.

Present Value

The **net present value (NPV)** is the present value of revenues less the present value of costs. Suppose that an investment costs $100 today and that it is expected to result in revenues of $60 a year for two years. The net present value equals

$$NPV = \frac{\$60}{(1 + r)} + \frac{\$60}{(1 + r)^2} - \$100$$

At a 10 percent rate of interest, $r = 0.10$,

$$NPV = \$60(0.90909) + \$60(0.82645) - \$100$$
$$= \$94 - \$100$$
$$= -\$6$$

The net present value of this project is negative, which means that the project would cost more than the revenue it would generate and probably wouldn't be undertaken. However, suppose the cash flow projection is $70 per year for two years rather than the $60 per year. Increasing the cash flow projection would increase the net present value to $21; in which case the project probably would be undertaken.

The net present value approach is fine in principle but can be troublesome in practice if not used appropriately. The situation illustrated in the previous paragraph with the change in cash flow projections from $60 to $70 illustrates the primary problem. All it takes for the executive in charge of capital allocation to say "go ahead with the project" is for the cash flow projection to be increased until the NPV is positive. So, when capital is allocated according to the NPV calculations, division managers have an incentive to fiddle with cash flow projections until the NPV of the project they support is positive. Another common problem with the use of NPV analysis for allocating capital is that the managers' forecasts of future revenues often depend on advertising and sales promotions but the costs of these promotions are not considered to be costs associated with the capital requests. This creates an upward bias in the calculation and thus a greater likelihood a project will be undertaken. Since the present value is the process of measuring future cash flows in terms of today's purchasing power, an obvious difficulty with relying on NPV calculations to allocate capital is measuring revenue and cost projections. At one telecommunications company, for example, the argument for a major switch-expansion project omitted the cost of the additional capacity required to link the new switches to all the other locations in the network. Having initially approved the program, senior managers were dismayed to watch the capital budget more than double. They finally halted construction.[1]

Even if the costs and revenues are appropriately measured, if the firm's objective is incorrect, the capital-budgeting process will fail. For example, a company trying to maximize return on assets (ROA) would reject any investment with an expected ROA that was lower than the current rate, even if it was higher than the cost of capital. In other words, the company would pass up opportunities to create shareholder wealth. Alternatively, if the current ROA was less than the cost of capital, the company or business unit could improve its ROA by undertaking any new investment with a return greater than the current rate even if it was lower than the cost of capital. Suppose that a firm's current ROA is 6 percent and the firm is considering undertaking a project that promises to yield an ROA of 7 percent. The project looks to be a no-brainer; the firm would definitely choose to allocate capital to it. However, if the firm's cost of capital was 8 percent, the firm would be losing economic profit by investing in this new project.

Just as economic profit better measures the actual performance of a company than accounting profits, using the discounted value of the future economic profit of a project as the decision criterion for determining whether to fund the project is better than the net present value of accounting profits. It is the present value of economic profits that tells us whether the project will create value. If the capital costs are not taken into account in the capital budgeting process, then management is treating capital as if it were free. Whenever some item with value is free, much more is wanted than is available. The same occurs when capital is thought to be free. Every division head would want to get the division's projects funded, but there would not be enough capital to fund every project. Management would have to set a limit on overall capital spending and then ration the dollars to the projects on some basis other than economic profit, thereby reducing the value of the firm. Using economic profit in the decision making creates a situation in which the top executives provide capital to the operating divisions, but only at a price—the cost of capital. And, not only must the cost of capital be included in the calculations, but all costs, direct and indirect, of the project must be accounted for. In this way, those projects promising to create value for the firm will be funded and those not creating value will not be funded.

The Canadian company Laurentian Bakeries allocated capital based solely on the basis of net present value calculations for the first several years of its existence. The costs were those directly attributable to the project, not any secondary costs such as effects on employees or the environment. After several years, the executives of the company found that a few of the projects they had funded had not been successful because either the costs were not all-inclusive or the cost of capital had not been used as the decision metric. A careful review of the capital allocation procedure revealed that they not only had to consider the cost of capital in their calculations, but they had to consider all opportunity costs of a project. For instance, any new projects had to be consistent with their business strategies. A project that was not consistent could lead to declines company-wide even though the project's net present value was positive. In addition, possible environmental impacts of a new project had to be taken into account. If a new facility somehow degraded the environment, the costs of future clean-up could be detrimental to the company. The third major factor the company had to take into account was impacts the project might have on employees and their families. If the new project somehow damaged morale in another part of the company, company-wide declines might result from the project even though the project looked to be profitable.[2]

Laurentian Bakeries exemplifies how the capital allocation process ought to occur in most firms. For any proposed project, all costs are taken into account and cost and revenue projections are as accurate as possible. Then the net rate of return is compared to the cost of capital to see if the project adds value (or the net benefits are discounted at the cost of capital). In the net present value formula used earlier in this chapter to show how a project with two years of revenue of $60 per year and costs of $100 would be evaluated, r is the cost of capital:

$$NPV = \frac{\$60}{(1 + r)} + \frac{\$60}{(1 + r)^2} - \$100$$

Then, if the *NPV* is positive, we are saying that the project is adding positive economic profit. In short, a firm should allocate capital only to those projects that generate positive economic profit.

Options

The history of option pricing is disussed at:

http://www.library.hbs.edu/merton/about.htm and http://www.pbs.org/wgbh/nova/stockmarket/formulaleft.html

In 1995–1996, the personal computer (PC) assembly business was in turmoil. Gateway was one of the few players making money. Amid tremendous uncertainty about what would happen in the industry, managers had to decide whether to exit or remain in business even as they lost money. Similarly, in 2002 the telecommunication business was in a deep depression. The executives of companies like Lucent had to decide whether to divest some lines of business or to exit the business altogether. The net present value calculations suggested they should exit immediately. But was net present value the best criterion to use?

Capital is limited and must be allocated to those projects that will generate economic profits. But most projects requiring significant shares of a firm's capital are long term and don't return anything for several time periods. The uncertainty of the capital allocation process is huge and mistakes are likely. A company can't simply sit on the sidelines refusing to use capital either; missing opportunities can be as disastrous as undertaking the wrong opportunities. Every company is presented a multitude of opportunities to use capital. Some of these opportunities need not use capital today but instead can be deferred until some future point in time. How do companies evaluate opportunities like these? A common approach is not to value them until they mature to the point where an investment decision

The Aladdinpower handheld electric generator was introduced in 2002 and can be used to produce power for a range of electrical items including cell phones, PDAs, pagers, and CD players. The generator gives those using mobile electrical devices an option—they need not devote resources to ensuring the electrical devices are fully charged.

can no longer be deferred. At that time, the opportunities join the pool of other investments under consideration for funding and net present value analysis determines which get funded.

This approach ignores a very important aspect of the allocation process. In general, the opportunity to start, stop, or modify a business activity at some future time is different from the opportunity to invest in it now. If a decision regarding whether or not to exploit an opportunity can be deferred, the crucial decision to invest or not can be made after some uncertainty is resolved or when there is no more time to delay a decision.

In financial terms, an "opportunity" is analogous to an **option**. With an option, you have the right, but not the obligation, to buy or sell something at a specified price on or before some future date. For instance, a **call option** on a share of stock gives you the right to buy that share for, say, $100 at any time within the next year. Clearly, if the share is currently worth $110, the option is valuable; it is said to be "in the money." But the option has value even if the stock is worth only $90 because the stock price could rise in the next few months and exceed $100 before the year passes.[3]

Many corporate opportunities have the same features as financial options. These are called **real options**. When a firm makes an initial investment in a project, it is paying an entry fee for a right, but it is not obligated to continue that project at a later stage. Spending now may not create cash flows but instead may provide the opportunity to invest again later, depending on how things look. This can be valuable. Consider Hybridon Inc., a small Canadian biotech firm that had to choose whether to move a promising anti-cancer technology into pre-clinical testing or to delay that hugely expensive undertaking until more assurance of the potential success of the technology was forthcoming. If Hybridon Inc. moved ahead, the expense would be a serious drain on the company's resources. The company had raised about $75 million in capital but the average cost of phase I and II clinical tests was $400,000 per month, and the cost of the final phase ran $1.5 million per month. With the length of the various phases of clinical testing, Hybridon, Inc. could run out of money. Moreover, there was no certainty the project would be completed. The probability of making it through phase I was about 75 percent, through phase II about 48 percent and then from phase III to regulatory filing and commercialization about 67 percent. So, the probability of making it from where the company was in 1995 to commercialization was only about 24 percent (67 percent × 48 percent × 67 percent). What should the CEO of the company do? He identified two possible routes other than continuing on. One would be to partner with a large pharmaceutical company that had the resources to take the technology through the testing into commercial development. This route would limit the profit payoff to Hybridon, Inc. The second was to spin the technology off into a separate company and seek capital for that company. This route would eliminate a potentially huge source of economic profits for Hybridon, Inc.

The most important aspect of the choices facing the CEO of Hybridon, Inc., was that none of the routes had to be selected at this time. The company could commit enough capital to enter into the phase I testing and then reconsider the financing routes at various stages during or after phase I. Thus, rather than looking at a commitment of as much as $100 million in one form or another to make it through all the testing phases, the company was looking at spending only about $500,000 per month.

Since the research, development, and commercialization of the technology could be carried out in stages, the CEO could, at each stage, evaluate further commitments and choices and decide whether to continue or to change directions.[4] Changing the problem from one of a full commitment now to one of a small commitment in order to consider a full commitment later is the value of thinking about capital expenditures in terms of real options.

Rubbermaid's expansion into China involved a series of steps. The initial investment in manufacturing and the sales organization that would have had to be created was extensive. A net present value analysis indicated that costs exceeded forecasted revenues. However, an options analysis showed that a smaller investment to create links to a Chinese company made more sense, allowing Rubbermaid two years to determine whether to fully enter the Chinese market.

Pharmaceutical companies spend about 16 percent of their revenues on R&D. Basic research starts with the synthesis of chemical compounds. For every drug that reaches the market, more than five thousand have been tested without success. One in every four hundred of these chemical compounds enters preclinical trials, and of these one out of two is tested on humans (phase I and phase II trials). Of these drugs, one out of three enters phase III clinical tests and, finally, one out of two of these is marketed. The whole process can take up to ten years and cost between $100 million and $200 million per drug. As we saw in the example with the biotech firm Hybridon, Inc., the process of getting a pharmaceutical in the market is very expensive but does take place in steps. It is not necessary to spend the entire

$200 million at one time. Companies can invest in basic research or outsource to university labs or private labs. If a result looks promising, further investment can lead to preclinical trials. Each additional investment depends on the success of the program to date and the prospects for future success.[5]

Valuing Real Options

Links to *NPV* and real options can be found at

http://www.investmentscience .com/?source=overture&wid=01

Many aspects of business have characteristics resembling financial options. Spending to create a new or stronger brand may have some immediate payoff, but it also creates opportunities for brand extensions later. The decisions to add a product-line extension, raise or lower price, relocate, close a plant, enter a new market—indeed, most business decisions—have aspects of an option. But how much are these options worth? How much should a company pay for flexibility?

Consider a company pondering whether it should build a new $50 million chemical plant. Suppose that of the total expected $50 million in cost, there are initial expenditures of about $500,000 associated with plant planning and environmental permits. The company can analyze the entire project today as if its only choice is to go forward and commit the entire $50 million or not to proceed at all. But the company does not face an all-or-nothing choice. Instead, it can invest the $500,000 now and then see about getting environmental approval. If it does so, it can go forward and invest $49.5 million. If not, it can abandon the project without spending the $49.5 million.

For additional links to real options, see

http://www.real-options.com/

For a primer on real options, visit
http://www.adainc.com/ approach/rov.html

The Tennessee Valley Authority (TVA) contracted out for two thousand megawatts of power instead of building its own plants. In some cases, the TVA paid for options to buy power but never exercised them. The options were a more efficient buffer against unexpected demand than, say, building a nuclear power plant that might not be needed.

In 2000 John Deere and Home Depot decided to offer a joint product. Deere would manufacture a lawn mower/tractor to be sold exclusively by Home Depot. Home Depot initially projected about 100,000 units to be sold per year. Soon, Home Depot increased that forecast to 300,000 units. With a potential business of 300,000 units per year, John Deere invested in a manufacturing facility focused solely on the Home Depot mower that would be most efficient at annual production of 300,000 units. The investment was considerable—many millions of dollars. The investment was not considered as an option; instead, Deere went ahead with construction. The problem was that within a very short time, the economy fell into a recession and Home Depot was requesting fewer than 100,000 units. If Deere had structured the investment as an option, it could have avoided being stuck with a huge expenditure on a factory that was not being utilized to full capacity.

How much is flexibility worth? In other words, how much is an option worth? The answer can be determined using an option-pricing formula used to value financial options.[6] The equation below is the **Black–Scholes option pricing formula**; it defines the value of a call option:

$$C = SN(d_1) - Ke^{(-rt)} N(d_2)$$

whereas
C = theoretical call premium
S = current stock price
t = time until option expiration
K = option striking price

r = risk-free interest rate
N = cumulative standard normal distribution
e = exponential term (2.7183)

$$d_1 = \frac{ln(S/K^2) + (r + \frac{s^2}{2})t}{s\sqrt{t}}$$

$$d_2 = d_1 - s\sqrt{t}$$

s = standard deviation of stock returns
ln = natural logarithm

You can find option pricing
calculators at:

http://www.freeoptionpricing.
com/models/wmbsm.asp
http://www.numa.com/derivs/
ref/calculat/option/calc-opa.htm
http://www.hoadley.net/options/
BS.htm

Fortunately, we don't have to solve this equation every time we want to determine the value of an option. Others have already done that and have created on-line calculators that will provide an option value.[7] All that is necessary is to know the value of the five important variables:

- The value of the project: the present value of the project's expected economic profit, S
- The cost to exercise the option: the one-time incremental investment required to exercise the option, K
- The risk-free rate of return, r
- The time to expiration of the option, T
- The project volatility: a measure of the potential variability of the project's future value, s

Consider, for example, a biomedical firm considering entering a new market and launching a new product. The company, Biomed, needs $4 million to begin product development and manufacturing and another $12 million in two years for its market launch. Biomed's executives plan to spend $500,000 each quarter for the first two years and then an additional $13 million in the first quarter of the third year ($10.7 in present value terms) to launch the product. The business plan assumes the launch would be successful, leading to a sustainable business with a total market value at the end of three years of $19.5 million.

Since Biomed must wait three years to obtain $19.5 million, the present value of that $19.5 million, at a 10% discount rate, is $14.5 million. Since Biomed must spend a total of just under $4 million to carry out tests and another $10.7 million in present value terms in two years to launch the product, the *NPV* is a negative $200,000 or so. On this basis, the investment is questionable; it is a huge undertaking for what appears to be a loss. However, Biomed is not obligated to undertake the market launch. It can carry out the tests and then undertake the launch if business conditions are strong enough to make the launch profitable. But, if it does not want to pursue the launch in two years, it need not spend the additional $13 million.

The numbers to be plugged into an option pricing calculator are:

- S, today's value of the business opportunity, $14.5 million
- K, cost to exercise the option, $10.7 million
- r, risk-free rate of return, 5 percent
- T, time to expiration of the option/time to market launch, two years
- s, volatility of the underlying asset/volatility of the value of the business opportunity, 40 percent per year

The resulting option value is approximately $5 million. This tells us that the current value of Biomed's option to launch is $5 million. The value of the option is positive because of the volatility or upside potential of the project. If two years from now business conditions are terrific and all other prospects look the same as they do now, then there will be a very high payoff to the launch. If two years from now business conditions are poor or other negative information is obtained, the product will not be launched and the $13 million will not be needed; there will be no losses associated with the launch.

The Value of Real Options Embedded in Companies   When the so-called dot.com companies were trading at extremely high stock prices in the late 1990s, many analysts were arguing that the valuation was correct because of the value of real options embedded in the stock price. Others called the high prices irrational exuberance. Who was correct? Given the performance of stocks between 1999 and 2003, it would seem that irrational exuberance clearly described what was going on. But was there any value to the real options firms had at that time—value that was embedded in the stock prices?

Let's see what the value of Amazon.com's options that are embedded in its stock price are. In February 2000, Amazon.com stock was trading at about $64 per share. With a per-share price of $64 and 345 million shares outstanding, Amazon's market value was nearly $22 billion. Given that Amazon had yet to earn a positive accounting profit, the stock price was based either on investor speculation or on the value of Amazon's future business opportunities—its real options. We can use the Black–Scholes options pricing formula to determine whether the stock price was justified.

Let's consider Amazon.com's business as of February 2000. At this time, Amazon's forecasted sales growth for its existing business, as reported in annual statements and analyst reports, was about 48 percent per year for five years followed by a rate of 40 percent per year for another five years. Most analysts expected Amazon to generate an accounting profit margin of 6 to 8 percent on average during this period. Using these projections and the expected profit margin and then determining the present value by discounting at the average cost of capital, we can say that Amazon's existing businesses were expected to generate an accounting profit of about $12 billion. Dividing $12 billion by the 345 million outstanding shares of stock means investors were attributing a value of $35 per share to existing businesses.

The difference between $35 per share and the actual price of $64 per share ($29 per share) is the amount not attributable to the future prospect of Amazon.com's existing business. If this is the embedded value of real options, investors believed that Amazon would create a very large amount of new business in the future.

If Amazon's real options value was $29 per share, then its total real option value was $10 billion (multiplying $29 by the 345 million shares of stock outstanding). Ten billion dollars is a huge amount of new business. How much new business would have to be undertaken over ten years to create an option value in February 2000 of $10 billion? We can use the option pricing formula to answer this question. Since we have the value of the option—$10 billion—we need the values for volatility, the cost of exercising the option, the risk-free rate, and time until the option expires to come up with a value for *S*, the market opportunity.

We'll assume the volatility of the value of the new business to be the same as Amazon's historical stock price volatility: s = 100 percent. Let's assume the time until the option has to be exercised to be two years. Finally, let's assume that Amazon.com will earn zero economic profit (cover all opportunity costs) in the new business. This means that $S/K = 1$. So, the value of the potential market, S, will equal the cost of exercising the option. Plugging these numbers into the Black–Scholes option pricing calculator, we find that the real options value of $10 billion is about 54 percent of the new market investment necessary to create that new business. Thus, the imputed market opportunity, S, necessary to generate an option value of $10 billion is about $19 billion. Given that Amazon.com had invested only about $2 billion for the three previous years, a $19 billion investment in a two-year period seems pretty much beyond possibility. We would have to say that much of Amazon's $64 stock price was pure speculation rather than based on options that the company might have had. Given that on March 1, 2002, Amazon.com's stock price was $14, that conclusion makes sense.[8] Carrying out similar exercises for many dot.com companies over this period would yield the same conclusion—a great deal of the stock price in 2000 reflected exuberance—or just pure speculation.

Managing the Value of the Options Since a firm's value contains some elements of the business opportunities open to the firm in the future, a manager may want to manage the value of these options and thus maintain or increase shareholder value. Let's consider an example of a firm that is looking into six projects. The data associated with the projects are presented in Tables 12.1 and 12.2. The projected cash flow in each case is $100 million. The capital expenditure required in the first and second cases is $90 million each, while the rest of the projects require $110 million each. The net present value is positive for projects 1 and 2 and negative for the rest. Thus, using traditional methodology, the firm would undertake expenditures of $180 million for projects 1 and 2 and forgo the remaining projects.

The time until it is now or never is zero (now) for projects 1 and 3, two years for projects 2 and 6, six months for project 4, and one year for project 5. Project 1 is one that would be invested in now, while project 3 is one that the firm should not consider. For both of these projects, a now-or-never decision has to be made: Time has run out—that is, there is no more possibility of delay—no options.

The cash flows from the remaining projects are uncertain. The volatility (standard deviation) of the cash flows each year is estimated to be 0.3 for projects 2 and 5, 0.2 for project 4, and 0.4 for project 6.[9]

Project 2 is promising; its net present value is positive. Project 6 has a net present value that is negative, but it is still something the firm might want to get into later. It will not be a now-or-never decision for two years, and the volatility of its cash flows is high. Project 5 also may be something to undertake later because it has a year to go and a moderate volatility. Project 4 will most likely not be considered because a decision must be made in only six months and, with a low volatility, there is not much likelihood that it will come into the money before time runs out.

Table 12.1
NET PRESENT VALUE OF SIX PROJECTS

	Project (millions of $)					
	1	2	3	4	5	6
Asset value	$100	$100	$100	$100	$100	$100
Capital cost	$90	$90	$110	$110	$110	$110
NPV	$10	$10	–$10	–$10	–$10	–$10

Table 12.2

OPTION VALUATION OF SIX PROJECTS

	Project (millions of $)					
	1	2	3	4	5	6
Asset value	$100	$100	$100	$100	$100	$100
Capital cost	$ 90	$ 90	$110	$110	$110	$110
Time (years)	0	2	0	0.5	1	2
Asset capital value to cost ratio	1.111	1.248	.909	.936	.964	1.021
Volatility	0	0.3	0	0.2	0.3	0.4
Call value	$10	$27.23	0	$3.06	$10.42	$23.24
Decision	Now	Maybe now	Never	Probably never	Maybe later	Probably later

Examining business situations as real options encourages executives to deal with uncertainty proactively rather than merely attempting to buffer against or avoid uncertainties. Most managers fear high levels of uncertainty, but the real options approach shows that a higher level of uncertainty can be valuable. Uncertainty widens the range of potential outcomes. This is bad if a now-or-never decision has to be made but good if the decision can be deferred. As time passes, the option value of a project will change; without some intervention, the option value will decline because the volatility of the asset value decreases as time runs out. Consider project 6. Its volatility measure is 0.4 and its value-to-cost ratio is 1.021. Now let a year pass and suppose none of the project's variables change. The year difference causes both the volatility measure and the value-to-cost ratio to change. The volatility measure falls from .4 to .2 and the value-to-cost measure declines from 1.021 to 0.964. These new values move the project from the "probably later" region to the "maybe later" region. Despite its initial promise, the only way the project will end up being undertaken is if some force alters its value.

The executives of the firm examining the six projects could simply wait until each one must be either dismissed or invested in. But, rather than simply waiting, it may be possible to change the value of the real option. The managers could try to change an option value by increasing the value of a project or decreasing its capital costs. This is no different from what managers try to do to increase economic profit: Increase the value of assets and decrease capital costs. The difference is that the option value will also rise if the likelihood that the project's value will change increases; that is, if volatility rises. A manager may, therefore, want to increase the volatility of a project's potential cash flow.

Use of Real Options in Business

Intel has invested over half a billion dollars in more than fifty companies that are developing products that will use Intel's chips. Intel has considered many of these investments as real options. For some startups, the biggest challenge is product development. Intel can throw dollars or software developers at this problem and thus increase the value of the startup. For other startups, the biggest challenge is the evolution of the product market, something Intel is less able to influence. In these cases, Intel lets the market evolve and makes further investments only after market conditions warrant.

The pharmaceutical industry's R&D operations now consist of large numbers of alliances with small biotech companies. In the past, the large companies had to manage a huge portfolio of product development programs within their research departments. Today, they manage a portfolio of biotech alliances. For example, in December 1997, Biogen Inc. announced that it had signed an agreement with Merck & Co. to develop and bring to market an asthma drug. Biogen received an up-front payment of $15 million from Merck, plus a potential $130 million in payments over several years. With each payment Merck obtained the option to continue.[10]

In the 1990s, Enron Corp. opened three gas-fired power plants in northern Mississippi and western Tennessee that were inefficient—deliberately so. The plants would generate electricity at an incremental cost 50 to 70 percent higher than the industry's best. Most of the time, the operating costs of these new plants would be too high for them to compete. But by building less efficient plants, the company saved millions of dollars on construction. It would let the plants sit idle, then fire them up when demand increases and prices rise. When the price of a megawatt-hour of electricity in parts of the Midwest soared briefly—from $40 to an unprecedented $7,000—Enron used the plants briefly. Enron's new plants were, in effect, options: They gave the company the opportunity but not the obligation to produce electricity.

Hewlett-Packard has experimented with real options since the beginning of the 1990s. In the 1980s, HP customized ink-jet printers for foreign markets at the factory, then shipped them in finished form to warehouses. Customizing at the factory is cheaper than customizing in the field. But HP kept guessing wrong on demand and ending up with, for example, too many printers configured for French customers but not enough for Germans. Executives realized that it would be smarter to ship partially assembled printers and then customize them at the warehouse, once it had firm orders. Although local customization costs were higher, HP saved $3 million a month by more effectively matching supply to demand. Increasing the cost of production was the price HP paid for the option to delay configuration choices until the optimal time. Since then, more HP products have gotten the real options treatment.

Ford and GM were both considering offering GPS systems in their cars in the early 1990s. However, the companies managed the real option of introducing those systems quite differently. It would seem that each firm possessed the same options and faced the same decision about investing in them. GM's system, called OnStar, was designed to provide navigation and other assistance to drivers. Ford's system, Wingcast, produced in a joint venture with Qualcomm, was supposed to offer full Internet access. GM exercised the option by introducing its system in Cadillac models in 1996 and now offers it on most of its products. But, the OnStar system is not being sought after by customers; only a few are paying to continue the system once the initial contract expires and yet GM has to continue funding it. Ford has as yet to introduce Wingcast. Ford extended the now or never period, which has enabled it to learn more about the possible returns from the project.

Considering economic decisions as real options is not really all that new. Real option analysis has been a part of economic instruction since lectures were first given. Anyone who has taken an introductory economics class will recall the decision about whether to shut down a project temporarily or permanently when revenues don't cover variable costs. If it is possible that prices will rise sufficiently in the near future to restart the project, then embarking on a liquidation or permanent shut-down may not be the best choice. The option to restart can be seen as a call option to capture the profits of the project, with the strike price being the variable cost. The value of that option will depend on the volatility of prices and the time until the now or never decision must be made.

Intuitively, most executives use option theory to some extent. No executive can afford to ignore the idea that the value of a long-term project might change over time as the environment around it shifts. So what we have discussed here should not be all that alien to executives; thinking about capital allocation in terms of real options may prove valuable; it may enable an executive to formulate solutions that otherwise would not have been evident.

CASE REVIEW *Merck and Medco*

Some executives at Merck worried that Medco would not benefit Merck. The risk involved—an expenditure of $5 billion to $6 billion—was very high. What should Merck do?

Merck might have been able to structure the acquisition of Medco as a real option. Let's suppose that Merck can purchase the right to acquire Medco in two to three years and in the meantime utilize Medco's resources. This would allow Merck to determine whether the synergies between Merck and Medco are sufficient to induce Merck to finish the acquisition. If the synergies do not materialize during that time, then Merck can choose not to complete the acquisition, being out only the amount that it and Medco agree to. This would be a real option.

Recall that the Black–Scholes option pricing formula requires the following:

- S, today's value of the business opportunity
- K, the cost to exercise the option
- r, risk-free rate of return
- T, time to expiration of the option/time to market launch
- s, volatility of the underlying asset/volatility of the value of the business opportunity

Thus the value of the option would depend on the value of the underlying asset, the value of Medco to Merck; the length of time, three years; the variability of the asset value, and the cost to exercise the option, $5 billion to $6 billion.

We aren't given much information in this case. We do not know the value of the business opportunity, nor do we know whether Medco would have been willing to enter into such an agreement with Merck. Nevertheless, let's use what information we have and some we assume to calculate the option value. The following are the values we'll use:

- S, today's value of the business opportunity, $50 billion (assuming ten years of sales at $5 billion per year, in present value terms)
- K, the cost to exercise the option, $6 billion
- r, risk-free rate of return, 5 percent
- T, time to expiration of the option/time to market launch, three years
- s, volatility of the underlying asset/volatility of the value of the business opportunity, 1.4

Using the Black–Scholes option pricing formula, the value of the option is $1.29 billion. Thus, rather than spending $5 billion to $6 billion, Merck could have spent $1.29 billion—just 20 percent of the total purchase amount—and then devoted three years to managing the option so as to increase its value. Merck could have used Medco's distribution channels to see if they were valuable; it could have increased its relationships through Medco to increase the value of Medco to Merck.

SUMMARY

1. Capital budgeting is the process of calculating the present value of income streams generated by alternative investment projects and then comparing that value to the cost of the capital.
2. Net present value is the present value of the income stream generated by an investment project minus the present value of the cost of that project.
3. Projects expected to generate cash flows with a positive net present value are undertaken; those with a negative net present value are forgone.
4. An option is an opportunity. It provides the opportunity to purchase something or carry out an activity but does not require that the item be purchased or the activity carried out.
5. A call option is the right but not the obligation to purchase a financial instrument at some point in the future.
6. A real option is the opportunity but not the obligation to purchase capital or make an investment at some point in the future.
7. An option's value depends on the value of the underlying asset, time, and risk.
8. A project could have a negative net present value and yet still have value as an option. If the likelihood that the value of the asset will rise is large or the time until a final decision has to be made is long, an option will have value.
9. As the time until a now-or-never decision has to be made decreases, the value of an option approaches the net present value of the project or zero, whichever is larger.

KEY TERMS

net present value (NPV)
option

call option
real option

Black–Scholes option
pricing formula

EXERCISES

1. Managers are often faced with decisions requiring the value of being flexible. Flexibility can be purchased through special features in capital equipment, or it can be obtained by investing in training, routines, or flexible contracts. The flexibility is not free, however. The special features in capital equipment are expensive, as are training and other investments.

   a. Compare a net present value analysis of the investment in flexible capital equipment and an option analysis of the same.
   b. Suppose the demand for the output of the capital was predictably volatile—high during cer-

   tain months and low during certain months. How would that change the analysis?
   c. Suppose the demand for the output of the capital was uncertain but had high volatility. How would that change the analysis?

2. Managers often use the option to wait, intuitively comparing the value of an investment today with the uncertain value of the same investment later. Investing in either period could have positive value. The problem is to choose the strategy with the highest value. Explain why the decision rule for investing now is: *If net present value is greater than the value of the option to wait, then invest now.*

3. Middleton Steel Co. is considering whether to temporarily close one of its manufacturing plants. If it does close the plant, it faces costs of shutting down and then starting back up, the costs of criticism from the city in which the plant is located, and the costs of customer abandonment as some customers purchase products elsewhere. If it does not close the plant, it will experience substantial losses because revenues will not cover variable costs.

   a. What would a net present value analysis say about the decision?

   b. How could an option strategy be developed? What is the option? What is the underlying asset?

4. The marketing director of National Midland Mortgage has been arguing with senior management about building a $50 million publishing facility. Other managers worried about the assumptions in the analysis that support the investment—an increase in the number of mortgages processed and a reduction in processing costs. What if the mortgage market did not grow as expected?

   a. Should National Midland invest in the publishing facility?

   b. What assumptions might the marketing director have made to make the investment look worthwhile?

   c. Could the problem be analyzed as an option strategy? Explain.

5. How can an option be managed? Suppose a firm has the opportunity to enter a new market. The cost of that entry is $20 million. The firm could spend just $2 million to form a joint venture with another firm already in that market. This would allow the firm to reconsider complete and independent entry later on. Explain the option and explain how the option could be managed.

6. Bob Davies must decide whether to invest $100,000 in his own business or in another local business. Both investment projects have an expected life of five years. The cash flow of each is as follows:

Year	Davies	Other
1	$20,000	$10,000
2	30,000	10,000
3	40,000	30,000
4	10,000	40,000
5	5,000	50,000

Suppose the risk of the projects is the same and is accounted for by a risk premium of 6 percent per year. Would either investment make sense? Which would be better?

7. An oil company recently evaluated a proposed investment for improvements in a particular type of refining equipment. According to the analysis, such improvements would require an investment of $15 million and would result in an incremental after-tax cash flow of $2 million per year for nine years following the year of the investment.

   a. If the interest rate is 10 percent, what is the net present value of this project?

   b. If the interest rate is 15 percent, what is the net present value of this project?

   c. What interest rate would you argue makes most sense in evaluating this project?

   d. If the cash flow was highly uncertain, having a volatility of 0.6, would the net present value analyses in parts a and b make sense?

   e. If the cash flow had the volatility indicated in part d and the project could be carried out in stages, with a $5 million investment in the first year and then a $12 million investment five years out, and if the value-to-cost ratio was 0.8, would the investment in stage 1 make sense?

8. Using the following information, determine which of the six projects should be funded now, which should never be funded, and which should be managed to increase the potential of funding them in the future.

	Project (millions of $)					
	1	2	3	4	5	6
Asset value	$200	$200	$200	$200	$200	$200
Capital cost	$190	$180	$210	$210	$200	$220
Time (years)		2	1	0	1	2
Value-to-cost ratio volatility	0	0.3	0.4	0	0.3	0.5

CHAPTER NOTES

1. See Harol H. Koyama and Robert Van Tassel, "How to Trim Your Capital Spending by 25 Percent," *The McKinsey Quarterly*, no. 3 (1998). Available at www.mckinseyquarterly.com (retrieved February 14, 2002). Available by subscription only.

2. See Case number 9A95B029 from the Richard Ivey School of Business, "Laurentian Bakeries" by Rob Barbara, David Shaw and Steve Foersler for an interesting presentation of the capital allocation process in Laurentian Bakeries. (London, Ontario, CA: Ivey Publishing).

3. A put option is the right to sell a share of stock at a specific price within a certain time but does not obligate the owner of the option to sell the share of stock.

4. For a great deal more information about Hybridon, see case 9B02N009, Neil D. Maruoka and James E. Hatch, *Hybridon, Inc.*, Richard Ivey School of Business, Ivey Cases, (2002), www.Ivey.uwo.ca/cases.

5. The use of options at Merck is outlined quite well in an interview with Merck's chief financial officer, Judy Lewent, in *Harvard Business Review*, (January/February, 1994): 89.

6. The Black-Scholes formula is the easiest method to use to price options, but it has limitations. It's based on a model in which options can be exercised only at the terminal date. That's more restrictive than where options can be exercised at any time prior to the terminal date. Nevertheless, it represents a reasonable approximation to the appropriate valuation.

7. You can find option pricing calculators by carrying out an Internet search using "Black-Scholes option pricing" or just "option pricing." Examples of such calculators are available at www.margrabe.com/OptionPricing.html or http://www.Colorado.EDU/engineering/alleman/downloads/Optimize.xls.

8. For more on Amazon.com and other real option evaluations, see Alfred Rappaport and Michael J. Mauboussin, *Expectations Investing* (Cambridge, Mass.: Harvard University Press, 2001).

9. For more on the use of real options in evaluating projects, see Timothy A. Luehrman, "Strategy as a Portfolio of Real Options," *Harvard Business Review*, Vol. 76 (September/October 1998): 94.

10. Martha Amram and Nalin Kulatilaka, *Real Options* (Cambridge, Mass.: Harvard Business School Press, 1999).

CHAPTER 13

Strategic Behavior:
The Theory of Games

CASE *Unilever and P&G*

Unilever and Procter & Gamble had been engaged in fierce competition over many decades, yet were in an equilibrium of sorts. There was a tacit understanding that any sudden and major shifts in policy would produce losses for both firms. As a result, neither firm attempted to best the other in price cutting without

providing sufficient notice to the other firm. Neither firm sought market share from the other by introducing new products without sufficient notice to the other that a new product would be introduced. And neither firm advertised directly against the competitor, that is, compared products in advertisements. Thus, an announcement that a price cut would occur or that a new product would be introduced would always provide lead time before the action was undertaken. Unilever was going to change this situation, however. It was going to introduce a new product without advance notice. Is this a good strategy?

Games

Strategic behavior involves the interdependence of actions; what one does affects and is affected by what others do. This is what **game theory** attempts to describe.[1] Depending on who is speaking, either managers have a lot to learn from game theory or game theory is useless. Although expressions such as *game theory, zero-sum game,* and *prisoner's dilemma* have become part of everyday language, game theory has been largely ignored by business. Many look upon game theory as principally a toy of academic theorists.

There is no doubt that all managers are absorbed in their own firm's situations. However, putting themselves in the shoes of competitors and focusing on the competitors' probable reactions to various strategies can be a useful exercise. This is what game theory can do for the manager. "I use game theoretic equations in business and in life, not with the expectation that all outcomes will be optimal, but rather that bad decisions will be minimized."[2] The chief financial officer of Merck responded to an interviewer's question about Merck's acquisition of Medco and its effects on the attitudes of Merck's competitors by stating that game theory forces you to see a business situation from two perspectives: yours and your competitor's.[3]

Game theory doesn't provide a solution—it's a way of thinking about the future. It can help managers to understand that the world of business is one of interdependence.

Games may be cooperative or noncooperative. The originators of game theory, John Von Neuman and Oscar Morgenstern viewed economic behavior as cooperative and so saw game theory as describing cooperative behavior. John Nash saw economic behavior as non-cooperative. He viewed something like J. Pierpoint Morgan going along with colleagues as long as it suited him but then going against the colleagues when that suited him. Thus, Nash extended game theory to the non-cooperative sets of behaviors. Within each type of game theory, there are two types of decision-making processes. The first is *sequential*. Players make alternating moves, first one then the other. Each player, when it is his turn, must look ahead to how his current actions will affect the future actions of others and his own future actions. The second kind of interaction is *simultaneous*, as in the prisoners' dilemma we discussed in previous chapters. The players act at the same time, ignorant of the others' current actions. In this case players have to try to determine what actions others will take.

Sequential Games

In **sequential games,** each player has to figure out the other players' future responses and use them in calculating his or her own best current move. Consider the situation experienced by the small, upstart SunCountry Airlines. SunCountry's transformation from a charter airline to a regularly scheduled carrier became official June 1, 1999. Six days later, a Northwest executive distributed an electronic memo to Northwest personnel stating, "Effective immediately, all parts support to SunCountry is terminated until further notice." A SunCountry executive said that this move was a competitive attack against the airline, a slap against a tradition that is meant to help all carriers by keeping air travel an attractive mode of transportation. He said the industry would be rife with long flight delays if carriers didn't help each other obtain parts on short notice. Officials at two other major U.S. airlines also said that collaboration on parts and tools is widespread, intended for the good of the entire industry. The cost of keeping sufficient hardware inventories in every city would be enormous. Within a few days, at least seven SunCountry flights experienced multihour delays in Minneapolis–St. Paul and Detroit because the airline had to scramble for parts or tools from sources in other cities. SunCountry executives dejectedly exclaimed that if Northwest could disadvantage SunCountry and inconvenience its customers, Northwest would see that as a win.

What did SunCountry do wrong? Why was it not prepared for the competitive response on the part of Northwest? Most likely, SunCountry failed to look ahead and then reason back.

Suppose the situation facing Northwest and SunCountry is as illustrated in Figure 13.1. SunCountry must decide whether to enter the airline market. If SunCountry enters and Northwest does not respond, SunCountry will experience a substantial gain, say $60 million. But is it likely that Northwest will not respond? To make its entry decision, SunCountry must look ahead and reason back. It knows that if it converts from commuter to the full-fledged airline, then Northwest will experience a substantial reduction in business, say $50 million. Northwest loses less business, only about $20 million, if it makes it difficult for SunCountry to operate. Northwest can do this by refusing to provide equipment on loan. SunCountry can reason that Northwest will respond to SunCountry's entry by breaking with tradition and not loaning the equipment.

Of course, the answer provided here depends on the assumptions made about the end of the game and future effects. Nevertheless, the example points out that in a sequential game situation, the players must look ahead and reason back to the present. SunCountry did not do this, assuming instead that what had occurred in the past would continue. Notice also that the sequential game provides an opportunity to consider the decisions as real options. Perhaps SunCountry could have made a series of steps leading to its conversion to a full-fledged airline, thereby testing Northwest's response prior to investing the entire amount without having a full understanding of the response.

Links to game theory resources:

http://www.economics.harvard.
edu/~aroth/alroth.html

http://levine.sscnet.ucla.edu/

http://www.sunysb.edu/
gametheory/Links.htm

http://www.gametheory.net/

Simultaneous Games

In **simultaneous games,** neither player has the benefit of observing the other's completed move before making his own. It is not enough simply to put yourself in your opponent's shoes since if you did, you'd only discover that your opponent is doing the same thing. Each person has to place himself simultaneously in both his own and the other person's shoes and then figure out the best moves for both sides.

Consider the situation where firms must decide whether to devote more resources to advertising. When a firm in any given industry advertises its product,

Figure 13.1

A GAME TREE

This road map is called a decision or game tree. The way a game tree is used is not to take the first branch and follow it, but to go to the end and reason backward, outlining the branches that define the best path.

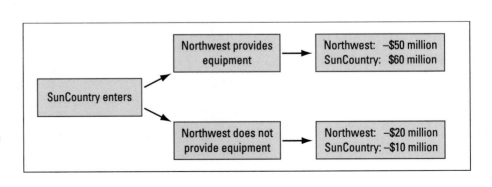

its demand increases for two reasons. First, people who had not used that type of product before learn about it, and some will buy it. Second, other people who already consume a different brand of the same product may switch brands. The first effect boosts sales for the industry as a whole; the second redistributes existing sales within the industry.

Let's consider the cigarette industry as an example. Assume that the matrix in Figure 13.2 illustrates the possible actions that two firms might undertake and the results of those actions. The top left rectangle represents the payoffs, or results, if both A and B advertise; the bottom left shows the payoffs when A advertises but B does not; the top right shows the payoffs when B advertises but A does not; and the bottom right shows the payoffs when neither advertises.

If firm A can earn higher profits by advertising than by not advertising, whether or not firm B advertises, then firm A will surely advertise. If a player has a strategy whereby one course of action outperforms all others no matter what the other players do, it is called a **dominant strategy**. Firm A compares the left side of the matrix to the right side and sees that it earns more by advertising no matter what firm B does. If A advertises, then A earns 70 if B also advertises and only 40 if A does not advertise but B does. If B does not advertise, then A earns 100 by advertising and only 80 by not advertising. The dominant strategy for firm A is to advertise. The dominant strategy for firm B also is to advertise. Firm B will earn 80 by advertising and 50 by not advertising if A advertises. Firm B will earn 100 by advertising but only 90 by not advertising if A does not advertise. Notice that both firms would be better off if neither advertised; firm A would earn 80 instead of 70, and firm B would earn 90 instead of 80. Yet the firms cannot afford to not advertise because they would lose more if the other firm advertised and they didn't. This is the prisoner's dilemma game we discussed in Chapter 6.

Sometimes one player has a dominant strategy but the other does not. Suppose that the payoffs for the two cigarette firms are such that firm A is better off advertising no matter what firm B does, but firm B is better off advertising only if firm A advertises. This case is illustrated in Figure 13.3. In contrast to the previous situation, the best strategy for firm B depends on the particular strategy chosen by firm A. Firm B does not have a dominant strategy.

A dominant strategy is a dominance of one of your strategies over your other strategies, not of you over your opponent. A dominant strategy is one that makes a player better off than she would be if she used any other strategy, no matter what strategy her opponent uses. Just as a dominant strategy is uniformly better than every other strategy, a **dominated strategy** is uniformly worse than some

Figure 13.2

DOMINANT STRATEGY

Firm A finds that advertising is its best choice no matter what firm B does. Firm B finds that advertising is its best choice.

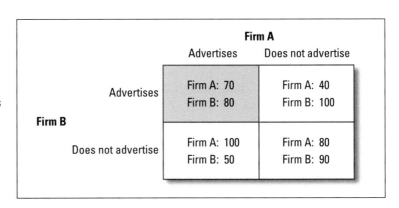

		Firm A	
		Advertises	Does not advertise
Firm B	Advertises	Firm A: 70 Firm B: 80	Firm A: 40 Firm B: 100
	Does not advertise	Firm A: 100 Firm B: 50	Firm A: 80 Firm B: 90

Figure 13.3
MIXED STRATEGIES

Firm A has a dominant strategy. Firm B does not. Firm B is better off advertising only if firm A advertises.

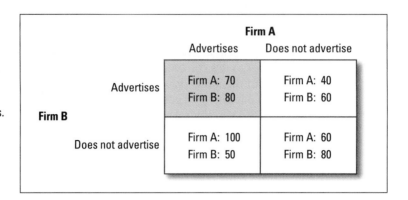

other strategy. You choose your dominant strategy if you have one and can be sure that your rival will choose hers if she has one. You also avoid your dominated strategies if you have any; you eliminate them from consideration.

Once all dominated strategies have been eliminated from consideration, you often face a problem of circular reasoning: What is best for you depends on what is best for your opponent, and what is best for your opponent depends on what is best for you. In some cases, there is an equilibrium strategy. In others, there is more than one equilibrium. And in still others, there is no equilibrium.

Let's consider a price war between two Internet booksellers, Amazon.com and BN.com. Each company has a core of loyal customers, but there is also a group that is price-sensitive. Through market research, the companies know how they will do if they respond to the other's pricing in a certain way. Amazon.com's response plan is the following: If BN.com sets the price discount at $0.50, we will not follow. Instead, we will set a lower discount, $0.40, and thus make some profit from the sales to our loyal customers. If BN.com charges a higher price (lower discount), we will raise our price but by less, thus getting some of the price-sensitive customers. For each $0.10 increase in BN.com price (or reduction in the discount), we will raise our price by $0.05. This relationship of Amazon.com's best response to all possible prices of BN.com is shown in Figure 13.4.

Suppose the two booksellers are alike in having similar costs, equal pools of loyal consumers, and similar drawing power over price-sensitive consumers. Then the relationship of BN.com's best response to all possible prices of Amazon.com is illustrated by an identical chart. The two separately are engaged in circular

Figure 13.4
EQUILIBRIUM

Amazon.com responds to each price BN.com may set.

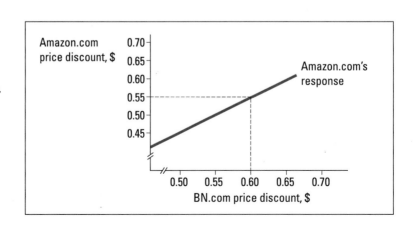

Figure 13.5

NASH EQUILIBRIUM

The responses of the two Internet booksellers to the other's price changes leads to an equilibrium, a position from which neither wants to change.

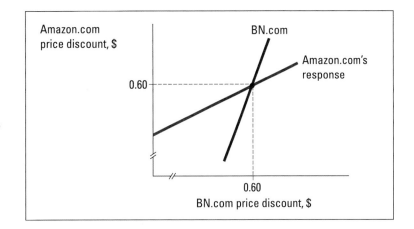

thinking. Amazon.com's manager says: "If he charges $0.50, I should charge $0.60. But knowing that I am thinking in this way, he will charge not $0.50; instead, will charge his best response to my $0.60, and that is $0.65. Then I should charge $0.70, not $0.55, but then . . ." Where does this end? Combining Amazon.com's response line to BN.com's response line, as illustrated in Figure 13.5, we can show what equilibrium is.

In this case, there is a combination of strategies in which each player's action is the best response to the action of the other players. Given what the other is doing, neither wants to change his own move. This is called a **Nash equilibrium**. A Nash equilibrium means that no player wants to change strategies given what other players are doing.

The Nash equilibrium is named after John Nash, the mathematician and economics Nobel Prize laureate whose life story was told in the book and movie *A Beautiful Mind*.

There can be more than one Nash equilibrium. In fact, some games have many equilibria; others, none. Suppose you are talking on the telephone with a business associate and the connection is broken. Do you call your associate or do you wait for her to call you? If you call, you might get only a busy signal because she is also calling. If you wait, neither of you might call. What is best for you depends on what your associate does, and vice versa. There are two equilibria to this problem. In one, you call and she does not; in the other, she calls and you do not. The problem is that without some rule of behavior, you may end up with a busy signal or no call. You could prevent this problem by announcing at the beginning of each phone conversation who will call if the connection is broken. Of course, this is very inefficient. No one wants to make such an announcement at the beginning of each call. What arises then, is a *convention*. A typical convention is that the person who called originally calls again.[4]

Components of the Game

A game is a situation of strategic interdependence. The outcome of your choices (strategies) depends on the choices of another person or persons. The decision makers involved in a game are called players and their choices are called moves. A game is defined by its features—the players, the players' perceptions, the rules to be followed, and the limits or boundaries of the game. A strategic situation

eBay has created a way that individual buyers and sellers can interact through Internet auctions. A seller offers an item for sale and prospective buyers bid for the item. The highest bidder at the end of the allocated time period purchases the item. The equilibrium is one of Pareto optimality—no one can be made better off without harming someone else—in game theory called a Nash equilibrium.

cannot be analyzed without defining these characteristics. Once they are defined, then it is possible to consider whether changing one of the features will alter the strategic situation.

Number of Players

To be successful, a firm must have a distinctive capability and must match that capability to the appropriate market. Consider the decision to enter a new market or to begin a new business. The firm must determine whether it has something distinct, some value it can add. In game-theory terminology, the firm must determine whether it has any value in any game.

Do you want to be a player? Approximately 670,000 new businesses are started each year in the United States. How many ask themselves what value they are bringing to the game before they enter? This should be an obvious question, since it determines whether the activity has even a small chance of being successful. But the question is rarely asked and when it is, the answer is rarely obvious. It's easy to misjudge what it would really be like to be in the game. Just think of the SunCountry situation noted above. SunCountry failed to consider its value in the game—that is, what value did it bring to the game?

Consider the story of NutraSweet and Holland Sweetener in the late 1980s. Aspartame is a low-calorie, high-intensity sweetener known by Monsanto's brand name, NutraSweet.[5] It was the key to the success of diet Coke and diet Pepsi in the 1980s. NutraSweet made over half a billion dollars in 1985. The business had 70 percent gross margins. Such profits usually attract entry, but in this case entry was barred by a patent on the sweetener and because the process of creating the sweetener was expensive and difficult. Monsanto had a distinct capability—its monopoly. It had also created another strategic asset—the NutraSweet brand name as represented by its trademark "swirl."

Monsanto's patent was to expire in 1987. In 1986 the Holland Sweetener Company began building an aspartame plant in Geleen, the Netherlands, to challenge Monsanto's hold on the aspartame market. Holland Sweetener was a joint venture between the Japanese Tosoh Corporation and DSM (Dutch State Mines).

Holland Sweetener failed to anticipate Monsanto's reaction. With the expiration of NutraSweet's European patent in 1987, Holland attacked the European market, but Monsanto fought back with aggressive pricing. Before Holland's entry, aspartame prices had been $70 per pound. After Holland's entry, the prices fell to about $22 per pound. At this low price, Holland was losing money. The only reason Holland Sweetener survived was that it convinced the European courts to impose antidumping duties on Monsanto.

Holland Sweetener was being courted by Coke and Pepsi to enter the U.S. market, but it failed to look at the game in terms of how Coke and Pepsi saw it. Neither Coke nor Pepsi had any real desire to switch over to generic aspartame, since neither company wanted to be the first to take the NutraSweet logo off its products. If only one switched, the other would most certainly gain market share. What Coke and Pepsi wanted was a lower price. This they received; new contracts with Monsanto led to savings for the two companies of $200 million a year.

Holland Sweetener's added value in the game was zero. It had no distinct capability. But its entry into the game was worth a lot to Coke and Pepsi.[6] It could have used that value to create value for itself. Before entering a game, assess the value you add to the game. In other words, define your distinctive capability and consider the imitability of that capability. If you have a high added value, you'll do well in the game. But if you don't have much added value, you won't do well unless you can figure out whether anyone stands to gain from your entry. Those players may be willing to pay you to play. If none of these conditions hold, you should ask whether it makes sense to play the game.

Limiting supply can enhance the value one brings to a game. How can the supply be limited? The supplier must have a distinct capability—a product or a supply network that is not easily imitated, for example. It must create barriers to entry that limit the number of firms in the industry. In the market, a firm must distinguish itself from rivals in order to increase the value that firm brings to a game. It must reduce the price elasticity of demand and the cross-price elasticity of demand. Monsanto did that with its swirl logo for NutraSweet and Intel did it with its "Intel inside" campaign.

As noted in Chapter 9, sometimes it is necessary to have a critical mass of customers. At least up to some point, the more people that use America Online, for instance, the more everyone values it because that's where they'll find more people online. The more people that use Microsoft Office, the more valuable the software becomes. Companies that need a critical mass of customers often subsidize initial customers. Both AOL and Microsoft did this. Newspapers and magazines subsidize readers in order to create more value for advertisers. In a few cases, the newspapers are given away. The publication generates its revenue solely through advertising.

Intel and Microsoft have a symbiotic relationship, each depending on the other. However, Intel was not comfortable with just relying on Microsoft to provide software that would require ever-faster microchips. Hence, Intel brought in more players, subsidizing activities that would require new microprocessors.

Many companies are bringing more players into the game and thereby increasing those firms' purchasing power; for example, by joining together to purchase health care for employees.

Rules

John Sculley, CEO of Apple Computer in 1992, reacted to the dismal performance of the computer industry in 1991 by stating that Apple's challenge "is not only to stay ahead of our competition, but . . . to find some way to change the rules of the game."[7] What did Sculley mean?

Apple was a huge success from its founding in 1976 until IBM entered the personal computer market in 1981. By 1980, new entrants had flooded the market. Almost every firm had a different configuration of hardware and software, making links between machines virtually impossible. IBM changed that. It's open system fostered imitators and clones. By 1992, the majority of buyers could not distinguish between IBM and no-name PC brands. As a consequence, price competition had become the rule. Apple had a peculiar position in the industry. It was the only alternative standard for PCs other than the MS-DOS/Intel standard. Apple's once-distinctive capability of graphics and a mouse-driven operating system had been eroded by Windows. In fact, Apple no longer had a distinctive capability. What was its value in the game? Virtually none. If it was to survive, it had to change the game. But how?

Apple might change the number of players, attempting to bring in more complementary firms—software companies that would use the Mac standard. But what would induce firms to enter the industry in order to use the Mac standard when they could use the Microsoft standard and appeal to more customers? Could Apple use rules or perceptions to alter the situation? Perhaps Apple had to change the boundaries of the game—to look to the next computer revolution. It might begin to focus on the Internet and the Web. By the time Apple was looking at changing the boundaries, others had already done that. Sun was producing the Netserver machines called dumb machines or Net PCs. And, in 1997, Microsoft and Intel combined to introduce a set of common technical standards to help manufacturers build Net PCs. Microsoft and Intel had defined the new boundaries.

An important rule of most games involves the government. Antitrust provisions limit what firms can do. International trade rules limit what firms can do. We'll discuss these in Chapter 15. The story of the entry of SunCountry Airlines into the Northwest Airlines' area is one of changing the rules of the game. Northwest changed the implicit rule of sharing equipment so that each airline did not have to maintain a full inventory at each terminal. SunCountry assumed the rule would not change; Northwest changed it.

Perceptions

Different people view the world differently. The way people perceive a game influences the moves they make. Thus, any description of a game must include how people perceive the game—even how they believe other people perceive it, how they believe other people believe the game is perceived, and so on. Consider the age-old problem of dividing candy among two children. The solution is to have one kid cut the bar and the other get first pick. The candy bar will be divided as equally as possible unless the child dividing the bar knows that the other child prefers the edges or the top more than the first child does. Then the child doing the dividing can cut the candy bar so that the second child chooses a smaller piece. Perceptions are important.

Game theory requires all the players to be *rational*. Being rational simply means that a person does the best he can, given how he perceives the game and how he evaluates the various possible outcomes of the game. It does not mean people do not misperceive situations or make mistakes. It means not consistently making the same mistakes. Two people can be rational and yet perceive the game quite differently. One person may have better information than the other. But if the second doesn't know what the first knows, she's not being irrational but is seeing things differently. The difference in information naturally leads to a difference in perceptions, even to misperceptions. People can guess wrong and still be rational: They're doing the best they can given what they know.

Boundaries

One more feature of a game is its scope or boundary. Real-life strategic situations have no boundaries. But a game without boundaries is too complex to analyze. Thus, a game is analyzed as being separate from every thing else going on. Nevertheless, a game's boundary should not restrict thinking. Wal-Mart had its greatest success when it was rapidly expanding into small towns across the United States. It effectively limited each game to the region in which a new store was being added. Each local druggist would fight the battle with Wal-Mart, each local florist would fight with Wal-Mart, and so on. None of the local firms thought beyond the boundaries, say, by attempting to link several small firms in different local markets.

Prisoner's Dilemma Revisited

Prisoner's dilemma situations arise so often in business that they are worth examining in detail. The **prisoner's dilemma** results in an outcome where all parties are worse off than would be the case if the parties could agree to another set of behaviors. Since the prisoner's dilemma has an outcome that is less than the best, the result is called *inefficient*. The inefficiency means that the parties have an incentive to escape from the dilemma. In a situation of private property rights, voluntary exchange, and free entry and exit, inefficiencies will be competed away—driven out of the market. The same holds for prisoner's dilemmas.

Wal-Mart and Procter & Gamble are known as tough companies with which to do business. Over the years P&G built up a reputation for being a "self-aggrandizing bully of the trade."[8] Wal-Mart, on the other hand, was renowned for demanding that its suppliers offer it the lowest prices, extra service, and preferred credit terms. In 1992 Wal-Mart instituted a policy of dealing directly with manufacturers, refusing to deal with brokers and manufacturers' representatives. It would do business only with vendors that invested in customized electronic-data-interchange technology and put bar codes on their products. Because of the volume and growth of Wal-Mart, manufacturers had little choice but to fall in line.

In the past, P&G would dictate to Wal-Mart how much P&G would sell, at what prices, and under what terms. In turn, Wal-Mart would threaten to drop P&G merchandise or give it poorer shelf locations. This adversarial relationship began to change in the mid-1980s. Sam Walton and P&G's vice president for sales decided to reexamine the relationship between the companies. After a great deal of research and communication, the two companies began to work toward mutual benefits. P&G took over responsibility for managing Wal-Mart's inventory of P&G products. P&G received continuous data by satellite on sales, inventory, and prices for different sizes of its products at individual Wal-Mart stores. This information allows P&G to anticipate, say, Pampers sales at Wal-Mart, determine the number of shelf racks and quantity required, and automatically ship the orders. Wal-Mart pays P&G for the products after the merchandise is sold to the end consumer. Wal-Mart is P&G's biggest customer, generating about 10 percent of P&G's total revenues.[9] Those who find themselves in a prisoner's dilemma will look for ways to escape.

Credible Commitments

Two ways of escaping from a prisoner's dilemma situation have been identified One way is to change the payoff structure and the other is to play the game repeatedly. To change the payoffs, firms make **commitments**. A commitment is an action that ties one party into a certain behavior that other parties know will result. A typical action-movie scene shows two drivers steering their cars madly at each other. Neither wants to crash into the other but neither wants to be the first to pull off the road, since each thinks the other will eventually pull off. Who wins? Usually, if a game of chicken proceeds to the finish, both parties lose. One party can win by taking some action that tells the other party there is no option. This is usually what occurs in the movies. For instance, if one driver rips the steering wheel off and throws it out the window and the other driver sees this, the second knows the first driver cannot now choose to pull off. The only outcome is for the second driver to pull off the road.

The most common commitments firms make are introductory offers, warranties, money-back guarantees, advertising, launching expenditures, and staking a reputation derived from elsewhere. These involve sunk costs and demonstrate to customers that the firm is here to stay—that its claims are credible. For instance, guarantees are difficult to fake. A low-quality product would break down frequently, making the guarantee quite costly for the firm. Thus, the higher the quality of the product, the better the guarantee offered by the firm.

In addition to providing information about quality, guarantees force competitors to disclose information about the relative qualities of their products. Once the highest-quality product appears with its guarantee, consumers have some information about the quality of that product—and also about the quality of all remaining products. They know that products without guarantees are not of the highest quality. Without other information about a product that has no guarantee, consumers might assume the quality of that product to be no better than the average quality of all such products. This places the producer of the second-best product in a difficult position. If it continues to offer no guarantee, consumers will think its product is worse than it really is, but its guarantee cannot match that of the highest-quality product. Thus, the producer of the second-best product must offer a guarantee of its own, but the terms of its guarantee cannot be quite as good as those for the best product.

In the end all producers must either offer guarantees or live with the knowledge that consumers rank their products lower in quality. The terms of the guarantees will in general be less liberal the lower a product's quality. Producers would rather not announce that their product is of lower quality by offering stingy warranty coverage, but failure to offer something makes consumers think the quality level is even lower than it is.

When Japanese automobile companies entered the U.S. market, they faced the difficulty of convincing consumers of the quality of their cars. Although the manufacturers knew that their products were of high quality, their potential customers did not. In fact, many believed that Japanese goods were shoddy imitations of Western products. "Made in Japan" had become synonymous with cheap and crummy. Accordingly, Japanese manufacturers offered more extensive warranties than had been usual in the market. Customers soon came to see that "Made in Japan" meant quality. During the 1970s and 1980s, U.S. auto producers offered warranties that were not as extensive—for example by not providing "roadside assistance," something the German and Japanese producers were providing. Consumers rightly viewed U.S. cars as being of lower quality.

Advertising is a similar statement of commitment. We have just spent millions of dollars drawing your attention to our product, the advertiser implicitly says. "If we intended to disappoint your expectations, to withdraw from the market, or to produce a poor-quality product, spending that money would be a foolish thing for us to have done." The advertisement assures the reader that the product is good, but not because it says that the product is good. Rather, the assurance that the product is good comes from the mere fact that the advertiser advertises.

In 1994, Rupert Murdoch's New York *Post* averted a price war with the rival *Daily News* by creating the perception that it was ready to start one. In the summer of 1994, Murdoch's *Post* was test-marketing a cut in the newsstand price to 25 cents and had demonstrated its effectiveness on Staten Island. In response, the *Daily News* raised its price from 40 cents to 50 cents. Under the circumstances, this seemed remarkable. As the *New York Times* commented, it was as if the *Daily News* was daring the *Post* to follow through with its price cut across all of metropolitan New York.

There was more going on than this. Before dropping the price to 25 cents, the *Post* had previously raised its price to 50 cents. The *Daily News* had opportunistically stuck at 40 cents. As a result, the *Post* was losing subscribers and advertising revenue. While the *Post* viewed the situation as unsustainable, the *Daily News* didn't see any problem, or at least appeared not to. The *Daily News* apparently thought that the *Post* would stick to a 10-cent premium—that it didn't have the will to counter the *Daily News*'s opportunistic behavior.

The *Post* needed to mount a show of strength, to demonstrate to the *Daily News* that it had the financial muscle to launch a retaliatory price if necessary. The goal was to convince the *Daily News* without incurring the cost of a full-blown war.

The *Post* cut prices to 25 cents on Staten Island. Sales of the *Post* surged, and the *Daily News* discovered that its readers were very willing to switch papers to save 15 cents. It became clear that disastrous consequences would befall the *Daily News* if the *Post* extended its price cut throughout New York City.[10] As a result, the *Daily News* buckled under, raising its price to the 50 cents desired by the *Post*. Both papers extended the higher price throughout their territories.

Establishing credibility means that you are expected to carry out your unconditional moves, keep your promises, and make good on your threats. Commitments are unlikely to be taken at face value. Credibility must be earned.

Credibility requires finding a way to prevent going back. Reputation can be one of the most important commitments. If you try a strategic move in a game and then back off, you may lose your reputation for credibility. Wal-Mart has an unconditional commitment to everyday low prices. It has established its reputation with many years of maintaining low prices. Had Wal-Mart periodically lowered prices a few days and then raised them, the low-price guarantee would have little value.

A straightforward way to make your commitment credible is to agree to a punishment if you fail to follow through. This can be done with a contract. A broken contract typically results in significant damages and expenses so that the injured party is not willing to give up on the contract easily. For example, a producer might demand a payment from a supplier that fails to deliver on time.

Repeated Transactions

The second way to emerge from a prisoner's dilemma is to "play the game" several times. Engaging in **repeated trials** means that customers and firms can learn about each other. Customers will learn through experience which are the quality firms and products, and firms will learn which are the quality customers.

When repeated transactions between players will occur, players have an incentive to cooperate. A cartel, for instance, enables the players to avoid a dilemma. The only problem is that the players in the cartel have an incentive to cheat on the cooperative agreement. A cartel has to find ways to discover whether cheating has in fact occurred and, if so, then determine who has cheated. Trust can break down for all sorts of reasons. Behind every scheme to encourage cooperation is usually some mechanism to punish cheaters. A prisoner who confesses and implicates his collaborators may become the target of revenge by the others' friends. The prospect of getting out of prison more quickly may look less alluring given the knowledge of what waits outside. On the other hand, there is no solution that achieves reciprocal cooperation in a one-time game. Only in an ongoing relationship is there an ability to punish. A collapse of cooperation carries an automatic cost in the form of a loss of future profits. If this cost is large enough, cheating will be deterred and cooperation sustained.

End-of-Game Problem

A one-time game and a repeated game have the same problem if there will be an end to the repeated game and everyone knows when that end will occur. The problem is that cooperation ends when there is no longer any time left to punish; since no one wants to be left cooperating while the others cheat, no one cooperates. This is true no matter how long the game is, provided the end time is known. Right from the start, players look ahead to predict the last play. On the last play, there will be no future to consider, and the dominant strategy is to cheat. The outcome of the last play is a foregone conclusion. Since there is no way to affect the last play of the game, the penultimate play effectively becomes the last one to consider.

Given this discussion about the incentive to cheat, it is quite amazing that cooperation occurs in the real world all the time. Why, if everyone has an incentive to cheat, would we observe so much cooperation? In the real world, games are repeated a finite number of times but the last period is not known. This means that cooperation can be a dominant strategy and mechanisms for penalizing cheaters can be effective. Let's consider two common ways to control cheating on cooperative relationships.

Tit-for-Tat When rivals do not cooperate, how can you penalize them? One of the more popular suggestions is **tit-for-tat,** a variation of the eye-for-an-eye rule of behavior: Do to others as they have done to you. The strategy has the participants cooperate in the first period and from then on mimic the rival's action from the previous period. Tit-for-tat is as clear and simple as you can get. It never initiates cheating but it never lets cheating go unpunished. The problem with tit-for-tat is that the slightest possibility of misperception can result in a complete breakdown. Any mistake echoes back and forth. One side punishes the other for a defection and this sets off a chain reaction. The rival responds to the punishment by hitting back. This response calls for a second punishment. At no point does the strategy accept a punishment without hitting back. What tit-for-tat lacks is a way of saying "enough is enough."

Suppose that two competitors, Big Roy and Crazy Bob, are matching each other's price in a tit-for-tat strategy. They start out peacefully, matching the prices.

Round	Big Roy	Crazy Bob
1	$100	$100
2	$100	$100
3	$100	$100

Suppose that in round 4 Big Roy misinterprets Crazy Bob's actions as a price cut.

Round	Big Roy	Crazy Bob
3	$100	$100
4	$100	$100M misperceived as $95
5	$ 90	$100
6	$100	$ 85
7	$ 80	$100
8	$100	$ 75

The single misunderstanding, $95M for $100M, echoes back and forth. In round 5 the misperception of a $90 price is punished with an $85 price in round 6.

Scorched-Earth Policy The tit-for-tat strategy indicates commitment, but its dynamic characteristic creates problems for misperceptions. A different enforcement rule is the **scorched-earth policy.** When Western Pacific attempted to acquire the publishing company Houghton Mifflin, the publishing house responded by threatening to empty its stable of authors. John Kenneth Galbraith, Archibald MacLeish, Arthur Schlesinger Jr., and others threatened to find new publishers if Houghton Mifflin were acquired. Western Pacific withdrew its bid and Houghton Mifflin remained independent.

This scorched-earth policy is one example of devices game theorists call strategic moves. A strategic move is designed to alter the beliefs and actions of others in a direction favorable to yourself. The distinguishing feature is that the move purposefully limits your freedom of action. The lack of freedom can have strategic value. It changes other players' expectations about your future responses, and you can turn this to your advantage.

Picture a rivalry between two microchip manufacturers, Intel and AMD. In the absence of any unconditional moves, the two companies simultaneously choose their strategies. Each company must decide between a low or high level of marketing and advertising. The game is illustrated in Figure 13.6.

Each side has two strategies, so there are four possible outcomes. Both sides regard a high-advertising race as the worst scenario. This is payoff 1 for each firm.

Figure 13.6

PAYOFF MATRIX

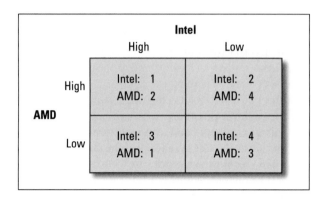

Each side's second-worst outcome is pursuing low advertising while the other goes all out. AMD likes best the situation in which it pursues high advertising and Intel follows with a low effort. For Intel, the best situation is when both sides make low effort. Low effort is the dominant strategy for Intel. Because AMD can anticipate Intel's action, the best response for AMD is high advertising. The equilibrium of the game is the top right cell where Intel gets its second-worst payoff.

To improve the situation, Intel needs to make a strategic move. Suppose that Intel *preempts*. It announces it will pursue an extensive amount of advertising and marketing (the high choice) before AMD reaches its decision. This turns the simultaneous game into a sequential game. If Intel pursues low advertising, AMD responds with high and Intel's payoff is 2. If Intel pursues high advertising, AMD responds with low and Intel's payoff is 3. Therefore, Intel should announce high and expect AMD to respond low. This is the equilibrium of the sequential game. It gives Intel a payoff of 3, more than the 2 it got in the simultaneous game. Commitment to an action or response rule transforms an otherwise simultaneous game into a sequential game. Although the payoffs remain unchanged, a game played with simultaneous moves in one case and sequential moves in another can have dramatically different outcomes.

Uncertainty

Game theory can become quite complex. Many of these complexities are beyond what might be useful to managers and to us, but one additional topic we should discuss is uncertainty. In the cases we've discussed, we've assumed that players knew the results of all actions with certainty (except perhaps the end period). In the real world, such knowledge is unlikely and uncertainty about profits can translate into an uncertainty about actions. This is why considering most situations with an eye to options can be valuable.

Almost every business decision involves some uncertainty. A seller does not know how a potential buyer values a good or service so does not know how high a price can be driven without losing the sale. An employer does not know the ability of a new employee at the time of hiring. A supplier might not know the costs of providing a manufacturing firm certain inputs before agreeing to supply them. How is it possible to make a decision without knowing exactly what consequences will follow?

The first component of a decision in the face of uncertainty is knowledge of the relative likelihood of the alternative possible outcomes. The process begins by listing all the possible outcomes that could follow a decision and assigning probabilities to them. Then, the expected value of the outcome can be calculated. Suppose, for example, a coin is flipped. If it comes up heads, you win $100; if tails, nothing. The probability of each outcome is one-half. What is the expected value of this event? The average payoff would be approximately $50, because the toss would come up heads about half the time. The **expected value** from the single coin toss is the probability that the event occurs weighted by the payoff if it occurs plus the probability that the event does not occur weighted by the payoff if it does not occur. In the example, the expected value is

$$(\$100 \times 0.5) + (\$0 \times 0.5) = \$50$$

In the example where SunCountry is considering entering the airline business in competition with Northwest, suppose SunCountry believes there is a 50–50 chance that Northwest will retaliate. SunCountry then figures an expected profit from entering of

$$0.5(-\$50 \text{ million}) + 0.5(\$60 \text{ million}) = -\$25 \text{ million} + \$30 \text{ million} = \$5 \text{ million}$$

In this case, the rule of looking forward and reasoning backward still has Sun-Country entering the market, since the expected profit of $5 million exceeds the expected profit of $0 from not entering. A change in beliefs can change that outcome. Suppose that SunCountry believes there is a 75 percent probability that Northwest will retaliate and only a 25 percent probability that it will not retaliate. Then the expected value or profit for SunCountry from entering is 0.75($–50 million) + 0.25($60 million) = –$37.5 million + $15 million = –$22.5 million.

The application of the probabilities of Northwest's response is obviously extremely important. Where does SunCountry get them? They come from a careful analysis of the position of the opponent. SunCountry might know that Northwest's reputation has value in other markets and that the airline has relations with suppliers, the government, and customers. In this case the probability of 0.75 of Northwest's retaliating would be reasonable. Or SunCountry might know that the new manager of Northwest is unlikely to devote funds to retaliating against SunCountry. In this case the probability of retaliation would be very low. One thing that SunCountry might have gained by pursuing the entry in stages is knowledge of the probabilities of certain actions by Northwest Airlines.

How people respond to risk depends on how risk-averse they are. If you were offered the choice of receiving $50 for sure and having a 50 percent chance of receiving $100 and a 50 percent chance of receiving nothing, which would you pick? The expected value is $50, but either $100 or $0 could occur. Most people would take the sure bet, $50. People tend to prefer a certain outcome to a gamble with the same expected return. In economics terminology, people who prefer the sure thing over the bet when the expected return is the same are risk-averse.

Suppose the amount of money offered "for sure" declines. How low would this sum have to go before you preferred the gamble to the certain outcome? The more risk-averse you are, the further the amount would have to be lowered. The difference between $50 and the amount at which you would take the gamble is called the **risk premium**. If, for example, you would switch from taking the sure thing to taking the gamble at $40, you have a $10 risk premium. Your risk premium is a measure of how cautious you are toward this particular gamble. In any situation, the risk premium is defined to be the difference between the expected return of the gamble and the amount of money that, if received for sure, the individual regards as equivalent to the gamble. The risk premium is the answer to the question: How much money would you be prepared to give up to rid yourself of this risk?

The size of the risk premium depends on the psychology of the individual—how cautious or adventurous the person is. It also depends on the likelihood of the event's occurring and on the size of the potential loss. A given individual has different risk premiums toward different risks, and different individuals facing the same risk can have different risk premiums.

Risk aversion and risk premiums have been measured by observing people's behavior: the amount of insurance people purchase, the types of crops farmers plant, the types of cars people purchase, the occupations people choose, and so on. Psychologists find that women, older people, married people, and firstborns tend more than others to avoid risks. Commission salespeople have been found to be less risk-averse than average, while public-sector employees and bankers are more risk-averse than average. Studies have found that CEOs are more willing to take risks than lower-level managers, that managers in small firms are more willing to take risks than managers in large firms, and that managers with a graduate degree are more willing to take risks than managers with just a bachelor's degree or high school education.[11] The rich and successful are consistently found to be less risk-averse than those who are less rich and successful.

Suppose a consumer regularly purchases a particular brand of detergent and a new detergent is being introduced. A risk-averse consumer prefers a sure thing to an uncertain prospect of equal expected value. Thus, if the consumer expects the new detergent to work just as well as the one regularly chosen, then the new one will not be purchased. There is risk associated with using a new product. The consumer prefers the sure thing—the current brand—to the risky prospect of a new product.

Firms recognize the risk aversion of consumers and attempt to overcome it. The new detergent may have a lower price than the existing brand. The firm may offer free samples to induce the consumer to try the new brand. Alternatively, ads may attempt to make the consumer think that the expected quality of the new product is higher than the certain quality of the old product.

Risk aversion can also explain why well-known chains often do better than local stores. A consumer driving through the town, knowing nothing about the local stores, sees a brand with which she is familiar. Even if the local store offered a better-quality product than the national chain, the chain has the advantage of being better known—of providing less risk.

CASE REVIEW *Unilever and P&G*

Recall that in our beginning chapter Case, Unilever was going to introduce a new product without giving any advance notice to its competitor, something it had previously always done. Was this a good strategy? Did Unilever look ahead and reason back? What would the outcome of the preemptive strike by Unilever be?

The two firms were in a situation of a prisoner's dilemma but had moved away from the inefficient solution to the efficient one by cooperating. The repeated play of the game between the two firms had enabled them to evolve to this situation of cooperation. Now Unilever was thinking about changing that situation. The question Unilever must answer is whether its actions would provoke a price/product/advertising war that would lead to a much worse situation for both firms than was currently the case or whether its actions would enable it to increase market share and profits no matter what P&G's response was. Given the history of cooperation, it seems reasonable to assume that P&G would retaliate. The only way that P&G would not retaliate is if retaliation would be more harmful than not retaliating. The fact that the two companies were currently cooperating means that both expected the other to retaliate in the event of unilateral action. Thus, what Unilever has to determine is whether there are actions it could take that would stop P&G from retaliating. Just as the New York *Post* had forced the *Daily News* to increase its price, could Unilever force P&G not to retaliate by demonstrating that doing so would hurt P&G even more in some way?

Suppose Unilever knows that P&G has no product readily available that it could introduce to retaliate against Unilever's new introduction. What would P&G do in such a case? Would it lower prices on all existing products just to penalize Unilever? Would it devote additional funds to research in order to come up with other products it could then introduce in an attempt to penalize Unilever?

Once the Unilever executives answer these questions and assign probabilities to various outcomes, it can then solve the game to see whether there is a Nash equilibrium.

SUMMARY

1. A game is defined to be a situation of strategic interdependence. Its components are players, the players' perceptions, the rules to be followed, and the limits or boundaries of the game.
2. The rules of a game may be defined by laws or government definitions, by societal convention, or by the actors themselves.
3. The boundaries of a game define where the game is played—locally, nationally, globally, and so on. A sequential game is one in which players take turns. Each player must look ahead and reason back.
4. A simultaneous game is one in which all players make their moves at the same time. Each player will begin by asking whether there are dominant strategies or dominated strategies.
5. A dominant strategy is a strategy that is best for player A no matter what player B does.
6. A dominated strategy is a strategy that is not best for a player.
7. An equilibrium strategy is one in which neither player has an incentive to change.
8. A prisoner's dilemma is a game in which both players have a dominant strategy and end up in an inefficient equilibrium. The only ways to avoid a prisoner's dilemma result are commitment and repeated transactions.
9. Commitment includes sunk costs—actions such as guarantees, warranties, and expenditures on advertising. Commitments also include credible actions, such as the willingness to enter into a price war.
10. Cooperation may be a result of repeated transactions.
11. There is often an incentive to cheat on a cooperative agreement. Enforcement mechanisms are used to restrict cheating. Tit-for-tat is an enforcement mechanism whereby what one does to you, you return. The scorched-earth policy is an enforcement policy whereby all other options are made untenable.
12. Uncertainty is introduced into game theory by placing probabilities on the various potential actions and deriving the expected actions or expected value of actions.

KEY TERMS

game theory	Nash equilibrium	scorched-earth policy
sequential game	prisoner's dilemma	expected value
simultaneous game	commitment	risk premium
dominant strategy	repeated trials	risk aversion
dominated strategy	tit-for-tat	

EXERCISES

1. The Federal Trade Commission prohibits bait-and-switch, defined as an alluring but insincere offer to sell a product or service that the advertiser does not intend or want to sell. To protect consumers from bait and switch, California requires that automobile ads list the serial number of the advertised car and the number of cars available at an advertised price. Why would governments restrict bait and switch?

2. Texas Instruments once announced a price for random-access memories that wouldn't be available until two years after the announcement. A few days later, Bowmar announced that it would produce this product and sell it at a lower price than Texas Instruments. A few weeks later, Motorola said it, too, would produce this product and sell it below the Bowmar price. A few weeks after this, Texas Instruments announced a price that was one-half of Motorola's. The other two firms announced that, after reconsidering their decision, they would not produce the product.

   a. What was Texas Instruments' reason for announcing the price of a product two years before it was actually for sale?

   b. Under what conditions would Motorola not have rescinded its production decision?

3. Explain how a strategy of increasing expenditures on advertising could deter market entry.

4. Under what conditions would a first-mover strategy not be beneficial?

5. Suppose you are the manager of a firm that has discovered an innovation that enhances the power of a microchip 1,000 times. What would you do with that unique resource—your innovation? Would you sell the chip to Intel and Motorola and allow them to market the chip under their own brand? Would you sell the chip directly to computer manufacturers such as IBM and Macintosh under your own firm's label?

6. Suppose you are the owner-operator of a gas station in a small town. Over the past twenty years, you and your rival have successfully kept prices at a very high level. You recently learned that your rival is retiring and closing his station in two weeks. What should you do today?

7. Which of the following might create first-mover advantages?

   a. Maxwell House introduces the first freeze-dried coffee.

   b. A consortium of U.S. firms introduces the first high-definition television.

   c. Wal-Mart opens a store in Nome, Alaska.

   d. Merck introduces Arogout, the first effective medical treatment for ulcers.

8. Coke and Pepsi have sustained their market dominance for nearly a century. General Motors and Ford have lost their dominance. What is the difference between the two cases.

9. In a situation that occurs only once, if you advertise and your rival advertises, you will each earn $5 million in profits. If neither of you advertises, your rival will make $4 million and you will make $2 million. If you advertise and your rival does not, you will make $10 million and your rival will make $3 million. If your rival advertises and you do not, you will make $1 million and your rival will make $3 million.

   a. Set up the situation in a matrix form.

   b. Do you have a strategy that you will choose no matter what your rival does?

   c. Is there a strategy your rival will choose no matter what you do?

   d. What is the solution or equilibrium?

   e. How much would you be willing to pay your rival not to advertise?

10. You and your rival must simultaneously decide what price to advertise in the weekly newspaper. If you each charge a low price, you each earn zero profits. If you each charge a high price, you each earn profits of $3. If you charge different prices, the one charging the higher price loses $5 and the one charging the lower price makes $5.

a. Find the equilibrium when there are no repeated transactions.

b. Now suppose there are repeated transactions. If the interest rate is 10 percent, what will be the outcome?

11. You are considering entering a market serviced by a monopolist. You currently earn $0 economic profits, while the monopolist earns $5. If you enter the market and the monopolist engages in a price war, you will lose $5 and the monopolist will earn $1. If the monopolist doesn't engage in a price war, you will each earn profits of $2.

a. There are two possible solutions or equilibria. What are they?

b. Will you enter?

12. Not all games possess a Nash equilibrium. In other words, there are games in which there is no set of strategies that represent the best strategy for each player contingent on what the other players do. Determine whether the game presented in Figure 13.7 has a Nash equilibrium. The game involves introducing a new product.

Figure 13.7

PAYOFF MATRIX FOR A NEW PRODUCT INTRODUCTION

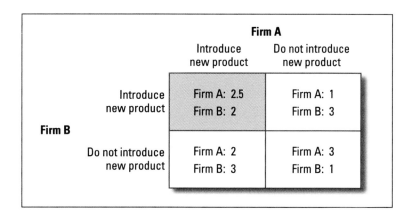

		Firm A	
		Introduce new product	Do not introduce new product
Firm B	Introduce new product	Firm A: 2.5 Firm B: 2	Firm A: 1 Firm B: 3
	Do not introduce new product	Firm A: 2 Firm B: 3	Firm A: 3 Firm B: 1

CHAPTER NOTES

1. When the young men of Princeton were playing poker in the early 1930s, they were being observed by a new member of the faculty, mathematician Johann von Neuman, who then captured their actions in mathematical models. The economist Oskar Morgenstern convinced Neuman that his mathematical structure would explain economic behavior. The result of their observations was the book *Theory of Games and Economic Behavior*. (Princeton, NJ: Princeton University Press, 1947).

2. William B. Hakes, "Readers Report, Game Theory Wasn't Meant to Be a Forecasting Tool," *Business Week*, July 13, 1998, p. 9.

3. Nancy A. Nichols, "Scientific Management at Merck," *Harvard Business Review*, Vol. 72 (January/February 1994): 97.

4. For more on conventions, see H. Peyton Young, "The Economics of Convention," *Journal of Economic Perspectives* 10, no. 2 (Spring 1996): 105–122.

5. This story comes from Adam M. Brandenburg and Barry J. Nalebuff, *Co-opetition* (New York: Doubleday, 1996).

6. Think about how Holland Sweetener might have created options and thus created value rather than simply jumping in with both feet.

7. Case 9-792-081, Apple Computer 1992, Harvard Business School, by David B. Yoffie, Jeff Cohn, and David Levy.

8. "Pritchett on Quick Response," *Discount Merchandiser*, April 1992, pp. 64–65.

9. Nirmalya Kumar, "The Power of Trust in Manufacturer–Retailer Relationships," *Harvard Business Review*, Vol. 74 (November/December 1996): 92–106.

10. This example is discussed in detail in Brandenburg and Nalebuff, *Co-opetition*, p. 198.

11. Kenneth R. MacCrimmon and Donald A. Wehrung, *Taking Risks: The Management of Uncertainty* (New York: Free Press, 1986).

PART V
Looking Outside the Firm

Most business strategy deals with issues the manager can control, but certain factors affect a firm that are beyond the control of the manager. Nonetheless, many of these outside factors are things the manager should be aware of and knowledgeable about. For instance, some managers think they need not worry about or consider events taking place in other parts of the world because their firms only do business domestically. Similarly, many managers think they can ignore the government when defining strategy. These views can be very costly.

In this section, the issues of globalization and the government are discussed. During the past decade, globalization has become one of the most widely referred to topics of concern in business. It has become a controversial social issue as well, with many environmentalists, activists, and labor unions staging protests at meetings of international bodies. Globalization refers to the fact that business has become more than simply a domestic issue. It is not uncommon for companies to have manufacturing facilities in foreign countries, sell of goods and services in several nations; and acquire resources from all over the world. This is all part of globalization. Each of these transactions requires the exchange of currencies. Thus, an understanding of the market in which currency is exchanged is essential for firms that operate internationally. But it is not just the international companies that are affected by exchange-rate changes—companies that have no foreign operations or exports can be affected by exchange rate changes as well. In Chapter 14, problems resulting from exchange-rate changes are examined and methods of minimizing ill effects from exchange-rate changes are discussed.

Chapter 15 deals with the government. As any person who has experience in business knows, a single chapter on government and business can barely scratch the surface of the government's involvement in and influence on business. There are so many laws and regulations affecting business that the simple list of those in the United States exceeds one thousand telephone book-sized pages. Laws regarding business actions that are or are not allowed affect business strategy. Managers must be aware of these laws for defensive purposes, but can also use the laws to their advantage by making them part of the firm's basic strategy. Similarly, governmental rules and regulations must be understood and their effects either minimized or used to create value. In Chapter 15 we discuss the primary areas in which the government intervenes in business—antitrust and economic and social regulation. We also briefly discuss some of the more important international regulatory agencies and their rules and regulations.

CHAPTER 14

Globalization

The Automakers and the Yen

During the period from 1980 to 1985, the executives of General Motors claimed that the company had difficulty competing because of the rising value of the dollar. Between October 1980 and February 1985, the dollar had risen 63 percent generally against currencies of U.S. trading partners and 26 percent specifically

against the yen. According to Roger Smith, then CEO of GM, the value of the Japanese yen put tremendous pressure on U.S. manufacturers by lowering the cost of autos manufactured in Japan relative to those manufactured in the U.S. Ford pleaded with Washington to help get the dollar down to 180 yen; GM and Chrysler agreed. The U.S. auto manufacturers argued that a weaker dollar would help blunt the continuing competitive pressure from imported cars. They told anyone who would listen that a strong dollar got them into their current poor sales position and a weak dollar would get them out.

The rapid fall of the dollar, beginning in 1985, brought renewed hope to executives of the Big Three auto companies. But, even as the dollar fell, American automakers lost an additional 5 percent market share. Why hadn't the falling dollar corrected the declining market share?

Exchange-Rate Fluctuations

Virtually every business consultant is talking about globalization; every new how-to book in business mentions the term; and most business magazines commonly carry feature stories on it. What is globalization? Some people say it is the homogenization of everything—that McDonald's and Wal-Mart will exist in every city and every city will look the same. Most people refer to it as the recognition that business has to do with more than just the domestic U.S. economy. Globalization is more general than this. It refers to cross-border activities as well as borderless transactions; the location of a manufacturing facility in more than one country; the sales of goods and services in several nations; and the acquisition of resources from many nations.

Whether we are driving to work in a Japanese car, wearing clothes manufactured in China, or having a French wine with dinner, we are using products originally purchased with currencies traded through the foreign-exchange market. An understanding of this market is essential to firms that operate internationally because they are exposed to foreign-currency fluctuations. But it is not just the international companies that are affected by exchange-rate changes. In fact, changes in exchange rates can often affect the operating profit of companies that have no foreign operations or exports. Today, every executive must have some understanding of international trade, exchange rates, and exchange-rate risk.

Foreign Exchange

In most instances, when consumers in the United States buy a foreign product, they see only the U.S. dollar price. They don't see the price denominated in yen, pounds, pesos, or other currency. Usually it is the business that must trade dollars for yen or dollars for pesos in order to purchase the Mitsubishi TV or the Nestlé chocolate. The business must carry out a transaction in the foreign-exchange market in order to acquire the foreign products it sells or uses in the production of its final good.

Foreign exchange is foreign money, including paper money and bank deposits such as checking accounts. When someone with U.S. dollars wants to trade those dollars for Japanese yen, the trade takes place in the foreign-exchange market, a global market in which people use one currency to purchase another. The foreign-exchange market involves participants buying and selling currencies all over the world. Trading takes place throughout most of each day—starting in Tokyo; moving west to Singapore and Hong Kong; continuing to Zurich, Frankfurt, and London; and then ending in New York, Chicago, and San Francisco. Participants in the market include individuals, corporations, commercial banks, and central banks.

An **exchange rate** is the price of one country's money in terms of another country's money. A shirt manufactured in Tijuana, Mexico, sells for 20 U.S. dollars in San Diego and for 250 pesos in Mexico. Where would you get the better buy, Tijuana or San Diego? Unless you know the exchange rate between U.S. and Mexican currencies, you can't tell. The exchange rate allows you to convert a foreign-currency price into its domestic currency equivalent, which can then be compared to the domestic price. For example, on January 17, 2003, the exchange rate between the Mexican peso and the U.S. dollar was $1 = 10.60Ps. This means that 250Ps is equivalent to $23.58. Thus, the shirt was less expensive in San Diego than in Tijuana.

Websites of important international organizations include:

http://www.worldbank.org
http://www.wto.org

Current exchange rates are available at:

http://moneycentral.msn.com/investor/market/rates.asp

Exchange rate data are available at:

http://www.economagic.com/fedny.htm

Several nations, their currencies, and the symbols for those currencies are noted below.

Country	Currency	Symbol
Australia	Dollar	A$
Austria	Schilling	Sch
Belgium	Franc	BF
Canada	Dollar	C$
China	Yuan (RMB)	¥
Denmark	Krone	DKr
Finland	Markka	FM
France	Franc	FF
Germany	Deutschemark	DM
Greece	Drachma	Dr
India	Rupee	Rs
Iran	Rial	RI
Italy	Lira	Lit
Japan	Yen	¥
Kuwait	Dinar	KD
Mexico	Peso	Ps
Netherlands	Gilder	FL
Norway	Krone	NKr
Russia	Ruble	Rub
Saudi Arabia	Riyal	SR
Singapore	Dollar	S$
South Africa	Rand	R
Spain	Peseta	Pts
Sweden	Krona	SKr
Switzerland	Franc	SF
United Kingdom	Pound	£
Venezuela	Bolivar	B
European Economic Community	Euro	€

Spot rates are quoted in the *Wall Street Journal*'s "Money & Investing" section, in the *Financial Times*' "Markets" section, and in most daily newspapers. A representation of the daily listings is shown in Table 14.1. The rates quoted are those occurring at a specific time, 4:00 P.M. Eastern time. The time is listed because the rates fluctuate throughout the day as the supply of and demand for currencies change. Each country for which foreign exchange is traded is noted along with its currency name in parentheses, such as "Brazil (Real)." In the first column is the U.S. dollar equivalent of the nation's currency—real, for instance—for the previous and current days. In the third and fourth columns are the exchange rates, the number of reals necessary to purchase one U.S. dollar for the current and previous days. For instance, on January 17, 2003, the Canadian dollar was selling for 0.6521 U.S. dollars; the U.S. dollar was selling for 1.5334 Canadian dollars.

The exchange rates listed in Table 14.1 are called **spot rates**—the rate of exchange at any given time. How is the spot rate determined? An exchange rate is determined by the demand for and supply of a currency. A country's currency is demanded by businesses wanting to purchase the goods and services of that na-

Table 14.1

EXCHANGE-RATE TABLES

January 17, 2003

The New York foreign-exchange selling rates below apply to trading among banks in amounts of $1 million and more, as quoted at 4:00 P.M. Eastern time by Bankers Trust Co., Dow Jones Telerate Inc., and other sources. Retail transactions provide fewer units of foreign currency per dollar.		
Country	**U.S. $ Equivalent**	**Currency per U.S. $**
Brazil (Real)	.2967	3.37
Australia (Dollar)	.5917	1.69
Bahrain (Dinar)	2.6525	.3770
European Community (Euro)	1.067	.9372
Britain (Pound)	1.6134	.6198
Canada (Dollar)	.6524	1.5334

tion and by investors wanting to purchase the financial assets of that nation. The supply of a country's currency is provided by businesses of that nation wanting to purchase the products of other nations and investors of that nation wanting to purchase financial assets of other nations.

If Micron in Boise, Idaho, sells $1 million worth of microchips to a manufacturer in France, the exchange of the chips requires an exchange of currencies. The manufacturer in France must offer the equivalent of $1 million in euros. A banker in France might arrange for the exchange with a banker in San Francisco, offering to buy 1 million U.S. dollars for some amount of euros. This is a demand for dollars and a supply of euros. Similarly, if a U.S. bank wants to purchase a Mexican bond in order to earn higher interest rates, the bank must purchase Mexican pesos with dollars. This creates a demand for pesos and a supply of dollars. Thus, both real transactions (the sale and purchase of goods and services) and financial transactions (the sale and purchase of financial assets) determine the exchange rate. The relative amounts of currencies offered in the foreign-exchange market determines the exchange rate between currencies.

The foreign-exchange market for dollars and euros is illustrated in Figure 14.1. The price measured on the vertical axis is the exchange rate, dollars per euro; the quantity measured along the horizontal axis is the quantity of euros. The demand for euros represents the U.S. demand for European goods and financial assets. To purchase these items, euros are needed. The U.S. consumers must buy euros. The higher the price—that is, the higher is $/€—the lower the quantity of euros demanded. The supply of euros represents the European demand for U.S products and financial assets. To buy these U.S. items, European buyers must offer euros in exchange for dollars. The higher the price—that is, the higher is $/€—the higher the quantity of euros offered.

An increase in the demand for European goods and services means an increase in the demand for euros, illustrated as an outward shift of the demand curve in Figure 14.1. This leads to a higher price—that is, higher exchange rate—for euros. The dollar depreciates (the euro appreciates).

Between the end of World War II and 1973, most of the world was on a fixed-exchange-rate system: The exchange rates were determined by law. When fixed exchange rates were abandoned by the major industrial countries in March 1973, the world did not move to purely free-market-determined floating exchange rates.

Figure 14.1

EXCHANGE-RATE DETERMINATION

The demand for and supply of euros is represented. The exchange rate is determined by the equilibrium between supply and demand.

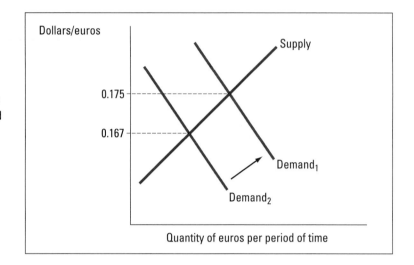

Currency rates are available at
http://www.x-rates.com

The major industrial counties have allowed their central banks to intervene to keep their currencies within certain ranges, and many smaller countries have fixed or pegged their rates to a major currency such as the dollar or the pound. In fact, only forty-eight nations allow their exchange rates to be determined in the free market. The European Union nations fixed their own currency rates to the euro in 1999, and prices were listed both in the domestic currency value and the euro until January 1, 2002. On that date, the euro began circulating, and the national currencies—such as the Italian lira, German mark, and French franc—were no longer considered legal tender as of July 1, 2002.

Some nations rely on another country's currency as legal tender. *Dollarization* refers to the practice whereby a nation adopts the U.S. dollar as its currency either explicitly using the dollar and doing away with any other currency or fixing the exchange rate between the dollar and the domestic currency and enabling trade to occur with either. In nations where price stability has been a problem, people have engaged in unofficial dollarization by choosing (as a store of value) to use the dollar rather than their own domestic currency even though the practice was not legally sanctioned. Official dollarization occurs when a country adopts the U.S. currency as its legal tender. In January 2001, El Salvador adopted the U. S. dollar as its currency. Panama has used the U.S. dollar as a national currency since 1904, and Ecuador dollarized in 1999. Other nations are considering dollarization as well. Mexican president Vicente Fox met with U.S. president George W. Bush in 2001 to discuss the dollarization of Mexico. In Canada, which experienced a 36 percent decline in the value of its currency between 2000 and September 2002, there was some discussion about adopting the U.S. dollar as its currency. But even with some nations adopting the U.S. dollar and others the euro, there remain many different currencies and thus a foreign-exchange market for the buying and selling of currencies.

Arbitrage and the Law of One Price

In Chapter 2 we discussed the **law of one price**—an identical good should sell for the same price in different locations (exclusive of transportation and transaction costs). This is true across national borders as well as within a country—the exchange rate between currencies adjusts to ensure that the law of one price holds. For instance, suppose a Mini Cooper sells for $30,000 in the United States and ¥744,000 in Japan. At the exchange rate of 124 yen per dollar (or 0.00806 dollars per yen), the dollar price of the MiniCooper in Japan would be $60,000. If the costs of transportation are negligible and there are no other costs or restrictions, arbitrage should occur. People will buy the car in the United States and ship it to Japan. This process should raise the price in the United States and lower it in Japan. The yen price might fall to ¥310,000 and the dollar price rise to $25,000. At the exchange rate of 0.00806 dollars per yen, the prices would be equivalent.

In foreign-exchange markets the law of one price is called **purchasing power parity (PPP)**. Purchasing power parity essentially argues that in the absence of impediments to trade, all tradable goods must sell at the same price everywhere, allowing for the cost of transportation. Purchasing power parity will come about as all arbitrage opportunities are exploited. This occurs as goods and services are traded, people migrate, and companies are able to transfer best practices and technology worldwide. But because these activities do not occur instantaneously, adjustments can take considerable time.

Arbitrage occurs whenever a profitable opportunity exists for buying something in one market and simultaneously selling it in another market. It occurs with goods and services as well as with financial assets. Thus, purchasing power parity should hold for both goods and services and for financial assets.

Investors search the world for the highest return on their investments. They have to consider exchange-rate changes in determining where to invest. A U.S. bond is denominated in U.S. dollars, while a British bond is denominated in British pounds. If the U.S. bond pays 10 percent interest, that interest is paid in

The law of one price says that identical items will sell for the same price once adjusted for exchange rates and transportation costs. Yet, the price of a can of Coca-Cola in Korea will not be identical to the price of a can of Coca-Cola in the United States. Why? Tariffs, taxes, and other governmental restrictions affect the functioning of the law of one price.

dollars. Similarly, if the British bond pays 5 percent interest, that interest is paid in pounds. If you are a U.S. citizen, you will ultimately want dollars and thus want to compare the returns on the two bonds in terms of dollars. If you buy the U.K. bond, you exchange dollars for pounds at the time you purchase the bond. You are subject to exchange-rate changes—that is, you are exposed to exchange-rate risk. When the bond matures, you receive the principal and interest in pounds and must exchange them for dollars. If the exchange rate remains the same, then the return on the U.K. bond is 5 percent. If, however, the exchange rate changes between the time you buy the bond and the time it matures, your return may be more or less than 5 percent.

Suppose the exchange rate is $1 = £0.6 when you purchased the bond and the bond sells for £100 and promises a 5 percent return in one year. You need $167 to buy the bond. A year later the bond matures and you receive the principal of £100 plus 5 percent interest for a total of £105. At the exchange rate of $1/£.6, the £105 is converted into $175. Because you paid $167 for the bond initially, the interest return in dollars is $8 or 5 percent. However, suppose the exchange rate for the pound has gone up from $1/£0.6 to $1/£0.58 during the period you held the bond. Then, the £105 proceeds from the bond are changed into $181 (£105 × $1/£.58 = $181). You are better off than you would have been if the exchange rate had not changed. You paid $167 for the bond initially and received $181: $8 in interest and another $6 in exchange-rate return, for a total of $14. This is a return of 8.4 percent. The return from the U.K. bond is the U.K. interest rate plus the percentage change in the exchange rate, not simply the U.K. interest rate. The percentage change in the exchange rate is 3.4 percent, so the dollar return from the U.K. bond equals the 5 percent interest paid in British pounds plus the 3.4 percent change in the exchange rate, or 8.4 percent.

When the pound increases in value, foreign residents holding pound-denominated bonds earn a higher return on those bonds than the pound interest rate. When the pound depreciates, it takes more pounds to convert to the domestic currency so the pounds received at maturity are worth less to the foreign resident than the pounds originally purchased, and the foreign resident's return from the U.K. bond is lower than the interest rate on the bond. For instance, in our example, if the pound had depreciated 5 percent—gone from $1/£0.6 to $1/£0.63—the dollar return would have been zero.

If the U.K. bond is returning a greater amount in dollar terms than the U.S. bond, then U.S. residents will purchase U.K. bonds. This drives up the price of U.K. bonds relative to U.S. bonds and lowers the return on U.K. bonds relative to U.S. bonds. Once again, arbitrage tends to force the rates of return toward equality. When the rate of return or interest rate tends to be the same on identical assets (when returns are measured in terms of the domestic currency), it is the law of one price in operation and is called **interest rate parity** (**IRP**). Because capital flows quickly (instantaneously in most cases), interest rate parity tends to occur more rapidly than purchasing power parity, although governmental regulations or restrictions of capital flows mean that interest rate parity may not hold in the short run. But, whether or not purchasing power parity and interest rate parity exist at any point in time, the main point is that there are market forces in operation tending to drive the prices to equality. When parity does not exist, there are profit opportunities and arbitrage will occur. And since entrepreneurs seek those economic profits, profit opportunities do not last very long before someone acquires them.

Exchange-Rate Exposure

In the example of the last section illustrating how the exchange rate between the U.S. dollar and U.K. pound affects the rate of return on an investment, we noted that the holder of the asset (the bondholder) was exposed to exchange-rate changes. A firm may be exposed to exchange-rate changes if items on the balance sheet—such as debt, payables, and receivables—are denominated in a foreign currency. Since these items have to be converted or translated into the currency of the country in which the headquarters is located at the end of the fiscal year, an exchange-rate change can affect their value. For example, Laker Airways, a U.K.-based company, figured it did not have to worry about exchange-rate changes between the pound and the dollar because any changes would just create offsetting behaviors on the part of British and American tourists. Although fewer British tourists would visit the United States when the dollar was strong, more Americans would travel to Britain. The two effects seemed, at least theoretically, to offset each other. But this appearance was misleading. When the dollar was declining in 1980, Laker financed new aircraft purchases in dollars, increasing its debt—debt that was denominated in dollars. When the pound weakened relative to the dollar, the airline couldn't pay its interest costs and was forced into bankruptcy. It had not considered the effects of exchange-rate changes on its balance sheet.

Exchange-rate risk is simple in concept: a potential gain or loss that occurs as a result of an exchange-rate change. But, who loses and who gains? If an individual owns a share in the German company Daimler-Chrysler, he or she will lose if the value of the euro drops. But what happens to the individual owning the shares of a company based in the United States and doing business in Germany? The firm's subsidiary in Germany may lose, but the firm itself may not if exchange rates have changed.

Types of Exposure

The task of gauging the impact of exchange-rate changes on an enterprise begins with measuring its *exposure;* that is, the amount, or value, at risk. The most common problem arises when an enterprise has foreign affiliates keeping books (accounting records) in the respective local currency. For purposes of consolidation, these records must be translated into the reporting currency of the parent company. This is called **balance sheet exposure**.

A company could reduce balance sheet exposure by refusing to do business in any other country but its home one. But this doesn't guarantee solving the problem of exchange-rate exposure. Consider a company that does not do any business across national borders. For instance, Lincoln Electric is a U.S. manufacturer of small motors that, until the 1990s, sourced domestically, sold exclusively in the home market, and had no foreign debt. It would seem that the company had no exposure to changes in exchange rates. However, its operating profit was exposed to changes in the yen–dollar rate because the company competed in the United States with Japanese manufacturers. When setting a dollar price in the United States, the Japanese companies considered their yen costs. In a year when the yen and the dollar were at purchasing power parity, Lincoln Electric's dollar costs would equal the dollar-equivalent costs of its Japanese competitors. But if Japan experienced a higher inflation rate than the United States, then Lincoln Electric's position would depend on whether purchasing power parity held. If the yen weakened in line with purchasing power parity, the competitive position of Lincoln Electric would not change. If, however, the yen weakened relative to the dollar by an amount more than required by purchasing power parity, the dollar-equivalent costs of the Japanese companies would be less than the costs of Lincoln Electric and the competitive position of Lincoln Electric would weaken. Lincoln Electric is exposed to exchange rate changes because it competes with foreign firms. This is called **market-based exposure.**

How much market-based exposure a company has depends on whether it does business globally, whether it competes domestically with foreign competitors if it does not export or import, and the selling environment in which the firm operates. Consider a domestic firm that sources domestically but competes with foreign firms in the domestic market. When the value of the foreign firms' home currencies falls, then those firms' costs fall. If the demand in the domestic market is highly price-elastic, then the foreign firms' lower costs will likely lead to lower prices. The domestic firm must follow suit or lose substantial business. Yet, because the domestic firm's costs did not decline, its profits will decline.

Now consider a domestic firm that sources domestically and competes with foreign firms but has a demand that is very price-inelastic. In this case, when exchange rate changes alter the competitive position of the foreign firms, the domestic firm does not have to worry about matching lower prices. The price inelasticity of demand means that customers are not as likely to alter their purchases by switching from the domestic firm to the foreign firms.

How does a firm reduce its exchange-rate exposure? If it has balance sheet exposure, it has to reduce those aspects of its business that have to be translated from one currency to another. Perhaps the most straightforward way to do this is to locate in the country where the firm does most of its business. In this way, most of the balance sheet will be defined in the same currency. What factors are important in deciding where to locate facilities? The size of the local market plays an important role because the firm can utilize those facilities to sell in that market. Obviously, a country's political climate is important. Locating in a country that might confiscate property at any time is a high-risk proposition for a firm thinking about spending millions of dollars in building facilities. Another important factor is the availability of labor and relevant technology.

If a firm decides to establish a facility in another country, it has to determine whether to build from scratch or to acquire existing facilities and whether to do the project alone or in an alliance or joint venture with a domestic firm. Each decision involves tradeoffs and cost-benefit calculations. For instance, when Jabil, a computer hardware manufacturer, was looking to expand internationally, it had to decide which countries to establish facilities in. It could not simply manufacture in the United States and ship to customers around the world; the shipping and handling costs were too high. It had to locate near its major customers.

It explored Asia, Latin America, and Europe. In Europe it examined the Czech Republic, Poland, and Hungary, among other nations. It ruled out the more industrial European nations such as Germany and France because the government rules and regulations made doing business there too costly. It liked particular areas in the Czech Republic and Hungary because they were close to major customers for whom Jabil manufactured as an original equipment manufacturer (OEM).

Jabil narrowed its choices down using cost-benefit analysis: The local labor force, the cost of doing business, the stability of the government, the stability of the currency, and other factors had a role in the analysis. Once it chose a location, it had to determine whether to build new facilities, whether to acquire and adapt existing facilities, and how fast to construct the facilities. Because the marginal cost of constructing facilities from scratch as opposed to acquiring and adapting existing facilities was small, it decided to construct new facilities. The question then was how fast to construct the facilities. Firms always have tradeoffs on the speed of construction and the costs and revenues associated with the project. Consider Figure 14.2, which shows the costs and revenues associated with speed of construction. The costs decline as the length of time needed to construct the facilities increases. To speed the construction up requires more labor at higher pay, more materials at higher costs, and so on. The revenue associated with the output from the plant is higher the faster the construction is and the quicker the output can be manufactured and sold. The profit-maximizing length of time taken to establish the facility is given by point T. This is the length of time at which the difference between the present value of revenue and cost is greatest.

After Jabil had gone through its analyses (its due diligence) and completed construction of facilities, it was not going to change to another country because exchange rates changed. The location of a manufacturing facility involves long-term commitment. Exchange-rate risk is more a short-term problem. Locating a facility only to minimize exchange-rate exposure may be a costly decision. Events could cause the firm to be subject to even greater exchange-rate risk in future years. You'll notice that in the above review of Jabil's actions, nothing about exchange-rate exposure arose. Seldom does a firm select a location for its facilities based on reducing exchange-rate risk. Most such decisions are based on resource costs (a firm wants a lower-cost source of labor or materials) or distribution costs (a firm wants to be close to the final market).

Once a firm has established facilities in more than one country, it is subject to balance sheet exposure. A firm must select the currency in which it invoices. It may select the invoicing currency so that its cash flows and assets are primarily defined in one currency. Its choice could benefit customers but put it at more exchange-rate risk, or it could reduce its exchange-rate risk by placing the burden of that risk on customers. For example, suppose Jabil is choosing to invoice in either

Figure 14.2

TIME AND PROFIT TRADEOFF

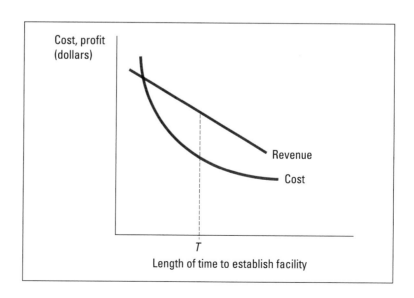

U.S. dollars or Czech koruna. If it selects the koruna, then its Czech customer has no worry about exchange-rate changes, but Jabil does. It has to translate the koruna back to the dollar. If Jabil invoices in dollars, then it is the Czech customer who must translate back to the domestic currency. Jabil will select the invoicing currency that maximizes profit and that depends on the price elasticity of demand. If the Czech customer has no other sources of the equipment, then the demand for Jabil hardware will be very price-inelastic; Jabil can shift the exchange-rate risk to the customer. However, if Jabil is just one among a few or several sources of equipment, and the price elasticity of demand is high, then Jabil will not be able to shift the risk to the customer.

Using Financial Markets to Reduce Exposure

A firm need not make long-term commitments, such as establishing manufacturing sites or changing the invoicing currency, to reduce exchange-rate exposure. Instead, it may turn to the foreign-exchange market and arrange forward contracts. The **forward market** allows corporations to establish the exchange rate between two currencies for settlement at a fixed future date. This is known as **hedging** or covering exchange-rate exposure. The **forward rate** is fixed at the time the contract is made, but payment and delivery are not made until the value date. The most common forward contracts—often called just **forwards** are for one, two, three, six, and twelve months. Whether the exchange rate changes in a direction expected by the firm or in the opposite direction does not matter. The firm is obligated to buy or sell the currency at the agreed-upon rate.

For a primer on hedging, visit http://www.boscia.com/ a260pages/Group02/Intacct.html

Another hedging practice is to use **currency futures**. Currency futures are similar to foreign-exchange forwards in that they are contracts for delivery of a certain amount of a foreign currency at some future date and at a known price. In practice, they differ from forward contracts in important ways. One difference between forwards and futures is standardization. Forwards are for any amount, as long as it's big enough to be worth the dealer's time, while futures are for standard amounts, each contract being far smaller that the average forward transaction. Futures are also standardized in terms of delivery date. The normal delivery dates for currency futures are March, June, September, and December, while forwards are private agreements that can specify any delivery date that the parties choose. Both of these features allow the futures contract to be tradable; a party could buy or sell an existing futures contract. Another difference is that forwards are traded by phone and telex and are completely independent of location or time. Futures, on the other hand, are traded in organized exchanges such as the London International Financial and Futures Exchange (LIFFE) in London, Singapore International Mercantile Exchange (SIMEX) in Singapore, and the International Money Market (IMM) in Chicago. In a forward contract, whether it involves full delivery of the two currencies or just compensation of the net value, the transfer of funds takes place once: at maturity. With futures, cash changes hands every day during the life of the contract, or at least every day that has seen a change in the price of the contract. This daily cash compensation feature reduces the possibility of one party's failing to deliver on the contract. Forwards and futures serve similar purposes and tend to have identical rates, but they differ in their applicability. Most large companies use forwards; futures tend to be used whenever credit risk may be a problem.

With a forward contract one can lock in an exchange rate for the future. There are a number of circumstances, however, in which it may be desirable to have more flexibility than a forward provides. For example, a computer manufacturer in California may have sales priced in U.S. dollars as well as in euros in Germany. Depending on the relative strength of the two currencies, revenues may be realized in either euros or dollars. In such a situation, the use of forwards or futures would be inappropriate: There's no point in hedging something you might not have. What is called for is a foreign-exchange option: the right, but not the obligation, to exchange currency at a predetermined rate.

A **foreign-exchange option** is a contract for future delivery of one currency in exchange for another, where the holder of the option has the right to buy (or sell) the currency at an agreed-upon price—the strike or exercise price—but is not required to do so. The option seller is obliged to make (or take) delivery at the agreed-upon price if the buyer exercises the option. In some options, the instrument being delivered is the currency itself; in others, the trade involves a futures contract on the currency. *American options* permit the holder to exercise the option at any time before the expiration date; *European options* permit the holder to exercise the option only on the expiration date.

Consider the situation faced by a major U.S.-based potato chip company. It agreed to purchase 15 million punt worth of potatoes from a supplier in County Cork, Ireland.[1] Payment of 5,000,000 punt was to be made in 245 days' time. The dollar had recently declined against the punt, making the cost of the potatoes to the U.S. firm higher. How could it avoid any further rise in the cost of imports? The CFO of the potato chip company decided to hedge the payment. He had obtained dollar/punt quotes of $2.25 spot ($2.25 for each punt) and $2.39 for 245 days forward delivery. In other words, the foreign-exchange market was anticipating that the dollar would fall relative to the punt. But what if the dollar rose in the next few months? This would make the $2.39 price much too high. The CFO decided to buy a call option. With this action, he was paying for downside protection while not limiting the possible savings that could be obtained if the dollar fell. If the dollar rose to $2.19, the CFO would not exercise the option and would purchase the punt at the spot rate of $2.19. But if the dollar fell to $2.39, the CFO could exercise the option and purchase the punt at $2.25.

This simple example illustrates the lopsided character of options. Futures and forwards are contracts in which two parties exchange something in the future. They are thus useful to hedge or convert known currency or interest rate exposures. An option, in contrast, gives one party the right but not the obligation to buy or sell an asset under specified conditions while the other party assumes an obligation to sell or buy that asset if that option is exercised. The option enables one to offset the risk of movements in exchange rates in one direction only.

When should a company use options in preference to forwards or futures? As we saw in the case of real options in Chapter 12 the price of an option is directly influenced by the outlook for the asset's volatility: The more volatile, the higher the price. So if a firm believes the exchange rate is more volatile than the market says its is (via the price of the option), then purchasing an option makes sense. In other words, the firm believes the option should have a higher price than what the market says. When a firm believes the likely change in exchange rates is in a specific direction, then purchasing an option to protect against unexpected changes in the other direction makes sense.

Forwards and options can be combined in a hedging strategy. While the forward contract allows the firm to reduce uncertainty about the price of a foreign currency, it does not eliminate foreign-exchange risk. A firm that had entered into a forward contract to purchase pounds at a price of £1.55/1$, but found that the spot rate was £1.5/1$ at the time the contract expired, would have an opportunity cost of £0.05/1$; if it had not locked into a forward contract, it would have been better off by £0.05/1$. Because the forward contract locks the firm into the transaction, the firm risks the possibility that future spot prices may be more favorable. A firm could purchase a put option, allowing but not obligating the firm to sell foreign exchange at a specified price. For instance, suppose the firm purchases a put option to sell pounds at a current price of £1.5/1$ and the spot rate at the time the forward contract matures is £1.55/1$. The firm can exercise the put option by using the forward contract to purchase pounds at £1.5/1$ and using the put option to sell those pounds at £1.55/1$.

Firms may combine a forward contract and put and call options in order to hedge risk. Suppose a forward contract specified that a firm would purchase dollars at a price of ¥120/$1 and the firm wanted to be sure it did not lose out if the price of yen changed. The firm could purchase both a put option and a call option. Suppose the firm purchases a call option with an exercise price of ¥108/$1. This means the firm can buy dollars at ¥108/$1. That protects the firm if the value of the yen rises above the forward rate. To protect itself against falling yen values, suppose the firm purchases a put option with an exercise price of ¥132/$1. This means the firm can sell dollars at a price of ¥132/$1. If, at the time the forward transaction is to occur, the spot price of yen has declined to ¥140/$1, the firm could exercise the call option and buy dollars at a price of ¥108/$1. But it still has to purchase dollars at the forward rate of ¥120/$1. It does this by acquiring yen on the spot market at ¥140/$1 and using those yen to purchase dollars at the lower price of ¥120/$1.

As you might have gathered by now, hedging in foreign-exchange markets can be complicated. Foreign exchange hedging activities can sometimes begin to override consideration of the market in which one is buying or selling goods and services. For instance, in Australia, the cotton growers hedged the Australian dollar between US60cents and US65cents in 2002 but they did not hedge the US dollar cotton price. When the US dollar cotton price dropped to a near 30-year low, it meant that the Australian cotton growers would lose money each time they exercised an option contract. As a result, many refused to meet their forward contract agreements; simply walking away from the contract.[2]

Visit the World Intellectual Property Organization's website at
http://www.wipo.org/

The Global Capital Market

Capital markets are global: Capital flows in and out of countries at the touch of a button. Understanding the global capital market is important to all managers, not just those doing business in more than one nation.[3] Interestingly, the world's economies were almost as globalized a hundred years ago as they are now. Capital mobility (the flow of capital across national borders) reached a peak at the beginning of World War I and then declined until about 1960. It took until 2000 to reach the 1918 level again.[4] Managing used to be easier in many respects. From 1945 until the 1980s, the world consisted of a series of closed national economies, each with its own unique set of factors of production. These economies competed with one another on the basis of manufactured goods. What determined the standard of living of any one of them was the effectiveness with which a country produced the goods that it exported. Savings were channeled within these national economies by a capital market that interacted with other countries only at the margin.

When the world gave up exchange-rate controls in the 1970s, the capital market began changing. Large multinational banks had foreign-exchange trading rooms that were quick to spot opportunities to profit from floating rates. They discovered that they could borrow for a short period, such as ninety days, in one currency at one rate and lend in another currency at a higher rate, while protecting themselves from foreign-exchange movements with a forward exchange contract. These institutions began profiting from arbitrage opportunities. But arbitrage sometimes turned into speculation. For example, if you believed that the U.S. dollar was going to decline against the Japanese yen, you could simply borrow dollars and convert them into yen. If the yen appreciated as you expected, you would sell the yen after it has risen in value, convert it back into dollars, pay off the U.S. dollar loan, and pocket the amount by which the dollar had depreciated relative to the yen less the interest on the loan. Or if you didn't want to borrow, you could buy a foreign-exchange call option or a forward exchange contract. Of course, if you took a position and were wrong about the price movement, you lost money.

The Asian Crisis

In the late 1990s, most Asian nations fell into very deep recessions. Japan's economy declined 10.7 percent, Korea's 43 percent, Malaysia's 31 percent, Thailand's 40 percent, and Indonesia's 72 percent from their highs in the early 1990s. In comparison, the U.S. economy declined 34 percent during the Great Depression. These Asian economies had such great difficulties primarily because Japan's economy, which comprises two-thirds of the sum of all Asian economies, did not have the financial structure to handle the huge capital outflow that occurred.

After World War II, the Japanese government developed a financial system to support the recovery of Japanese industry. With a devastated economy, Japan needed foreign capital and high domestic savings to support the manufacture of goods, particularly for export. To facilitate this, the banking system ensured that there was no risk of default by corporate borrowers. All loans were secured by collateral, and large corporations were part of industrial groups, the *keiretsu*. Each *keiretsu* had a bank committed to supporting all members of the group. Behind the banks stood the ministry of finance and the Bank of Japan.

This structure enabled large Japanese manufacturing companies to operate with much more debt than would have been considered reasonable in the United States. For example, as recently as 1990, Japanese firms had about ¥1 of equity for every ¥3 of debt. In contrast, the average for publicly traded U.S. corporations was $1 of debt for each $1 of equity.

The Japanese banks were government sanctioned and supported and were expected to own equity in the corporations to which they lent funds. Roughly 75 percent of all Japanese stock is held by banks or insurance companies or by other members of the company's industrial groups. As a result of this structure, stockholders do not count; capital is not allocated by the wishes of the stockholders.

The initial result of the Japanese structure (copied by Korea and other Asian nations) was to jump-start development and lead to rapid rates of growth. But when the foreign-exchange market was liberalized and the global capital market began moving capital quickly from one investment to another no matter the country, the industrial structure of Japan proved too rigid. It could not prevent outflows of capital or depreciation of equity values.

The Breakdown of Barriers

Asia was not the only area in which markets were not allowed to function freely. Prior to 1990, major shares of most economies were protected from competition by government regulations, including capital controls, product-market restrictions, and labor restrictions. Most governments limited the entry of certain products, declared the inconvertibility of local currency, imposed onerous approval processes for acquisitions of companies by foreigners, dictated very high labor costs through minimum wages and benefits, and even set constraints on the hours stores were allowed to remain open. Governments influenced the allocation of capital in the economy and had a primary role in setting interest rates because of their monopoly on printing money and their ability to raise taxes.

These barriers restricted the mobility of capital and the transplant of best practices. If more efficient firms are not able to enter a market to compete with existing firms, then the existing firms will not have to be as efficient. The agricultural industry in France is a great illustration of this situation. Despite low levels of productivity, farmers in France were protected from competition for decades. By protecting that industry for so long, the government was able to avoid the disruption of displacing large numbers of people who had been in farming families for centuries. But the French agricultural market was much less productive than agricultural markets in other nations and the French public paid much more for their domestic produce than did consumers in other nations. In Japan, restrictions have kept competition to a minimum in most industries. The low level of competition, in turn, has resulted in many highly unproductive sectors. Since the Japanese companies are, in general, not as efficient as those in other parts of the world, the only way the companies could compete abroad was to be heavily subsidized by the Japanese government either in direct grants or by restricting domestic competition.

Anti-dumping duties are listed at http://www.wto.org/english/ thewto_e/whatis_e/tif_e/ agrm7_e.htm

Whenever a movement toward openness and global markets occurs, groups threatened by these developments turn to the government for help. As local producers and local labor are faced with external competition, they lobby the government for protection. In some cases, new restrictions on imports are imposed, as with U.S. steel producers in 2002; in others, subsidies are provided, as with most agricultural sectors. But even with such restrictions, managers and citizens in general in one country can no longer limit their understanding of events to what is happening in their own economies. Capital will flow to where its risk-adjusted value is highest. Entrepreneurs will seek ways around, over, and through barriers. This means that countries wanting to raise the standards of living of their citizens will be competing, in a sense, to provide the most desirable economic environment. Countries will need to attract the capital that will increase productivity, employment, and economic growth.

Emerging Markets

Emerging markets are now considered the major growth opportunity in the evolving world order. Coca-Cola, for example, predicts that its $2 billion investment in China, India, and Indonesia, which together account for more than 40 percent of the world's population, can produce sales in those countries that double every three years for the indefinite future, compared with Coke's 4 percent to 5 percent average annual growth in the U.S. market in the past decade.

An emerging market is an economy where the standard of living is low—the real gross domestic product per capita is below about $700 a year. The phrase *emerging markets* is being adopted in place of the previous designation *less developed countries* (LDCs). This change indicates how the perception of these countries has changed. They are considered markets, not simply extremely poor countries that need assistance from the industrial nations.[5]

Tariffs and Other Restrictions

Free trade based on comparative advantage maximizes world output and allows consumers access to higher-quality products at lower prices than would be available in the domestic market alone. If trade is restricted, consumers pay higher prices for lower-quality goods and world output declines. Protection from foreign competition imposes costs on the domestic economy as well as on foreign producers. When production does not proceed on the basis of comparative advantage, resources are not used in their most efficient manner. Why, then, are restrictions placed on trade? The primary reason is due to politics: Some group or groups would be hurt by free trade, so they lobby the government for protection. The most common arguments used to rationalize protection are to save jobs, to enhance national defense, and to protect new industries until they are old enough to compete.

If foreign goods are kept out of the domestic economy, it is often argued, jobs will be created at home. This argument is based on the idea that domestic firms will produce the goods that otherwise would have been produced abroad, thus employing domestic instead of foreign workers. The problem with this argument is that only the protected industry would benefit. Since domestic consumers will pay higher prices to buy the output of the protected industry, they will have less to spend on other goods and services, which could cause employment in other industries to drop. If other countries retaliate by restricting entry of U.S. exports, the output of U.S. firms that produce for export will fall as well.

Table 14.2 shows estimates of consumer costs and producer gains associated with protection in certain Japanese and U.S. industries. The first column lists the total cost to domestic consumers, in terms of higher prices paid, for each industry. The second column lists the dollar cost to consumers of saving one job in each industry. Notice, for instance, that the total cost to consumers due to restrictions in the Japanese chemical products industry exceeds $15 million and the cost of one job saved is $2.4 million. Yet the producer gained only $8.5 million, as shown in column 3.

Another common argument for industry protection is for national defense reasons. It is argued that certain industries, such as shipbuilding, should be protected from foreign competition. It is interesting to look at the industries that receive some sort of protection on the basis of national defense: shipbuilding

Table 14.2

COSTS OF
GOVERNMENT
CONSUMER
PROTECTION LAWS

	Consumer Costs		Producer Gains
	Total (millions of U.S. $)	Per job saved (millions of U.S. $)	(millions of U.S. $)
Japan			
Food and beverages	58,395	762	43,210
Textiles and light industry	8,979	485	3,341
Metals	5,162	974	2,546
Chemical products	15,500	2,385	8,466
Machinery	21,587	287	12,286
United States			
Food and beverages	2,947	488	1,775
Textiles and light industry	26,443	148	12,242
Chemical products	484	942	222
Machinery	542	348	157

Sources: Data are drawn from Yoko Sazanimi, Shujiro Urata, and Hiroki Kawai, *Measuring the Costs of Protection in Japan* (Washington, D.C.: Institutes for International Economics, 1995); and Gary C. Jufbauer and Kimberly Ann Elliott, *Measuring the Costs of Protection in the United States* (Washington, D.C.: Institute for International Economics, 1994). Table is presented in William Boyes and Michael Melvin, *Economics,* 5th ed. (Boston: Houghton Mifflin, 2002).

(including the building of yachts and sailboats), copper, steel, basic metals, nuclear power, aeronautics, railroads, transportation, and others.

Another common argument is that new or emerging industries require protection. Once they mature and get big enough to achieve economies of scale, they won't need the protection any longer. This is called the infant industries argument. The problem with this argument is that the protected industries typically don't become efficient enough to compete without protection. In a sense there is no incentive for these industries to become efficient since once they do, the politicians might reduce the barriers to entry.

The government may protect industries from competition with the use of tariffs, quotas, and subsidies. A **tariff** is a tax on imports or exports. Every country imposes tariffs on at least some imports. Some countries also impose tariffs on certain exports as a means of raising government revenue. Brazil, for instance, taxes coffee exports. Export tariffs in the United States are forbidden by the Constitution.

The effect of a tariff is illustrated in Figure 14.3, which shows the domestic market for oranges. Without international trade, the domestic equilibrium price, P_d, and quantity demanded, Q_d, are determined by the intersection of the domestic demand and supply curves. If the world price of oranges, P_w, is lower than the domestic equilibrium price, this country will import oranges. The quantity imported will be the difference between the quantity Q_1 produced domestically at a price of P_w and the quantity Q_2 demanded domestically at the world price of oranges.

When the world price of the traded good is lower than the domestic equilibrium price without international trade, free trade causes domestic production to fall and domestic consumption to rise. The domestic shortage at the world price is met by imports. Domestic consumers are better off, since they can buy more at a lower price. But domestic producers are worse off, since they now sell fewer oranges and receive a lower price for the ones they do sell.

If a tariff of T (the dollar value of the tariff) is imposed on orange imports, then the price paid by consumers is $P_w + T$ rather than P_w. At this higher price, domestic producers will produce Q_3 and domestic consumers will purchase Q_4. The tariff has the effect of increasing domestic production and reducing domestic consumption, relative to the free-trade equilibrium. Domestic producers are better off since the tariff has increased their sales of oranges and raised the price they receive. Domestic consumers pay higher prices for fewer oranges than they would with free trade.

Quotas are limits on the quantity or value of goods imported and exported. A quantity quota restricts the physical amount of a good. For instance, in 2000 the United States allowed only 1.5 million tons of sugar to be imported. Even though the United States has no comparative advantage in producing sugar, unlike nations such as the Dominican Republic or Cuba, the quota allowed U.S. firms to produce about 6 percent of the world's sugar.

Other restrictions on free trade include subsidies, government procurement rules (must purchase from domestic producers), and health and safety standards. Government standards for products sold in the domestic marketplace can have the effect of protecting producers from foreign competition. The government of Japan once prohibited foreign-made snow skis from entering the country because they were not safe on Japanese snow. Several European nations banned U.S. beef because hormones approved by the U.S. government are fed to beef cattle. In the late 1960s, France required tractors sold there to have a maximum speed of 17 miles per hour; in Germany, it was 13 miles per hour; and in the Netherlands it was 10 miles per hour. Tractors produced in one country had to be modified to meet the requirements of the other countries, thereby raising the prices of the foreign-made tractors relative to domestic ones. Most governments subsidize some

Figure 14.3

A TARIFF ON THE IMPORT OF ORANGES

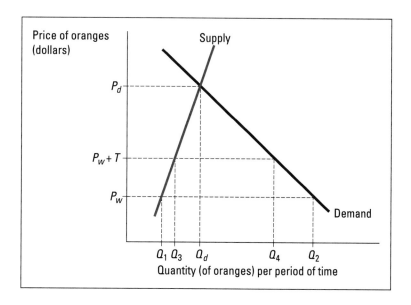

industries in their nations to protect them from harm due to foreign competition. Nearly every nation subsidizes agriculture, but a list of subsidized industries would be extensive.

CASE REVIEW *The Automakers and the Yen*

The rapid fall of the dollar, beginning in 1985, brought renewed hope to executives of the Big Three auto companies. But, after five years of holding ground, American automakers lost an additional 5 percent market share from 1985 to 1988. Why hadn't the falling dollar corrected the declining market share?

Everything else being the same, a falling value of the dollar would make U.S. autos less expensive in other nations. For instance, suppose a BMW produced in Tennessee has a price tag of $40,000. Suppose the dollar-to-euro rate of exchange is $1 to €1.4. This would mean that the BMW would have a euro price tag of €1.4/1$ × $40,000 = €56,000. If the value of the dollar declined, the exchange rate would change from $1 = €1.4 to, say, $1 = €1.1. In this case, the euro price of the BMW produced in the United States would be €44,000. This is a significant reduction in the price of the car in Europe—a 21 percent decline. With a price elasticity of, say, 0.8, the 21 percent decline in price would increase sales by 16.8 percent.

So what could have happened to keep the sales of U.S. auto manufacturers from rising when the value of the dollar declined? If the foreign auto manufacturers lowered the price of their cars to match the falling dollar or if the U.S. manufacturers raised the price of their cars to offset the falling value of the dollar, sales of U.S.-manufactured autos would not increase. Suppose, for instance, that BMW of America raised the U.S. price of the car from $40,000 to $50,000 when the dollar declined to $1/€1.1. The euro price of the car would then be €55,000, a small decline in price from €56,000. Or suppose that Daimler-Benz lowered the price of its €56,000 Mercedes to €44,000 following the decline of the dollar. Then, the reduction in the price of the BMW of America car resulting from the dollar decline would not cause foreign buyers to switch from the Mercedes to the BMW.

SUMMARY

1. An exchange rate is the rate or price at which one currency trades for another.
2. The law of one price means that price (or interest rate) differences of identical goods in different markets will only be large enough that a profit cannot be made by simultaneously buying and selling the good in the different markets.
3. Purchasing power parity (PPP) means that identical goods should have the same price in different countries once adjusted by the exchange rate. Interest rate parity (IRP) means that identical financial assets should have the same rates of return once adjusted by the exchange rate.
4. Foreign-exchange risk is the risk that a change in the exchange rate will adversely affect profits.
5. Forward and futures contracts are agreements to buy or sell foreign exchange at a specified time in the future at a specified rate.

6. An option to buy foreign exchange is a contract that allows but does not require the purchaser of the option to purchase foreign exchange in the future at a specified rate.

7. Foreign-exchange exposure consists of two types: balance sheet, or contractual, exposure and market-based exposure. Market-based exposure depends on whether rivals are foreign or domestic and whether the demand is price-elastic or price-inelastic.

8. Trade restrictions imposed to benefit domestic producers take the form of tariffs and quotas. A tariff is a tax on an exported or imported good. A quota is a limit on the quantity of a product or the value of a product that can be imported.

9. Arguments used to rationalize trade restrictions include the protection of jobs, enhancement of national defense, and protection of infant industries.

KEY TERMS

foreign exchange	interest rate parity (IRP)	forwards
exchange rate	balance sheet exposure	currency futures
spot rate	market-based exposure	foreign-exchange options
law of one price	forward market	tariff
purchasing power parity (PPP)	hedging	quota
arbitrage	forward rate	

EXERCISES

1. An overvalued currency is one that is expected to decline in value relative to other currencies. What is the effect on a firm that produces in the country whose currency is overvalued and sells to other nations?

2. Suppose you are managing a firm that produces in each of the countries listed below and sells according to the description. How would you protect the firm from exchange-rate changes? How would you expect downturns in the United States to affect your business?

   a. A small country that conducts all of its trade with the United States.

   b. A country that has no international trade.

   c. A country whose policies have led to a 300 percent annual rate of inflation.

   d. A country that wants to offer exporters cheap access to the imported inputs they need but to discourage other domestic residents from importing goods.

   e. An industrialized and large economy such as the United States' or Japan's.

3. What does it mean to say that a currency appreciates or depreciates in value? Give an example of each and briefly mention what might cause such a change. Explain how each change could affect a firm's sales when the firm produces in one nation and sells to others.

4. Illustrate the exchange-rate effect of a change in tastes prompting German residents to buy more goods from the United States. How would this affect the sales of a firm that produces in the United States but sells to German residents.

5. Your firm needs to raise $10 million for an expansion. How would you propose the money be raised?

   a. if your firm sells only domestically

   b. if your firm sells in several nations

   c. if your firm is privately owned—has issued no shares of stock

6. Explain the effects of an increase in the value of the domestic currency on a firm's revenues under each of the following conditions:

   a. The firm sells only domestically

   b. The firm purchases supplies from other countries

   c. The firm sells products domestically and in other countries

d. The firm has manufacturing plants located in other countries

7. Your firm has manufacturing facilities in an emerging market. That country decides to impose trade restrictions requiring that all companies be majority-owned by local firms. How would you deal with this change?

8. You are being clobbered by exchange-rate changes. You decided to minimize the exchange-rate risk. How would you proceed? Describe the tradeoffs of minimizing exposure via the financial markets and establishing manufacturing sites in countries in which you do business.

9. Mexico and the United States are the only producers and consumers of a certain type of electronic switch. The demand for and supply of the electronic switch in each country is given below.

UNITED STATES

Price (dollars)	Quantity Demanded (millions)	Quantity Supplied (millions)
20	10	4
40	8	6
60	6	8
80	4	10

MEXICO

Price (pesos)	Quantity Demanded (millions)	Quantity Supplied (millions)
190	5	2
380	4	6
570	3	10
760	2	14

a. Suppose there is free trade and that the exchange rate is 9.5 pesos to the dollar. What is the equilibrium price?

b. Which country will export the switches to the other country?

c. Suppose the United States imposes a tariff of $100 per switch. What will happen to imports and exports?

d. Suppose the exchange rate changes to 10 pesos to the dollar. How does that change answers to parts a, b, and c?

10. The Lincoln Electric Company is the maker of a new electrical motor bought only in Europe and the United States. In the United States the demand for this product is

$$Q_u = 20 - 2P_u$$

and the supply is

$$Q_u = 5 + 3P_u$$

where P_u is the price in dollars and Q_u is the quantity in thousands of units per month.

In Europe the demand is

$$Q_e = 45.5 - 3P_e$$

and the supply is

$$Q_e = -5 + 2P_e$$

Where P_e is the price in euros and Q_e is the quantity in thousands of units per month.

Using the current exchange rate, determine the price of the product in each country(ies).

Suppose the United States imposes a tariff of $T = 0.1 Q_e$. How will this affect the price in the United States? In Europe?

11. A firm has a manufacturing plant in China and sells its product in the United States and Europe. Its costs are

$$TC = 50Q - 10Q^2 + Q^3$$

which are defined in RMB, the Chinese currency. Its demand in the United States is

$$Q_u = 20 - 2P_u$$

and its demand in Europe is

$$Q_e = 45.5 - 3P_e$$

where P_u is dollars and P_e is euros.

a. Using current exchange rates, determine the profit-maximizing prices and quantities.

b. Explain or demonstrate what it would mean if the dollar price of the RMB declined while the euro price of the dollar remained constant.

c. Explain what balance sheet exposure would be for this firm.

d. Explain what market-based exposure this firm would have.

e. Explain how the firm might hedge the risks associated with the exposure.

CHAPTER NOTES

1. The Irish punt was fixed against the euro in 1999. This case took place prior to that date.
2. Stephen Wyatt, "Cotton Farmers Face Crisis Over Hedging" *Australian Financial Review,* May 24, 2002, p. 1.
3. An interesting view of the effects of a global capital market on economic development is provided in Lowell Bryan and Diana Farrell, *Market Unbound: Unleashing Global Capitalism* (New York: Wiley, 1996).
4. Michael A. Clemens and Jeffrey G. Williamson, "Wealth Bias in the First Global Capital Market Boom, 1870–1913," Harvard Working Papers, May 2002 (http://post.economics.harvard.edu/faculty/jwilliam/papers/Wealth_Bias.pdf).
5. Interesting discussions of capital flows in these countries can be found in *Risk Management in Emerging Markets: How to Survive and Prosper* by *Carl Olsson* (London: Financal Times Management, 2002) and *Emerging Markets: A Practical Guide for Corporations, Lenders, and Investors* by *Jeffrey C. Hooke* (New York: John Wiley & Sons: 2001).

CHAPTER 15

Government and Business

CASE *Microsoft*

The Justice Department accused Microsoft of anticompetitive business practices, claiming the company had illegally used its market power to try to destroy the competition in a key segment of the high-technology industry. Ninety percent of the world's personal computers use Microsoft's Windows operating system, the

master program that runs a computer. The government claimed that Microsoft used Windows' dominance to gain unfair advantage in another business—providing access to the Internet. In 1995, Microsoft began giving Windows users its Internet browser at no extra cost. This took business away from other browser providers, in particular, Netscape Communications. Microsoft also allegedly told computer manufacturers who wanted to install Windows on their machines that they could do so only if they agreed to install Microsoft's browser, too. The Justice Department said that Microsoft should be forced either to remove its browser from Windows or to include a rival browser. Microsoft argued that forcing the company to include competing software would be like requiring Coca-Cola to include three cans of Pepsi in every six-pack it sells and that making Microsoft remove Internet technology from Windows would be like telling Coca-Cola that it must take something out of its formula. Was Microsoft a corporate bully or just the best player in the game? How might have Microsoft avoided the antitrust action?

Government Intervention in Business

Managers have to see the connection between concerns originating outside the firm and the market strategies adopted by the firm. They have to be aware of government rules and regulations and to understand how they affect business.

Consider an industry in which price and entry have been regulated for many years. Now suppose a deregulatory initiative provides a new definition of the competitive arena, allowing existing firms to expand their areas of operations and new firms to enter and attempt to attract business through lower prices. Without a strategy to deal with the change, incumbent firms will flounder. This could be seen in those nations that turned from government run economies to market based economies during the 1980s and 1990s. In the United States the electrical utility industry provided a good illustration of the difficulty of making a change to competition after years as a protected, regulated monopoly. Many electrical utility companies floundered, jumping from business to business, attempting to define what they would be in a new competitive environment, if regulatory commissions ever enabled competition to occur.

Consider another situation. A firm is contemplating a merger with a former competitor. It carries out due diligence of the merger, at considerable expense, and then makes an offer for the company. The Justice Department and/or Federal Trade Commission then intercede, disallowing the merger. Had the firm known what the government would do, it may have saved itself considerable money. This occurred in 1996 to Rite Aid, the nation's largest drugstore chain, when it decided to acquire Revco, the second-largest drugstore company. Rite Aid operated 2,760 stores nationwide and Revco 2,100, which would have made the combination more than twice the size of its closest competitor, Walgreen Co. The Federal Trade Commission (FTC) disallowed the merger on the basis of possible anticompetitive effects that might occur after the merger. The CEO of Staples, who had faced a similar situation when the company's attempt to merge with Office Max was denied by the FTC, was asked: "During a merger attempt, a company not only has to run its own business, but it must plan for the combined company once the merger is accomplished. And, it must fight the FTC or Justice Department. How can it all be done?" The CEO responded that it was indeed very expensive: "You have to identify individuals who are accountable only for dealing with the merger. We had about 20 people working full time who were pulled off their normal jobs, letting the majority continue to focus on the business at hand. And, a kazillion outsiders: lawyers, accountants, and economists."[1]

In this chapter we discuss the interaction between government and business. We look at the two main approaches the government uses to intervene in the activities of business—antitrust policy and regulation. Antitrust policy is an attempt to ensure that businesses compete "fairly." Guidelines of behavior and accepted types of behavior are defined, and firms that do not comply are sued. Regulation involves a more active role for government. There are two types of regulations—economic and social. Economic regulation focuses on a single industry and ranges from the government's prescribing the pricing and output behavior to actually running and operating the business. Social regulation, which applies across all businesses, involves health and safety standards for products and the workplace, standards for protecting the environment, and other government restrictions on the behavior of firms and individuals.

Antitrust Policy

Antitrust regulation in the United States is based on the Sherman, Clayton, and Federal Trade Acts. The Sherman Act of 1890 makes illegal "every contract, combination, or conspiracy in restraint of trade" and declares that "every person who shall monopolize, or attempt to monopolize, or conspire to monopolize shall be deemed guilty of a felony." The 1914 Clayton Act built on the Sherman Act with a list of practices that could entail anticompetitive effects in certain situations, including tying arrangements, exclusive dealing, mergers, and interlocking boards of directors. Antitrust policy in the United States is the responsibility of two federal government agencies—the Antitrust Division of the Department of Justice and the Federal Trade Commission—and each state's attorney general. When the Federal Trade Commission was created in 1914, it was given authority to stop *unfair* methods of competition. In 1931, it was given the power to protect consumers from unfair or deceptive acts.

Antitrust activities tend to focus on large firms because large firms typically have more market power. The theoretical basis for government intervention in the activities of the large firm is the comparison between perfect competition (a large number of small firms) and monopoly (one large firm). Figure 15.1 illustrates a perfectly competitive market, with price and quantity determined at the equilibrium between demand and supply. The consumer surplus—the bonus consumers receive from a free market—is the difference between what they would be willing and able to pay (the demand curve) and the price they actually pay.

Now consider what would happen if this same industry were controlled by one firm: The market supply would be offered by one firm, a monopoly, rather than the large number of firms offering identical competitive products as is the case in perfect competition. As shown in Figure 15.2, the monopolist would produce where $MR = MC$. The market demand would have an associated marginal revenue since the monopolist would have to lower price to sell a larger quantity. The market supply would be the amount the monopolist would be willing and able to supply at each price—represented by the monopolist's marginal cost curve (which is equal to the sum of the individual perfectly competitive firms' marginal cost curves).

For an overview of US antitrust laws, visit

http://www.ftc.gov/bc/
compguide/index.htm
http://www.antitrust.org/
http://www.usdoj.gov/atr/

Figure 15.1

PRICE, QUANTITY, AND CONSUMER SURPLUS IN A PERFECTLY COMPETITIVE MARKET

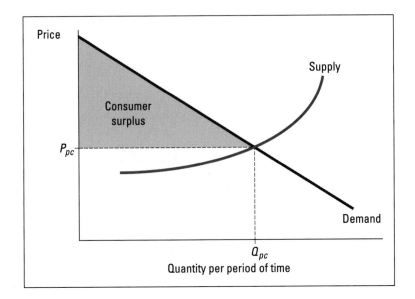

Figure 15.2

PRICE, QUANTITY, AND CONSUMER SURPLUS WHEN A MARKET IS MONOPOLIZED

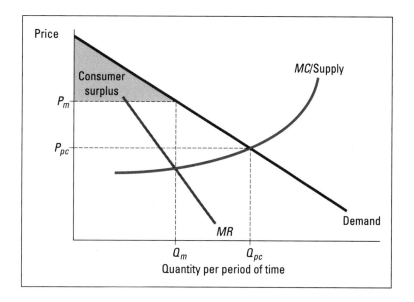

In the perfectly competitive market, firms together produce Q_{pc} and sell that quantity for P_{pc}. The monopoly produces Q_m and charges a price P_m. Thus, less is produced and a higher price is charged when the market is monopolized. In addition, consumer surplus is reduced. This comparison has given antitrust authorities the impetus for focusing on large firms.

What is a large firm? The government has used a definition based on a measure of the control a firm has over its market. The **Herfindahl–Hirschman index (HHI)** is a measure of concentration—how dominant one or a few firms are in a market. The index is calculated as

$$HHI = (size)^2 + (size)^2 + \ldots + (size)^2$$

where $(size)^2$ is the size of a firm squared. An industry in which each of five firms has 20 percent of the market would have an HHI of 2,000. If the largest firm had 88 percent of the market and each of the others 3 percent, the HHI would be 7,780. The higher the HHI, the more dominated the market is by a single firm.

In merger cases, the government will calculate the HHI index that would result following the merger to see whether it is too high or whether it increases too much. In 1992, the Department of Justice and Federal Trade Commission issued horizontal merger guidelines that antitrust enforcers have since used to judge the competitive effects of proposed mergers. The guidelines stipulate that where the postmerger HHI exceeds 1,800, it will be presumed that mergers producing an increase in the HHI of more than 100 points are likely to create or enhance market power or facilitate its exercise. But the guidelines also provide a process for overcoming an anticompetitive presumption. This involves showing that a "merger is not likely to create or enhance market power or to facilitate its exercise if entry into the market is so easy that market participants, after the merger, either collectively or unilaterally could not profitably maintain a price increase above premerger levels." In other words, not only must the market be concentrated, it must be possible for the dominant firm(s) to maintain price increases without facing significant pressure from lower-priced rivals.

The degree to which these guidelines are followed by the FTC varies. In 2001, the commission approved the $3 billion merger of AmeriSource Health Corp. and

Bergen Brunswick Corp. The deal brought the HHI to 2,700, with an increase of 450 points. Nevertheless, the commissioners supported the companies' claim that combining the nation's third- and fourth-largest prescription drug wholesalers would result in efficiencies not possible without the merger. FTC rulings have not been consistent, however. Boeing was allowed to merge with McDonnell Douglas, even though it meant a virtual monopoly in the domestic commercial-airplane manufacturing market. The acquisition of MCI Communications by WorldCom was put into serious doubt while the FTC examined its effects on the market because the combined company might control 50 percent of the Internet "backbone." Southern Pacific was allowed to merge with Union Pacific and thus to control a major share of the rail lines, but other mergers were disallowed. What are the criteria for blocking some deals and not others? The reality is that the interpretation of the statutes by the courts and government authorities changes from administration to administration. Thus, a manager must be aware of what the current administration is expecting from its antitrust officials.

There have been several phases of antitrust policy in the United States. The first began with passage of the Sherman Antitrust Act in 1890 and lasted until about 1914. In this period, litigation was infrequent. The courts used a **rule of reason** to judge firms' actions: Being a monopoly or attempting to monopolize was not in itself illegal; to be illegal, an action had to be unreasonable or unfair in a competitive sense, and the anticompetitive effects had to be demonstrated.

The second phase of antitrust policy began in 1914 with the passage of the Clayton Antitrust Act and the Federal Trade Commission Act. Operating under these two acts, the courts used the **per se rule** to judge firms' actions that were potentially monopolizing tactics; the mere existence of these activities was sufficient evidence to lead to a guilty verdict.

In the Reagan 1980s, the only legitimate subject of antitrust enforcement was price fixing. For a decade, this translated into virtually no antitrust action by the government. Since then, the antitrust regulators have argued that there are justifications above and beyond price fixing that require antitrust enforcement. These tactics include tying, forcing customers to buy one product to get another (the Microsoft case); exclusive dealing, pressuring distributors to dump competitors' wares (this was the main issue in suits against Anheuser-Busch and against Kodak); and standard setting wherein a standard becomes the dominant or only one in use (again, the Microsoft case).

Action against alleged violators of the antitrust statutes may be initiated by the U.S. Department of Justice, by the Federal Trade Commission, by state attorneys general, or by private plaintiffs. Since 1941, the FTC and the Justice Department together have filed nearly 2,800 cases; since 1970, however, private suits have outnumbered those filed by the Justice Department and the FTC combined by about ten to one.

Antitrust laws are directed toward "creating a level playing field" by restricting the anticompetitive actions of large firms. Nearly eighty countries now have such laws, although the degree of restrictiveness varies. Each country's antitrust laws are primarily directed toward its domestic firms, but the laws can also affect foreign companies' ability to enter the domestic market or even spill over into other countries' markets. For instance, a merger or alliance between two companies from the same country could affect competition in other countries. Boeing, a manufacturer of civil aircraft, acquired McDonnell Douglas, an ailing smaller firm. This merger was applauded by U.S. antitrust authorities (FTC, Justice) but decried by the European Union's competition commission, which feared that the merger would reduce competition in Europe to the detriment of Boeing's European rival, Airbus. A merger or an alliance between two companies from different countries could also affect competition in the two markets in different ways. For example, the alliance between British Airways and American Airlines was seen in the United States as an increase in competition, while in the United Kingdom it was viewed as a reduction in competition.

Compared to other countries, the United States is restrictive in terms of allowing certain types of business behavior. When the per se rule was emerging in the United States during the 1920s and 1930s, most European nations had no antitrust laws at all and cartels flourished. Today, many nations continue to support cartels and cooperative behavior that is illegal in the United States.

At least part of the explanation for the differences among nations lies in the growth and development of the various countries following World War II. The economies of Europe and Japan were severely damaged by the war. As the losers, Germany and Japan were occupied and their laws rewritten by the occupying forces. Thus, their antitrust laws resemble those of the United States. However, because Europe and Japan were not concerned with large business but instead with businesses that were too small to compete in world markets, the antitrust laws were never enforced. Businesses had to be large enough to achieve economies of scale, and for several decades it seemed that only U.S. firms were of sufficient size. Hence, while the United States was worrying about large businesses becoming too powerful, other countries were attempting to increase the sizes of their businesses. Only since the 1970s have the European countries begun to institute and enforce antitrust laws along the lines the United States has followed since the 1940s.

Defense Against Antitrust as a Strategy

Competitive strategy means that a firm must develop a distinctive capability that has value in the marketplace. To increase shareholder value, the firm often must differentiate itself, increase its size to benefit from economies of scale, or form alliances. Yet these same competitive strategies may be perceived as anticompetitive by the government antitrust agencies. In recent years, strategic alliances and other forms of cooperation have become an increasingly important part of business strategy, but collaborative arrangements often attract scrutiny by antitrust authorities. Problems can arise out of innocent actions that the government might view as having anticompetitive effects. For example, in the past ten years or so, antitrust enforcement has targeted or forbidden each of the following: the use by airlines of a clearinghouse that listed fares; licensing agreements and renegotiations involving patented products in the chemical and pharmaceutical industries; information sharing among competing hospitals; the exchange of advertising and marketing plans by infant-formula manufacturers through an industry trade association; and certain joint ventures in the online bond trading industry and foreign-exchange trading industry. A firm might think that it should be able to resist the use of its own equipment and supplies by rivals. But printer manufacturers such as Hewlett-Packard, Lexmark, Canon, and Epson were investigated by European regulators in 2002 regarding anticompetitive practices in the sale of ink cartridges. The market shares of these firms had been eroding due to a rise in the number of companies that refill original cartridges and sell them at a fraction of the price of a new one. The large manufacturers fought back by inserting a "killer" computer chip that makes it difficult for the cartridge to be refilled. This, the European regulatory authorities said, was anticompetitive.

The exchange of information, even in informal discussions, sometimes attracts antitrust attention. This can happen when businesspeople get together to talk about other things and inadvertently exchange information that they should not. For example, in one case, the court upheld the criminal price-fixing conviction of several realtors after one realtor discussed a commission-rate change at a dinner party with other realtors. Within months, each realtor present at the dinner party had adopted similar rates.[2] In another case, the FTC alleged that a respondent's representative met with officers of a competing firm and invited them to fix prices on certain products that both companies produced. The managers' defense was that they only went to their competitor's plant to see their competitor's low-cost production processes. It was not their intent to discuss prices. However, the complaint alleged that these discussions quickly turned to discussions about price.[3] In another case, airlines were forbidden to use a common clearinghouse to report fares. Although the clearinghouse enabled travel agents easy access to fares, the Department of Justice alleged that the eight airlines using the computerized fare-exchange system had unreasonably restrained price competition in the domestic air travel industry.

Discussions between or among competitors will often occur in the normal course of business through existing interfirm relationships such as joint ventures involving the competitors or because competitors are considering a merger or other formal relationship. Managers need to consider how antitrust laws and policies may require them to create certain internal structures or organizational designs to ensure that the flow of information is not interpreted as being anticompetitive. Also, managers attempting to negotiate a relationship with a competitor must be careful about what information is released, when it is released, and to whom it is released.

Pre-deal discussions with potential partners and suitors are settings where antitrust considerations can be important. The potential problem arises when such discussions take place between horizontal competitors and don't result in consummation of a deal.

There are limitations on which competitors can be licensed, which licenses can be exchanged, and which provisions can be written into license contracts. According to government guidelines, enabling your major competitor to sell your product through a licensing arrangement could be viewed as a reduction of competition.

The use of patents to dominate a market could also be viewed as anticompetitive. Patent policy allows the patent holder exclusive use, but this is not necessarily a problem as long as there are products that compete with the patented product. In the absence of such substitutes, managers have to be careful about their use of patents. Major pharmaceutical companies were investigated in 2001 regarding their use of patents to restrict the introduction of generic drugs.

Antitrust as Strategy

Being aware of what actions the antitrust authorities might scrutinize or disallow is important. But being defensive is not the only way antitrust is used as strategy. Outcomes that cannot be achieved through market action can sometimes be achieved through legal action. There are approximately ten times as many private antitrust suits filed each year as government suits. Refusals to deal are the most common type of case, followed by horizontal price fixing, tying or exclusive dealing, and price discrimination.

A firm may file a suit in an attempt to change a rival's market behavior. For example, Intel filed a suit against Advanced Micro Devices' (AMD) use of Intel's microcode. AMD then had to decide whether to copy Intel's microcode or create its own.

If it continued to copy Intel's microcode and then lost the lawsuit, the court might prevent the sale of the relevant AMD microprocessors. AMD changed its behavior.

The filing of a suit can change behavior even if the suit is not litigated. CIBA Vision Corporation agreed to a settlement with private plaintiffs not because it thought the suit was justified but because the cost and disruption to the business that would be required to litigate outweighed the cost of settlement.

Even the threat of private antitrust action can change behavior. In 1999, Virgin Air announced that it was considering an antitrust suit against the four major tour operators: Thompson, Airtours, First Choice, and Thomas Cook. Virgin Air claimed that travel agents owned by these companies sold their own companies' products before they offered the products of nonaffiliated tour companies. The announcement alone was sufficient to change the agents' behavior regarding Virgin.

International Competition and Antitrust Strategy

Managers must also be aware of the international antitrust and regulatory authorities. The World Trade Organization (WTO) was created by the General Agreement on Trades and Tariffs (GATT) in 1995 to deal with international trade disputes. As of 2002, the WTO had 133 members; 30 other countries had applied for admission. The WTO implements and enforces agreements in such areas as customs regulations, environmental restrictions, intellectual property rights, and dumping. The WTO has a permanent structure headed by a council of ministers representing member countries. The WTO requires a strict timetable for consultation, the presentation of arguments and evidence to a panel, the option of appeal to a dispute settlement body, and the mandatory implementation of the organization's decisions.

The most common case involving foreign firms deals with dumping. Under WTO rules, countries are allowed to impose antidumping duties on imports sold at below "normal value," which can mean the price in their home market or the cost of production. *Dumping* in a pure economic-theory sense occurs when a firm sells its products in a foreign market at a price that is below its average variable costs. In reality, dumping cases are filed whenever a foreign firm sells at a price that is below a domestic firm's price. Suppose the demand for a firm's product is price-inelastic in Europe and price-elastic in the United States. A European firm selling this product would maximize profit by setting a higher price in Europe than it does in the United States. But this profit-maximizing strategy would be subject to a dumping claim by the domestic U.S. firms selling that same product.

Typically, a firm or industry with complaints against foreign firms will appeal to domestic authorities and then either the plaintiff or the government agency will present a case to the World Trade Organization. Dumping cases are handled by two agencies of the U.S. government: the Commerce Department, which is charged with determining whether a company is a foreign producer, whether it is selling for less than fair value, and, if so, by how much; and the International Trade Commission (ITC), which decides whether U.S. industry has been injured by the dumping. A case begins when a U.S. company files a complaint with the Commerce Department's Import Administration Office, which reviews it to decide whether to launch a formal investigation. If the petition is accepted, the case moves on to the ITC, which makes a preliminary determination of whether the affected U.S. company is injured by the dumped imports. If the ITC decides there is an injury, the case moves back to the Commerce Department for a full-scale investigation.

Cases can be filed or begun by individual firms. For instance, the Asian economic crisis of the 1990s hurt U.S. textile businesses because the depreciations of the

Asian nations' currencies reduced the prices of Asian textiles. Imports of synthetic fiber fabric from Asia increased 51 percent and all fabric imports from Asia were up 35 percent during the late 1990s. The U.S. textile industry pursued antidumping action against Asian suppliers as a means of slowing down the competition.

As of the beginning of 2002, the United States had antidumping duties (essentially taxes on imports) on about 265 items from forty different countries, making it the largest user of antidumping taxes. The second-largest user is the European Union, which had about 150 duties. Antidumping duties have become a very popular strategy for domestic firms to use against rival foreign firms. From 1916 to 1970, there were about 15 dumping cases a year in the United States. In the 1980s and 1990s the pace rose to 60 per year. From the late 1990s to the early 2000s, the number was about 50 per year. Worldwide filings have followed that trend. About 1,600 cases were filed worldwide in the 1980s, which was twice the level of the 1970s. In the 1990s there were 2,500 cases filed, and in 2000, there were 272.[4]

The growing number of antidumping cases is a response to increased world trade. As we discussed in the previous chapter, free trade harms some parties, and the harmed parties want to offset or minimize the harm. The antidumping laws have become a substitute for other kinds of protection, such as tariffs, subsidies, and quotas.

Antidumping claims often bring counterclaims. Governments often file counterclaim suits on behalf of businesses. The growing trade deficit in the United States in the mid to late 1990s prompted the U.S. government to file charges against the European Union and other nations for discriminating against American products. For instance, the United States claimed that the European Union unfairly subsidizes Airbus Industrie through government support of a new flight-management system. The United States also accused the European Union of treating American cheese and wine products unfairly through European copyright and trademark practices. India was charged with imposing unfair requirements on American automakers seeking to set up operations there. South Korea was accused of unfairly restricting the ability of American construction companies to bid on airport work and restricting the import of American beef. The list goes on and on.

Whether the claims are valid is, in most instances, irrelevant. If the businesses can get the domestic authorities to impose sanctions against foreign firms or to file actions in the World Trade Organization, the domestic businesses can benefit. In 1995, the United States came close to imposing punitive tariffs on Japanese luxury cars in retaliation against the exclusive ties between Japanese automakers and showrooms. Had the Japanese not instituted "voluntary" restraints, the United States would have carried out the action. This would eventually have reached the WTO. In 1997, the United States lost a case at the WTO in which it had argued that Fuji, Japan's market leader in photographic film and paper, was keeping Kodak out of the Japanese market by controlling distribution and retailing.

Government Regulation

More information on regulation can be found at
http://www.osha.gov/
http://www.regulation.org/

While antitrust policies are intended to prevent unfair or monopolistic practices but otherwise to leave business to act as it desires, regulation is a much more pervasive intervention into business by government. There are two categories of regulations: economic and social. Economic regulation refers to the prescribing of prices and output levels for a particular industry or line of business. Social regulation refers to prescribed performance standards, workplace health and safety standards, emission levels, and a variety of output and job standards that apply across all or several industries.

Economic Regulation

The government may restrict certain industries from participating in some activities or lines of business, such as banks not being able to issue insurance or sell stocks, or it may require businesses to serve certain markets, such as telephone companies and airlines being required to serve rural markets. But the greatest amount of economic regulation has to do with what is called the **natural monopoly**. In the 1930s, when most economic regulation came into existence, it was argued that a natural monopolist would be able to charge high prices and produce less as a consequence of its cost situation. The natural monopoly is one that arises from economies of scale. When economies of scale exist throughout the market, only one firm will end up supplying the market. That firm, because of its monopoly, will be able to charge high prices, earn huge profits, and keep other firms from entering the market. So the government authorities attempt to force the natural monopolist to price and sell as would a perfectly competitive firm.

Figure 15.3 illustrates how regulations would work. The monopolist would charge price P_m and sell quantity Q_m. The perfectly competitive firm would sell at a price equal to the market price; that price would be where the supply and demand curves are equal—P_r and Q_r. The regulations force the firm to sell more at a lower price. The way that the regulatory commissions determine what price to prescribe is to calculate average accounting costs and add a markup to those costs based on a fair rate of return on capital—called rate of return regulation.

Rate of return regulation refers to the situation in which an industry is told the prices it must charge and the quantities it must sell. Industries that have been subject to rate of return regulation include electric utilities, telecommunications, trucking, railroads, airlines, and cable television. Rate of return regulation works in the following way. Suppose an electric utility has $300 million of assets and the regulatory

Figure 15.3
RATE OF RETURN REGULATED FIRM

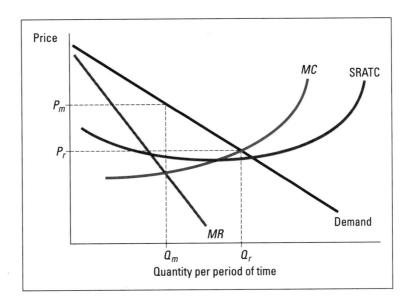

authority is allowing it to earn a 10 percent rate of return. The utility will then be allowed to earn accounting profits of $30 million. The utility will be allowed to set a price and sell a quantity that will yield this profit—as long as all customers are served.

You might notice that rate of return regulation creates an incentive for the regulated firm to increase capital costs. Because the rate of return the regulatory commission sets is applied to a firm's assets, the firm, in essence, is allowed to pass on cost increases to customers.

Regulatory bodies exist at both federal and state levels, and most industries have been subject to regulations at both levels. For instance, the electric utility industry was required to meet customer demands and provide electrical power at a rate prescribed by state corporation commissions. At the same time, the Federal Energy Regulatory Commission (FERC) regulates aspects of the power that cross state borders, and nuclear power plants are subject to federal regulations.

While it is likely that managers would be aware of economic regulations that affect their firms, it is important that managers subject to such regulation be aware of potential changes. Consider what is happening to the electrical and telecommunications industries. Rate of return regulation induced firms to purchase more capital than a competitive firm would acquire to produce the same level of output.

To reduce the amount of dust landing in the local Priam, Minnesota area, the Minnesota Pollution Control Agency required that the Minnesota Valley Alfalfa Producers plant add 140-feet to its emission chimney in 2002. The additional 140 feet will send the dust farther into the atmosphere so that it will be dispersed over a larger area.

Without the regulation, these excessive capital expenditures would become costly to the firm and its shareholders. This is what has occurred in electrical power generation and distribution and telecommunications. In an attempt to deregulate these industries, the government has been criticized by the companies for "stranding" their assets. The firms argue that if it were not for the demands of the regulatory authorities, they would never have invested so heavily in capital. As a result, it is argued, the regulatory authorities owe them compensation when the regulations are removed. The same stranded-asset argument is being used by local telephone companies—the Baby Bells—to attempt to restrict entry into local telephone markets until they can be compensated for the assets they acquired during regulation.

Visit the Federal Register's website at

http://www.archives.gov/federal_register/publications/about_the_federal_register.html

Social Regulation

Although a few industries have been deregulated in the past three decades—trucking, airlines, telecommunications, and, to a very limited degree, power generation and distribution—the number of government rules and regulations has grown tremendously. The reason is the growth of social regulation.

The following U.S. government agencies are concerned with social regulation:

- The Occupational Safety and Health Administration (OSHA), which is concerned with protecting workers against injuries and illnesses associated with their jobs
- The Consumer Product Safety Commission (CPSC), which specifies minimum standards for safety of products
- The Food and Drug Administration (FDA), which is concerned with the safety and effectiveness of food, drugs, and cosmetics
- The Equal Employment Opportunity Commission (EEOC), which focuses on the hiring, promotion, and discharge of workers
- The Environmental Protection Agency (EPA), which is concerned with air, water, and noise pollution

Social regulation is typically applied across all industries. For instance, all businesses are subject to OSHA standards or EPA requirements. Most of the arguments made in support of social regulation are based on the idea that without government intervention, the public would be harmed. More than ten thousand workers die in job-related accidents in the United States each year; air pollution is an increasing problem in many cities, leading to cancer and other diseases, which in turn means increased demands on health care agencies; hundreds of children are killed each year as a result of poorly designed toys; unfair discharges from jobs occur frequently. It is argued that without government regulation, these events would be much more serious and would impose tremendous costs on society.

Whether one agrees with these arguments or not, one has to recognize that there are costs to the regulations. It is expensive to administer the agencies and enforce the rules and regulations. The annual administrative costs of federal regulatory activities exceed $15 billion. The costs of complying with the rules and regulations have been estimated to exceed $300 billion per year. Complying with environmental regulations alone costs business more than $200 billion per year.[5] Added to the direct costs of regulations are the opportunity costs. For instance, the lengthy FDA process for approving new biotechnology has stymied advances in agriculture and placed many lives in jeopardy. Regulatory restrictions on the telecommunications industry have resulted in U.S. industries lagging behind those in other nations in the development of fiber optics. The total cost imposed on the U.S. economy from federal regulations has been estimated to be more than $600 billion a year, or $6,000 per household.

Does social regulation benefit the general public? To answer this question, we need to compare the costs and benefits of the regulations. But this is a difficult proposition. It requires us to answer the question: How much is a life worth? Simply asking the question offends many people. But answering the question is necessary to determine whether a regulation is worth its costs. To economists, life is worth what people are willing to pay to stay alive. Of course, that differs from person to person, but values could be used to place limits on what regulations to implement. For instance, using the extra pay that people require to take dangerous jobs, or calculating the total value of expenditures on smoke detectors and safer cars, could provide estimates of how much people value life. Although the estimates vary widely, none exceeds $10 million. Some economists thus argue that any regulation costing more than $10 million per life saved should not be implemented. Rules on unvented space heaters save lives for just $130,000 each; regulations on asbestos removal exceed $100 million per life saved. According to a comparison of costs and benefits, the first rule should be implemented but the second should not.

The cost-benefit test for regulation would limit regulations designed to benefit a very few at the cost of many. However, according to many economists, the cost-benefit test should also include the opportunity costs implied by interfering with the free market. If labeling is desired by the public, won't the public voluntarily pay the higher price for it? Why, then, is regulation necessary unless it is to benefit some special-interest group? If seat belts and antilock braking systems are desired by the public, won't the public voluntarily pay the price to have these safety systems? Why, if the market would ensure that what the public desires is produced at the lowest possible cost, is it necessary for the government to intervene in the economy and impose regulatory costs of $600 billion or more each year? The answer given is that regulations do not benefit the general public but rather benefit special interests. This is where business strategy comes into play.

Regulation as Strategy

As is the case with antitrust laws, managers must be aware of regulations—both as a defensive matter and possibly as an option in business strategy. Unanticipated changes in regulatory regimes can be disastrous to firms. The electrical utility industry with its stranded-asset costs is one instance in which the regulatory regime changed relatively slowly but still caught many firms unprepared. In many nations, regulations can be onerous and baffling and can change precipitously. Shifeng Group, a northern Chinese manufacturer of farm vehicles for the huge rural sector, had high hopes after beating out rivals and becoming the largest producer in China. Its goal was to sell 600,000 vehicles and reach $300 million in sales in 2002. But regulators in Beijing had other plans. They slapped state-owned Shifeng with a $110,000 fine and forced it to scale back production by 50 percent. The crime: The efficient producer was selling its products too cheaply—about $30 cheaper than its competitor's $700 price. Beijing officials are now setting minimum prices in more than twenty industries in order to stop price wars.

Many businesses use regulations as part of their business strategy. Attempts to gain a competitive advantage through manipulation of the regulatory process occur regularly. Defining used motor oil as a hazardous waste under the Resource

Conservation and Recovery Act (RCRA) would have increased the cost of oil changes for consumers and discouraged recovery and recycling of used oil; however, it would have guaranteed additional business for the Evergreen Company and members of the Hazardous Waste Treatment Council (HWTC), a trade association of companies that operate incinerators and other hazardous-waste facilities. The Business Council for a Sustainable Energy Future, a coalition of gas, wind, solar, and geothermal power producers and related firms, lobbied for deep cuts in greenhouse gas emissions. The Environmental Technology Council, a successor to the HWTC, wanted to ensure that various wastes, such as fluorescent bulbs, were covered by hazardous-waste regulations. The Alliance for Responsible Thermal Treatment (ARTT) wanted to prevent the burning of hazardous waste in cement kilns—and thereby eliminate its members' toughest competitors. Major utilities lobbied to require the sale of electric vehicles in California and the northeastern United States and have sought policies that would subsidize the purchase of electric cars. Ethanol producers attempted to secure a portion of the lucrative oxygenate market for federally mandated reformulated gasoline.

Rent seeking refers to the use of resources to obtain a transfer of wealth from some other group. Rent seeking does not increase output but merely transfers wealth. It occurs, in part, because firms can receive concentrated benefits through government action, while the costs are dispersed throughout the whole of society. In the case of sugar subsidies, for example, the benefits accrue directly to U.S. sugar producers, while the costs, estimated at $1.4 billion per year, are paid by sugar consumers in the form of higher sugar prices. When such policies are enacted, a narrow interest arguably wins while everyone else loses.

In the regulatory context, rent seeking typically consists of pursuing government intervention that will provide a comparative advantage to a particular industry. By restricting market entry or reducing output, regulations often reduce competition, create cartels, and increase returns. Thus, tariffs and licensing restrictions are regulatory measures commonly sought by rent seekers. Less direct measures can heighten preexisting comparative advantages or create a comparative advantage out of incidental differences in an industrial sector. For instance, one effect of environmental regulation is to give larger facilities benefits relative to smaller facilities. Small firms are vulnerable to regulatory costs. Reporting and other paperwork requirements consume a much greater percentage of the value of the small firm than of the larger firm.

A classic example of environmental policy by and for special interests is the 1977 Clean Air Act amendments that mandated the use of scrubbers on coal-fired power plants. Under the 1970 Clean Air Act, the EPA established a policy whereby all coal plants were required to meet an emission standard for sulfur dioxide. The original standard of 1.2 pounds of sulfur dioxide (SO_2) per million BTUs (British thermal units) of coal could be met in a variety of ways. Despite its apparent flexibility, the regulation had disparate regional effects. Most of the coal in the eastern United States is relatively "dirty" due to its high sulfur content. Western coal, on the other hand, is cleaner. By using western coal, utilities and other coal-burning facilities complied with the federal standard without installing costly scrubbers. Scrubbers were so expensive that many midwestern firms found that it was cheaper to haul low-sulfur coal from the West than to use closer, "dirtier" deposits. When the Clean Air Act was revised in 1977, eastern producers of high-sulfur coal sought universal scrubbing. The revisions to the act required coal plants to meet both an emission standard and a technology standard. In particular, the law contained "new-source performance standards" that forced facilities to attain a "percentage reduction in emissions." In other words, no matter how clean the coal was, any new facility would still be required to install scrubbers. This destroyed low-sulfur coal's comparative advantage.

A key component of the 1990 Clean Air Act amendments was a set of provisions governing the content of automotive fuels. The amendments required that oxygenates be added to gasoline in cities with high carbon monoxide (CO) levels and that reformulated gasoline be used in cities with high levels of ground-level ozone (smog). Both provisions created opportunities for the use of ethanol, a corn-based alcohol fuel. Midwestern agricultural interests wanted both provisions to require the maximum amount of oxygenates possible, in order to increase the demand for ethanol. The direct cost to consumers that would have resulted from the agricultural proposals was estimated to be somewhere between $48 million and $350 million a year.[6]

Firms and industries can enhance their rent-seeking activities by joining forces with "public-interest groups." In the environmental arena, for example, environmental activists may prefer a policy, such as tightening hazardous-waste regulations, while hazardous-waste treatment firms see such regulations as an opportunity to expand their market. The HWTC, alluded to above, joined with environmental groups in a series of lawsuits seeking to force the EPA to impose more stringent regulations on used-motor-oil management. This would have required the treatment of used oil before disposal, providing HWTC members with increased business. If used oil were regulated as hazardous waste, the costs of handling it would increase, as would insurance for potential environmental liability exposure. The primary effect would be to drive smaller firms out of the used-oil-collection business and reduce the overall percentage of oil collected for reuse, recycling, or energy recovery.

Chlorofluorocarbons (CFCs) were once the most widely used class of refrigerants. CFCs were found in virtually every air conditioner, refrigerator, and chiller throughout the world. CFCs were also used as propellants in aerosol cans, cleaning agents, and foam-blowing agents. Congress banned the use of CFCs in aerosol cans in 1978 when the United Nations sponsored negotiations with the purpose of drafting a treaty to protect the ozone layer. Interestingly, the regulations were not opposed by the CFC industry. DuPont, the world's largest CFC producer, called for a complete global phase-out. Foreign CFC producers were taking over DuPont's market share. Under a global phase-out, consumers would have no alternative but to replace CFCs and CFC-reliant equipment with substitutes designed and patented by DuPont and other American producers. Others got into the act as well, boosting the phase-out's overall cost.

An example of trade protectionism disguised as environmental protection is the European Economic Community's (EEC) 1989 ban on the importation of U.S. beef produced with bovine growth hormones. There was no credible scientific evidence linking hormones in American beef to health problems. Nevertheless, health concerns were the reason given by the EEC when they prevented U.S. beef to be imported. The United States has used environmental measures to restrict foreign imports as well. When corporate average fuel economy (CAFE) standards for automobiles were first enacted in the 1970s, Congress rejected alternative means of reducing automobile fuel consumption because they might encourage foreign imports. The CAFE standards that were adopted discriminated against high-end foreign manufacturers such as Mercedes-Benz, BMW, and Volvo. The CAFE standards are average fleet standards and thus are more troubling for manufacturers that do not make small cars with high fuel economy ratings.

The use of government rules and regulations to create a competitive advantage is not new and will not disappear. It is a strategy that a manager must be aware of in a defensive sense—to protect the firm from rent seeking by rivals—and must consider in the firm's portfolio of strategies.

CASE REVIEW *Microsoft*

Microsoft was accused of attempting to maintain a monopoly by bundling an Internet browser with its Windows operating system, which is used to run most personal computers. Microsoft's bundling of its Internet Explorer with its Windows operating system is an example of what antitrust authorities call monopolizing tactics of bundling and tying sales. The argument is that Microsoft bundled its web browser with its Windows operating system in order to drive other web browsers—primarily Netscape—out of the market. Moreover, manufacturers who purchased the Windows operating system to install on their machines were forced by Microsoft to include Internet Explorer and not other web browsers. If Netscape, for example, were provided, Microsoft would not provide Windows. This is called a tying arrangement.

During the trial, the regulatory authorities defined the market as single-user desktop machines with Intel processors. This was a very narrow definition that eliminated all of Microsoft's chief competitors, such as Apple and Sun, from the market. The narrow definition meant that the HHI was very high; within that market definition, Microsoft had the dominance, according to authorities, to act monopolistically.

Although Microsoft was found guilty, the verdict was controversial. Critics noted that at the time of Microsoft's actions, the market remained open for competitors, since the majority of households did not have personal computers. Moreover, while the theoretical argument is that a monopolist raises price and sells a smaller quantity in order to reap those monopoly benefits, the price of Windows has plummeted. Windows 3.0 was introduced in April 1990 at a price of $205. In November 1998, Windows 98 was introduced at a price of $169. When WordPerfect was the dominant word-processing software, prices had risen 35 percent but fell 75 percent after Microsoft's Word took the lead. In software markets where Microsoft has a product, prices have declined 65 percent, but in markets where Microsoft doesn't, prices have declined only 15 percent. If price gouging is the mark of a monopolist, Microsoft doesn't seem to qualify. Finally, with respect to the tying arrangement, critics noted that no other business has to worry about providing competitor's products with their own. Think about the *Washington Post,* for example, which dominates the market for newspapers in Washington, D.C. It does not provide the business section of the *New York Times* with its paper. Thus, the *Post* ties its business section to the rest of the paper.

Was Microsoft a monopolist? Did it carry out monopolizing actions? Or was it merely a corporate bully? The answers to these questions is that Microsoft was not a monopolist; it did compete vigorously, it did try to take over markets and run competitors out of markets.

SUMMARY

1. Antitrust policy is an attempt to enhance competition by restricting certain activities that could be anticompetitive.

2. The antitrust statutes have undergone several phases of interpretation. In the early years, a rule of reason prevailed; acts had to be unreasonable to be a violation of the statutes. Between 1914 and 1980, a per se rule applied more often. Under this policy, the mere existence of actions that could be used anticompetitively was a violation. In the early 1980s, the interpretations returned to the rule-of-reason standard. In the early 1990s, another attempt to tighten enforcement was made.

3. Antitrust laws are more rigorously enforced in the United States than elsewhere.

4. Economic regulation refers to the prescription of price and output for a particular industry. Social regulation refers to the setting of health and safety standards for products and the workplace as well as environmental and operating procedures for all industries.

5. Social regulation has increased even as economic regulation has decreased. Regulations raise the costs of doing business and increase the prices of products.

6. The World Trade Organization deals with international disputes. Antidumping is the issue that appears most often in claims brought to the WTO.

KEY TERMS

Herfindahl–Hirschman index (HHI)	rule of reason per se rule	natural monopoly rent seeking

EXERCISES

1. Using the demand and cost curves of an individual firm in oligopoly, demonstrate the effects of each of the following:

   a. the Clean Air Act

   b. The Nutrition and Labeling Act, which requires that the ingredients be listed on the outside of a package

   c. A ban on smoking inside the workplace

   d. A sales tax

2. Consider a firm with fixed costs and relatively small marginal costs:

   a. What price and quantity will the firm select to maximize profit?

   b. How could the large fixed costs serve as a barrier to entry?

   c. Under what conditions might the managers of the firm prefer regulation to free competition?

   d. How would you describe and illustrate stranded-asset costs?

3. Kodak has developed an important brand name through its advertising, innovation, and product quality and service. Suppose Kodak sets up a network of exclusive dealerships, and one of the dealers decides to carry Fuji and Mitsubishi as well as Ko-

dak products. If Kodak terminates the dealership, is it acting in a pro- or anticompetitive manner?

4. Would auctioning broadcast licenses be more efficient than having the Federal Communications Commission (FCC) assign licenses on some basis designed by the FCC? Explain.

5. Which of the three types of government policies—antitrust, social regulation, economic regulation—is the basis for each of the following? Who benefits from the policy?

   a. beautician education standards

   b. certified public accounting requirements

   c. liquor licensing

   d. Justice Department guidelines

   e. the Clean Air Act

   f. the Nutrition and Labeling Act

6. The Glaxo-Wellcome pharmaceutical firm has a monopoly on the AIDS drug AZT. As an active member of an AIDS-prevention organization, argue that regulation by the FDA has been harmful. As an executive of Glaxo-Wellcome, argue that FDA regulation has been beneficial.

7. Some airline executives have called for reregulation. Why might an executive of an airline prefer to operate in a regulated environment?

8. Discuss the claim that social regulation is unnecessary. Does the claim depend on whether the structure of an industry is primarily one of perfect competition or of oligopoly?

9. Suppose a monopolist is practicing price discrimination and a lawsuit against the monopolist forces an end to the practice. Is it possible that the result is a loss in efficiency? Explain.

10. In the 1990s, the Justice Department sued several universities for collectively setting the size of scholarships offered. Explain why the alleged price fixing on the part of universities might be harmful to students.

11. Suppose a consumer hires Bekins moving company to move his possessions from California to Utah and Bekins damages $3,000 worth of furniture and refuses to compensate him. The consumer in frustration says, "There ought to be a law!" Evaluate the situation.

12. "The Japanese are beating us at every step. We must act as they do. We must allow and encourage cooperation among firms and we must develop partnerships between business and government. The first place we should begin is with the aerospace industry. Let's use the government to transfer the resources no longer employed in aerospace to nondefense industries such as the environment and health." Evaluate this argument.

13. Discuss dumping and antidumping. Under what conditions is dumping the same as predatory pricing?

14. Using the following HHIs, do the following:
   a. Indicate in which market a merger would be allowed under Department of Justice guidelines.
   b. Provide an economic explanation for why this result would occur.
   c. Provide a numerical example illustrating why the result might not make economic sense.

IMPACT OF WORLDCOM'S ACQUISITION OF SPRINT (HHIs FOR LONG-DISTANCE VOICE, DATA, AND INTERNET BACKBONE MARKETS)

	Total Long-Distance Voice	Consumer Long-Distance Voice	Business Long-Distance Voice	Total Long-Distance Data
Premerger	3,209	4,133	2,921	1,730
Postmerger	3,881	4,441	4,105	2,290
Increase	672	308	1,184	560

	Long-Distance Data (except IP)	IP Standing Alone	Internet Backbone
Premerger	2,153	1,928	1,774
Postmerger	2,581	2,600	2,266
Increase	428	672	492

15. Suppose the state corporation commission decides that a fair rate of return for a local electricity producer would be 10 percent. Since the firm has assets of $400 million, the commission is allowing the firm to earn $40 million of accounting profits. The firm's demand is

$$P = 50 - 0.1Q$$

where P is the price per customer and Q is the number of customers served (in millions). The firm's costs are

$$TC = 10 + 5Q + 0.8Q^2$$

where TC is total accounting cost in millions of dollars. Thus, the accounting profit is

$$\text{Profit} = PQ - TC$$

Based on the rate of return regulation, determine the price the firm will charge and the quantity of customers served.

16. Using the information in Exercise 15, demonstrate the returns to the firm of increasing assets to $500 million.

CHAPTER NOTES

1. Del Jones, "Today's Issue: Some Lessons Learned in an Antitrust Fight. Guest CEO: Thomas Stemberg, CEO of Staples," *USA Today,* March 30, 1998, p. 5B
2. *United States* v. *Foley,* 1979-1 Trade Cas.(CCH) 62,577 (4th Cir. 1979).
3. *Quality Trailer Products,* 57 Fed. Reg. 37004, August 17, 1992.
4. Ronald A. Wirtz, "Anti-Dumping: The Free-Trade Antacid," *The Region,* December 2001, Federal Reserve Bank of Minneapolis.
5. Information on costs of compliance is available from www.sba.gov and www.cato.org.
6. See www.cato.org.

PART VI

Putting It All Together

Successful strategy requires the firm to choose the markets in which its distinctive capabilities yield competitive advantage. Since every firm is a member of an industry, is a part of a strategic group, and serves a variety of product and geographic markets, strategy begins with the analysis of that industry, that strategic group, and these markets. It then requires an analysis of what goes on inside the firm—the firm's organization, personnel, compensation, culture, and other issues. It must also consider external factors that influence the firm such as exchange rate exposure and the influence of governments on business. This analysis is referred to as a strategic audit. The audit considers the definition of the firm's distinctive capabilities and strategic assets, the markets in which they exist and might be deployed, and the extent to which they yield appropriable and sustainable competitive advantages.

The audit pulls together the topics and analyses presented in the first 15 chapters of this book. In each chapter we have examined an aspect of a firm's strategy to obtain and keep economic profits. We started by learning about the customer and how the firm can generate revenues. We then turned to a firm's costs and put revenues and costs together to find economic profit. The firm's profit maximizing strategies—the appropriation of profit—included both cost strategies and revenue strategies (price and non-price). If a firm is able to earn an economic profit, the owners and managers of the firm want it to continue earning a profit—to sustain its profit. But, since competitors enter the market and attempt to secure some of the profit for themselves, it is necessary to create barriers to entry. The barriers are never secure for long—entrepreneurs will seek ways over, under, around, or through the barriers. Thus, firms must continually seek ways to create profits and sustain those profits.

To understand what the firm must do, what strategies it must implement, one must know how all the factors influencing the prospects and behavior of the firm come into play. In this last chapter we'll discuss the elements of a strategic audit and then provide a simple example of a strategic audit using Southwest Airlines.

CHAPTER 16

Strategy and Management

CASE *Edward Jones Brokerage*

Edward Jones is only about the thirty-fourth-largest brokerage firm in the United States but is the most profitable. Its brokers operate out of one-person offices located in small communities and do business in these communities. Since 1981, Edward Jones has expanded its broker force at an annual rate of 15 percent, without making any acquisitions. It now boasts more than 2,500 partners.

The firm may be described as a federation of highly autonomous entrepreneurial units bound together by a strong set of values and beliefs. The entrepreneurial units are the brokers. Foremost among the values and beliefs these brokers have in common is that their job is to offer sound, long-term financial advice to customers.

The company was originally a financial department store—a source of one-stop shopping to satisfy all of a customer's financial needs, offering an array of financial services—but soon evolved into a financial services delivery system for rural America. In contrast to the larger brokerage houses, Jones does not manufacture the products it sells but instead is a distributor for the products of a few manufacturers such as Capital Research, Putnam, and Morgan Stanley, and Jones targets and sells its products only to individual investors.

Edward Jones now faces competition from the ebrokerage houses, the Internet companies. What is Edward Jones to do?

Strategy

Economic data sources can be found at

http://www.nber.org/data_index.html or

http://www.stat-usa.gov/

The SEC edgar site provides free company information at

http://www.sec.gov/edgar.shtml

In general terms, strategy is all about making tough choices; it is nothing more or less than utilizing *the economic way of thinking*. It involves recognizing and accounting for opportunity costs, comparing costs and benefits, and equating the marginal costs and marginal benefits of each possible action.

As we have discussed throughout this book, choices about what not to do are as important as choices about what to do. Deciding which target group of customers the company should serve is crucial, but so is deciding not to serve other customers. Deciding which services or features to offer is important, but so is deciding not to offer other features and services.

In this chapter we focus on the strategy creation process. In so doing we summarize the material we have discussed throughout this book. We end the chapter by discussing the role of management in strategy creation and implementation.

Strategic Positioning

Firms build success on finding and exploiting unique positions in industries. However, no successful position can remain unique forever. Success breeds imitation. Moreover, what is unique and valuable at one point will change as technology and/or consumer tastes change.

Xerox once dominated the copier market by focusing on the high-volume customer. This defined Xerox's customers as big corporations, which, in turn, determined its distribution method—the direct sales force—and the leasing rather than sale of machines.

Xerox prospered because it developed a distinct strategic position in its industry, based on a well-defined customer base, well-defined products, and a well-defined system of delivering those products to those customers. Xerox's success attracted IBM and Kodak to the market. IBM entered the market in 1970 with its first model, the IBM Copier I, aimed at the medium- and high-volume segments and marketed on a rental basis. Kodak entered the market in 1975 with the Ektaprint 100 copier, also aimed at the high-volume end of the market.

Neither IBM nor Kodak was able to differentiate itself clearly from Xerox or offer the same services at lower costs. Canon, on the other hand, chose to play the game differently. Whereas Xerox targeted big corporations Canon went after small companies and individuals; while Xerox emphasized the speed of its machines, Canon accentuated quality and price; and whereas Xerox employed a direct sales force to lease its machines, Canon used its dealer network to sell its copiers.

Time after time, in industry after industry, companies rise to fame and fortune only to see their once-formidable positions become susceptible to attack as new players enter the field from newly created strategic positions. Table 16.1 lists several market leaders in certain industries, along with the rivals who have emulated successful strategies and the latest innovator that has entered the market with a differentiated strategy.

Imitation or Innovation?

To be successful, a company must create and exploit a unique strategic position in its industry. Consider the following list of companies:

Table 16.1

MARKET LEADERS AND NEWEST INNOVATORS

Market Leaders	Rivals	Innovators
American Airlines	Delta	Southwest
	Northwest	
	United	
Hertz	Avis	Enterprise
	Budget	
General Foods (Maxwell House)	Nestlé (Nescafé)	Starbucks
	Procter & Gamble (Folgers)	
	Sara Lee (Douwe Egberts)	
Regional newspapers	Regional newspapers	*USA Today*
Xerox	IBM	Canon
	Kodak	
	Nicoh	
IBM	Compaq	Dell
	Hewlett-Packard	
	Toshiba	
Merrill Lynch	Dean Witter	Edward Jones
	Paine Webber	Charles Schwab
	Smith Barney	
U.S. Steel	Bethlehem	Nucor
	Inland	

Source: Information regarding these firms in Constantinos C. Markides, *All the Right Moves* (Cambridge, Mass.: Harvard University Business School Press, 1999), p. 12.

The Body Shop
Dell
Enterprise Rent-A-Car
E-Trade
Federal Express
Home Depot
MTV
Southwest Airlines
Starbucks
Swatch
USA Today

What distinguishes the companies on this list from other well-known firms is the relatively short time in which they achieved success and substantial market share. Most new entrants in a business fail within five years, and even those few that do not fail manage to capture only a small share of the market—perhaps 5 percent in five years. How did the companies listed above succeed? Instead of attacking the established competitors in their existing, well-protected positions, these companies created new strategic positions; they changed the rules of the game.

A company cannot settle for what it has. It must be on the lookout for new positions or others will find those new positions and exploit them at the expense of the incumbent firms. As obvious as this may sound, it is not what most companies do. Most firms take their current position and the established rules of the game as givens and focus on bettering each other at that same old game. They do not change the game.

Most companies that innovate are small players or new market entrants. It is rare to find a large firm that changes the game in the industry in which it is established. Xerox initially responded to Canon by ignoring it. Xerox's vice president at the time said, "We had been late to recognize market opportunities for low and mid range copiers and Japanese competitors like Canon were cutting into our market share."[1]

Recognizing that it had failed to respond appropriately, Xerox decided to go directly after Canon. Xerox introduced new products and restructured sales operations to create dedicated organizations for large system customers as well as small businesses, and it opened retail stores that sold small copiers. The outcome was a classic prisoner's dilemma: a situation in which both competitors occupied the same two strategic positions simultaneously, their own and each other's. As a result, the only way for either to gain an advantage was to become better than the other—through cost or differentiation or pricing strategies. As would be predicted in this situation, profit margins in the business declined sharply.

There are exceptions to the general rule that firms become entrenched and stale due to their success. In 1995 the low-cost brokerage firm Schwab had no Internet business. Three years later, more than half the company's total trading volume was carried out on Schwab's website. Until 1985, Intel engaged primarily in the production of dynamic random access memory products (DRAMs). By the early 1980s, the DRAM business had been turned into a commodity business and companies other than Intel were winning the price wars. Intel decided to exit the DRAM business and focus on microprocessors. Intel was again having to redefine its business in 2002 as microprocessors became commodities.

Irrespective of these examples, most incumbent firms tend to become complacent in their success—"If it ain't broke, don't fix it."

Innovation Is Not for Everyone

Realizing that incumbent firms become complacent in their success, many consultants are telling their clients that their companies should become strategic revolutionaries, breaking the rules of the game in their respective industries. Yet for every company that has succeeded by breaking the rules, there are probably ten others that failed by doing so. For every Southwest Airlines there is a People Express; for every Compaq Computer, an Osborne Computers; for every Virgin Atlantic, a Kiwi International; for every Body Shop, a Next Ltd.

The real issue for companies is not whether they should break the rules but when it makes sense to do so—what are the costs and benefits. Going after whatever fad of the month is being pushed by consultants and academics will not suffice.

An individual company's strategy depends on factors such as the nature of the industry, the nature of the game currently being played in the industry, the way value is created in the industry, the competitive position of the firm, technological change, and so on. These factors must be evaluated as they apply to each individual firm. After considering these factors, the firm may decide that, for itself, it makes no sense to break the rules. In fact, year after year, a list of the companies that create the most wealth for their shareholders would seldom contain more than two rule breakers. Most companies create wealth by trying to be better than their competitors.

The best way for a startup or a new entrant to play the game might be to break the rules. It often makes little sense to try to play the game the way the big established competitors in these businesses do. The established incumbents often have so many advantages that they could easily crush any new entrant that tries to play their game. Paul Cook, the founder of Raychem Corporation, said: "I think a more powerful way to compete is to avoid competition altogether. The best way to avoid competition is to sell products that rivals can't touch. When we started Raychem, the last thing we wanted to do was make products that giants like GE or Du Pont would also be interested in making."[2] In fact, evidence suggests that without the benefit of a technological innovation, it is difficult for any firm to successfully attack established industry leaders or to successfully enter a new market where established players already exist.

The decision to rush into a new position is not always the right one either. Everyone cannot be a revolutionary. The decision whether to break the rules should be based on a detailed cost-benefit analysis: What are the benefits of embracing a new strategic position and what are the costs of not embracing it? What are the costs and benefits of embracing a new strategic position?

The Strategic Audit

Successful strategy requires the firm to choose the markets in which its distinctive capabilities yield competitive advantage. Since every firm is a member of an industry, is a part of a strategic group, and serves a variety of product and geographic markets, strategy begins with the analysis of that industry, that strategic group, and these markets. This analysis is referred to as a **strategic audit**.[3] The audit considers the definition of the firm's distinctive capabilities and strategic assets, the markets in which they exist and might be deployed, and the extent to which they yield appropriable and sustainable competitive advantages.

The first step is the identification of the customer, what we introduced in Chapter 4 as "knowing your customer." What are the characteristics of the products that serve the customers' wants and needs? Are they commodity items or do they have many attributes? What are the dimensions of these attributes? How do consumers learn about them? How price sensitive are consumers? Are there ways to segment customers by elasticity? What markets are served? What are their geographic and their product dimensions? Which are growing and which contracting?

What Business Are We In?

Although very few executives actually ask themselves "What business is this firm in?" this may be the most important question one must answer in defining a firm's strategy. The definition of the business defines who the customers are, who the competitors are, what a firm sees as its competitive advantage; it also describes the game and the role the firm plays in that game.

There are different schools of thought on how to define a business. One way is that a company should define its business according to the product it is selling.

In this sense, Ford is in the car business, Boeing in the airplane business, and Philip Morris in the cigarette business. The second approach is that a company should define its business according to the customer function it is trying to fulfill. According to this definition, Ford is in the transport business, Boeing in the aeronautical business, and Philip Morris in the food business. The third perspective is that a company should define its business according to its portfolio of core competencies. According to this definition, Ford might be in the family entertainment business, Boeing in the manufacturing business, and Philip Morris in the marketing business.

The first approach limits the boundaries of the market, whereas the second and third approaches broaden the boundaries. Which approach should be used? It shouldn't matter; the outcome should be the same if the decision is reached in the appropriate manner. The golden rule of economics applies here as it does in every decision. The firm must compare costs and benefits: *The firm will define its boundaries at the point where the marginal benefits of stretching the boundary equal the marginal costs.* The difficult job is not to decide to use the first approach or the third approach, but rather to define the costs and benefits of the market boundaries.

Who Are Our Customers?

Most companies want to sell their products to everyone, but no company can afford to market to everyone. There are tradeoffs; there are opportunity costs of broadening the customer base. A firm has to decide who its possible customers are and then determine which of these customers it should target.

Enterprise Rental Cars extended the market boundary of rental cars. It achieved its position as the largest rental company by defining the market not just as people who rent cars at airports, but as people who rent cars anywhere. Enterprise positioned its 2,400 offices within a fifteen-minute drive of 70 percent of the U.S. population, and it offers to deliver the cars to customers' houses or places of business. Dell, on the other hand, narrowed the boundaries of the computer market by targeting experienced buyers. Dell did not want to attract first-time computer buyers because these people typically need a lot of support and service, both of which are costly.

One of the primary pitfalls in defining market boundaries is forgetting that every customer exacts an opportunity cost. Whenever a company is advised to narrow its customer base, the usual response is, "But we're making money on this type of customer!" The problem is that the full costs of satisfying that customer are not being considered: Perhaps an accounting profit is being earned on that customer, but is this accounting profit also an economic one? Another common pitfall is that firms do not want *not* to sell to a certain customer. It has to be recognized that there are customer sales that are beyond the market boundary and thus stretch the firm to inefficiency.

When considering the market boundary, the firm has to define how customers obtain information in the market. The manner of acquiring information can place a limit on the boundaries of the firm. For instance, if information is acquired through brand name, then the firm does not want to extend sales to the point where brand name is depreciated. Extending brand name from one market or market segment to another has its costs. Not only are resources stretched thinner, but the activities in one market or market segment will affect the brand name and thus affect the entire market. Nike, which has a solid brand name in sports shoes and apparel, decided to extend its brand name to golf balls and golf clubs. If these products did not maintain a high quality, the entire portfolio of Nike products would have been hurt.

Costs

A firm has to know its supply or value chain. As Chapter 9 indicated, technological changes have meant changes in supply chains. These changes could destroy a business and/or could lead to huge new opportunities.

The costs of doing business are the resource costs—the ingredients of the product or service. A firm has to acquire resources from somewhere. The suppliers to a firm define the vertical relationships of that firm—the relationships between the firm and the suppliers and distributors. In recent years these relationships have become a field of business study in themselves, known as *supply chain management*. The *management* part of this term has not changed—it means to think and solve problems in the ways described in this book. The *supply chain* aspect narrows the focus of the economic thinking and problem solving to the supply chain. The managers must define supplier relationships; that is, determine whether resources are better spent in developing and maintaining a relationship or in behaving as if the market were perfectly competitive. If the market is considered to be perfectly competitive, then the firm can acquire from any number of suppliers and it would make no sense to spend resources on relationship development. The field examines the logistics of inventory management—whether it is better to maintain a store of inventories or to acquire them just in time. The field examines the distribution of product—what the best way is to get the product to the customer.

The field of supply chain management must also consider the competitive or "game" situation between suppliers and final customer. Does the firm have a monopoly purchasing situation (called a monopsony)? What value does an individual supplier bring to the game?

Strategic Assets

Do you build your strategy on an assessment of which skills and capabilities you have, or do you first decide on a strategy and then decide which skills and capabilities to build? Different firms have taken different approaches. But in both cases, a firm's current stock of assets and capabilities—its strategic assets—will influence which activities the firm is able to best perform.

A strategic asset is something valuable that enables the firm to create a distinct position. For an asset to be valuable, it has to be rare (the demand for it must be greater than the supply); it can not be easy to imitate, and there can be no readily available substitutes. Even if the capability or resource you possess is valuable, if everybody else has it, it will not provide you with a competitive advantage.

The British company Laker Airways became very successful putting together holiday travel packages because it could do so at a low cost. Laker then entered the traditional airline business, going into competition with British Airways and several U.S.-based major airlines. The skills and competencies that Laker was transferring to the transatlantic airline business were not rare enough to provide the company with a sustainable advantage. The airline went bankrupt in 1982.

Wal-Mart's core competency was its point-of-purchase data collection, which allowed it to respond to changes in consumer tastes quickly and flexibly. This competence gave Wal-Mart an advantage over competitors during the 1980s. However, that advantage has now been effectively neutralized because other firms have imitated it.

Fit

A firm's distinctive capability must fit with the market in which it is doing business. A manager must define those markets in which a firm's distinctive capabilities and strategic assets are valuable. In addition, for both offensive and defensive purposes, the manager must determine whether there are other markets, linked by economies of scale or scope to the principal market, that it pays to serve even if there is no direct competitive advantage.

Architecture   Part of the determination of fit is the firm's architecture. Is the firm's organization appropriate for the firm's strategy? An important part of that architecture is the firm's reward system. What incentives are created by the reward system? Are they the incentives that are compatible with the firm's strategies.

If a strategy is to be successful, the firm's architecture must enable the firm to pursue that strategy in the most efficient manner. Strategic failure usually occurs when there is a poor fit between strategy and the firm's architecture. For instance, the combination of a hierarchical and bureaucratic organizational structure and a strategy calling for rapid new product development and continual improvement is a major misfit. Another common misfit is the existence of incentives that reward and encourage behaviors that are inconsistent with the firm's espoused strategy. Yet another common type of misfit is a culture that focuses on the short term—on meeting next year's targets or budget—while the strategy calls for long-term profit maximization.

Corporate Culture   Culture is to a corporation what it is to any other social system—a selection of shared beliefs, myths, and practices that make people feel invested in and attached to one another. In theory, a strong corporate culture can enhance corporate economic performance by increasing efficiency; that is, reducing costs. Shared beliefs, myths, and practices coordinate employee effort. The company's goals and practices are clearer, which enables employees to respond more quickly to events. These savings mean that companies with a stronger corporate culture can expect to enjoy higher economic performance.

The Executives

It is often argued that companies that last do so because the managers who run them are exceptionally good at what they do. They make better decisions and build better organizations. Through clear thinking and concerted effort, they achieve and maintain competitive advantage despite the vagaries of the marketplace. The clear thinking that is necessary is the type of thinking we have discussed in this text. Good leaders, good managers, are those who can solve problems, who can think. Strategy is thinking. It is not wishing. A wish-driven strategy, such as "We want to be the best at everything," would simply be unacceptable—it is impossible. The executives of Wilkinson-Match, the unsuccessful product of a merger between British Match and razor-blade manufacturer Wilkinson Sword, claimed that their merger would "give both companies substance." What does this tell us? Other mergers are made "to create critical mass" or "to become a global player." These statements are nothing more than wishes—wish-driven strategies. They make no sense because they forget that allocating resources to one use means that these resources cannot be used elsewhere. There is no free lunch. Executives must evaluate each feasible option by comparing its value and its cost, and that cost is what must be sacrificed in order to attain something. Tradeoffs—giving up something in order to get something else—lie at the heart of the executive's job. And this is what economics is about.

Illustration of a Strategic Audit: Southwest Airlines

To illustrate how an audit could be undertaken, let's examine Southwest Airlines. We'll just briefly discuss the various aspects of an audit—if you were carrying out an audit for clients or for your company you would need to perform a more detailed and in-depth examination.

What Is Southwest Airline's Distinctive Capability?

Southwest Airlines Co. was organized in March 1967 in response to a perceived need for improved air service between Houston, Dallas–Fort Worth, and San Antonio. During the mid-1960s service by existing airlines was poor; complaints about Braniff and Texas International were extensive and common.

The airline industry was highly regulated during this time and interstate carriers were subject to the regulations. Only those airlines flying within a single state could avoid the regulations. This was the niche Southwest saw itself in. The airline began flying three Boeing 737 aircraft with routes among only three Texas cities—Houston, Dallas, and San Antonio. This history dictated Southwest's distinctive capability—short-haul flights.

What Business Are We In?

Southwest defines itself as being in the business of transporting passengers. It views its competitors as more than just other airlines; competitors include automobiles, trains, trucks, and other surface transportation. The cross-price elasticity of demand between Southwest and other airlines (flying the same route) is positive, indicating that the airlines are indeed substitutes. Moreover, the value is high, about 1.8, indicating that for each 10 percent increase in fares by another airline, the demand for Southwest Airlines flights increases by about 18 percent. The cross-price elasticity between Southwest Airlines and other forms of transportation such as automobiles is positive but considerably smaller than the value between airlines. For each 10 percent increase in Southwest Airline fares between Phoenix and San Diego, the quantity of consumers driving the 350 miles between Phoenix and San Diego rises by only about 7 percent. That value varies from route to route and decreases the longer the route.

Who Are Our Customers?

Initially, Southwest saw its customers as Texas fliers—those traveling between San Antonio, Houston, and Dallas–Fort Worth. These fliers wanted efficiency and reliability but low prices as well. The airline began as an alternative to the automobile because the three cities to which it flew were only just over two hundred miles apart. Southwest's flights were particularly appealing to people located in any one of the three Texas cities who had one day of business in one of the other cities. These people wanted to travel from one city to the other, complete their business, and return home later in the day. Since Southwest flew many business passengers among just three cities, it did not pay much attention to transferring baggage or interfacing with connecting flights. What it wanted to do was deliver the passengers to the destination on time and to provide customers with a variety of flight times throughout the day.

Even though Southwest Airline's customers may be business customers, they are price sensitive. The price elasticity of demand for air travel in general has been estimated to be inelastic (with a value of about 0.2) with business travel much more inelastic than leisure travel. However, when the price elasticity is calculated for a particular flight on a particular airline, demand is elastic—the price elasticity of demand is larger than 1. The amount of price sensitivity varies according to the number of other airlines flying the same route, the distance of the route, and the ease of driving by automobile.

Price sensitive, short-haul, reliable, and on-time—these factors defined the Southwest Airline strategy. The company has maintained its focus on this strategy throughout its history.

The income elasticity of demand for Southwest Airlines is positive but less than 1. Each recession or dip in real gross domestic product leads to a decline in number of passengers, but a decline that is much smaller than that experienced by other airlines; for each 10 percent decrease in income, the demand for Southwest Airlines declines by only about 3 percent.

Costs

Southwest Airlines flies to airports that are underutilized and relatively close to a metropolitan area, flies just one type of aircraft, and uses a point-to-point route system as compared to the hub and spoke system used by other airlines. This is not the lowest cost approach. The use of secondary airports does reduce costs since the airport is underutilized, but fuel, the primary cost of an airline, constituting almost 16 percent of total expenses, is more costly for short-haul as compared to long-haul flights. Most fuel is consumed during take-offs and landings. Since short-haul flying requires more take-offs and landings, the plane consumes more fuel than if the flights were long-haul. Another more costly factor with short-haul flights is that maintenance on the aircraft is greater as the take-offs and landings create the most wear and tear on the equipment. A partial offset to these costs is the use of just one type of aircraft since it enables less training and inventory of parts. In addition to fuel costs, the short-haul flights mean that more planes have to be managed at the gate. Yet, even with these more costly aspects of Southwest's flights, its costs per passenger are only about 70 percent of the costs of other airlines. The cost per passenger mile for Southwest is about 7 cents; the next closest airline's costs exceed 10 cents per passenger mile.

Southwest's cost advantage is generated primarily from the productivity of its work force. The company "turns around" an aircraft in fifteen minutes (from time of arrival at gate to time of departure from gate) whereas other airlines are 2.5 to 3 times more than that. Southwest's gates are manned by a single agent with a ground crew of six or fewer, rather than the three agents and twelve ground crew members, which other airlines, on average, use. Southwest's pilots spend more time in the air than pilots at other airlines. Pilots at United, American, and Delta earn significantly more and fly fewer hours than the pilots at Southwest. Southwest also has only about one-half of the number of employees per aircraft and per passenger as compared to other airlines.

How is Southwest able to generate the high productivity and lower personnel costs that give it a competitive advantage? It is the personnel policies that make a difference. The company reports that: "recognizing that our people are the competitive advantage, we deliver the resources and services to prepare our people to be winners, to support the growth and profitability of the company, while preserving the values and special culture of Southwest Airlines."

The People Department—which is Southwest's term for human resources department—plays an important role in the company. It begins with the type of people Southwest Airlines hires. Teamwork is crucial. If someone says "I" too much in an interview, that person is not hired. Peer recruiting is relied on for hiring. For example, pilots hire other pilots.

The emphasis Southwest places on its employees—what it calls its family, is exemplified by the months following September 11, 2001. The airlines were shut down for a few days and passenger counts remained low for several months. Southwest was the only airline not to lay off, furlough, or provide unpaid leaves for employees. It was argued that a short-run disruption would increase costs and

Colleen Barrett is the President and Chief Operating Officer of Southwest Airlines. Informally known as Southwest's "chairman of fun," Barrett has been praised not only for creating the airline's unique culture, but also for shepherding the company through the more difficult times—including those encountered after September 11, 2001.

decrease revenues, but the long-term costs of employee disgruntlement and un-happiness would far override the short-term benefits from furloughing employees.

Corporate Culture

Southwest has a strong corporate culture developed on the foundation of team-work. Themes repeated again and again are: customer service, hard work, equal-ity, cost consciousness, dedication, fun, and most frequently, family. Flight attendants and pilots help clean the airplanes, help with customers, and even load bags. As noted above, there is a "people" department and the "culture commit-tee" has the assignment of ensuring that the values that brought Southwest to its current position are preserved.

Strategic Assets

Strategic assets for Southwest Airlines include leadership, culture, and reputation. The value of Southwest's culture is evidenced by the mediocre attempts by other airlines to mimic Southwest's style and performance. No other airline has been able to reduce costs to the extent Southwest has, and no other airline has been able to create that workplace environment, which results in greater productivity even with lower wages and salaries. Southwest's reputation as a reliable and low-cost airline has been developed by years of consistent performance. The number of complaints per passenger is far below those of its competitors.

Fit

A firm's distinctive capability must fit with the market in which it is doing busi-ness. Southwest has retained its use of one aircraft, short-haul flights, and use of minor airports that remain convenient to metropolitan areas. Its distinctive capa-bility has not changed and its fit with its market niche has remained since its founding.

The airline industry is an oligopoly—that is, an industry in which there are relatively few firms and entry is difficult. The ease of entry has increased since the deregulation of the airline industry that occurred in the 1970s. Nevertheless, an airline requires access to gates, capital to lease airplanes, and the ability to obtain permission to fly certain routes. Due to the difficulty of entering, most new en-trants initially serve as commuter airlines for the largest airlines—for example, the Delta connection, United Express, Mesa Airlines for America West, and so on. The distinctive capabilities of Southwest Airlines have kept these new entrants from directly taking on Southwest.

Leadership

While a number of experts attribute Southwest's accomplishments to its unwa-vering adherence to its low cost niche strategy, others argue that its real competi-tive advantage is its leadership. Herb Kelleher is often cited as the difference between Southwest and other companies. A few years ago, business experts noted that "The greatest obstacle to long term prosperity at Southwest may be Kelleher's mortality." In 2001, Herb Kelleher began the transition from active management to retirement; he announced that he would share responsibilities with the Vice Chairman and CEO, Jim Parker. The stock market value of the company did not change in response to that announcement. It is the company—not one individual—that determines profitability.

Economic Performance

Economic profit is calculated below using data from the Southwest Airlines' annual report.

Sales	5555.2
Expenses other than interest	4,924.0
Depreciation	345.8
Earnings before interest and taxes (EBIT)	631
Taxes on EBIT	136
Earnings before interest and after taxes (EBIAT)	495
assets	8,997
liabilities	4,938
Invested capital	4059
Times cost of capital (calculated using CAPM; beta = 0.9; industry beta = 1.11 using 60-month comparison to S&P 500)	10.29%
Capital charge	472.31
EBIAT	495
Less capital charge	(472.31)
Economic Profit	23

Table 16.2 shows the economic profit figures for various airlines calculated for the same time period—a one-year period. But remember that one year does not make a trend. While Southwest did not do as well as other airlines in this one year, over any five-year period since Southwest began operations, it outperformed all airlines, and over any ten-year period, Southwest's economic profit was more than double any other airline. Southwest has added value throughout its history.

Southwest's performance over the years has induced other airlines to try to copy its policies. For instance, in the mid 1990s, United and Continental began low cost airlines as divisions within their companies. They attempted to use Southwest's policies and procedures, but without the success of Southwest. Continental Lite was rolled out in October 1993. CALite relied more heavily on one stop and connecting passengers than Southwest and was not able to match Southwest's efficiency. United announced its low-cost airline on the West Coast in mid-1994. The goal was to cut costs by 30 percent, reducing costs per seat to 7.4 cents—to match Southwest's costs. The Shuttle, as United's low cost airline was called, was not able to reduce its costs to the 7.4 cents per passenger seat mile experienced by Southwest Airlines.

Table 16.2

**COMPARISON DATA
(ONE YEAR)**

	Alaska	AW	SW	Delta	United	American
Revenue	1618	2180	5468	15657	16932	17829
Expenses	1763	2357	4628	15104	18698	18322
Fuel cost ($/ga)	1.03	.88	.79	.67	.81	.78
Miles per passenger	886	958	662	942	1493	1560
Size fleet	95	138	355	831	604	978
Load factor (%)	69.2	70.5	70.5	72.9	72.3	71.9
Complaints per 100k passengers	2.04	7.45	.47	2.02	5.22	3.54
Economic Profit	37	26	23	332	194	−49

New Economy

Southwest's continued focus on its market niche has meant a selection of options that lower costs. In some cases this has meant the rejection of a new technology. And in other cases it has meant an adoption of a new technology. In the 1970s computer reservation systems and networks of airlines and travel agents dominated the airline markets. Travel agents were able to search for fares and book tickets from a terminal in their own office rather than by telephone. The largest system was Sabre, developed by American Airlines. Other systems were developed by United, TWA and JAL. The networks related to these systems expanded rapidly. It looked like a winner-takes-all market with Sabre being the winner. However, antitrust action against American ended the domination of Sabre. Southwest had never been part of such a network, so the decision did not hurt them and may, in fact, have benefited them. Although Southwest Airlines avoids travel agents, pays no commissions, and remains out of any reservation network, the company does not avoid technological improvements. Its greatest foray into the New Economy is its use of the Internet. Southwest began selling tickets over the Internet in 1996. The company developed a system that reduced costs and was easy for customers to use. Southwest is one of the fifty most searched for websites and is requested 1.5 times more often than the next airline. Southwest generates 30 percent of its revenues from Internet sales. In comparison, America West earns 12 percent of its revenues online. Southwest had booking costs of less than $1 compared to travel agent costs of $10 per ticket and internal personnel costs of $5 per ticket.

Southwest Airlines has adopted a technologically advanced pricing process. Airlines must forecast demand, forecast how many reservations will go unused, and price each seat in order to maximize profit. The task of setting prices is called revenue optimization. The airlines refer to it as yield management. It is a technically and conceptually complicated undertaking. For instance, overbooking is an attempt to gain the increased revenue obtained from flying full aircraft rather than leaving seats empty. The optimal overbooking point is reached when the marginal revenue from accepting one more reservation on a flight equals the marginal cost of that overbooking. The cost of overbooking must include not only the direct costs of paying off the customer, but the chance that a customer will choose not to fly the airline again. Most of the airlines, including Southwest, have outsourced yield management to firms that specialize in pricing solutions. Such firms include Manugistics, PROS Revenue Management, IDEAS, Siebel Systems, KANA, Just Enough, KhiMetrics, and ProfitLogic. These activities have generated as much as a 3 percent increase in profit margins.

Strategic Directions

At this stage Southwest Airlines has no close competitor and is the only airline consistently earning economic profit. We know that competitors want a piece of what Southwest has. What Southwest has to recognize is how competitors might attempt to capture some of Southwest's profits. Southwest Airline's short-haul approach has been shown to be more efficient than the hub and spoke system used by other airlines. Can we expect other airlines to adopt the short-haul structure? The answer is yes; and as mentioned above, other airlines have tried this. But these other attempts have not been successful; the other airlines have not been able to meet the costs of Southwest Airlines. One problem is that the new entrants have been offshoots of existing airlines and thus carried some of the cost baggage from their operations. Could a totally new entrant create a duplicate to Southwest Airlines that would capture market share? How can Southwest ensure this does not occur? Southwest's culture continues to enable the company to experience greater productivity than other airlines. This is the primary barrier that Southwest Airlines has erected. As long as that culture is effective and as long as employee productivity remains superior to that of other airlines, Southwest will retain its market.

Southwest Airlines currently has 355 planes (all Boeing 737's) serving fifty-nine airports in thirty states. This is a growth over thirty years from three planes and three airports in one state. The principal question for Southwest is how large it can become. Is there a stage at which it will have to move to a hub and spoke system or a stage at which it will not be able to maintain the efficiency of its short-haul approach? Southwest's competitive advantage is its cost structure (due to productivity, one type plane, lower gate and airport costs, Internet sales) and reliability. The company has to maintain these advantages in order to continue its performance. Rather than competition taking away these advantages, it seems that the greatest danger to Southwest's continued performance is its own decisions regarding whether or not to continue expanding.

Summary of the Strategic Audit

This illustration of a strategic audit is limited. As we previously noted, if this were an audit for a client or for the firm, a much more in-depth analysis would be required. One would need to calculate data on pricing, not merely refer to the pricing firms. One would need to examine the potential effect of entry from international carriers as well as the impact from JetBlue or other new low-cost point-to-point airlines. One would need to consider the impact of governmental regulations, governmental subsidies, the future cost of airplanes, and the impact of subsidies by the European Community to Airbus, the manufacturing competitor to Boeing. In addition, issues like branding, customer loyalty, firm architecture, and the potential erosion of culture would have to be examined in much more detail. In short, the audit provided here is very limited; it should encompass everything we have discussed in this text. Nevertheless, the purpose of presenting the audit of Southwest Airlines was not to provide a full-scale examination; instead it was to illustrate how strategy is developed and how economic thinking is the basis of strategy.

CASE REVIEW *Edward Jones Brokerage*

Edward Jones is only about the thirty-fourth-largest brokerage firm in the United States but is the most profitable. Edward Jones now faces competition from the ebrokerage houses, the Internet companies. What is Edward Jones to do?

The key elements of Edward Jones' strategy are an entrepreneurial culture revolving around small offices staffed by only one broker; an emphasis on long-term, low-turnover investing; and a strong focus on rural areas and on average American investors. Edward Jones does not have any in-house mutual funds, does not sell options or commodities, encourages clients to focus on the long term and ignore short-term fluctuations of the market, and recommends only high-quality stocks.

This strategy differentiates Edward Jones from other brokerage houses. In those other firms, there are many lines of business: Such a firm has investment bankers who take companies public and brokers who sell these companies' stock; its brokers sell options, calls, puts, commodities, and every other financial tool; the firm will manage its own mutual funds as well as other investment products.

The strategy also differentiates it from the ebusiness brokers who do nothing for a client but carry out the transaction. Edward Jones brokers evaluate the client and the client's goals; they recommend long-term investment approaches that avoid the vagaries of the market. The ebusiness brokers provide no such client service.

Edward Jones has differentiated itself; it has determined what its distinct capability is and created a niche where that capability has value. As long as it continues with this strategy, it will endure. If developments in the future mean that Edward Jones loses its competitive advantage or its advantage fails to have value in its market, then it will have to rethink and alter its strategy.

SUMMARY

1. Strategy involves tradeoffs—the recognition of opportunity costs.
2. A manager has to determine whether the firm has a distinct capability and, if so, whether it is being applied to appropriate markets.
3. Competition means that uniqueness will not last forever. Success breeds imitation.
4. When viewing a potentially profitable situation, a firm has to decide whether to imitate the successful firms in the market or to innovate. The answer depends on a comparison of costs and benefits.
5. The strategic audit is an analysis of the firm: where the firm is today. This audit is necessary prior to determining strategy.
6. The strategic audit requires an analysis of the market, the boundaries of the market, the firm's distinctive capabilities, and the fit between distinctive capabilities and the market.
7. Organizational fit is important to the implementation and success of strategy. This means that the firm's organization, architecture, and culture allow the most efficient path to the firm's strategic goal.
8. The strategic audit must consider the management and leadership of the firm. How are decisions being made? Are the managers thinking like economists?

KEY TERM

strategic audit

EXERCISE

1. Select an existing company and carry out a strategic audit.

CHAPTER NOTES

1. Quoted in John Seely Brown, "Research That Reinvents the Corporation," *Harvard Business Review* (January/February 1991): 102–111.
2. William Taylor, "The Business of Innovation: An Interview with Paul Cook," *Harvard Business Review,* Vol. 69 (March/April 1990): 97–106.
3. The term was first used by John Kay, *Foundations of Corporate Success* (Oxford: Oxford University Press, 1995).

Glossary

accounting profit revenue that exceeds costs, not including cost of capital (3)

added value value of output that exceeds cost of resources (3)

applied research research focused on bringing a final product to fruition (9)

arbitrage process of simultaneously buying in low-priced market and selling the identical item in high-priced market (2, 14)

architecture organization or structure of the firm (2)

average fixed costs (AFC) total fixed costs divided by quantity (5)

average total cost (ATC) total costs divided by quantity; per unit costs (5)

average variable costs (AVC) total variable costs divided by quantity (5)

backloaded compensation a compensation structure in which an individual receives less than his productivity is worth during the first years he is with the firm (11)

balance sheet exposure the items on a balance sheet whose value may be affected by exchange-rate changes (14)

basic research research devoted to solving a problem irrespective of final output (9)

Black–Scholes option pricing formula a means of determining a value for the right but not the obligation to undertake an action (12)

buyback a means of securing a contract—one party agrees to buy back a portion of the transaction between two parties (10)

call option the right but not the obligation to purchase an item (12)

cannibalization occurs when sales of one product by a firm reduce sales of another product by that same firm (8)

commitment expending resources on a particular action in order to demonstrate that the action will be carried out (13)

commodity market a market in which many sellers offer an identical item for sale (6)

comparative advantage when an activity by one person can be carried out with lower opportunity costs than could be done by another (2)

complements products that are used together (4)

constant returns to scale a doubling of all resources results in a doubling of output (5)

constraint a restraint or limit; the budget constraint indicates a limited amount that can be spent (2, Appendix)

consumer surplus the bonus provided consumers by a market; the difference between what buyers would be willing and able to pay and the market price (6)

contracts agreements to carry out certain transactions (10)

core competency the main thing a firm does (1)

corporate culture a set of collectively held values, beliefs, and norms of behavior among members of a firm that influence individual behaviors (10)

cost of capital the opportunity cost to creditors and investors—the amount a firm must pay investors so that they will not take their funds to another activity (3)

cost-plus pricing setting price according to a markup on average costs (8)

countercyclical goods when income goes up, quantity demanded of these goods goes down—income elasticity of demand is negative (4)

cross-price elasticity of demand a measure of the sensitivity of sales to a change in the price of a related item; percentage change in quantity demanded of item A divided by percentage change in price of item B (4)

currency futures contracts for delivery of a certain amount of a foreign currency at some future date and at a known price; similar in this way to foreign-exchange forwards (14)

customizing setting price according to an individual's willingness and ability to purchase an item (8)

cyclical goods when income goes up, quantity demanded of these goods goes up—income elasticity of demand is positive (4)

derivative in calculus, the change in a dependent variable that comes with a very small change in the independent variables (2, Appendix)

development readying the results of research for sale as a final product (9)

differentiated products products that are different in customers' minds (6)

diseconomies of scale a doubling of resources leads to less than a doubling of output (5)

dominant strategy an activity that will be carried out no matter what rivals do (13)

dominated strategy an activity that will not be carried out because there are better, more profitable activities no matter what rivals do (13)

downsizing reducing the size of the firm; cutting costs (5)

downstream an activity that uses a firm's output as inputs into its own production (10)

economic profit total revenue less total costs, including opportunity cost of capital (3)

economies of scale a doubling of resources leads to a more than doubling of output (5)

efficiency lowest cost (2)

efficiency wage wage that is higher than the equilibrium or market wage in order to induce increased productivity (11)

elastic measure of sensitivity of sales to changes in a determinant of sales (4)

exchange rate the rate at which two currencies are exchanged (14)

expected value value weighted by probability of occurrence (13)

experience goods goods whose attributes are discovered through trial (7)

externalities costs or benefits created by a transaction not paid for or received by the parties carrying out the transaction (2)

foreign exchange: currency not that of the domestic nation (14)

foreign-exchange options the right but not the obligation to buy or sell foreign exchange at some point in the future for a price determined now (14)

forward market market in which transactions to occur in the future are bought and sold today (14)

forward rate the price determined today for a transaction to take place in the future (14)

forwards contracts for delivery of a certain item at some future date and at a known price (14)

free ride occurs when someone receives benefits without paying for those benefits (11)

full-cost pricing pricing based on total costs (8)

function a rule that describes the relationship between variables (2, Appendix)

gains from trade the additional amount that an individual, firm, or nation can obtain by trading as compared to not trading (2)

game theory mathematical representation of strategic behavior (13)

golden parachutes compensation provided executives of a firm who are dismissed or otherwise lose a position with the firm (11)

greenmail payments provided to employees/executives of a target firm in the event of a hostile takeover (11)

hedging undertaking an action to offset some possible losses related to a separate transaction (14)

Herfindahl–Hirschman index (HHI) a measure of the degree of dominance of a firm or firms in a market; the sum of squares of sales—HI = $(size)^2 + (size)^2 + \ldots + (size)^2$, where $(size)^2$ is the size of a firm squared (15)

hold-up the situation in which one party to a transaction is able to force another to perform as the first desires (2)

horizontal integration occurs when a firm merges with or acquires a rival firm; the combining of firms at the same level of business (2)

hostages a means of ensuring that one party to a transaction carries out the transaction (10)

income elasticity of demand a measure of the sensitivity of sales to a change in income (4)

indifference analysis measuring consumer choice by examining the baskets of goods and services among which the individual is indifferent (4, Appendix B)

indifference curve a graph showing different combinations of goods among which the consumer is indifferent (4, Appendix B)

inelastic percentage change in quantity demanded is less than percentage change in price (4)

interest rate parity (IRP) occurs when interest rates in different nations are the same once adjusted for exchange-rate changes (14)

joint venture two or more firms joining together to produce (5)

law of diminishing marginal returns adding increasing amounts of a variable resource to a fixed amount of other resources initially increases output but eventually causes output to increase at a decreasing rate and finally to decrease (5)

law of one price identical items sell for the same price in different markets (2, 14)

limit price the price above which new firms will enter (8)

locked-in having to utilize a specific technology even though it is not the most efficient technology (9)

long run a period of time just long enough that everything is variable (4)

long-run average total cost (LRATC) total costs divided by quantity when there are no fixed costs (5)

make-or-buy decision the decision whether to carry out an activity in-house or to purchase the activity in the market (10)

marginal cost (MC) the change in cost divided by the change in quantity (5)

marginal rate of substitution (MRS) the slope of the indifference curve (4, Appendix B)

marginal relationship a relationship between two variables that looks at the difference or change between them (2, Appendix)

marginal revenue product the value of an additional resource to a firm; the marginal revenue multiplied by the marginal product (11, Appendix)

market-based exposure sales and/or costs of multinational companies may be affected by exchange-rate changes (14)

market failure a situation in which a free market does not allocate resources efficiently (2)

market share percentage of total sales made by one firm (1)

market structures the selling environments in which firms operate (6)

matrix an organizational structure designed to ensure efficient communication among disparate units (10)

meet-the-competition clause a low-price guarantee—matching any other firm's price (8)

M-form, multidivisional form an organizational structure designed to enable specialization (10)

mixed bundling occurs when a firm sells two or more products individually and also sells the products as one product (8)

monopolistic competition a selling environment in which there are many firms with differentiated products, where entry and exit can be carried out easily (6)

monopoly a selling environment in which only one firm sells a good or service (6)

most-favored-customer clause a firm guarantees that its customers will obtain the lowest price offered by the firm (8)

Nash equilibrium situation in which no one has an incentive to change current actions (13)

natural monopoly situation that exists when economies of scale persist throughout the entire market (15)

negative economic profit revenues are less than costs when costs include all costs (that is, the cost of land, labor, and capital) (3)

net present value (NPV) present value of earnings less present value of costs (12)

network a situation in which activities carried out by groups of people or firms using a specific technology have lower costs than if each person or firm uses different technologies (9, 10)

New Economy term referring to the technological changes occurring in information processing and management (9)

noncyclical goods products whose sales do not depend on income (4)

normal profit zero economic profit (3)

objective function the item being optimized; profit under profit maximization; cost under cost minimization; happiness under utility maximization (2, Appendix)

offsets a means of ensuring that an agreement is carried out (14)

oligopoly a selling environment in which just a few firms dominate the market (6)

options the right but not the obligation to carry out some activity (12)

outsourcing divesting activities so they are purchased in the market rather than created in-house (5)

Pareto efficient an outcome or equilibrium in which no one can be made better off without harming another (2)

partial derivative in calculus, measures a change in the dependent variable with respect to a very small change in one independent variable, everything else held constant (2, Appendix)

path dependence a situation in which certain actions or certain technologies are adopted simply because previous actions or technologies were adopted (9)

peak-load pricing prices differ depending on amount of demand—higher when demand is higher (8)

perfect competition a selling environment in which there are many firms selling identical products and in which entry and exit are easy (6)

perfect price discrimination each consumer pays exactly what each is willing and able to pay for a good or service (8)

per se rule a fixed rule of antitrust that an action is illegal no matter the circumstances (15)

personalized pricing pricing determined according to each individual's willingness and ability to pay (8)

piece-work rates compensation based on output (11)

poison pill a situation in which a firm acquired by another firm imposes large costs for the acquiring firm (11)

positive feedback externalities created by one person carrying out an activity spill over to or benefit all others also participating in those activities (9)

positive network externalities see *positive feedback* (9)

predatory price a price low enough to drive competitors out of business (8)

price elasticity of demand the sensitivity of sales to price changes; the percentage change in quantity demanded divided by the percentage change in price (4)

price taker a perfect competitor or commodity seller; the price one must sell at is determined by the market (6)

prisoner's dilemma a situation in which a rival's actions lead to a less than best solution (13)

producer surplus the difference between what a producer is willing and able to sell a good or service at and the market price (6)

production possibilities curve (PPC) a graph illustrating the limitations of resources (2)

product-line extension adding an attribute or component to an existing product (8)

public good a product that can be consumed by anyone and where one's consumption does not reduce the amount others can consume (2)

purchasing power parity (PPP) the prices of goods and services are the same in different nations once adjusted for exchange-rate changes (14)

pure bundling offering two products for sale only in combination (8)

quota a fixed amount that a supplier is allowed to offer for sale in a particular market (14)

real option the right but not the obligation to purchase an asset or carry out an activity (12)

rent seeking devoting resources to transferring income from one group to another (7, 15)

repeated trials carrying out activities more than once (13)

risk aversion avoidance of risk; when someone prefers a result with certainty over the possibility of receiving either a higher or lower result (13)

Risk premium the price that people will pay to avoid risk (13)

Rule of reason the idea that antitrust prosecution depends on the reasonableness of the action, that is, the circumstances surrounding the action (15)

scorched-earth policy a strategy for penalizing those who cheat on agreements—destroying all assets so that others cannot use them (13)

search goods products consumers must know about and understand characteristics of before they will purchase them (7)

second-degree price discrimination when the firm is able to group multiple units of the good and charge different prices for the different groups (8)

self-managed team a workplace organization designed to enlist the benefits of teamwork (10)

sequential game game in which decisions are made in steps, with each step taking place at a different point in time (13)

services items consumed immediately (7)

shareholder value the value of a firm to an investor (3)

short run a period of time just short enough that at least one resource is fixed (5)

short-run average total cost (SRATC) per unit costs; total costs divided by quantity when some costs are fixed (5)

simultaneous game game in which decisions are made at the same time (13)

spot rate current price (14)

standardized products products that are identical (6)

strategic asset an asset that enables a firm to create barriers to entry (7)

strategic audit the examination of the activities and potential success of a firm (16)

strategic behavior carrying out actions by considering the actions and reactions of others (6)

substitutes items that can be used in place of each other (4)

sunk cost expenditures that once made have no liquidation value (7)

supply chain management the management of the value chain; the process of creating and selling a good or service from raw materials through finished product to the consumer (5)

tariff a tax imposed on imported goods and services (14)

team a popular means of organizing the workplace—having output produced by groups of individuals (10)

third-degree price discrimination groups of customers pay a different price for the same product (8)

tipping point the point at which a disease becomes an epidemic (9)

tit-for-tat a strategy for penalizing those who cheat on agreements—doing unto others what they do to you (13)

total fixed costs (TFC) total costs of the fixed resources (5)

total quality management devoting resources to ensuring that quality is high—often implied that marginal revenue from quality is less than marginal cost of obtaining quality (1)

total variable costs (TVC) total costs of variable resources (5)

transaction costs costs involved in carrying out a transaction (2, 10)

tying selling one product by offering it for sale in combination with another product (8)

U-form, unitary form, functional form organizational form or structure of a firm that enables just one activity (10)

unit-elastic percentage change in quantity demanded is equal to percentage change in price (4)

upstream the firm that is a supplier to another firm (10)

using the market purchasing an activity from the market rather than carrying out the activity in-house (9)

value of the marginal product the value of a resource to a firm that sells its output in a commodity market (11, Appendix)

value pricing standard economic pricing where $MR = MC$ but the name value is attached to make it seem as if the customer is gaining something additional (8)

vertical integration occurs when a firm that is a supplier to another firm is merged with the second firm (2, 10)

wage compression occurs when wages of newly hired workers are near or above the wages of employees who have been with the firm for a long period of time (11)

winner-takes-all one firm or one technology completely dominates the market—becomes a monopoly (9)

zero economic profit revenue is just equal to total costs, including opportunity cost of capital (3)

Company Index

Subject Index

357

CHAPTER 8

Price Strategies

http://www.khimetrics.com

http://www.firstmonday.dk/issues/issue2/
different

http://ecommerce.internet.com/news/insights/
ebiz/article/0,3371,10379_759511,00.html

http://www.ftc.gov/bc/compguide/index.htm

http://www.dispatch.com/connect/
connect091800/424450.html

Case Study

http://www.fritolay.com

CHAPTER 9

The New Economy:
Technological Change and Innovation

E-commerce

http://ecommerce.internet.com/news/insights/
ebiz/article/0,3371,10379_759511,00.html

http://www.utdallas.edu/~liebowit/palgrave/
network.html

http://economics.about.com/library/weekly/
aa030198.htm

http://www.sims.berkeley.edu/resources/
infoecon/Networks.html

Speculative Bubbles

http://www.cnn.com/COMMUNITY/
transcripts/2000/3/gladwell/

http://www.economymodels.com/bubbles.asp

Case Study

http://compnetworking.about.com/cs/
dslvscablemodem/

CHAPTER 10

The Firm's Architecture:
Organization and Corporate Culture

http://www.companyculture.info/

http://www.koreatimes.co.kr/14_8/9807/
t4851233.htm

Corporate Governance

http://slate.msn.com/?id=2068448

http://www.corpgov.net/

http://www.oecd.org/EN/home/0,,EN-home-0-
nodirectorate-no-no-no-0,FF.html

http://www.encycogov.com/

http://www.corp-gov.org/glossary.php3

Case Study

http://www.monsanto.com/monsanto/
layout/default.asp

http://www.wyeth.com

http://www.pharmacia.com

http://www.jpmorgan.com

http://www.chase.com

CHAPTER 11

Personnel and Compensation

http://www.salary.com

http://www.ssrn.com/update/ern/
ern_personnel.html

Case Study

http://bwnt.businessweek.com/exec_comp/
2002/index.asp

CHAPTER 12

Capital Allocation: Real Options

Options

http://www.library.hbs.edu/merton/about.htm

http://www.pbs.org/wgbh/nova/stockmarket/
formulaleft.html

http://www.investmentscience.com/
?source=overture&wid=01

http://www.sdg.com/home.nsf/sdg/
Competencies--RealOptionsAnalysis

http://www.adainc.com/approach/rov.html

http://www.freeoptionpricing.com/models/
wmbsm.asp

http://www.numa.com/derivs/ref/calculat/
option/calc-opa.htm

http://www.hoadley.net/options/BS.htm